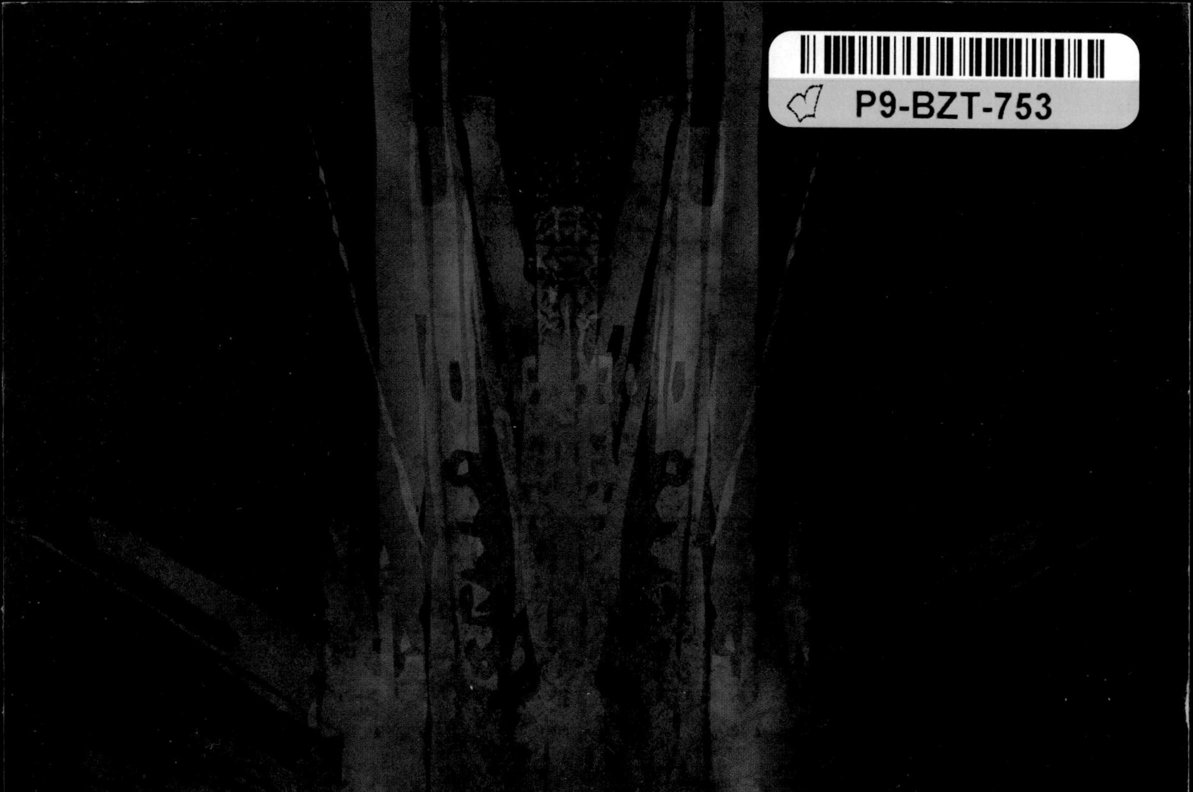

Sara Pezzini no longer possesses the Witchblade. Realizing the danger it would attract to her unborn child, Sara chose to give up the powerful artifact and passed it to a new bearer, Danielle Baptiste, who is still learning to control the Witchblade. The child's impending birth has set into motion events that will lead to war between the Angelus and the Darkness, the primal forces of Light and Dark in the universe.

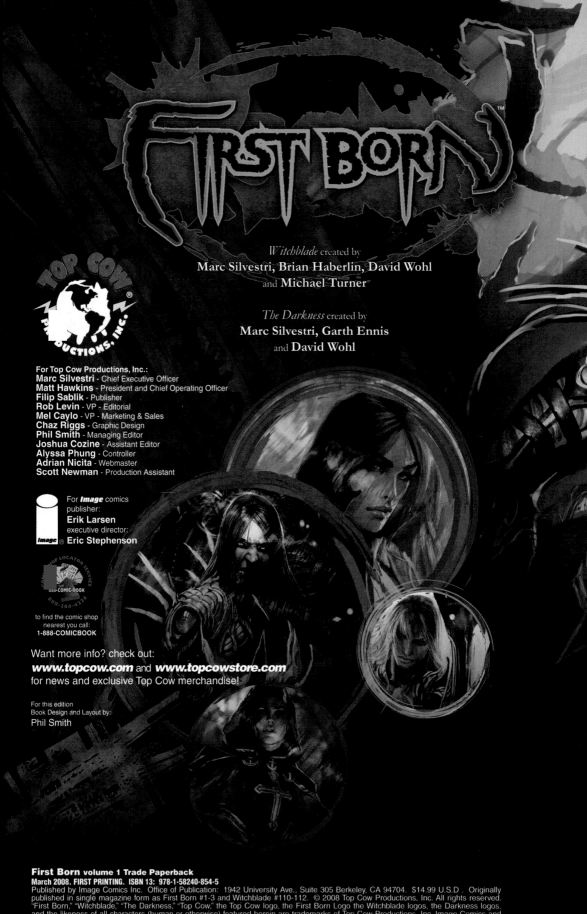

First Born

Witchblade created by
Marc Silvestri, Brian Haberlin, David Wohl
and **Michael Turner**

The Darkness created by
Marc Silvestri, Garth Ennis
and **David Wohl**

For Top Cow Productions, Inc.:
Marc Silvestri - Chief Executive Officer
Matt Hawkins - President and Chief Operating Officer
Filip Sablik - Publisher
Rob Levin - VP - Editorial
Mel Caylo - VP - Marketing & Sales
Chaz Riggs - Graphic Design
Phil Smith - Managing Editor
Joshua Cozine - Assistant Editor
Alyssa Phung - Controller
Adrian Nicita - Webmaster
Scott Newman - Production Assistant

For *Image* comics
publisher:
Erik Larsen
executive director:
Eric Stephenson

to find the comic shop
nearest you call:
1-888-COMICBOOK

Want more info? check out:
www.topcow.com and **www.topcowstore.com**
for news and exclusive Top Cow merchandise!

For this edition
Book Design and Layout by:
Phil Smith

First Born volume 1 Trade Paperback
March 2008. FIRST PRINTING. ISBN 13: 978-1-58240-854-5
Published by Image Comics Inc. Office of Publication: 1942 University Ave., Suite 305 Berkeley, CA 94704. $14.99 U.S.D . Originally published in single magazine form as First Born #1-3 and Witchblade #110-112. © 2008 Top Cow Productions, Inc. All rights reserved. "First Born," "Witchblade," "The Darkness," "Top Cow," the Top Cow logo, the First Born Logo the Witchblade logos, the Darkness logos, and the likeness of all characters (human or otherwise) featured herein are trademarks of Top Cow Productions, Inc. Image Comics and the Image Comics logo are trademarks of Image Comics, Inc. The characters, events, and stories in this publication are entirely fictional. Any resemblance to actual persons (living or dead), events, institutions, or locales, without satiric intent, is coincidental. No portion of this publication may be reproduced or transmitted, in any form or by any means, without the express written permission of Top Cow Productions, Inc. PRINTED IN CANADA

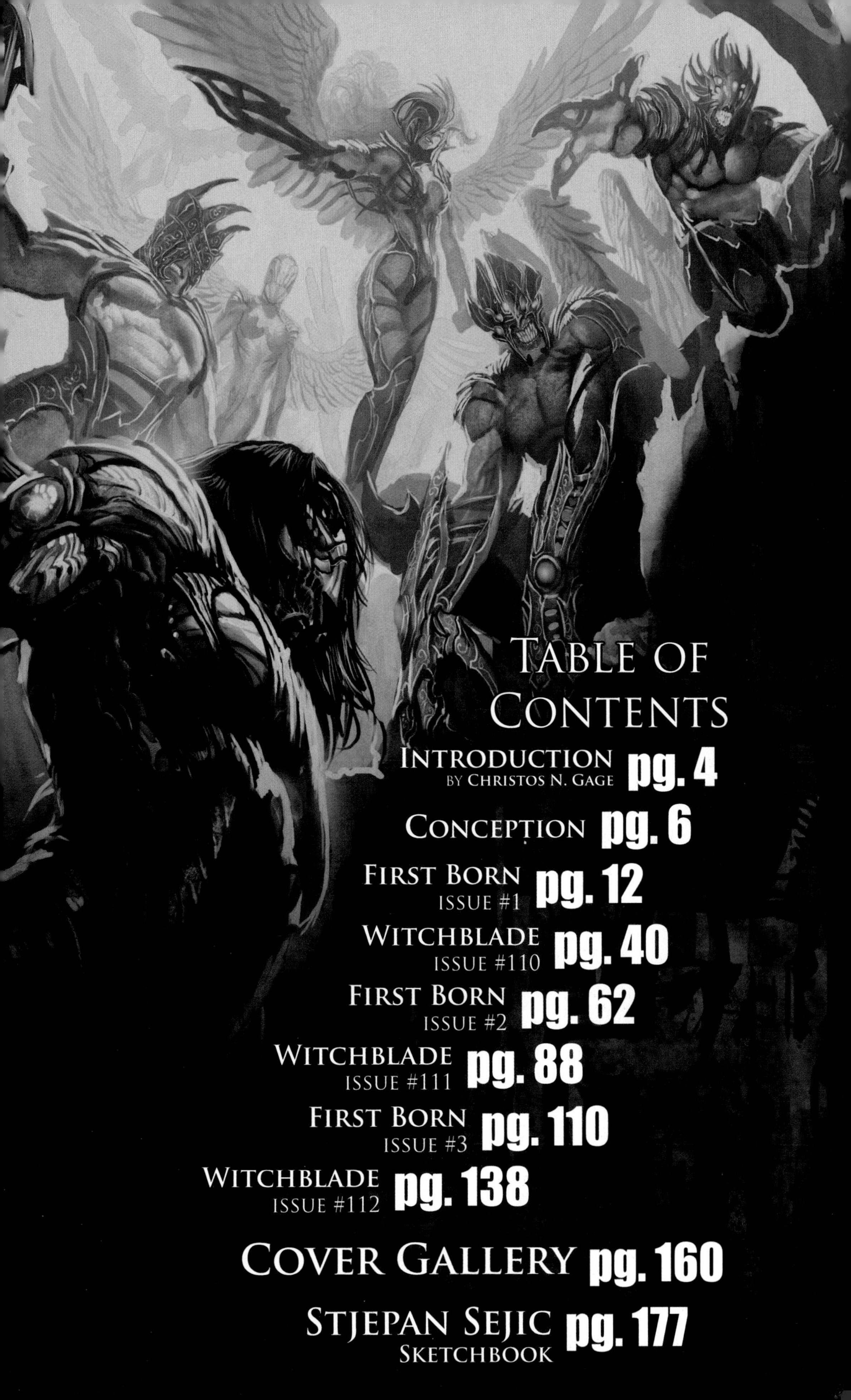

Table of Contents

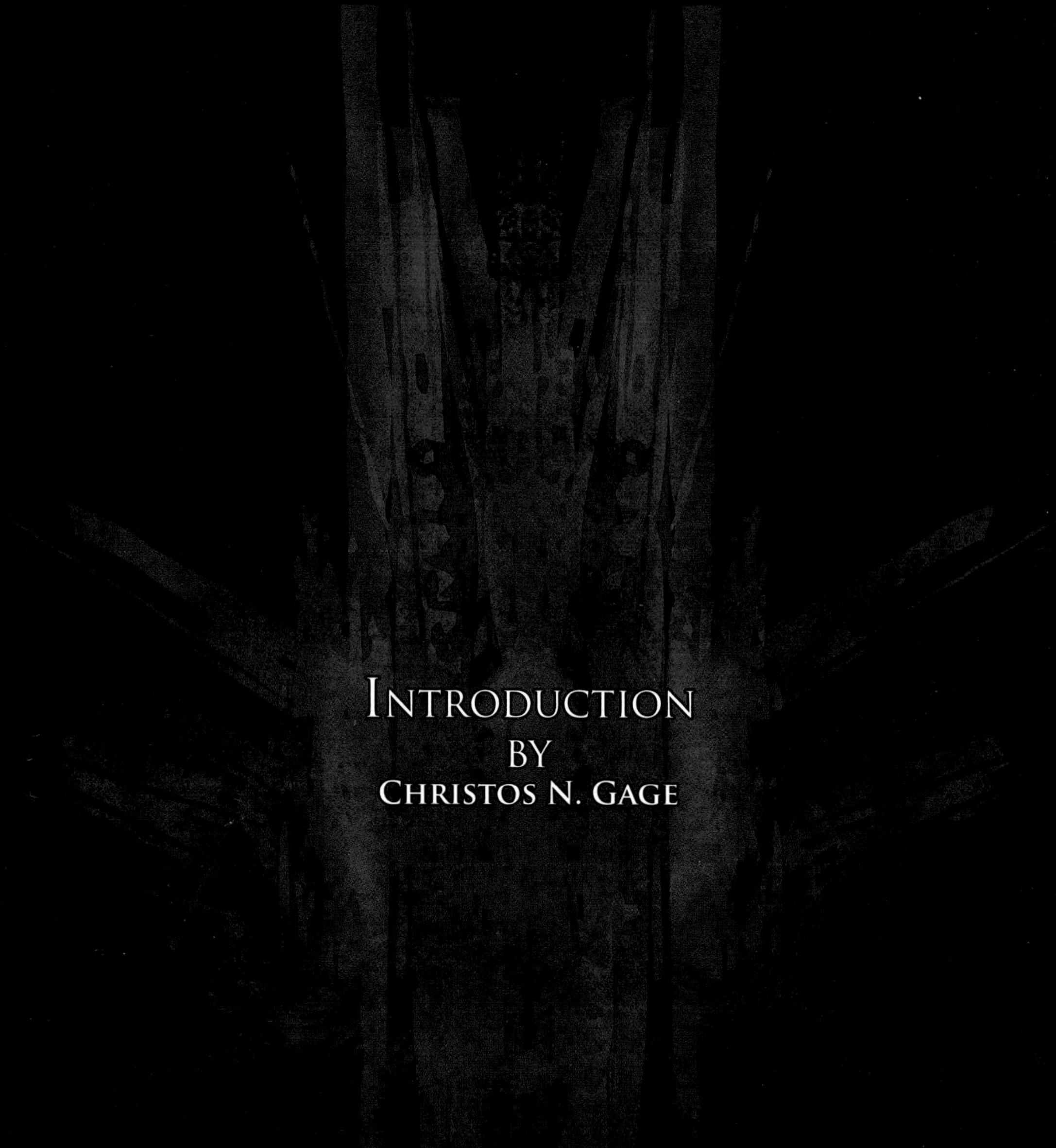

Introduction
by
Christos N. Gage

When Rob Levin asked me to write an introduction to the *First Born* collection, I wasn't sure I was the best choice. Oh, sure, I enjoyed it…a lot…although my humble opinion is hardly necessary here. There are plenty of no-brainer reasons to wholeheartedly recommend this book, not the least of which is the art. Stjepan Sejic is one of the most exciting young talents in the field, combining the grand tradition of fantasy painting with the tools of modern technology to create vibrant, exciting illustrations that never forget their purpose is to tell a story. The pencilers of the *Witchblade* issues are A-list veterans with experience at the highest level…and, I'm sorry, Kevin Nowlan inking? Are you kidding me? Aside from being a fan favorite, Nowlan is one of those rare figures other professional artists worship the same way fanboys like me worship them. Bottom line, if you have eyes, you'll find something to mesmerize you in these pages.

As for the writing, Ron Marz is a name I've come to associate with making me like characters I never much identified with before. His run on the *Silver Surfer* took a guy whose cosmic scale had always made him a bit distant to me, and – without de-powering or otherwise altering the Surfer's basic nature – enabled me to relate to him on a human level…no small feat, considering he's a space-faring alien. I couldn't think of a better person to handle the likes of the Witchblade and the Darkness, who in lesser hands could be boringly unbeatable. So it's not like I was hesitant about the creative side of things.

What gave me pause was the fact that – confession time – I'm not what you'd call a diehard fan of *Witchblade* or *The Darkness*. Sure, I've read and enjoyed their adventures, but more on a casual basis – a bit here, a bit there. I certainly don't have an encyclopedic knowledge of their histories.

And then I realized that might be a good thing. Because if you're like me – if you haven't been picking up these books regularly – I can tell you from personal experience that this is a perfect place to start. It's an epic adventure that gives you all you need to know about the backstory while always moving the characters and events forward. We still have the classic elements of the ancient, powerful Witchblade caught between the eternal struggle of the forces of Darkness and Light; everything that's made these books a success before remains. But there are also some very cool innovations, not the least of which is a pregnant protagonist. There's also a nice switch on the classic "girlfriend in jeopardy" trope found in comics – in this case the "girlfriend" is a tough, male New York cop, while Detective Sara Pezzini gets to play the hero's role. We also have an intriguing deepening of the nature of the Darkness, as we see quite clearly that Jackie Estacado doesn't fully control it – in fact, it may be quite the opposite. As for the Darkness itself and the Angelus, they aren't portrayed as analogues for Heaven and Hell (boring), or as figures used to bash religion (even more boring), but rather as forces of nature, crashing against each other explosively with our heroes caught in the middle, trying desperately to survive – a feeling all too familiar in the early 21st century.

If you've been reading *Witchblade* and *The Darkness* from day one, I have no doubt you'll enjoy this book. But if, like me, you have only a casual familiarity – or none at all – there couldn't be a better time to climb on board. So just do it already!

Oh, and ignore that high-pitched cackling from the shadows. He just works here.

Christos N. Gage
-Los Angeles, CA

THE UNIVERSE IN A NUTSHELL

New York city police detective **Sara Pezzini** is the bearer of the Witchblade, a mysterious artifact that takes the form of a deadly and powerful gauntlet. It would take years before Sara learned the artifact's true nature. The Witchblade was, in fact, the male offspring of the universe's primal forces...

...The Angelus and the Darkness. The Witchblade was conceived as a balance, meant to keep the fragile peace between the eternally struggling light and dark. Even after learning the Witchblade's true nature, Sara remained on the police force, investigating crimes that were deemed so mysterious or strange as to be unsolvable.

And then she realized she was pregnant.

The pregnancy wasn't simply unexpected, it was seemingly impossible, as Sara admitted she hadn't had sex in more than a year. But even though the pregnancy's origin remained a mystery, Sara resolved to keep the baby, embracing the opportunity to have the family she'd presumed would be denied to her.

So for the sake of her baby, Sara made the decision to give up the Witchblade, and pass it to a new bearer.

Danielle Baptiste, a dance student who also happened to be the daughter of Sara's police captain, accepted it.

Less an ally but not quite an enemy is **Jackie Estacado**, the current head of the New York-based Franchetti crime family. Estacado is also the present incarnation of The Darkness, with a seemingly endless army of shadowy creatures at his disposal.

The equal and opposite force to the Darkness is the Angelus the embodiment of the light. just as the Darkness takes a human host, so too does the Angelus. At present, though, the disembodied Angelus searches for a proper host, even as its cadre of winged, ethereal warriors furthers its plans

A sometimes ally to Sara is **Patience**, the present Magdalena, descended from the bloodline of Christ and armed with the Spear of Destiny. Traditionally, each generation's Magdalena is charged by the Catholic Church to seek out and destroy evil. Recently, however, Patience left the church's employ, and now operates on her own.

ON THE FOLLOWING PAGES

FREE COMIC BOOK DAY
TOP COW SUPPLEMENT 2007
FIRST BORN: CONCEPTION

written by: **Ron Marz**

art by: **Stjepan Sejic**

letters by: **Troy Peteri**

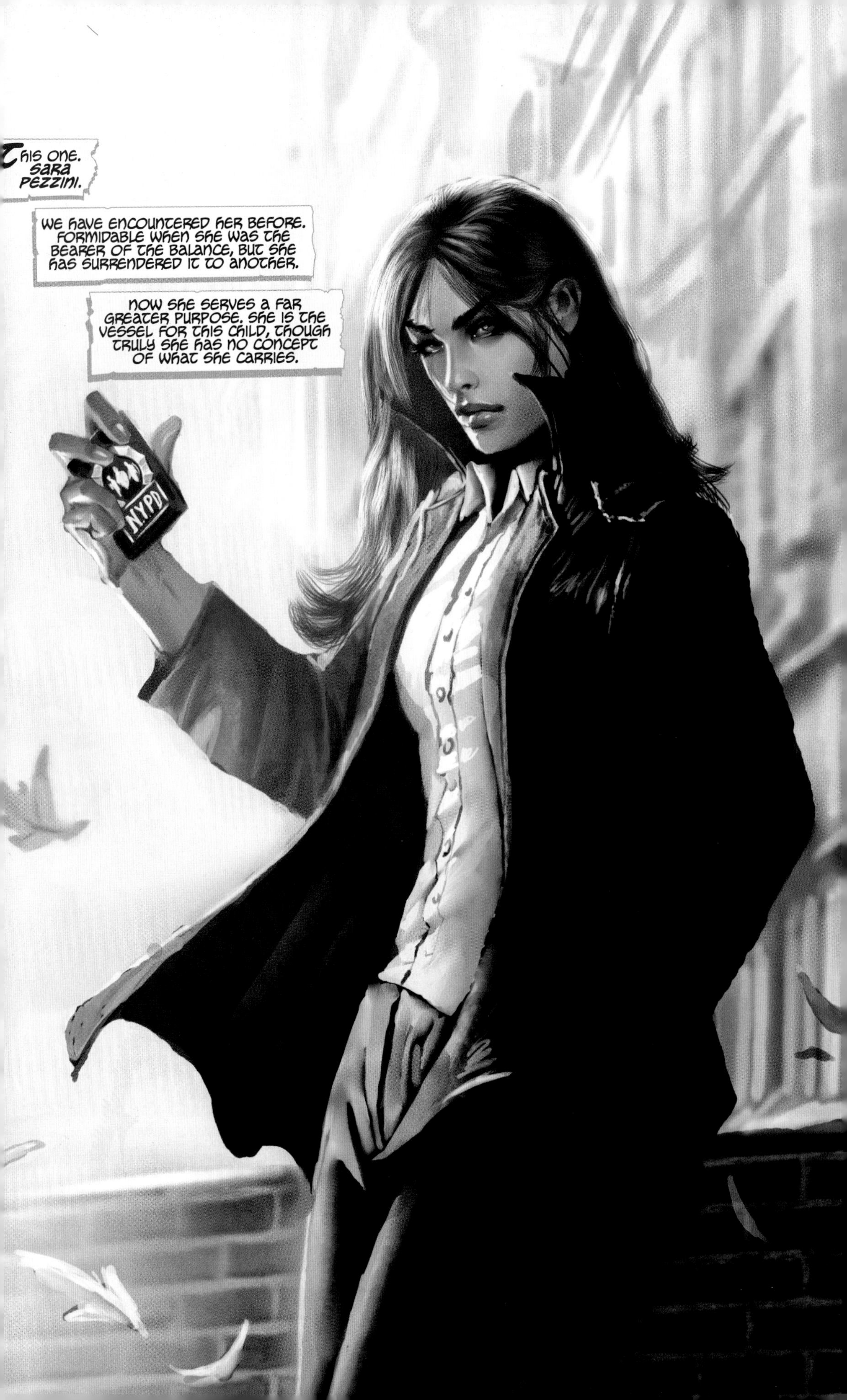
THIS ONE. SARA PEZZINI.
WE HAVE ENCOUNTERED HER BEFORE. FORMIDABLE WHEN SHE WAS THE BEARER OF THE BALANCE, BUT SHE HAS SURRENDERED IT TO ANOTHER.
NOW SHE SERVES A FAR GREATER PURPOSE. SHE IS THE VESSEL FOR THIS CHILD, THOUGH TRULY SHE HAS NO CONCEPT OF WHAT SHE CARRIES.
N.Y.P.D.

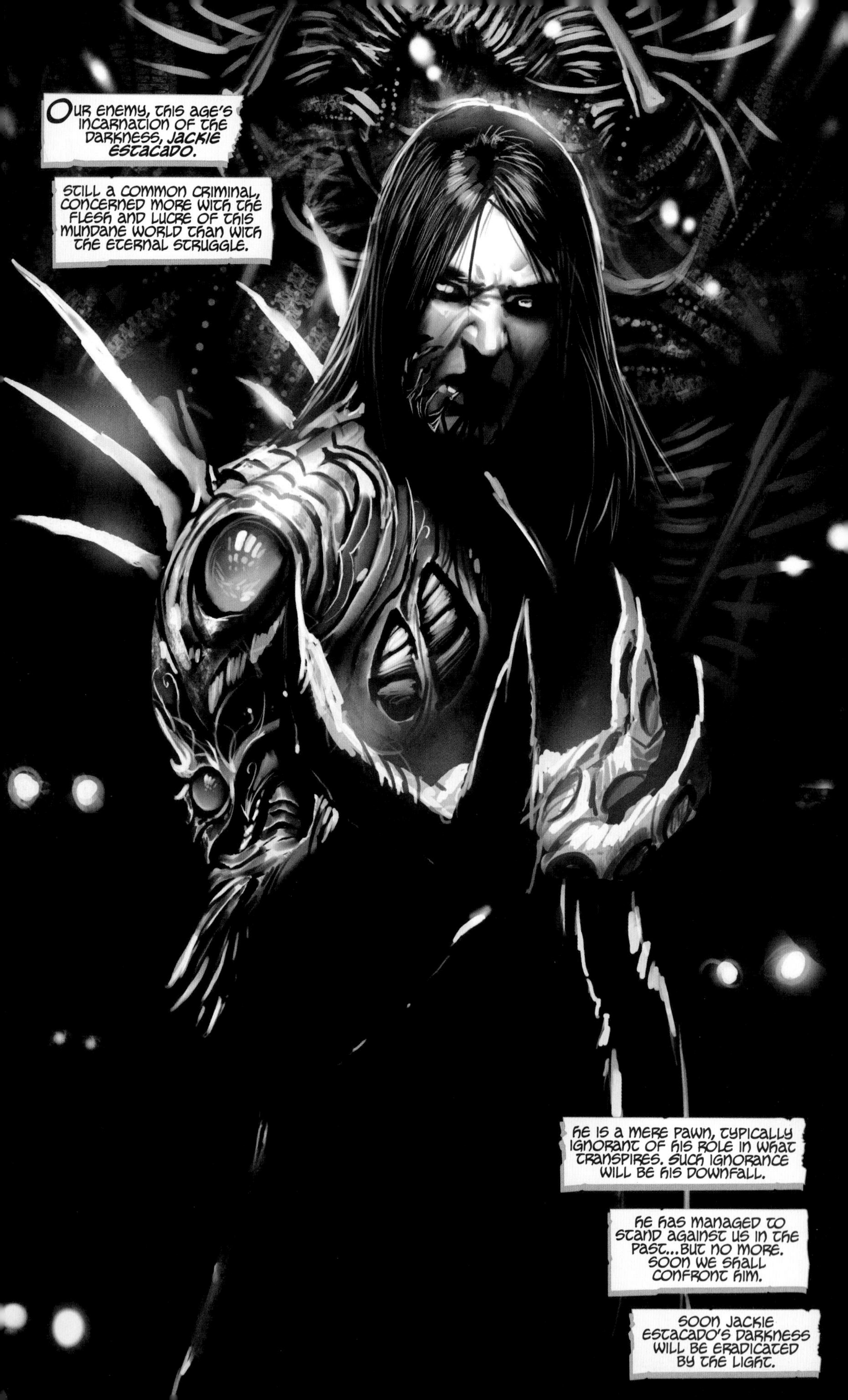
OUR ENEMY, THIS AGE'S INCARNATION OF THE DARKNESS, JACKIE ESTACADO.
STILL A COMMON CRIMINAL, CONCERNED MORE WITH THE FLESH AND LUCRE OF THIS MUNDANE WORLD THAN WITH THE ETERNAL STRUGGLE.
HE IS A MERE PAWN, TYPICALLY IGNORANT OF HIS ROLE IN WHAT TRANSPIRES. SUCH IGNORANCE WILL BE HIS DOWNFALL.
HE HAS MANAGED TO STAND AGAINST US IN THE PAST...BUT NO MORE. SOON WE SHALL CONFRONT HIM.
SOON JACKIE ESTACADO'S DARKNESS WILL BE ERADICATED BY THE LIGHT.

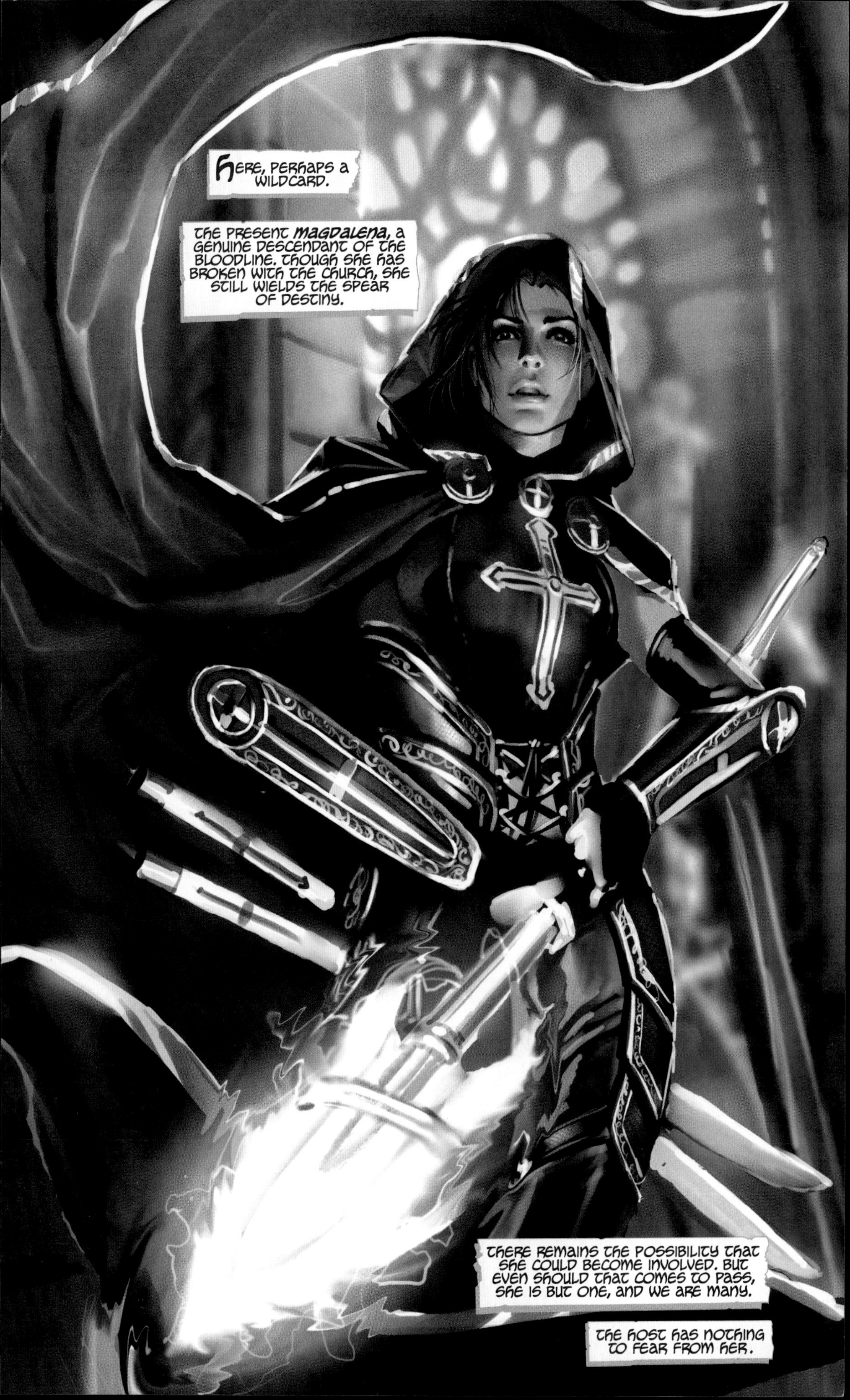
HERE, PERHAPS A WILDCARD.
THE PRESENT MAGDALENA, A GENUINE DESCENDANT OF THE BLOODLINE. THOUGH SHE HAS BROKEN WITH THE CHURCH, SHE STILL WIELDS THE SPEAR OF DESTINY.
THERE REMAINS THE POSSIBILITY THAT SHE COULD BECOME INVOLVED. BUT EVEN SHOULD THAT COMES TO PASS, SHE IS BUT ONE, AND WE ARE MANY.
THE HOST HAS NOTHING TO FEAR FROM HER.

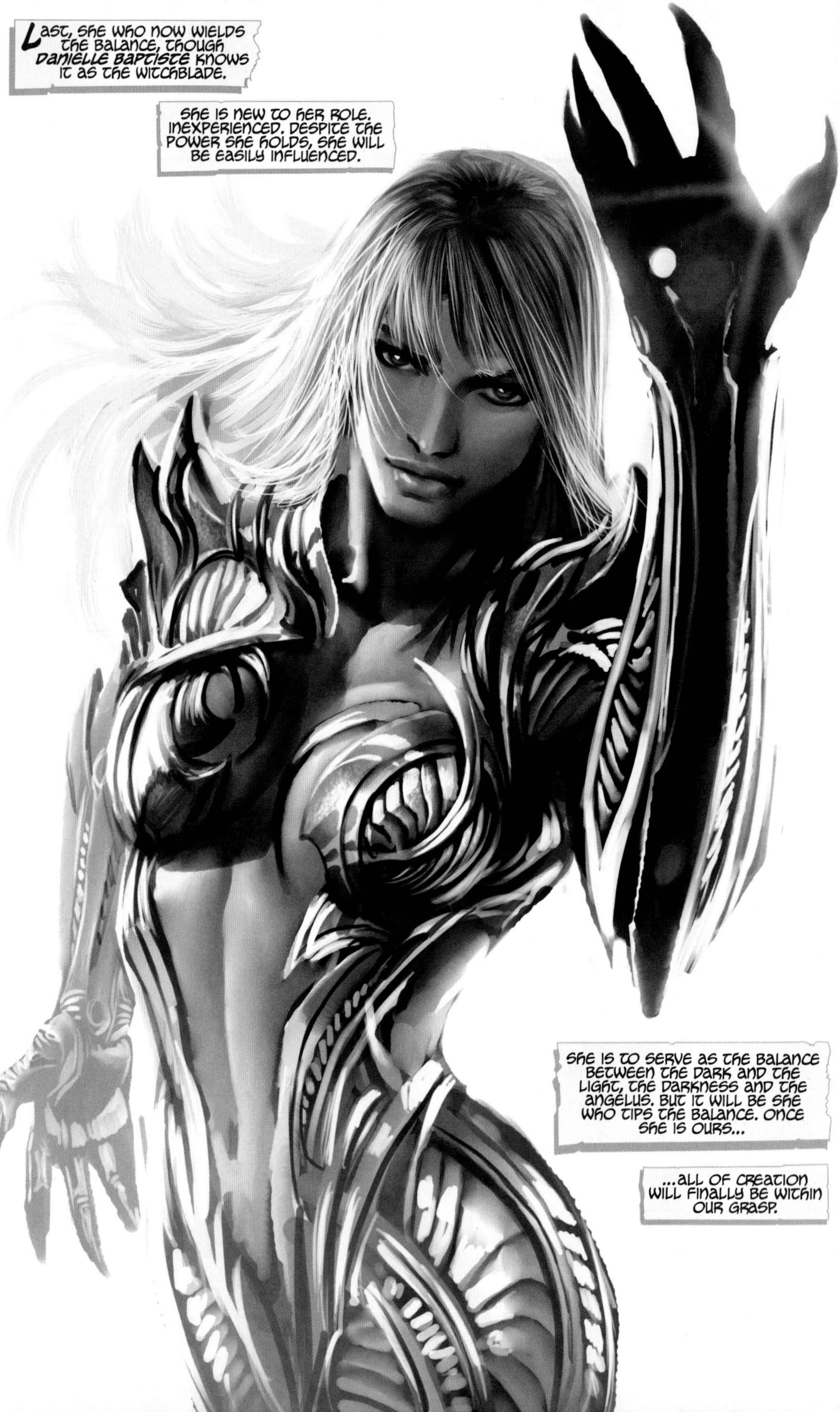
LAST, SHE WHO NOW WIELDS THE BALANCE, THOUGH DANIELLE BAPTISTE KNOWS IT AS THE WITCHBLADE.
SHE IS NEW TO HER ROLE. INEXPERIENCED. DESPITE THE POWER SHE HOLDS, SHE WILL BE EASILY INFLUENCED.
SHE IS TO SERVE AS THE BALANCE BETWEEN THE DARK AND THE LIGHT, THE DARKNESS AND THE ANGELUS. BUT IT WILL BE SHE WHO TIPS THE BALANCE. ONCE SHE IS OURS...
...ALL OF CREATION WILL FINALLY BE WITHIN OUR GRASP.

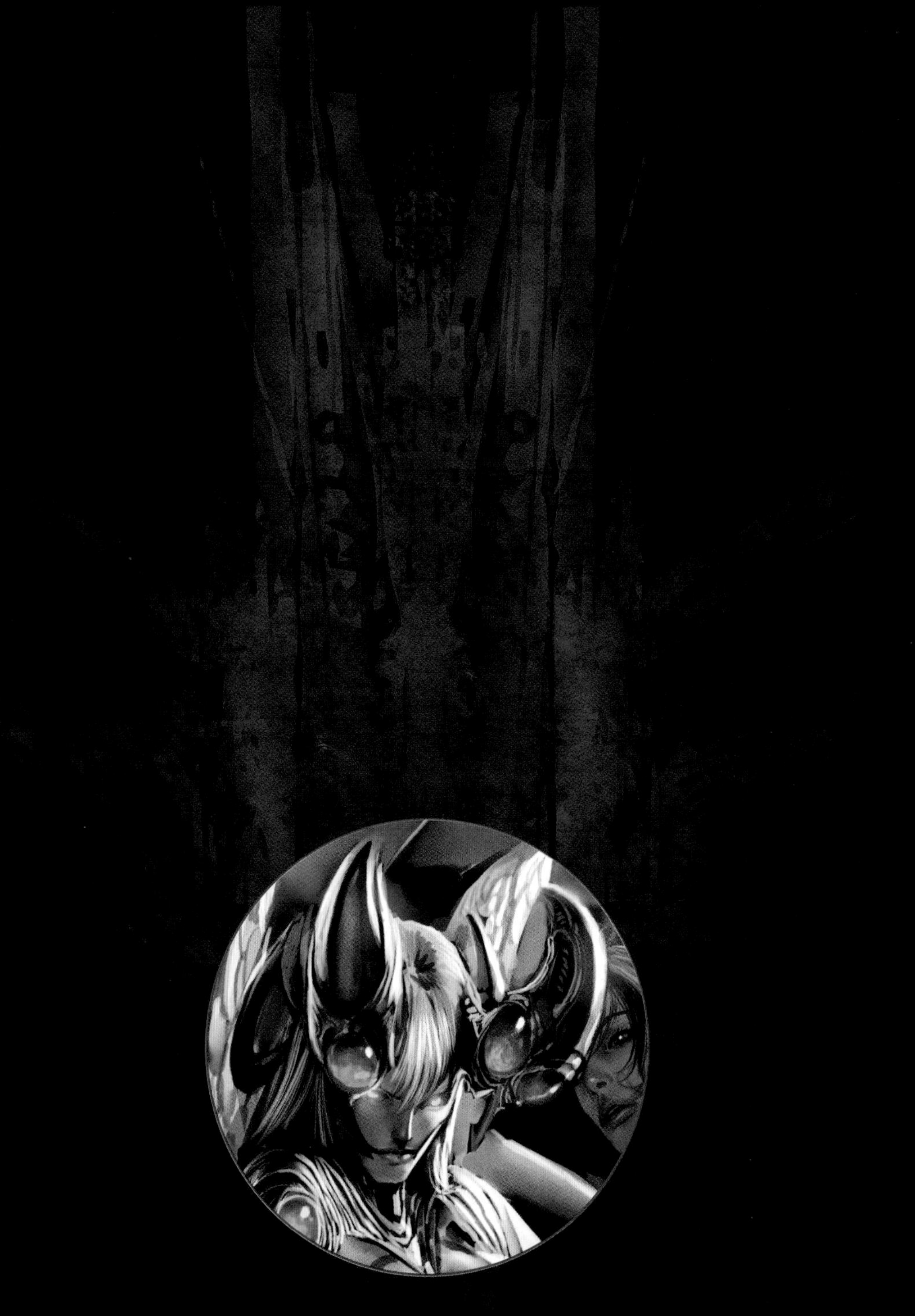

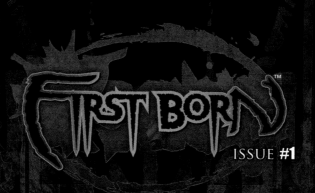

FIRST BORN™

ISSUE **#1**

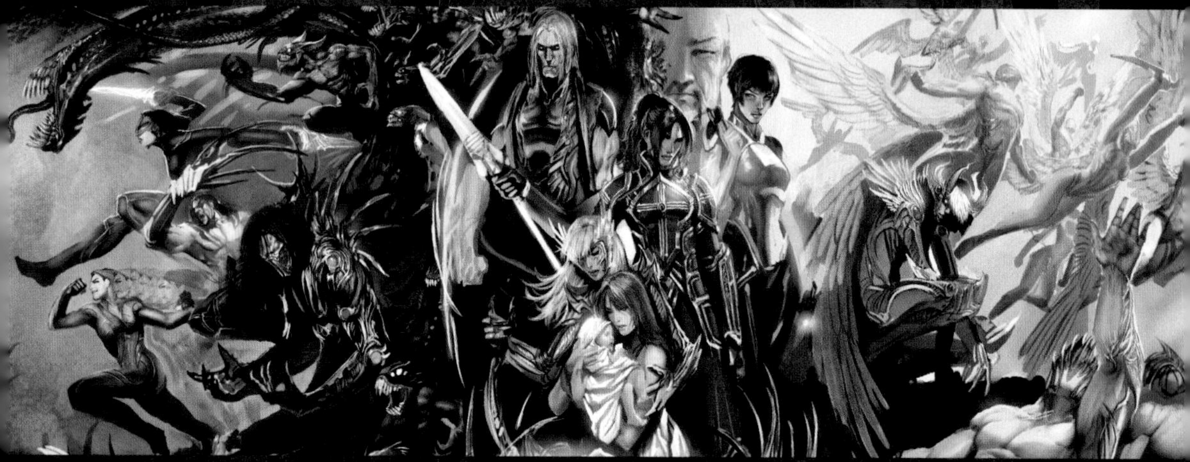

written by: **Ron Marz**
art by: **Stjepan Sejic**
letters by: **Troy Peteri**

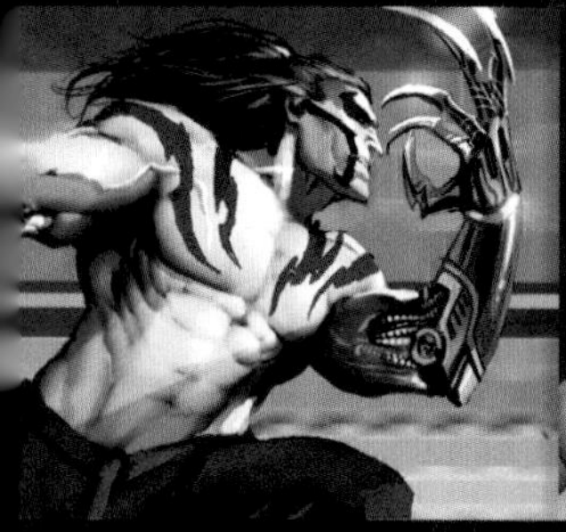
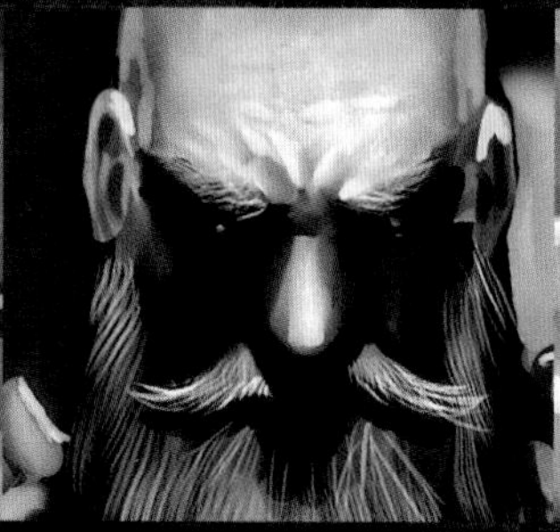
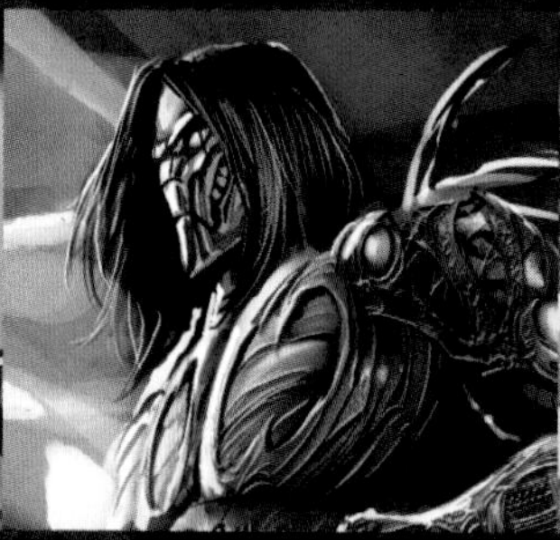
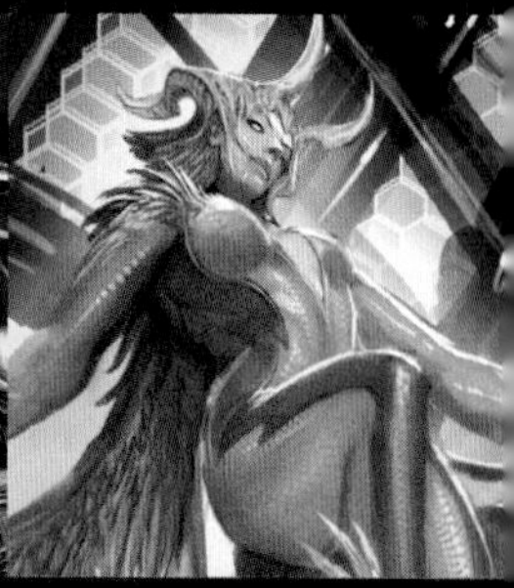

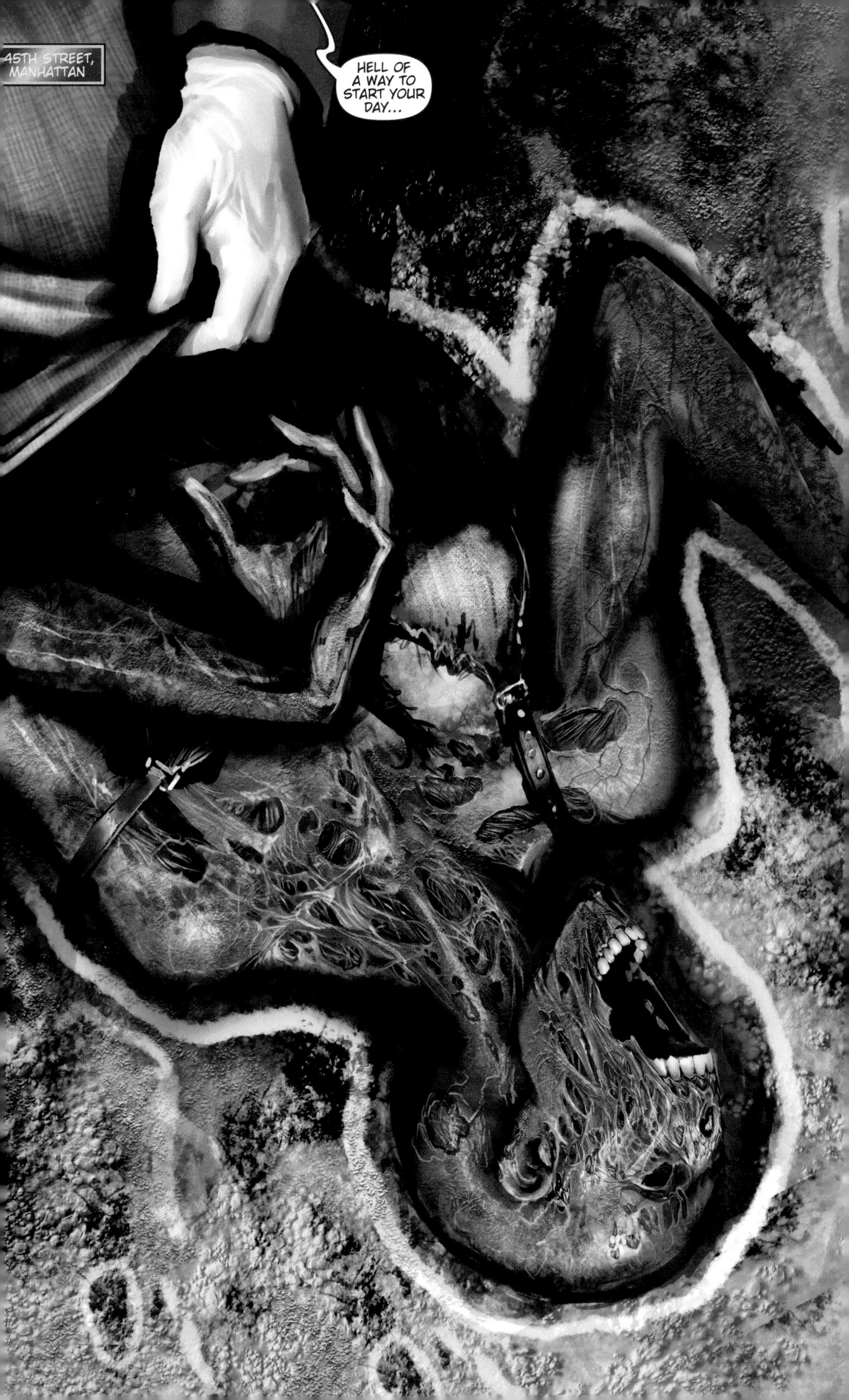
45TH STREET, MANHATTAN
HELL OF A WAY TO START YOUR DAY...

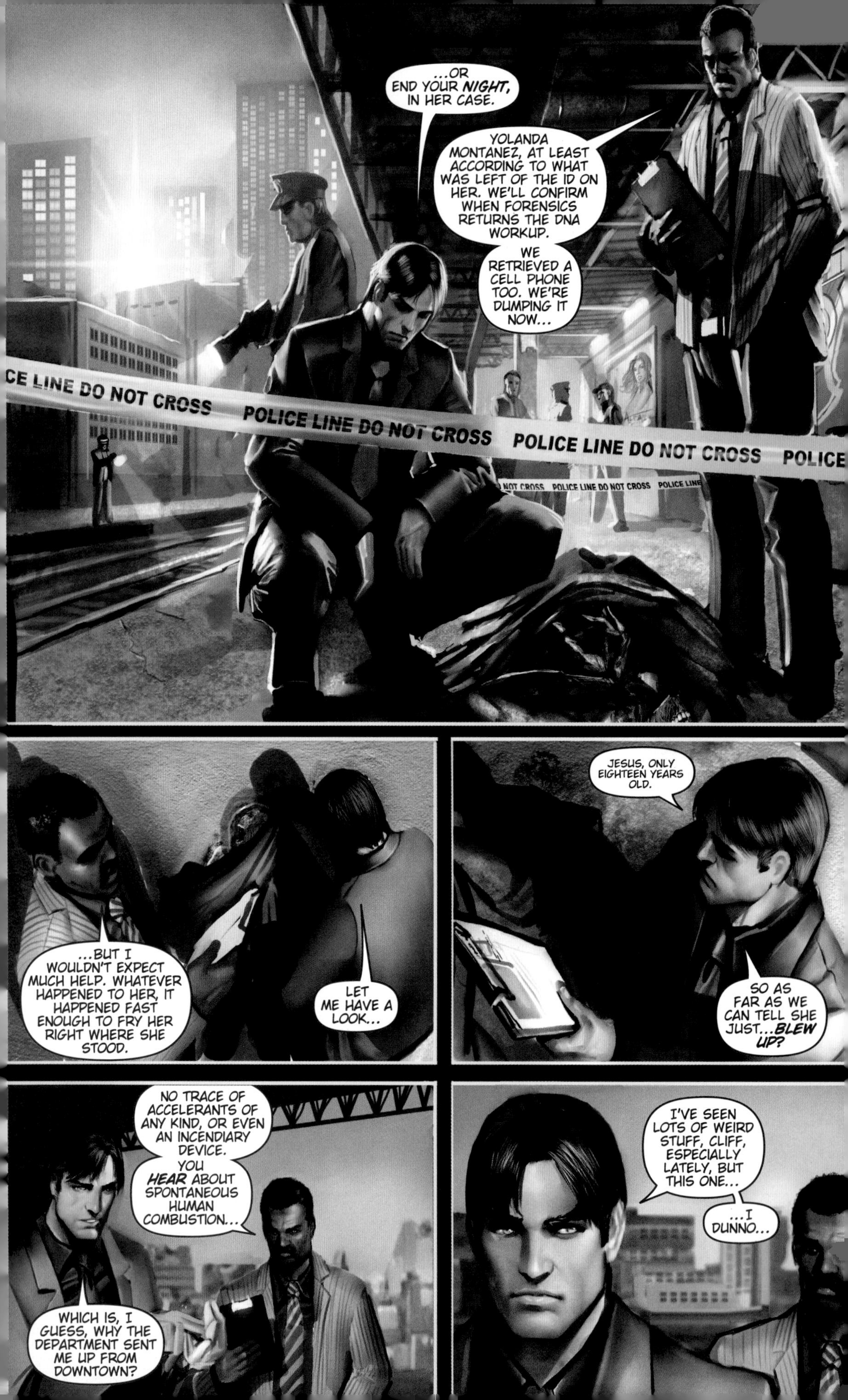
...OR END YOUR NIGHT, IN HER CASE.
YOLANDA MONTANEZ, AT LEAST ACCORDING TO WHAT WAS LEFT OF THE ID ON HER. WE'LL CONFIRM WHEN FORENSICS RETURNS THE DNA WORKUP.
WE RETRIEVED A CELL PHONE TOO. WE'RE DUMPING IT NOW...
POLICE LINE DO NOT CROSS
...BUT I WOULDN'T EXPECT MUCH HELP. WHATEVER HAPPENED TO HER, IT HAPPENED FAST ENOUGH TO FRY HER RIGHT WHERE SHE STOOD.
LET ME HAVE A LOOK...
JESUS, ONLY EIGHTEEN YEARS OLD.
SO AS FAR AS WE CAN TELL SHE JUST...BLEW UP?
NO TRACE OF ACCELERANTS OF ANY KIND, OR EVEN AN INCENDIARY DEVICE.
YOU HEAR ABOUT SPONTANEOUS HUMAN COMBUSTION...
WHICH IS, I GUESS, WHY THE DEPARTMENT SENT ME UP FROM DOWNTOWN?
I'VE SEEN LOTS OF WEIRD STUFF, CLIFF, ESPECIALLY LATELY, BUT THIS ONE...
...I DUNNO...

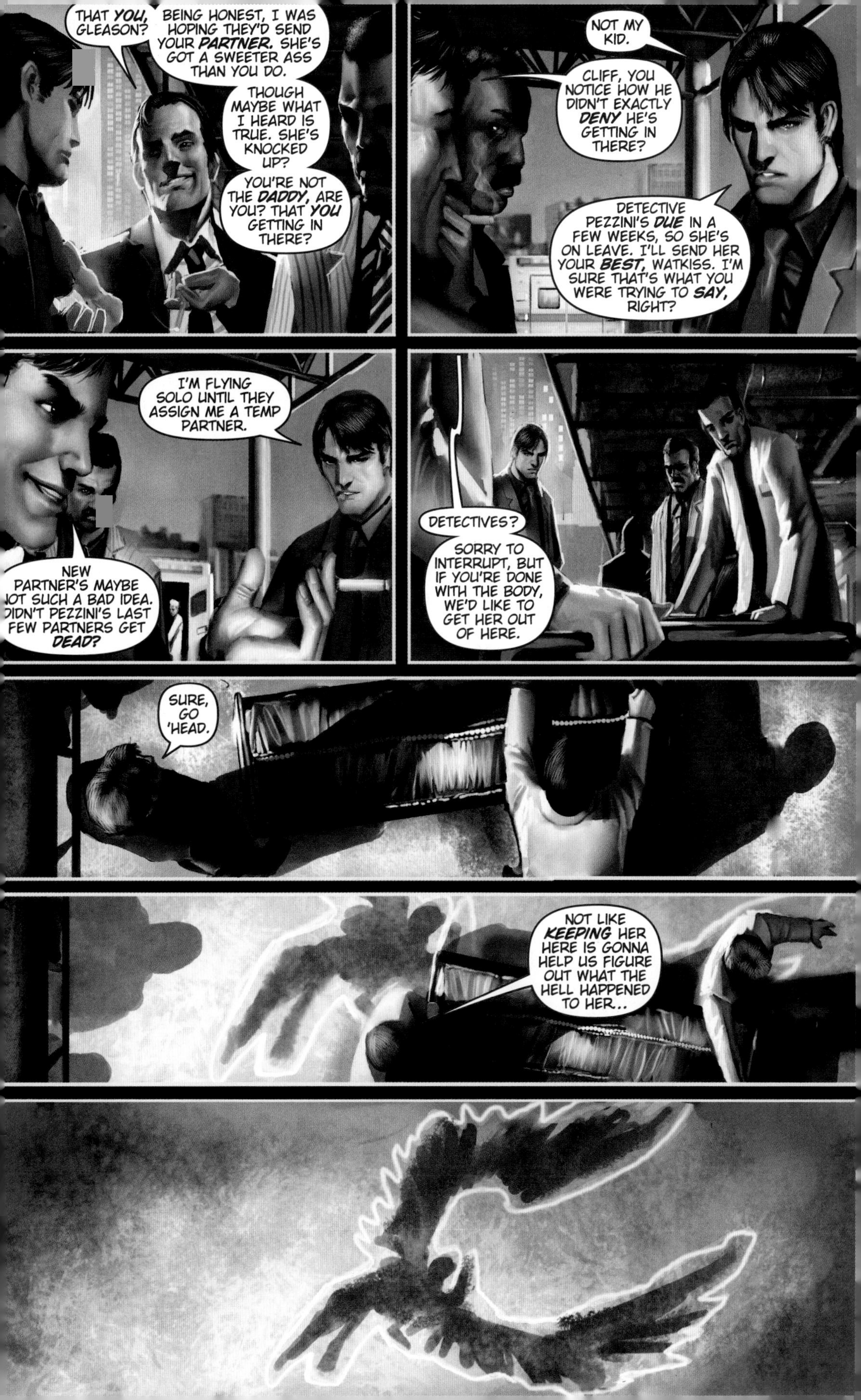
THAT YOU, GLEASON?
BEING HONEST, I WAS HOPING THEY'D SEND YOUR PARTNER. SHE'S GOT A SWEETER ASS THAN YOU DO.
THOUGH MAYBE WHAT I HEARD IS TRUE. SHE'S KNOCKED UP?
YOU'RE NOT THE DADDY, ARE YOU? THAT YOU GETTING IN THERE?
NOT MY KID.
CLIFF, YOU NOTICE HOW HE DIDN'T EXACTLY DENY HE'S GETTING IN THERE?
DETECTIVE PEZZINI'S DUE IN A FEW WEEKS, SO SHE'S ON LEAVE. I'LL SEND HER YOUR BEST, WATKISS. I'M SURE THAT'S WHAT YOU WERE TRYING TO SAY, RIGHT?
I'M FLYING SOLO UNTIL THEY ASSIGN ME A TEMP PARTNER.
NEW PARTNER'S MAYBE NOT SUCH A BAD IDEA. DIDN'T PEZZINI'S LAST FEW PARTNERS GET DEAD?
DETECTIVES?
SORRY TO INTERRUPT, BUT IF YOU'RE DONE WITH THE BODY, WE'D LIKE TO GET HER OUT OF HERE.
SURE, GO 'HEAD.
NOT LIKE KEEPING HER HERE IS GONNA HELP US FIGURE OUT WHAT THE HELL HAPPENED TO HER...

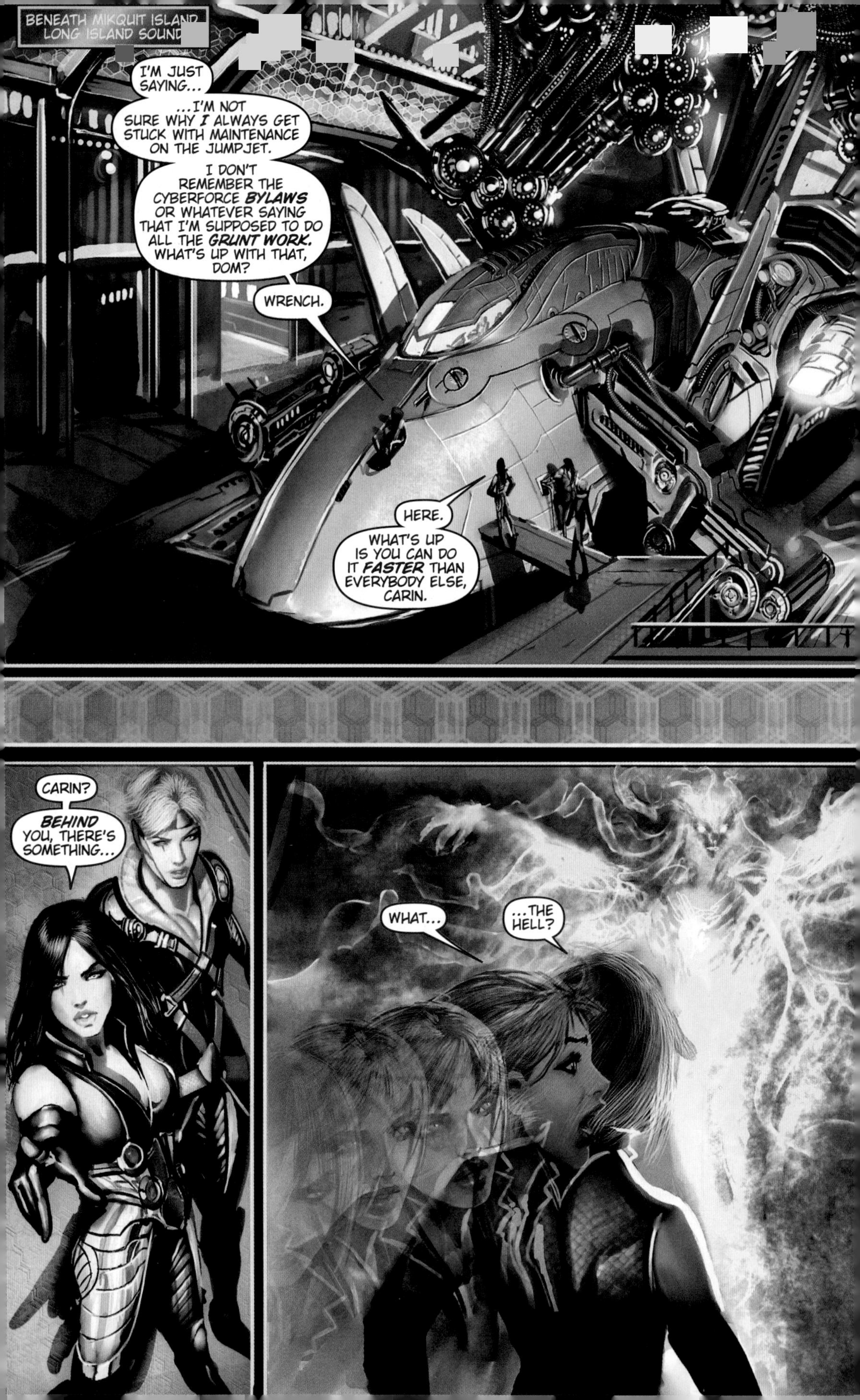
BENEATH MIKQUIT ISLAND
LONG ISLAND SOUND
I'M JUST SAYING...
...I'M NOT SURE WHY *I* ALWAYS GET STUCK WITH MAINTENANCE ON THE JUMPJET.
I DON'T REMEMBER THE CYBERFORCE **BYLAWS** OR WHATEVER SAYING THAT I'M SUPPOSED TO DO ALL THE **GRUNT WORK.** WHAT'S UP WITH THAT, DOM?
WRENCH.
HERE.
WHAT'S UP IS YOU CAN DO IT **FASTER** THAN EVERYBODY ELSE, CARIN.
CARIN?
BEHIND YOU, THERE'S SOMETHING...
WHAT...
...THE HELL?

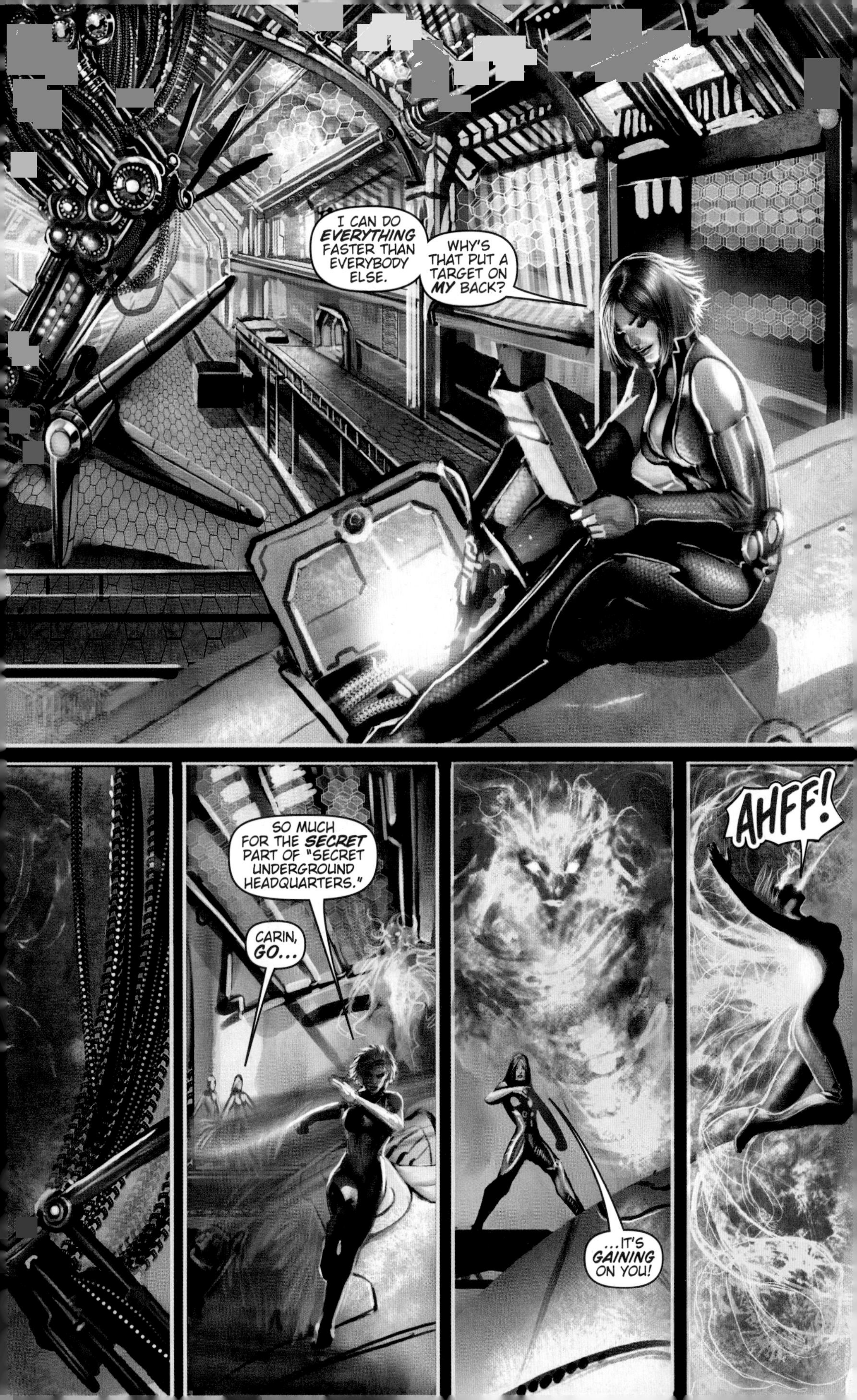
I CAN DO **EVERYTHING** FASTER THAN EVERYBODY ELSE.
WHY'S THAT PUT A TARGET ON **MY** BACK?
SO MUCH FOR THE **SECRET** PART OF "SECRET UNDERGROUND HEADQUARTERS."
CARIN, **GO...**
...IT'S **GAINING** ON YOU!
AHFF!

YES.

OH, YES, *THIS* WILL DO. *THIS ONE* IS STRONG ENOUGH TO CONTAIN ALL THAT I AM.

WHAT THE HELL JUST HAPPENED TO MY *SISTER?*

I DON'T EVEN KNOW IF THAT *IS* YOUR SISTER ANYMORE.

BALLISTIC, CYBLADE...

...BUY A *TICKET* IF YOU'RE JUST GONNA BE SPECTATORS.

THIS ONE IS CALLED *CARIN?*

OR *VELOCITY?*

I THANK YOU FOR HER. SHE IS A *WORTHY* VESSEL.

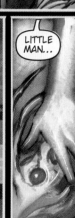

LITTLE MAN...

FIND A *DIFFERENT* WORTHY VESSEL.

CYBERFORCE PROTECTS ITS OWN.

...WHO ARE *YOU* TO REFUSE ME ANYTHING?

A*AGH!*

CASS, THAT'S STILL YOUR *SISTER.* OR AT LEAST *PART* OF HER IS.

BUT UNLESS YOU'VE GOT A *BETTER* IDEA...

DO IT.

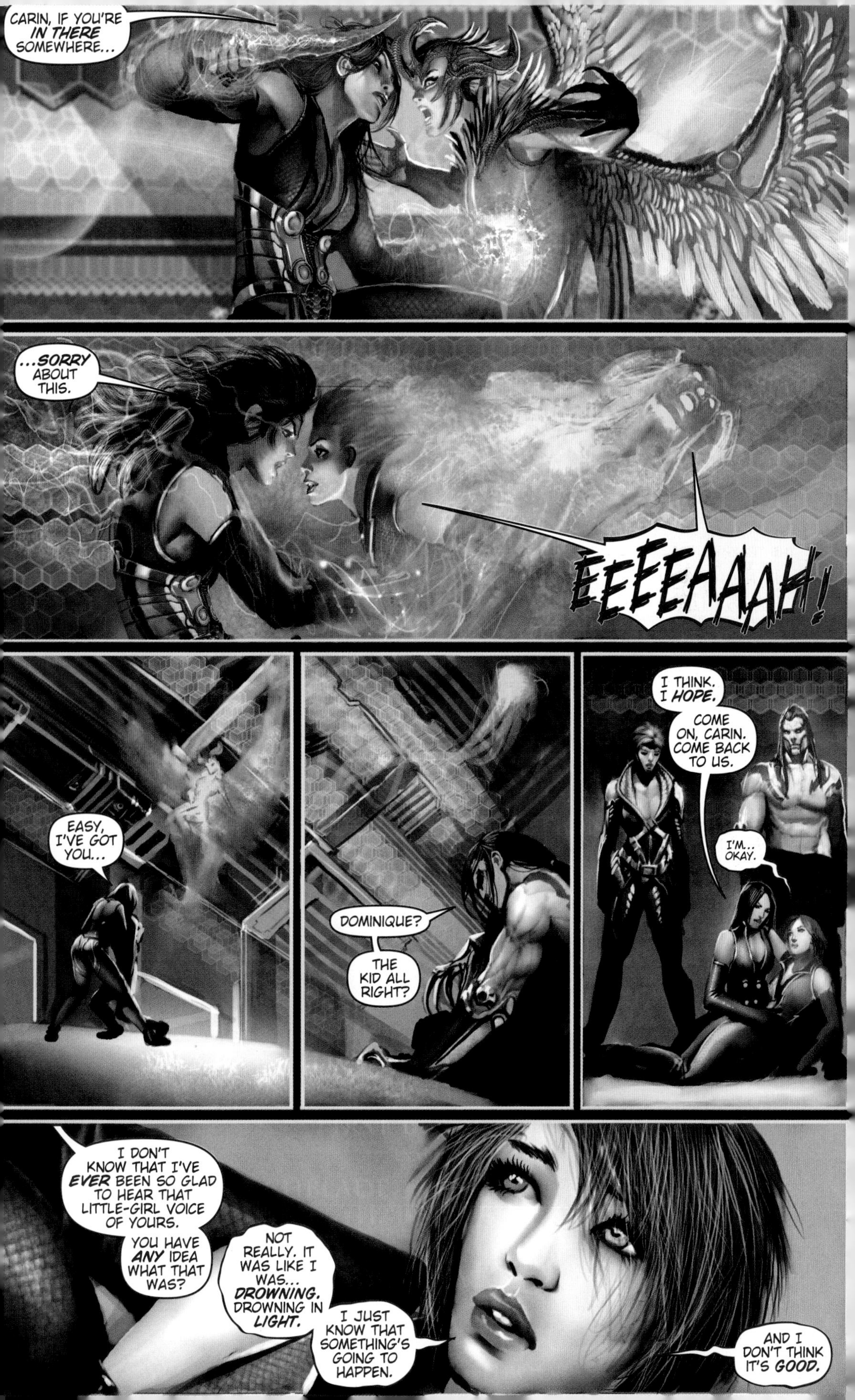
CARIN, IF YOU'RE **IN THERE** SOMEWHERE...
...**SORRY** ABOUT THIS.
EEEEAAAH!
EASY, I'VE GOT YOU...
DOMINIQUE?
THE KID ALL RIGHT?
I THINK. I **HOPE.**
COME ON, CARIN. COME BACK TO US.
I'M... OKAY.
I DON'T KNOW THAT I'VE **EVER** BEEN SO GLAD TO HEAR THAT LITTLE-GIRL VOICE OF YOURS.
YOU HAVE **ANY** IDEA WHAT THAT WAS?
NOT REALLY. IT WAS LIKE I WAS... **DROWNING.** DROWNING IN **LIGHT.**
I JUST KNOW THAT SOMETHING'S GOING TO HAPPEN.
AND I DON'T THINK IT'S **GOOD.**

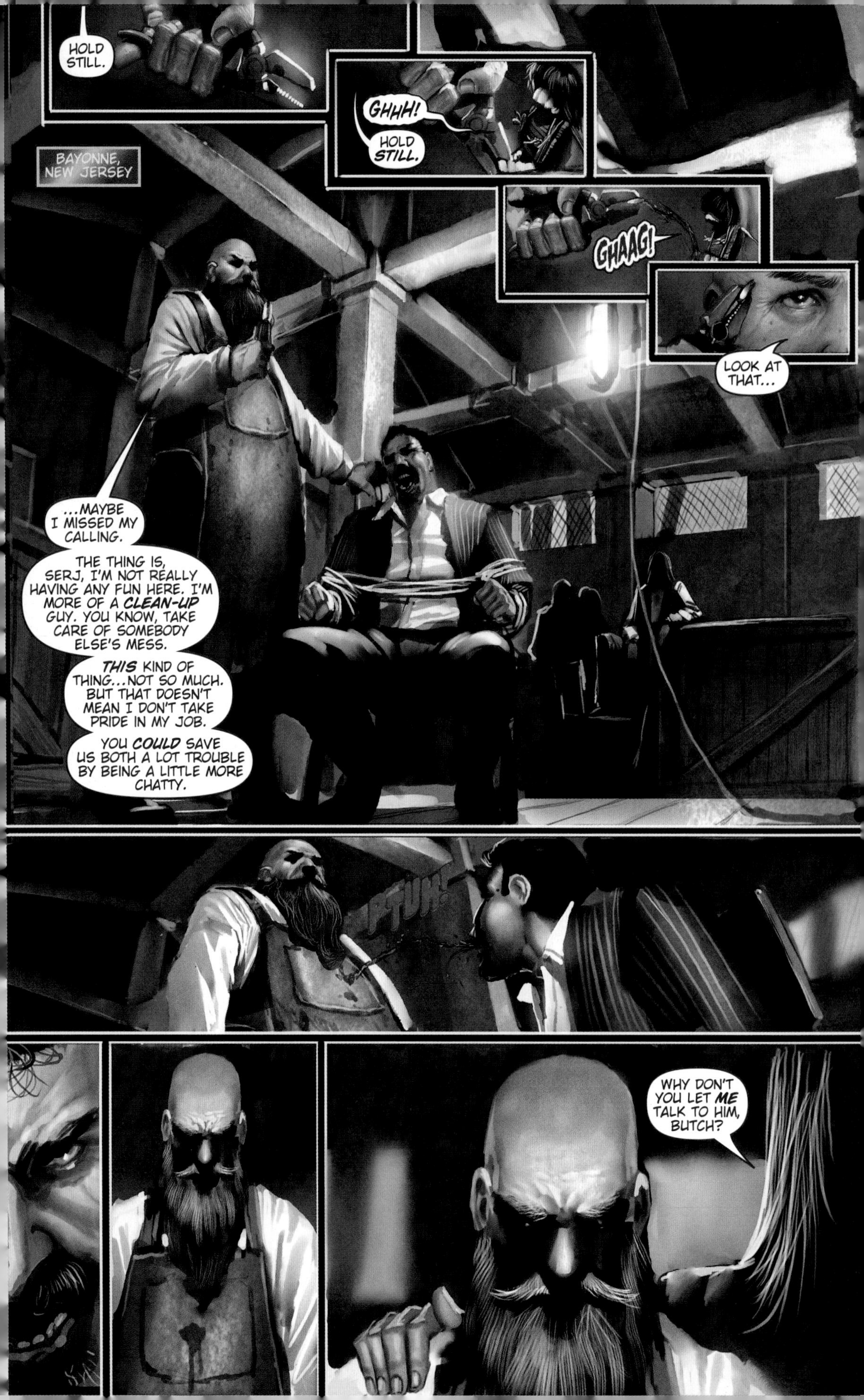
HOLD STILL.
GHHH!
HOLD STILL.
BAYONNE, NEW JERSEY
GHAAG!
LOOK AT THAT...
...MAYBE I MISSED MY CALLING.
THE THING IS, SERJ, I'M NOT REALLY HAVING ANY FUN HERE. I'M MORE OF A CLEAN-UP GUY. YOU KNOW, TAKE CARE OF SOMEBODY ELSE'S MESS.
THIS KIND OF THING...NOT SO MUCH. BUT THAT DOESN'T MEAN I DON'T TAKE PRIDE IN MY JOB.
YOU COULD SAVE US BOTH A LOT TROUBLE BY BEING A LITTLE MORE CHATTY.
PTUH!
WHY DON'T YOU LET ME TALK TO HIM, BUTCH?

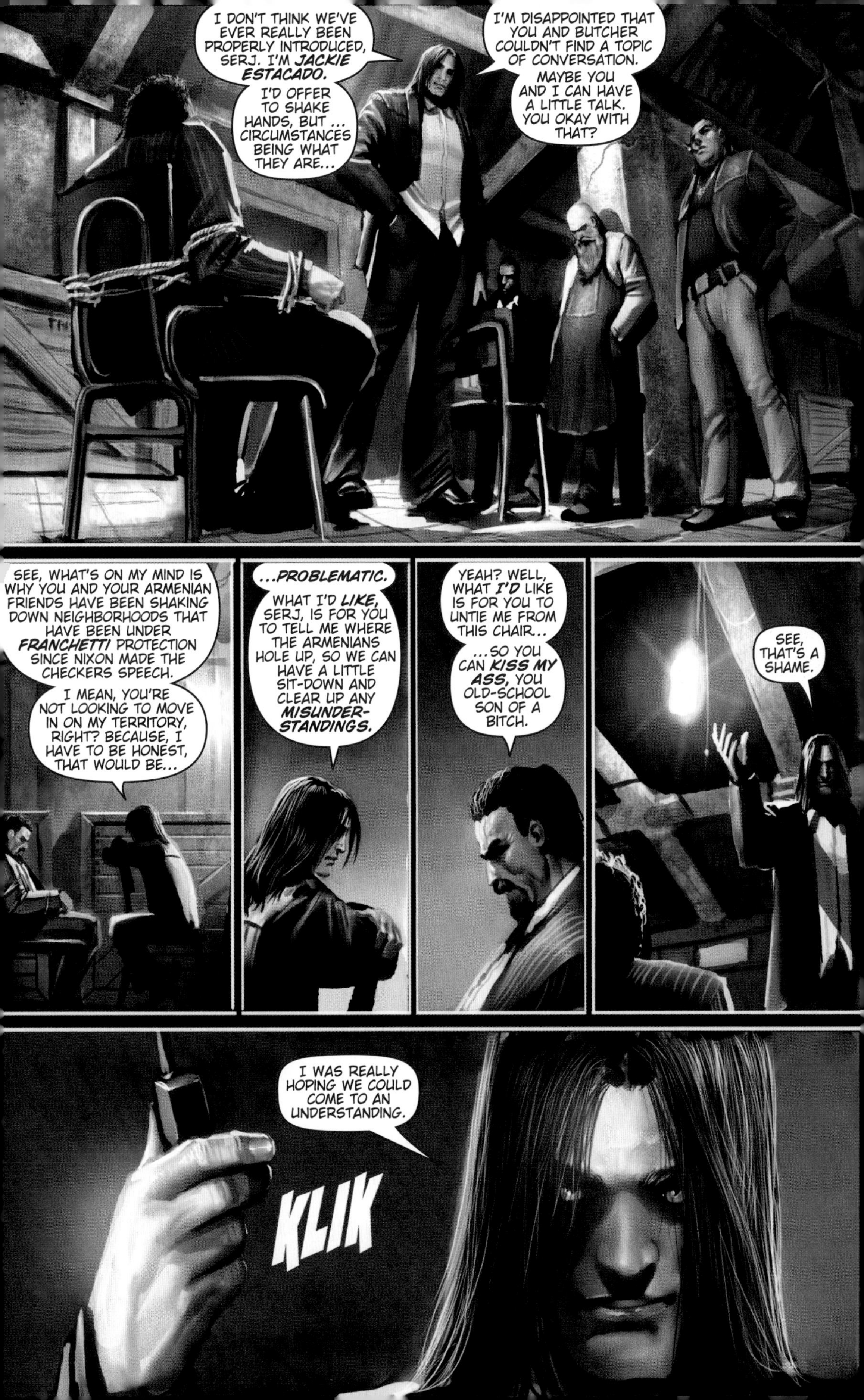
I DON'T THINK WE'VE EVER REALLY BEEN PROPERLY INTRODUCED, SERJ. I'M JACKIE ESTACADO.
I'D OFFER TO SHAKE HANDS, BUT ... CIRCUMSTANCES BEING WHAT THEY ARE...
I'M DISAPPOINTED THAT YOU AND BUTCHER COULDN'T FIND A TOPIC OF CONVERSATION.
MAYBE YOU AND I CAN HAVE A LITTLE TALK. YOU OKAY WITH THAT?
SEE, WHAT'S ON MY MIND IS WHY YOU AND YOUR ARMENIAN FRIENDS HAVE BEEN SHAKING DOWN NEIGHBORHOODS THAT HAVE BEEN UNDER FRANCHETTI PROTECTION SINCE NIXON MADE THE CHECKERS SPEECH.
I MEAN, YOU'RE NOT LOOKING TO MOVE IN ON MY TERRITORY, RIGHT? BECAUSE, I HAVE TO BE HONEST, THAT WOULD BE...
...PROBLEMATIC.
WHAT I'D LIKE, SERJ, IS FOR YOU TO TELL ME WHERE THE ARMENIANS HOLE UP, SO WE CAN HAVE A LITTLE SIT-DOWN AND CLEAR UP ANY MISUNDERSTANDINGS.
YEAH? WELL, WHAT I'D LIKE IS FOR YOU TO UNTIE ME FROM THIS CHAIR..
...SO YOU CAN KISS MY ASS, YOU OLD-SCHOOL SON OF A BITCH.
SEE, THAT'S A SHAME.
I WAS REALLY HOPING WE COULD COME TO AN UNDERSTANDING.
KLIK

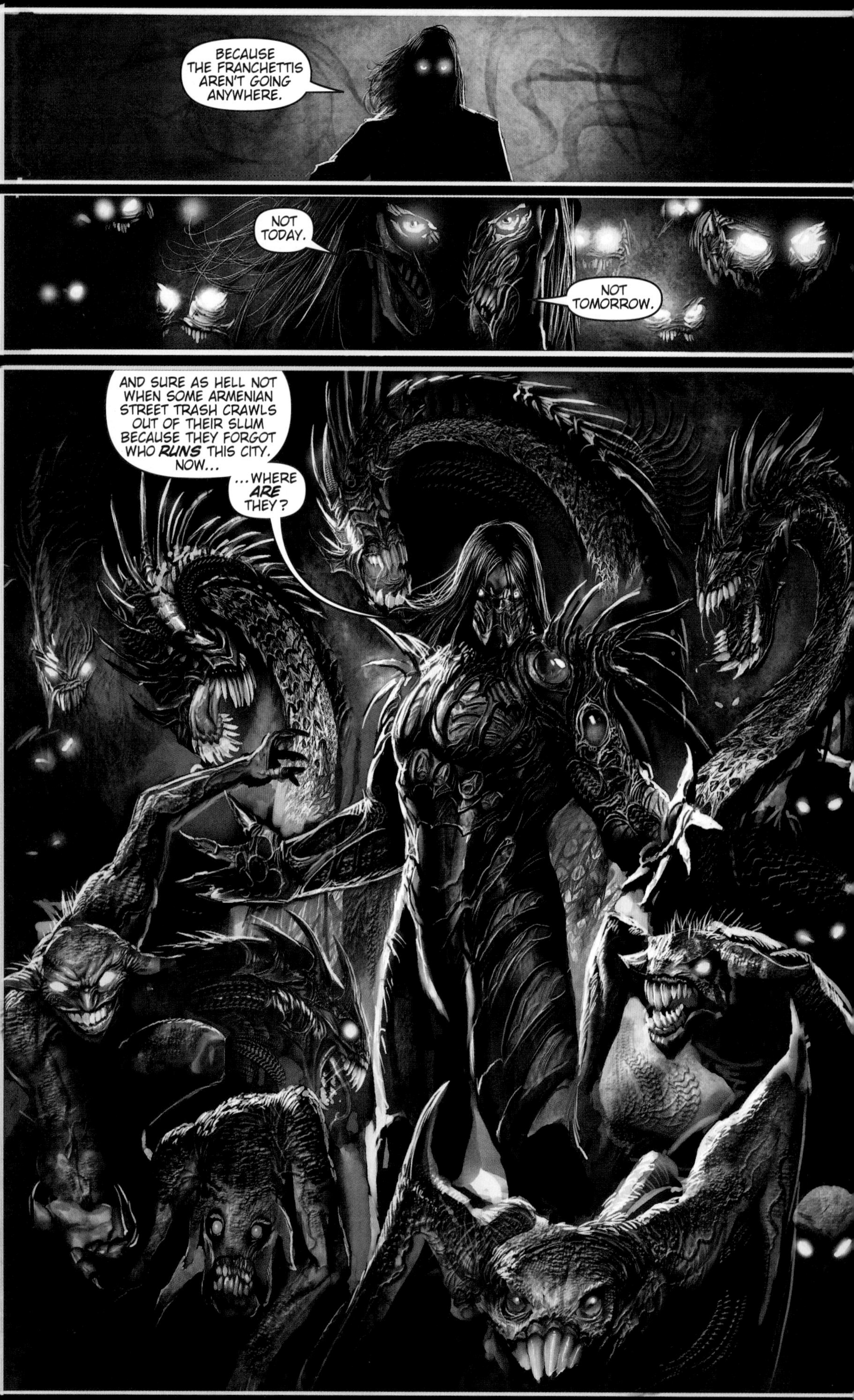
BECAUSE THE FRANCHETTIS AREN'T GOING ANYWHERE.
NOT TODAY.
NOT TOMORROW.
AND SURE AS HELL NOT WHEN SOME ARMENIAN STREET TRASH CRAWLS OUT OF THEIR SLUM BECAUSE THEY FORGOT WHO *RUNS* THIS CITY. NOW...
...WHERE *ARE* THEY?

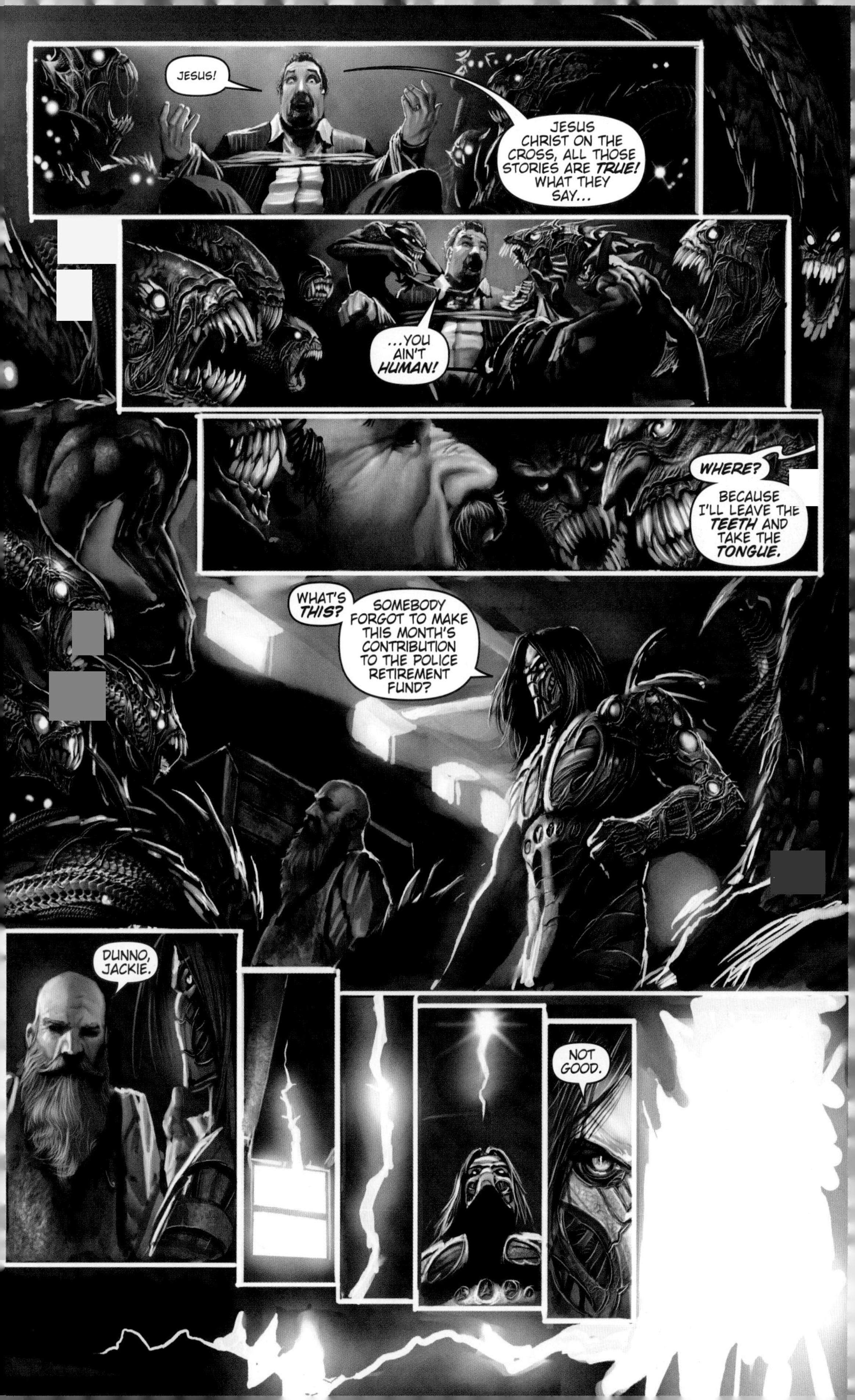
JESUS!
JESUS CHRIST ON THE CROSS, ALL THOSE STORIES ARE *TRUE!* WHAT THEY SAY...
...YOU AIN'T *HUMAN!*
WHERE?
BECAUSE I'LL LEAVE THE *TEETH* AND TAKE THE *TONGUE.*
WHAT'S *THIS?*
SOMEBODY FORGOT TO MAKE THIS MONTH'S CONTRIBUTION TO THE POLICE RETIREMENT FUND?
DUNNO, JACKIE.
NOT GOOD.

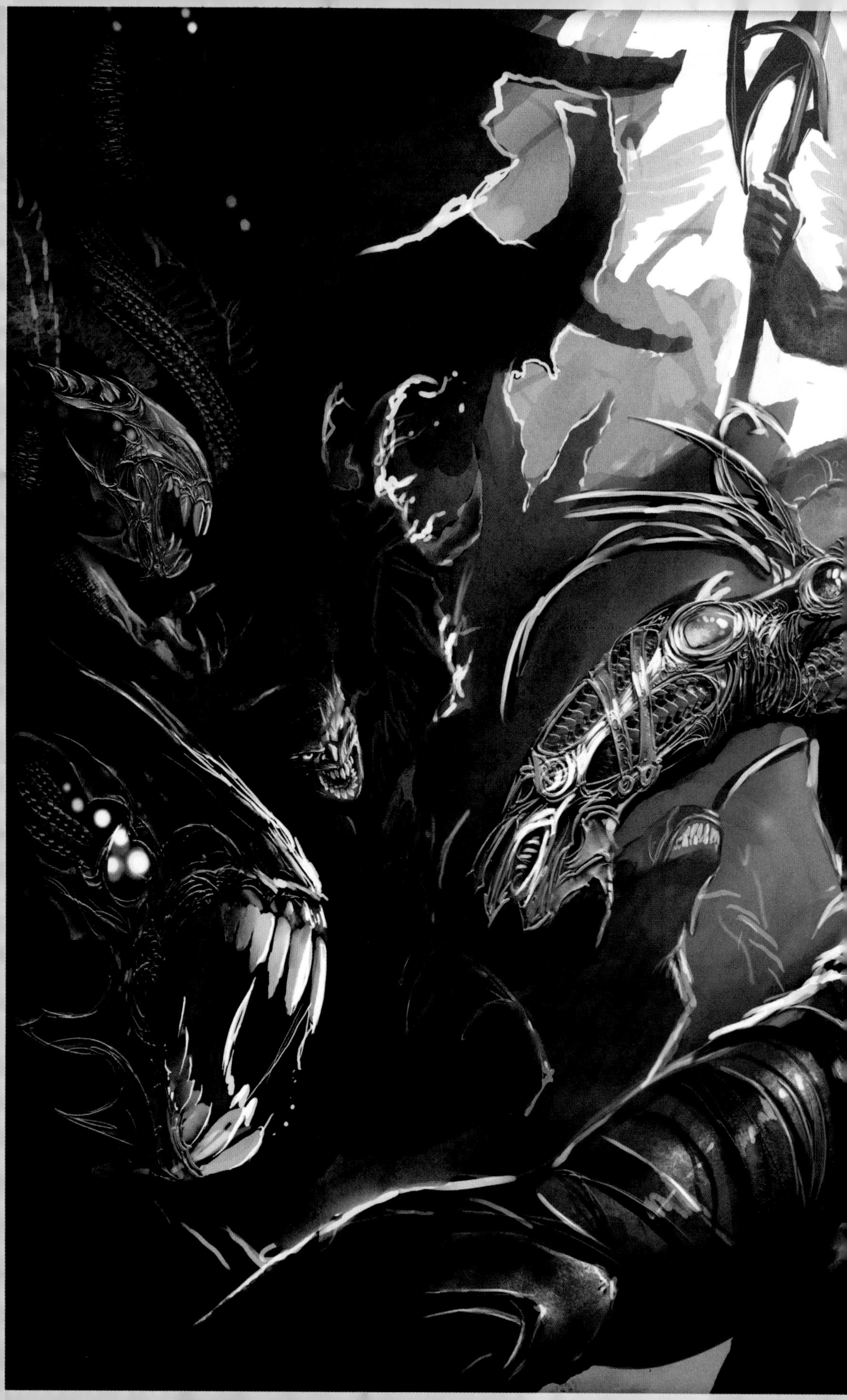

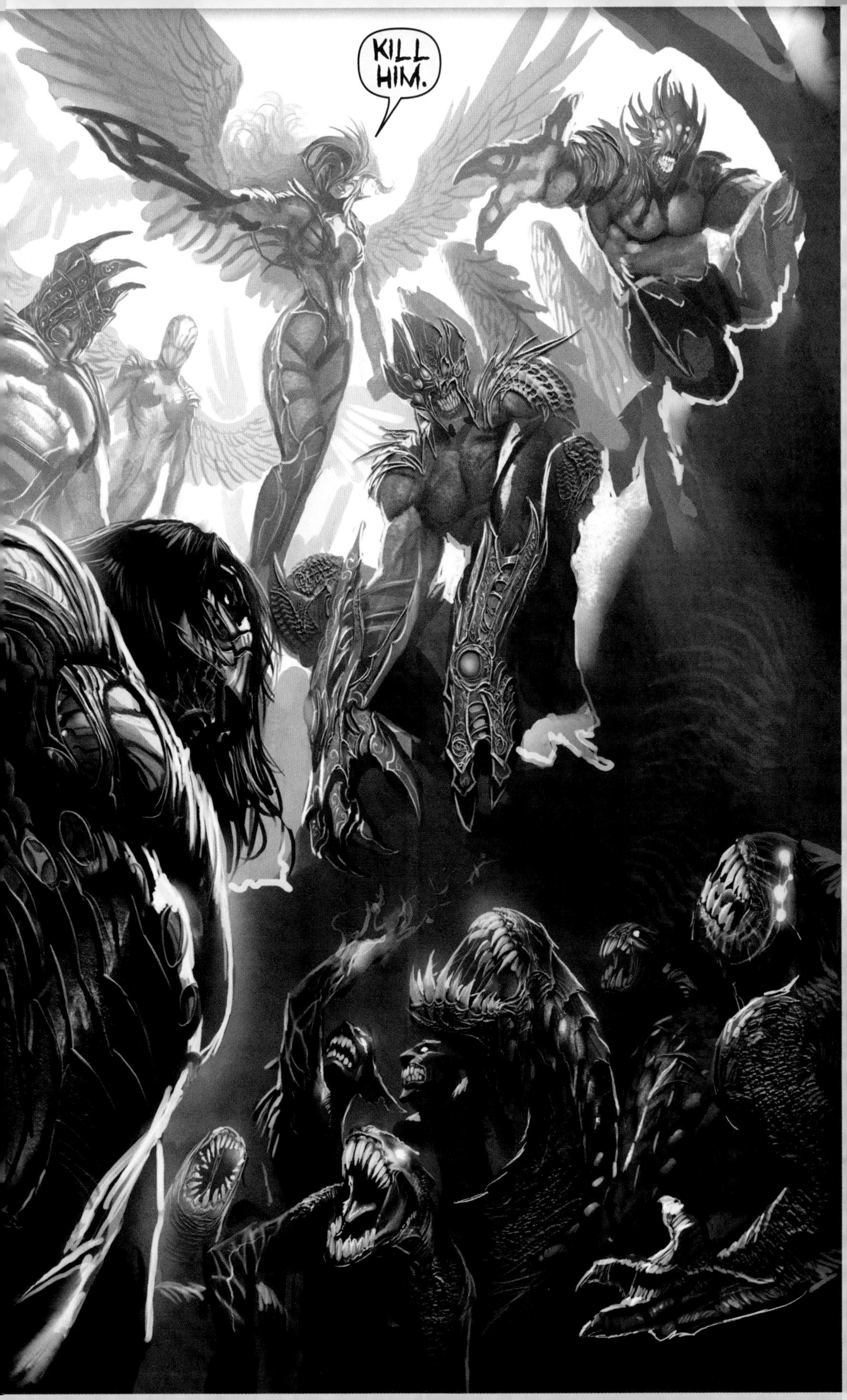
KILL HIM.

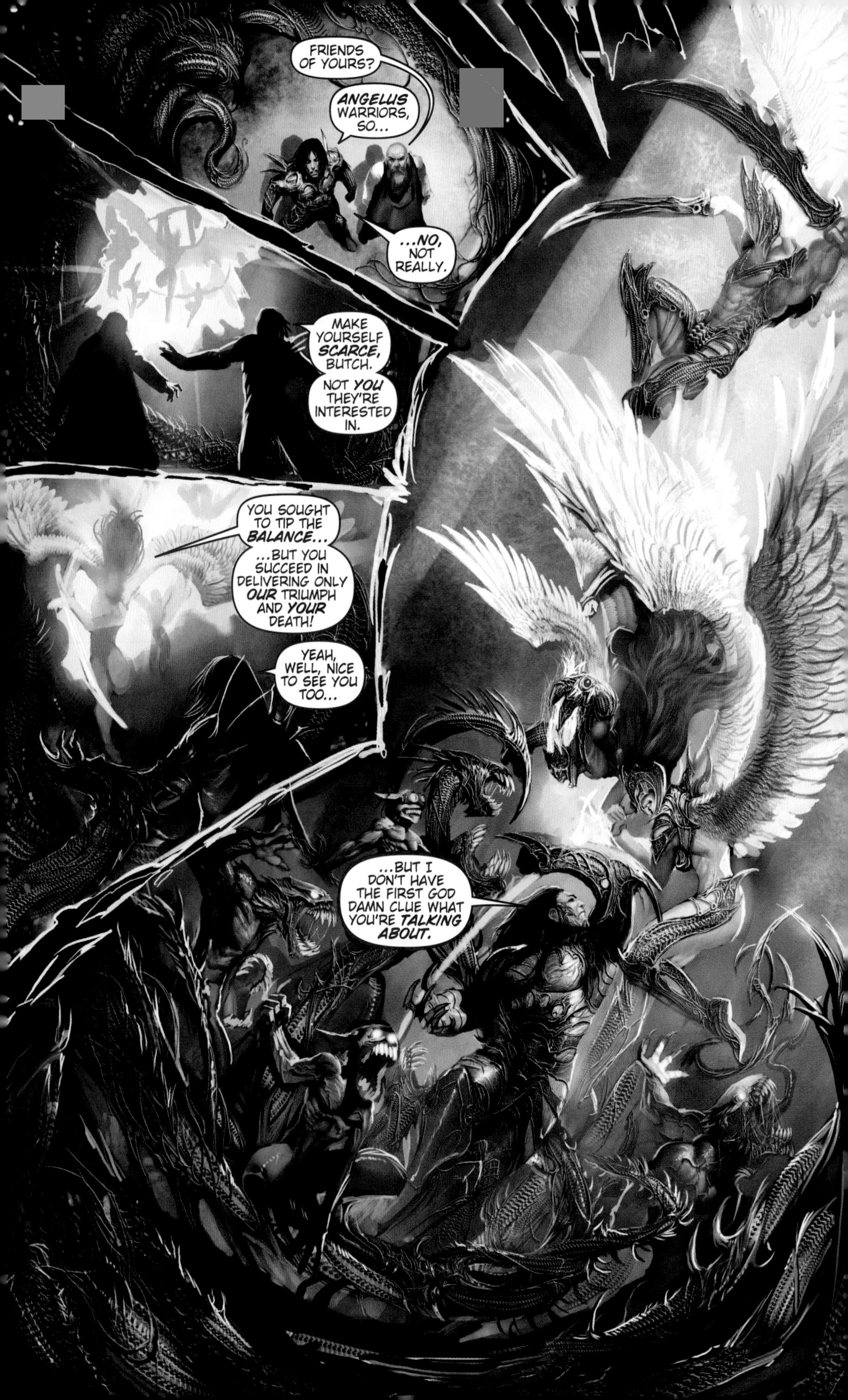
FRIENDS OF YOURS?
ANGELUS WARRIORS, SO...
...NO, NOT REALLY.
MAKE YOURSELF SCARCE, BUTCH.
NOT YOU THEY'RE INTERESTED IN.
YOU SOUGHT TO TIP THE BALANCE...
...BUT YOU SUCCEED IN DELIVERING ONLY OUR TRIUMPH AND YOUR DEATH!
YEAH, WELL, NICE TO SEE YOU TOO...
...BUT I DON'T HAVE THE FIRST GOD DAMN CLUE WHAT YOU'RE TALKING ABOUT.

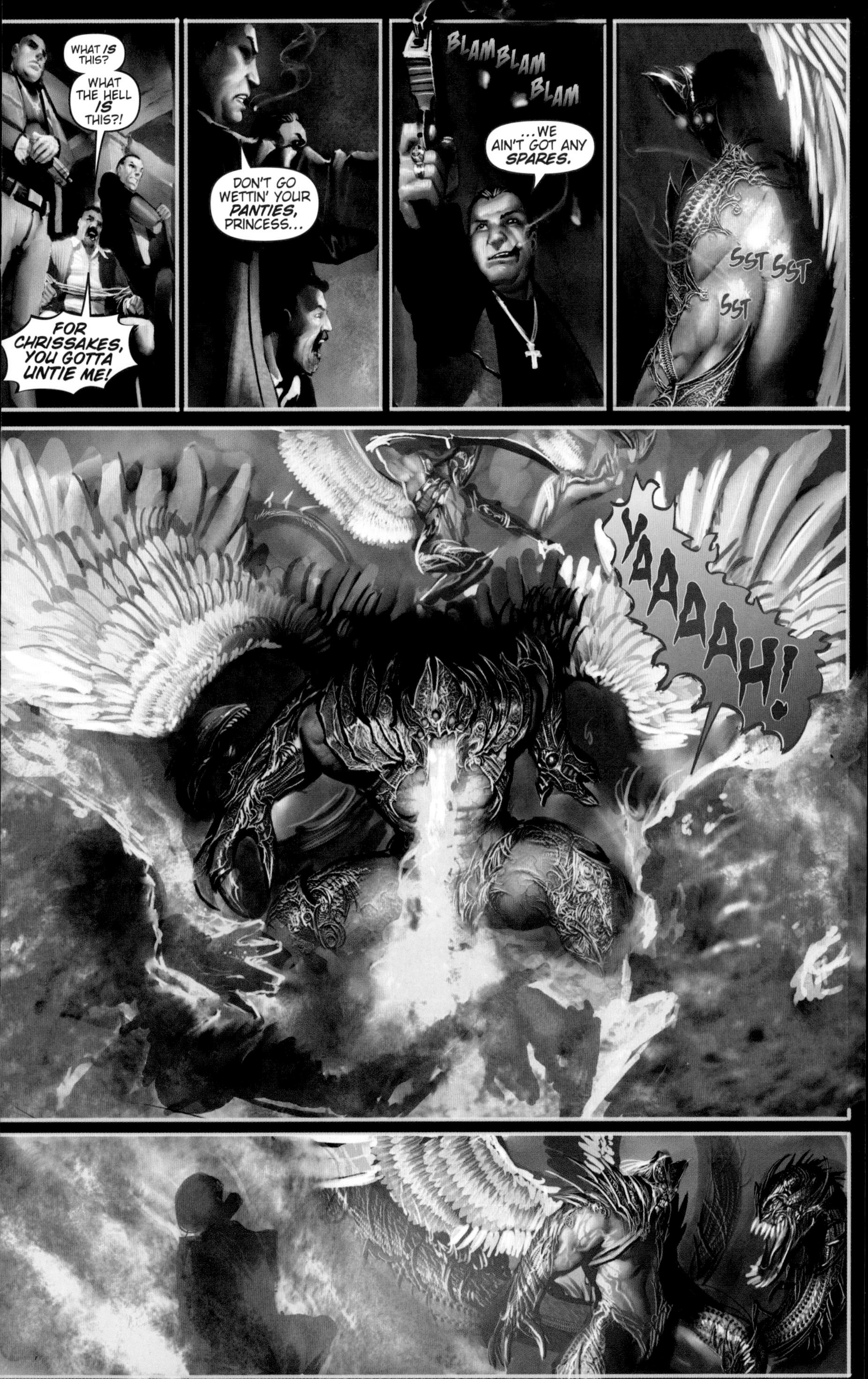
WHAT IS THIS?
WHAT THE HELL IS THIS?!
FOR CHRISSAKES, YOU GOTTA UNTIE ME!
DON'T GO WETTIN' YOUR PANTIES, PRINCESS...
BLAM BLAM BLAM
...WE AIN'T GOT ANY SPARES.
SST SST
SST
YAAAAAH!

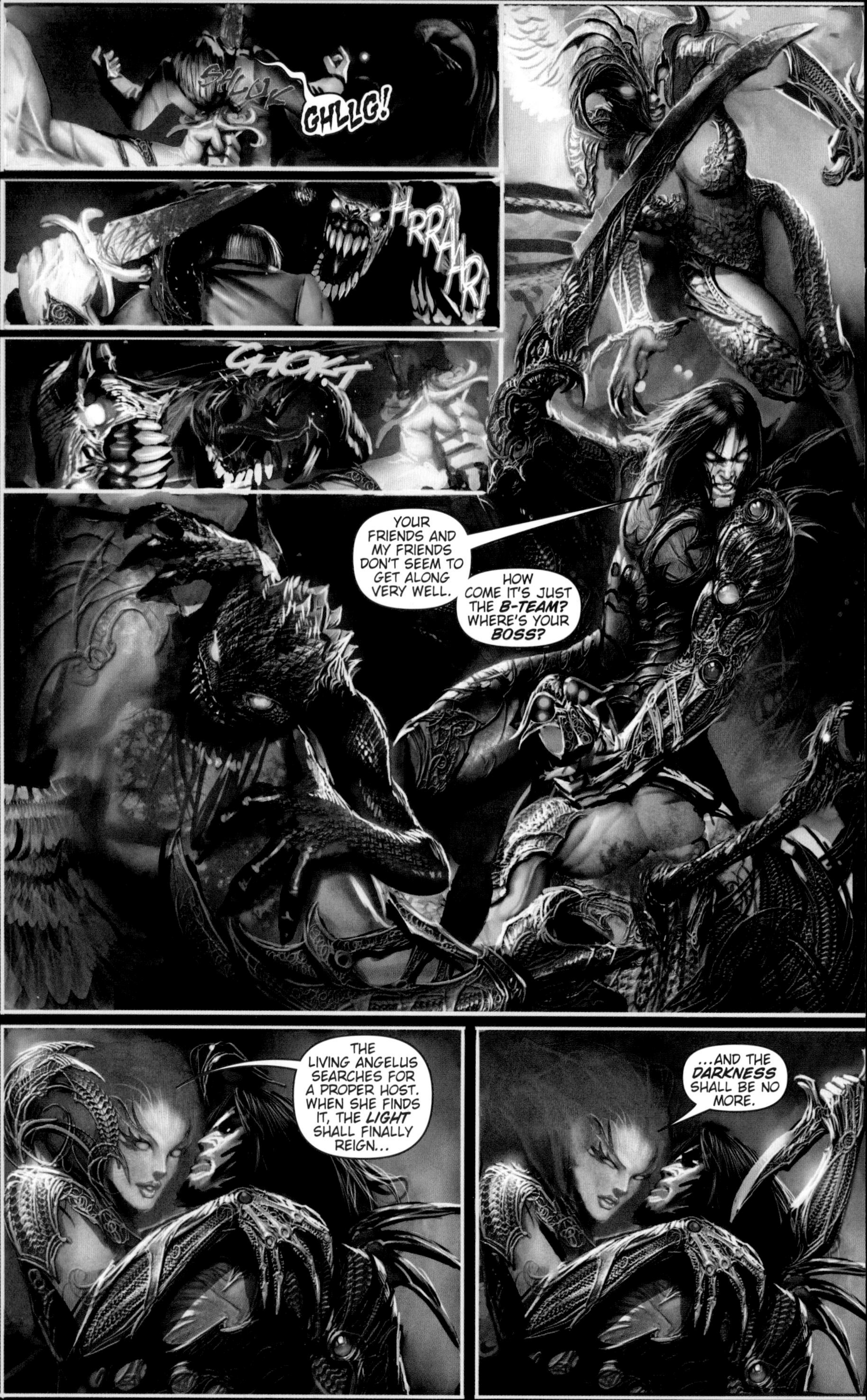
SHLUK
GHLLG!
HRRAAAR!
CHOK!
YOUR FRIENDS AND MY FRIENDS DON'T SEEM TO GET ALONG VERY WELL.
HOW COME IT'S JUST THE *B-TEAM?* WHERE'S YOUR *BOSS?*
THE LIVING ANGELUS SEARCHES FOR A PROPER HOST. WHEN SHE FINDS IT, THE *LIGHT* SHALL FINALLY REIGN...
...AND THE *DARKNESS* SHALL BE NO MORE.

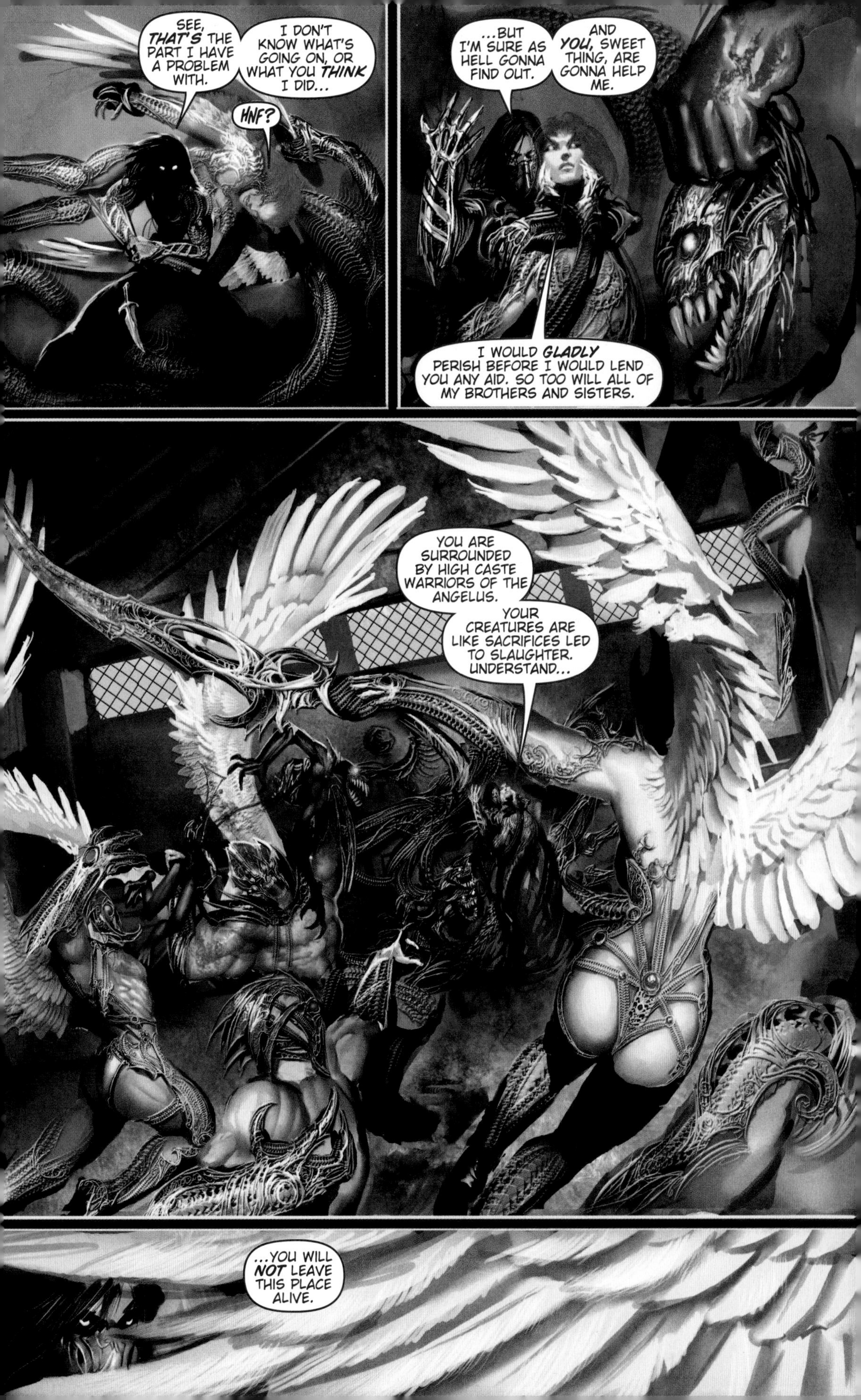
SEE, THAT'S THE PART I HAVE A PROBLEM WITH.
I DON'T KNOW WHAT'S GOING ON, OR WHAT YOU THINK I DID...
HNF?
...BUT I'M SURE AS HELL GONNA FIND OUT.
AND YOU, SWEET THING, ARE GONNA HELP ME.
I WOULD GLADLY PERISH BEFORE I WOULD LEND YOU ANY AID. SO TOO WILL ALL OF MY BROTHERS AND SISTERS.
YOU ARE SURROUNDED BY HIGH CASTE WARRIORS OF THE ANGELUS.
YOUR CREATURES ARE LIKE SACRIFICES LED TO SLAUGHTER. UNDERSTAND...
...YOU WILL NOT LEAVE THIS PLACE ALIVE.

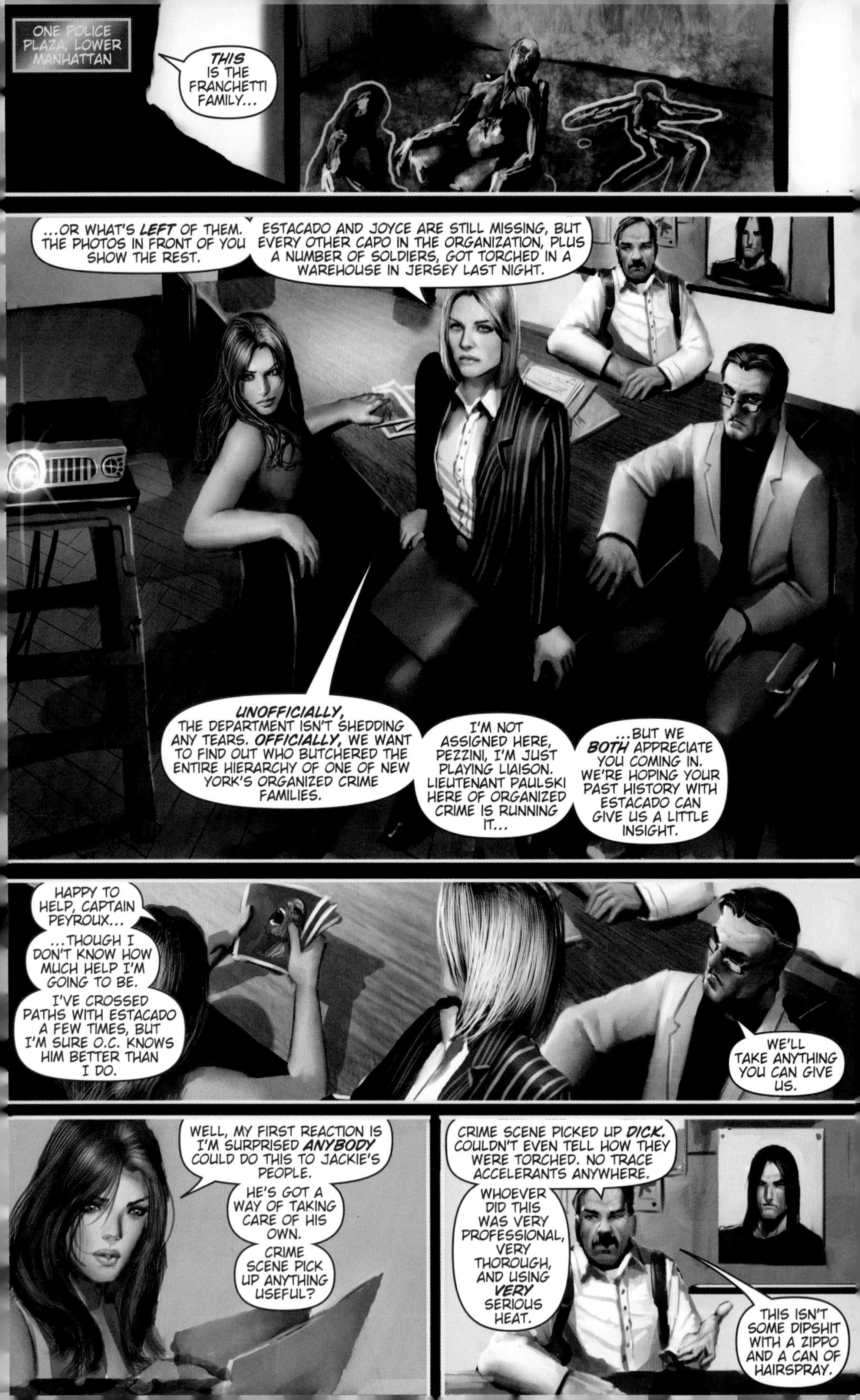

ONE POLICE PLAZA, LOWER MANHATTAN
THIS IS THE FRANCHETTI FAMILY...
...OR WHAT'S LEFT OF THEM. THE PHOTOS IN FRONT OF YOU SHOW THE REST.
ESTACADO AND JOYCE ARE STILL MISSING, BUT EVERY OTHER CAPO IN THE ORGANIZATION, PLUS A NUMBER OF SOLDIERS, GOT TORCHED IN A WAREHOUSE IN JERSEY LAST NIGHT.
UNOFFICIALLY, THE DEPARTMENT ISN'T SHEDDING ANY TEARS. OFFICIALLY, WE WANT TO FIND OUT WHO BUTCHERED THE ENTIRE HIERARCHY OF ONE OF NEW YORK'S ORGANIZED CRIME FAMILIES.
I'M NOT ASSIGNED HERE, PEZZINI, I'M JUST PLAYING LIAISON. LIEUTENANT PAULSKI HERE OF ORGANIZED CRIME IS RUNNING IT...
...BUT WE BOTH APPRECIATE YOU COMING IN. WE'RE HOPING YOUR PAST HISTORY WITH ESTACADO CAN GIVE US A LITTLE INSIGHT.
HAPPY TO HELP, CAPTAIN PEYROUX...
...THOUGH I DON'T KNOW HOW MUCH HELP I'M GOING TO BE.
I'VE CROSSED PATHS WITH ESTACADO A FEW TIMES, BUT I'M SURE O.C. KNOWS HIM BETTER THAN I DO.
WE'LL TAKE ANYTHING YOU CAN GIVE US.
WELL, MY FIRST REACTION IS I'M SURPRISED ANYBODY COULD DO THIS TO JACKIE'S PEOPLE.
HE'S GOT A WAY OF TAKING CARE OF HIS OWN.
CRIME SCENE PICK UP ANYTHING USEFUL?
CRIME SCENE PICKED UP DICK. COULDN'T EVEN TELL HOW THEY WERE TORCHED. NO TRACE ACCELERANTS ANYWHERE.
WHOEVER DID THIS WAS VERY PROFESSIONAL, VERY THOROUGH, AND USING VERY SERIOUS HEAT.
THIS ISN'T SOME DIPSHIT WITH A ZIPPO AND A CAN OF HAIRSPRAY.

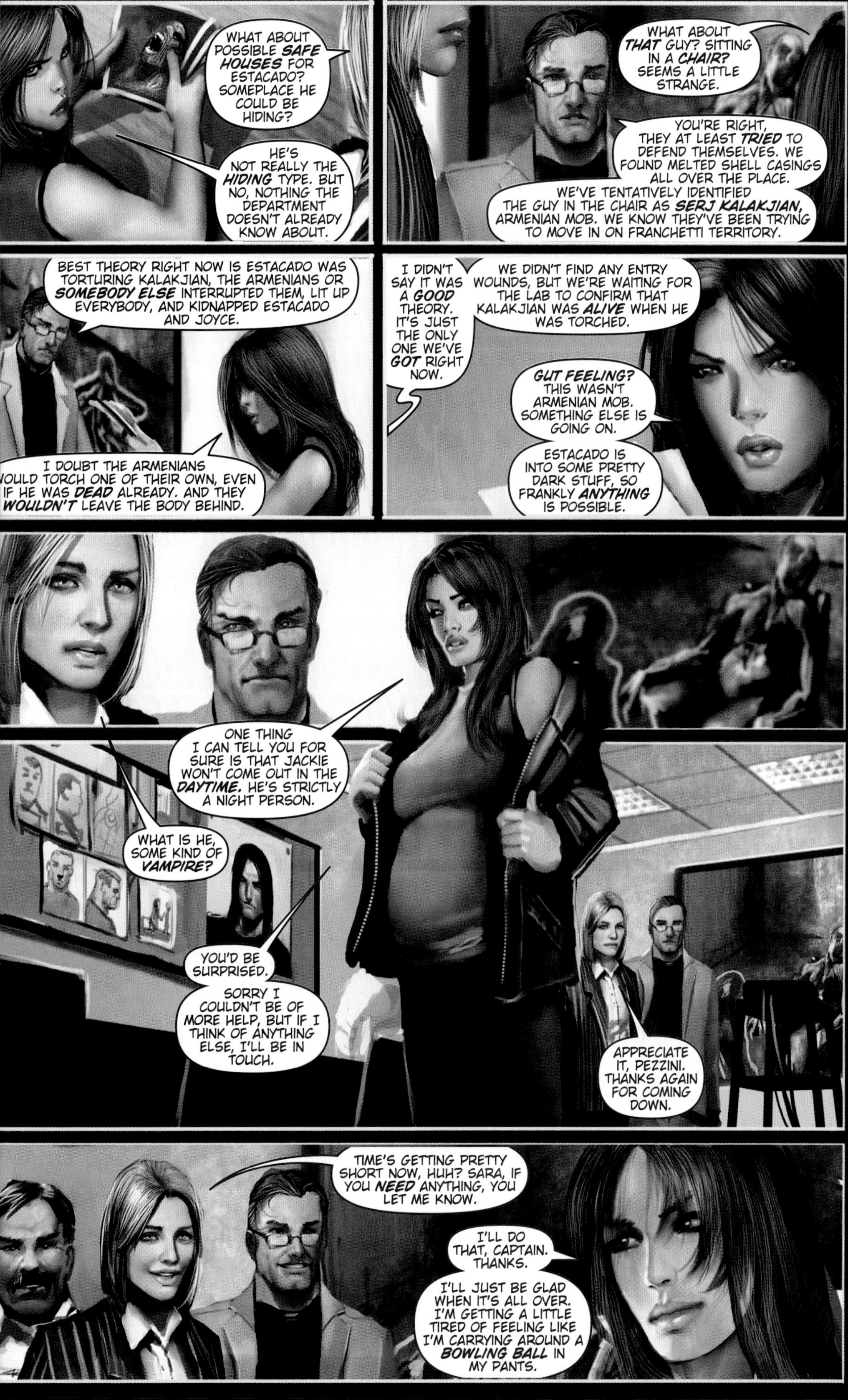
WHAT ABOUT POSSIBLE SAFE HOUSES FOR ESTACADO? SOMEPLACE HE COULD BE HIDING?
HE'S NOT REALLY THE HIDING TYPE. BUT NO, NOTHING THE DEPARTMENT DOESN'T ALREADY KNOW ABOUT.
WHAT ABOUT THAT GUY? SITTING IN A CHAIR? SEEMS A LITTLE STRANGE.
YOU'RE RIGHT, THEY AT LEAST TRIED TO DEFEND THEMSELVES. WE FOUND MELTED SHELL CASINGS ALL OVER THE PLACE.
WE'VE TENTATIVELY IDENTIFIED THE GUY IN THE CHAIR AS SERJ KALAKJIAN, ARMENIAN MOB. WE KNOW THEY'VE BEEN TRYING TO MOVE IN ON FRANCHETTI TERRITORY.
BEST THEORY RIGHT NOW IS ESTACADO WAS TORTURING KALAKJIAN, THE ARMENIANS OR SOMEBODY ELSE INTERRUPTED THEM, LIT UP EVERYBODY, AND KIDNAPPED ESTACADO AND JOYCE.
I DOUBT THE ARMENIANS WOULD TORCH ONE OF THEIR OWN, EVEN IF HE WAS DEAD ALREADY. AND THEY WOULDN'T LEAVE THE BODY BEHIND.
I DIDN'T SAY IT WAS A GOOD THEORY. IT'S JUST THE ONLY ONE WE'VE GOT RIGHT NOW.
WE DIDN'T FIND ANY ENTRY WOUNDS, BUT WE'RE WAITING FOR THE LAB TO CONFIRM THAT KALAKJIAN WAS ALIVE WHEN HE WAS TORCHED.
GUT FEELING? THIS WASN'T ARMENIAN MOB. SOMETHING ELSE IS GOING ON.
ESTACADO IS INTO SOME PRETTY DARK STUFF, SO FRANKLY ANYTHING IS POSSIBLE.
ONE THING I CAN TELL YOU FOR SURE IS THAT JACKIE WON'T COME OUT IN THE DAYTIME. HE'S STRICTLY A NIGHT PERSON.
WHAT IS HE, SOME KIND OF VAMPIRE?
YOU'D BE SURPRISED.
SORRY I COULDN'T BE OF MORE HELP, BUT IF I THINK OF ANYTHING ELSE, I'LL BE IN TOUCH.
APPRECIATE IT, PEZZINI. THANKS AGAIN FOR COMING DOWN.
TIME'S GETTING PRETTY SHORT NOW, HUH? SARA, IF YOU NEED ANYTHING, YOU LET ME KNOW.
I'LL DO THAT, CAPTAIN. THANKS.
I'LL JUST BE GLAD WHEN IT'S ALL OVER. I'M GETTING A LITTLE TIRED OF FEELING LIKE I'M CARRYING AROUND A BOWLING BALL IN MY PANTS.

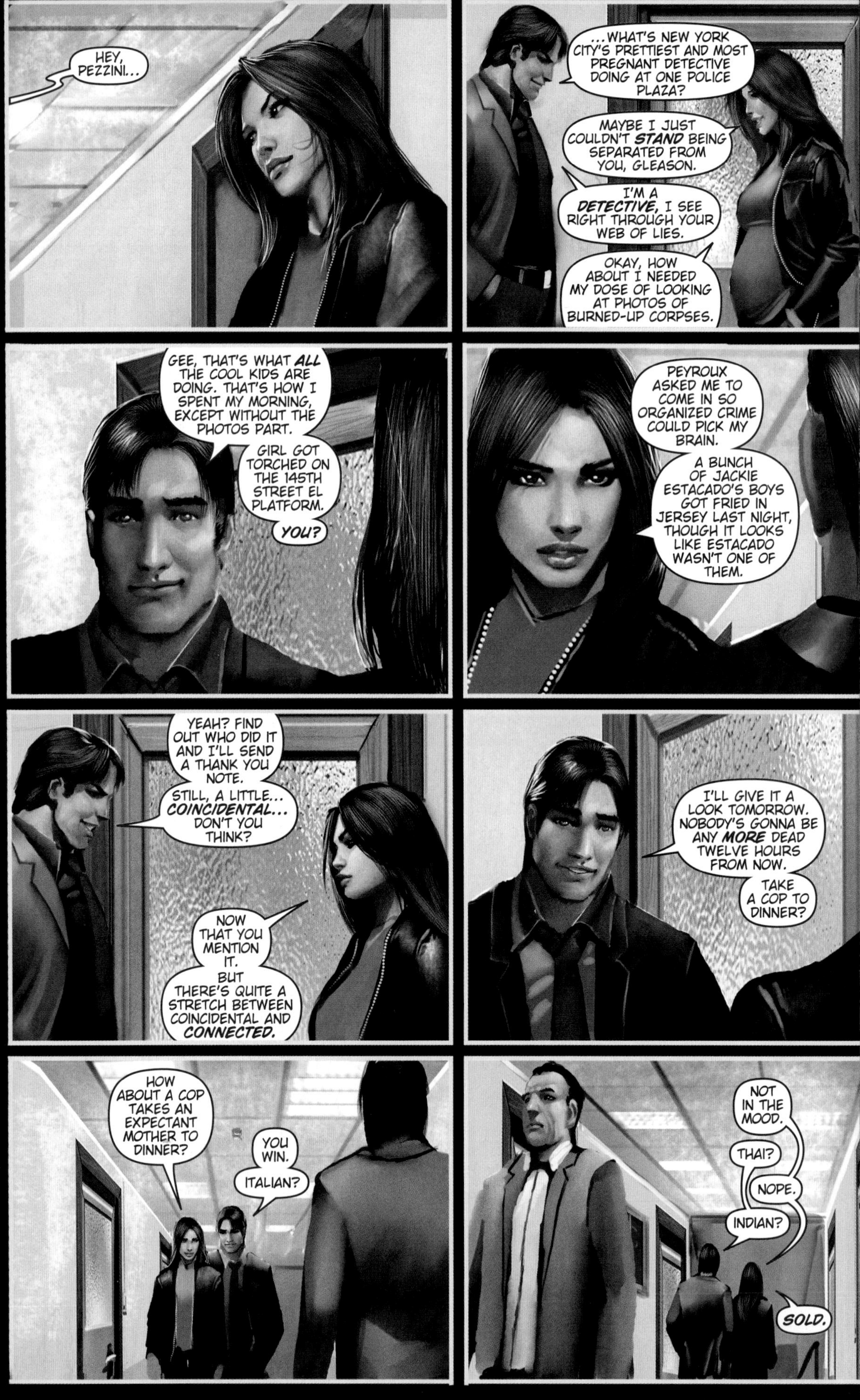
HEY, PEZZINI...
...WHAT'S NEW YORK CITY'S PRETTIEST AND MOST PREGNANT DETECTIVE DOING AT ONE POLICE PLAZA?
MAYBE I JUST COULDN'T STAND BEING SEPARATED FROM YOU, GLEASON.
I'M A DETECTIVE, I SEE RIGHT THROUGH YOUR WEB OF LIES.
OKAY, HOW ABOUT I NEEDED MY DOSE OF LOOKING AT PHOTOS OF BURNED-UP CORPSES.
GEE, THAT'S WHAT ALL THE COOL KIDS ARE DOING. THAT'S HOW I SPENT MY MORNING, EXCEPT WITHOUT THE PHOTOS PART.
GIRL GOT TORCHED ON THE 145TH STREET EL PLATFORM.
YOU?
PEYROUX ASKED ME TO COME IN SO ORGANIZED CRIME COULD PICK MY BRAIN.
A BUNCH OF JACKIE ESTACADO'S BOYS GOT FRIED IN JERSEY LAST NIGHT, THOUGH IT LOOKS LIKE ESTACADO WASN'T ONE OF THEM.
YEAH? FIND OUT WHO DID IT AND I'LL SEND A THANK YOU NOTE.
STILL, A LITTLE... COINCIDENTAL... DON'T YOU THINK?
NOW THAT YOU MENTION IT.
BUT THERE'S QUITE A STRETCH BETWEEN COINCIDENTAL AND CONNECTED.
I'LL GIVE IT A LOOK TOMORROW. NOBODY'S GONNA BE ANY MORE DEAD TWELVE HOURS FROM NOW.
TAKE A COP TO DINNER?
HOW ABOUT A COP TAKES AN EXPECTANT MOTHER TO DINNER?
YOU WIN.
ITALIAN?
NOT IN THE MOOD.
THAI?
NOPE.
INDIAN?
SOLD.

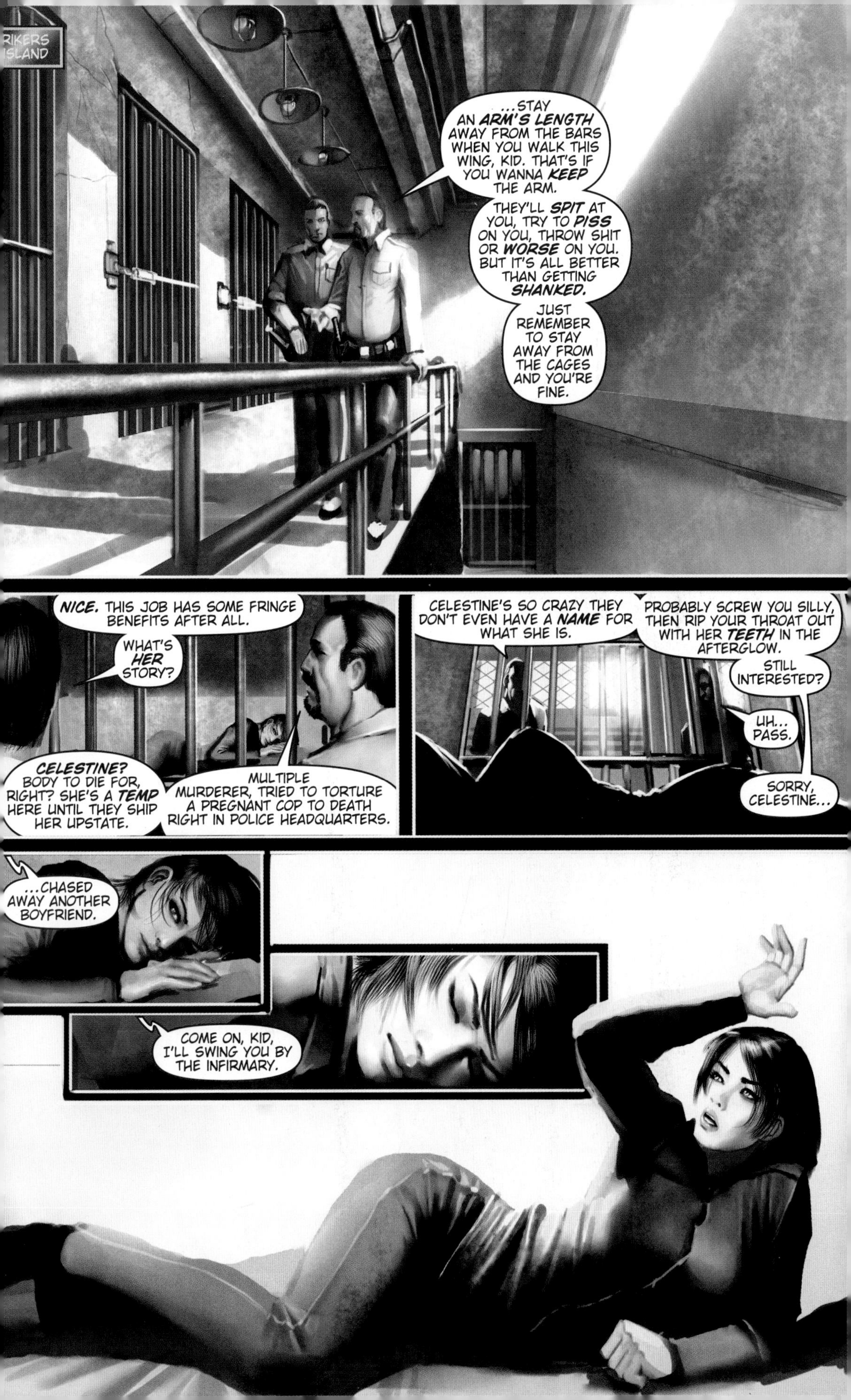
RIKERS ISLAND
...STAY AN ARM'S LENGTH AWAY FROM THE BARS WHEN YOU WALK THIS WING, KID. THAT'S IF YOU WANNA KEEP THE ARM.
THEY'LL SPIT AT YOU, TRY TO PISS ON YOU, THROW SHIT OR WORSE ON YOU. BUT IT'S ALL BETTER THAN GETTING SHANKED.
JUST REMEMBER TO STAY AWAY FROM THE CAGES AND YOU'RE FINE.
NICE. THIS JOB HAS SOME FRINGE BENEFITS AFTER ALL.
WHAT'S HER STORY?
CELESTINE? BODY TO DIE FOR, RIGHT? SHE'S A TEMP HERE UNTIL THEY SHIP HER UPSTATE.
MULTIPLE MURDERER, TRIED TO TORTURE A PREGNANT COP TO DEATH RIGHT IN POLICE HEADQUARTERS.
CELESTINE'S SO CRAZY THEY DON'T EVEN HAVE A NAME FOR WHAT SHE IS.
PROBABLY SCREW YOU SILLY, THEN RIP YOUR THROAT OUT WITH HER TEETH IN THE AFTERGLOW.
STILL INTERESTED?
UH... PASS.
SORRY, CELESTINE...
...CHASED AWAY ANOTHER BOYFRIEND.
COME ON, KID, I'LL SWING YOU BY THE INFIRMARY.

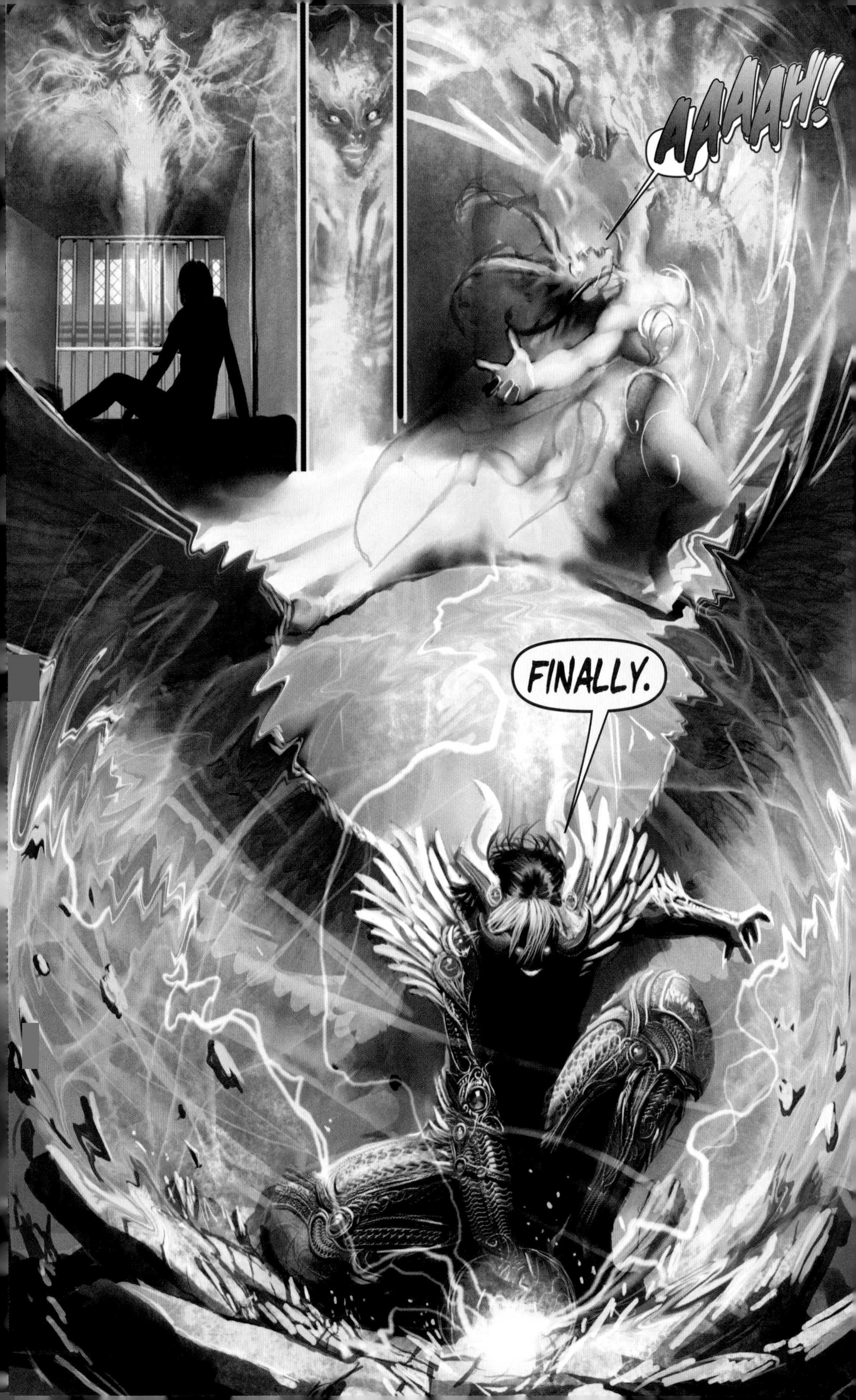
AAAAH!!
FINALLY.

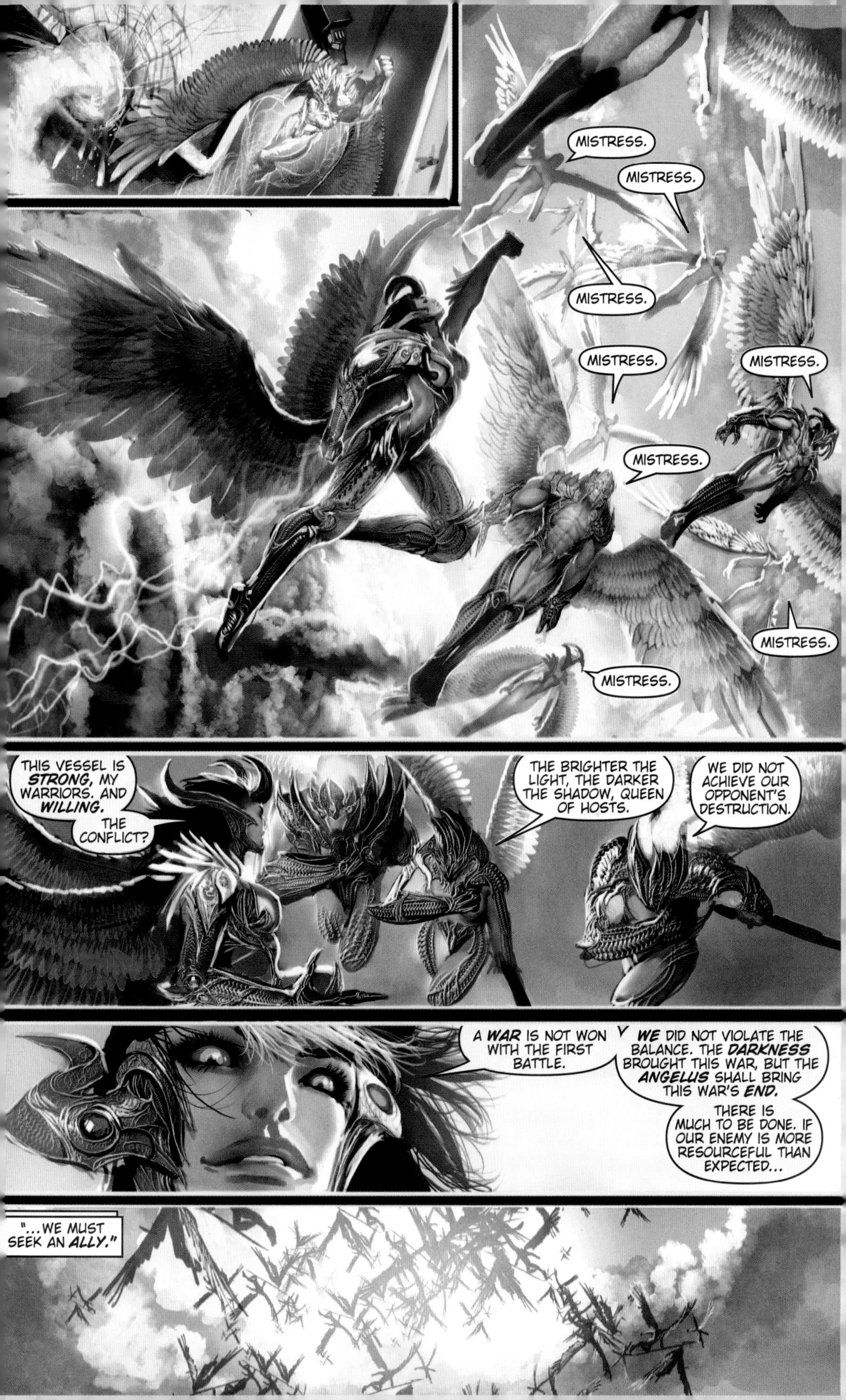

MISTRESS.
MISTRESS.
MISTRESS.
MISTRESS.
MISTRESS.
MISTRESS.
MISTRESS.
MISTRESS.
THIS VESSEL IS STRONG, MY WARRIORS. AND WILLING.
THE CONFLICT?
THE BRIGHTER THE LIGHT, THE DARKER THE SHADOW, QUEEN OF HOSTS.
WE DID NOT ACHIEVE OUR OPPONENT'S DESTRUCTION.
A WAR IS NOT WON WITH THE FIRST BATTLE.
WE DID NOT VIOLATE THE BALANCE. THE DARKNESS BROUGHT THIS WAR, BUT THE ANGELUS SHALL BRING THIS WAR'S END.
THERE IS MUCH TO BE DONE. IF OUR ENEMY IS MORE RESOURCEFUL THAN EXPECTED...
"...WE MUST SEEK AN ALLY."

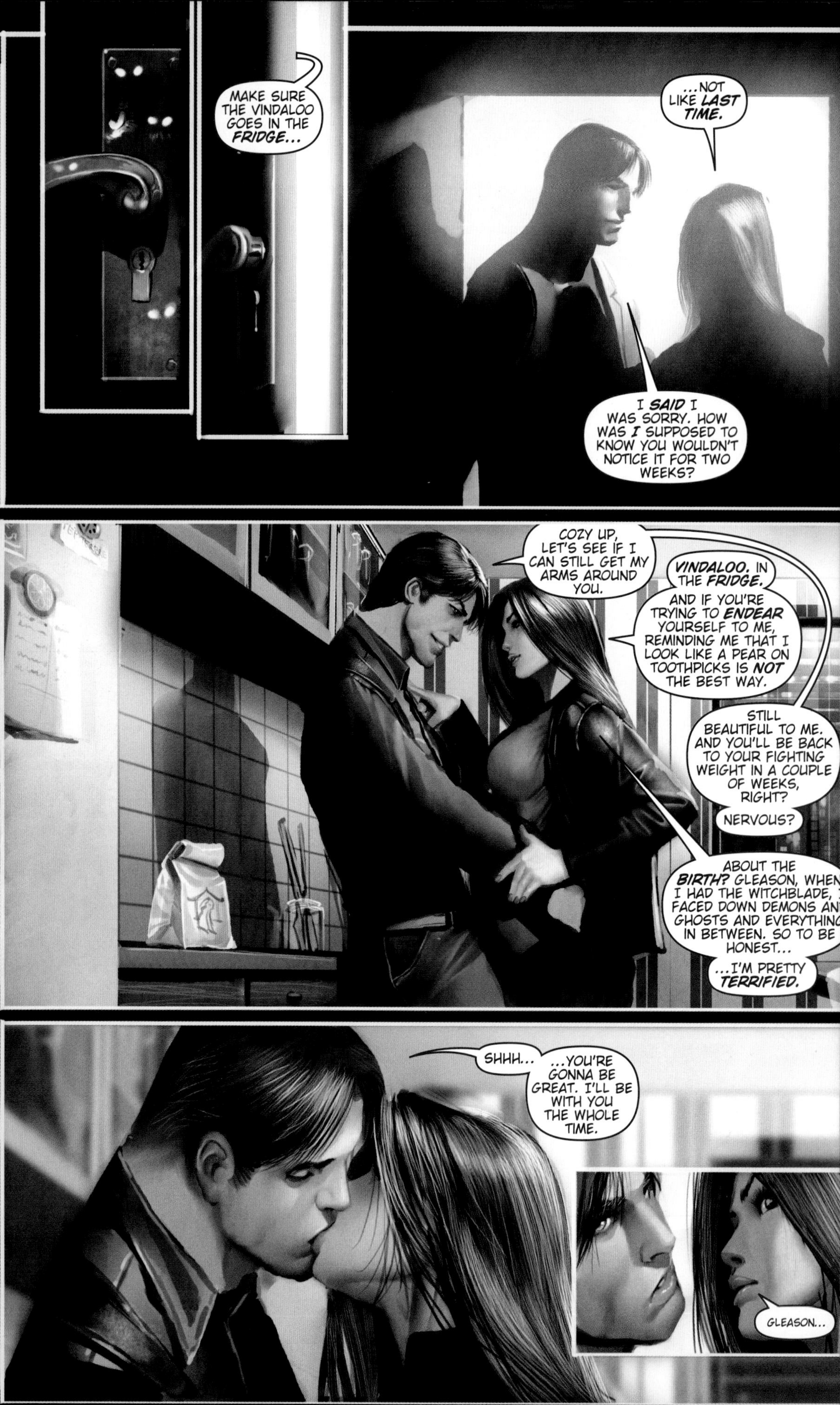

MAKE SURE THE VINDALOO GOES IN THE FRIDGE...
...NOT LIKE LAST TIME.
I SAID I WAS SORRY. HOW WAS I SUPPOSED TO KNOW YOU WOULDN'T NOTICE IT FOR TWO WEEKS?
COZY UP, LET'S SEE IF I CAN STILL GET MY ARMS AROUND YOU.
VINDALOO. IN THE FRIDGE.
AND IF YOU'RE TRYING TO ENDEAR YOURSELF TO ME, REMINDING ME THAT I LOOK LIKE A PEAR ON TOOTHPICKS IS NOT THE BEST WAY.
STILL BEAUTIFUL TO ME. AND YOU'LL BE BACK TO YOUR FIGHTING WEIGHT IN A COUPLE OF WEEKS, RIGHT?
NERVOUS?
...I'M PRETTY TERRIFIED.
SHHH...
...YOU'RE GONNA BE GREAT. I'LL BE WITH YOU THE WHOLE TIME.
GLEASON...

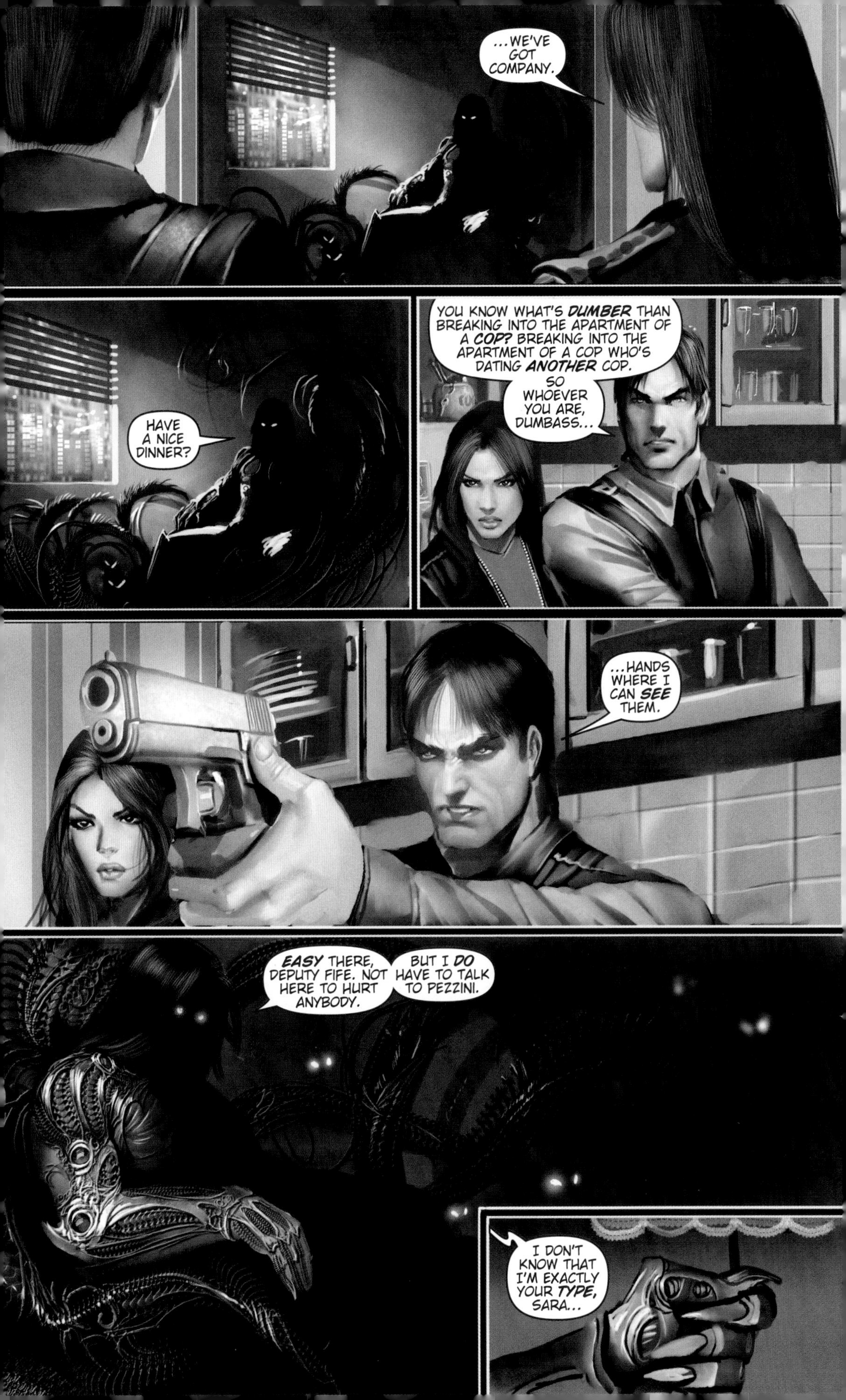
...WE'VE GOT COMPANY.
HAVE A NICE DINNER?
YOU KNOW WHAT'S DUMBER THAN BREAKING INTO THE APARTMENT OF A COP? BREAKING INTO THE APARTMENT OF A COP WHO'S DATING ANOTHER COP.
SO WHOEVER YOU ARE, DUMBASS...
...HANDS WHERE I CAN SEE THEM.
EASY THERE, DEPUTY FIFE. NOT HERE TO HURT ANYBODY.
BUT I DO HAVE TO TALK TO PEZZINI.
I DON'T KNOW THAT I'M EXACTLY YOUR TYPE, SARA...

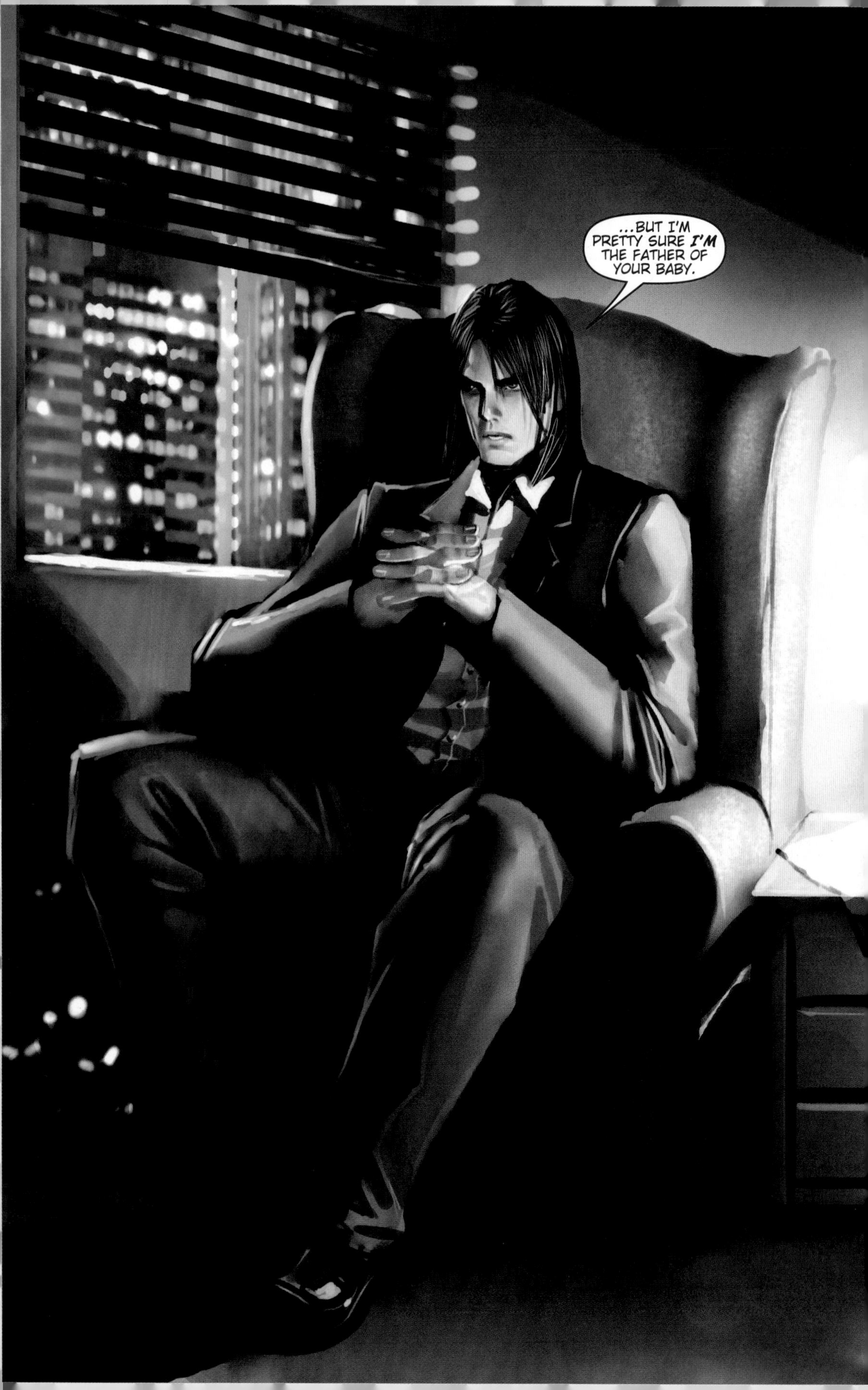
...BUT I'M PRETTY SURE *I'M* THE FATHER OF YOUR BABY.

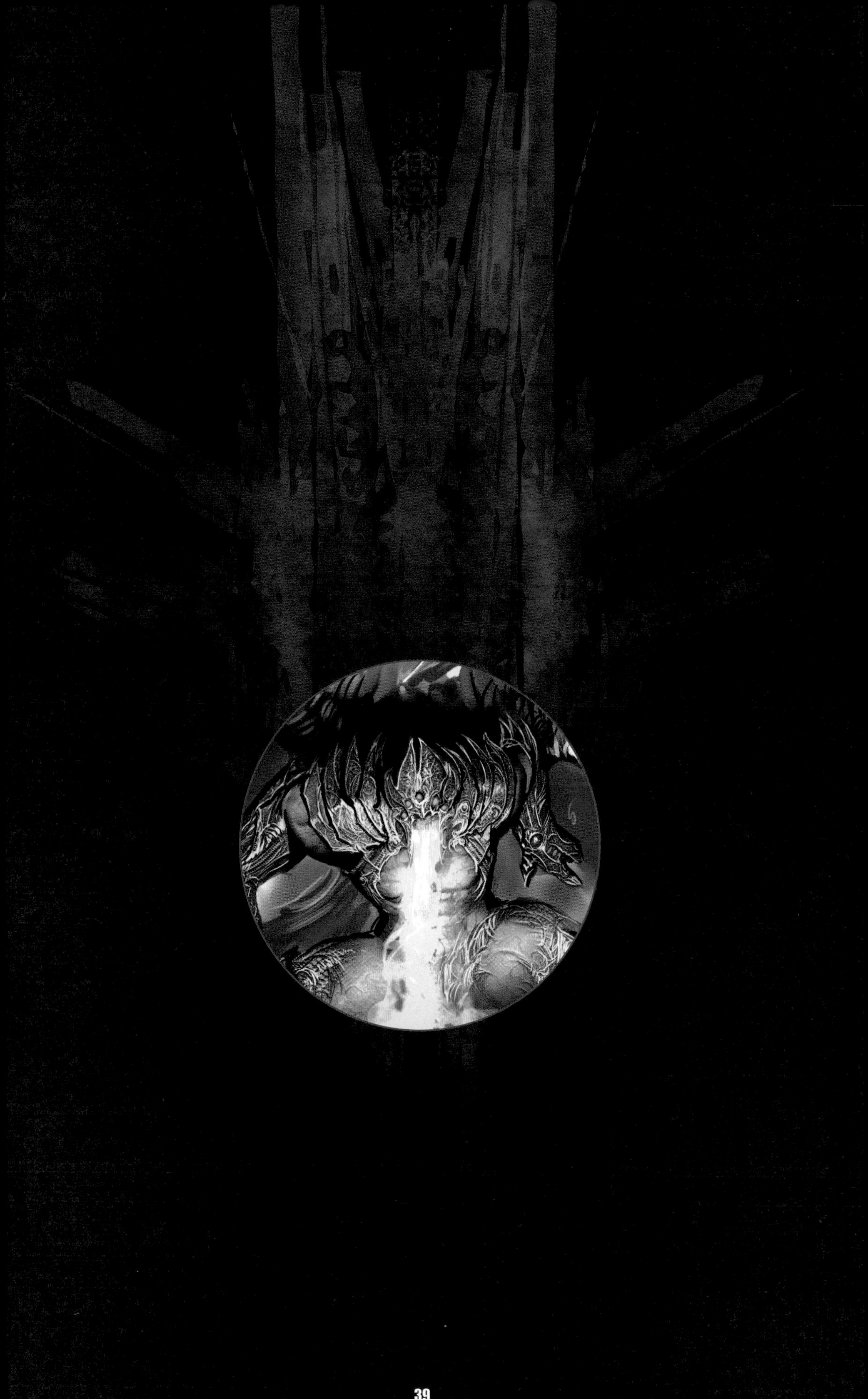

WITCHBLADE

FLIGHTS OF ANGELS, ISSUE #110

written by: **Ron Marz**
pencils by: **Luke Ross**
inks by: **Kevin Nowlan**
colors by: **Nathan Fairbairn**
letters by: **Troy Peteri**

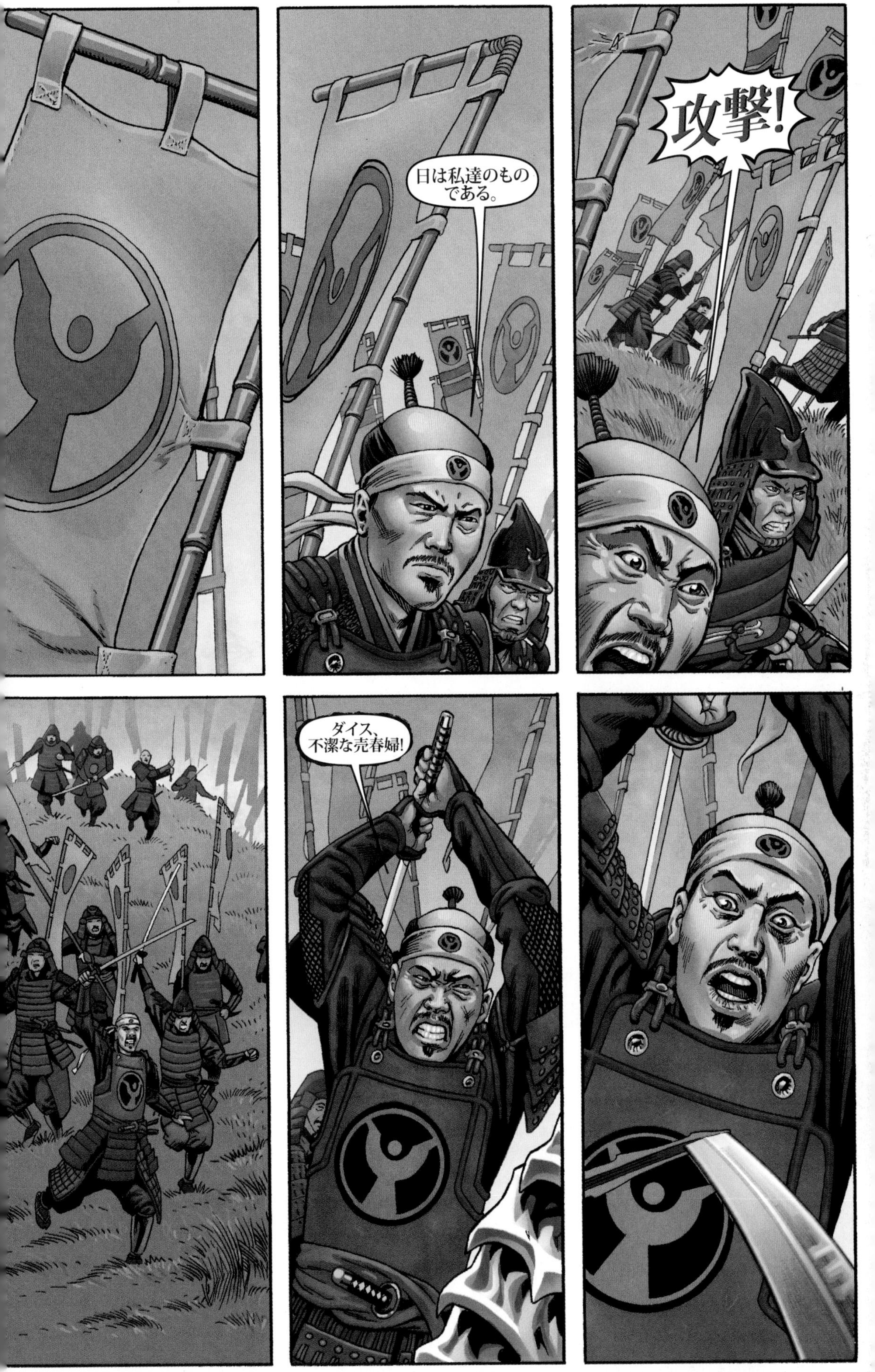
日は私達のものである。
攻撃!
ダイス、不潔な売春婦!

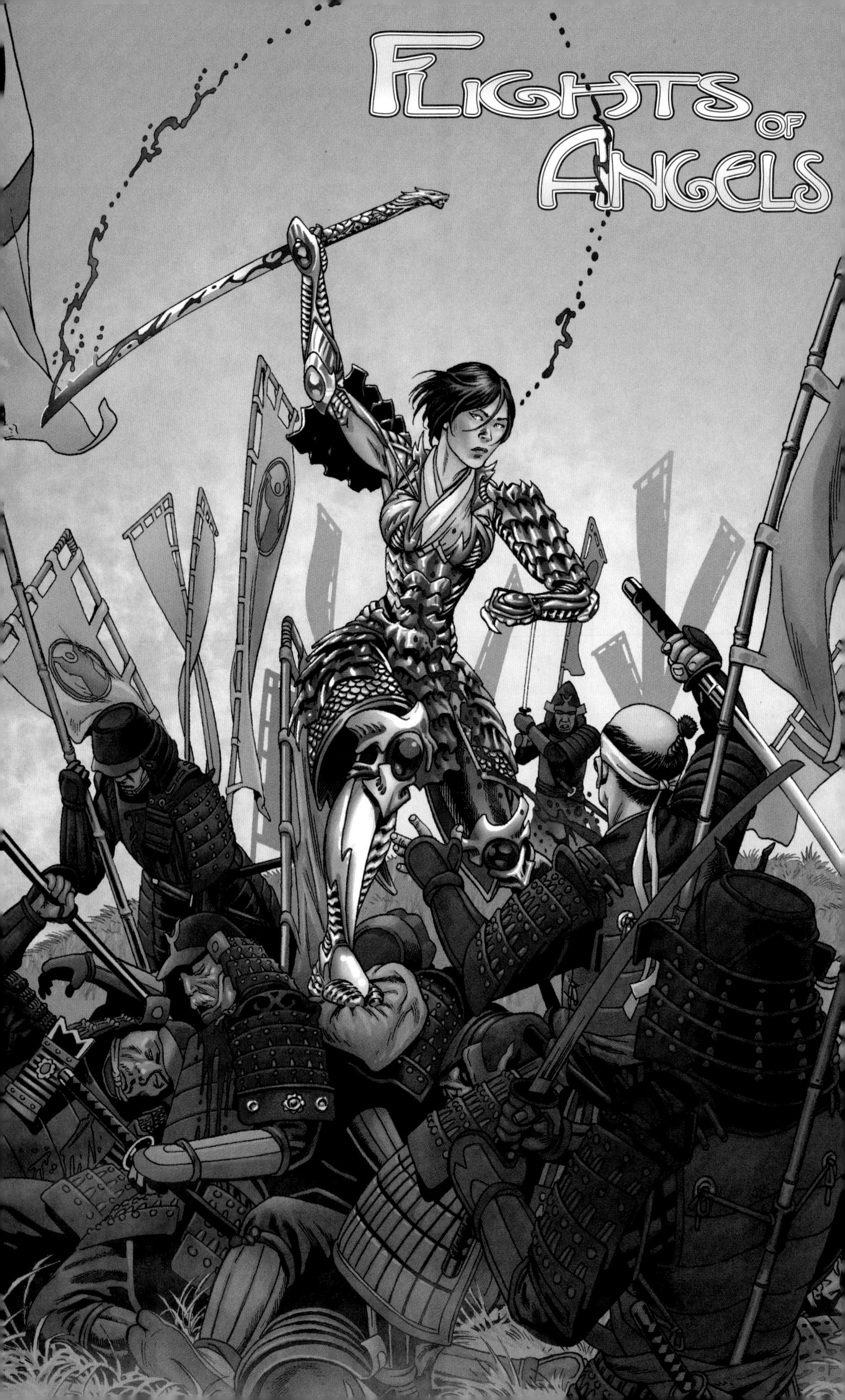
FLIGHTS OF ANGELS

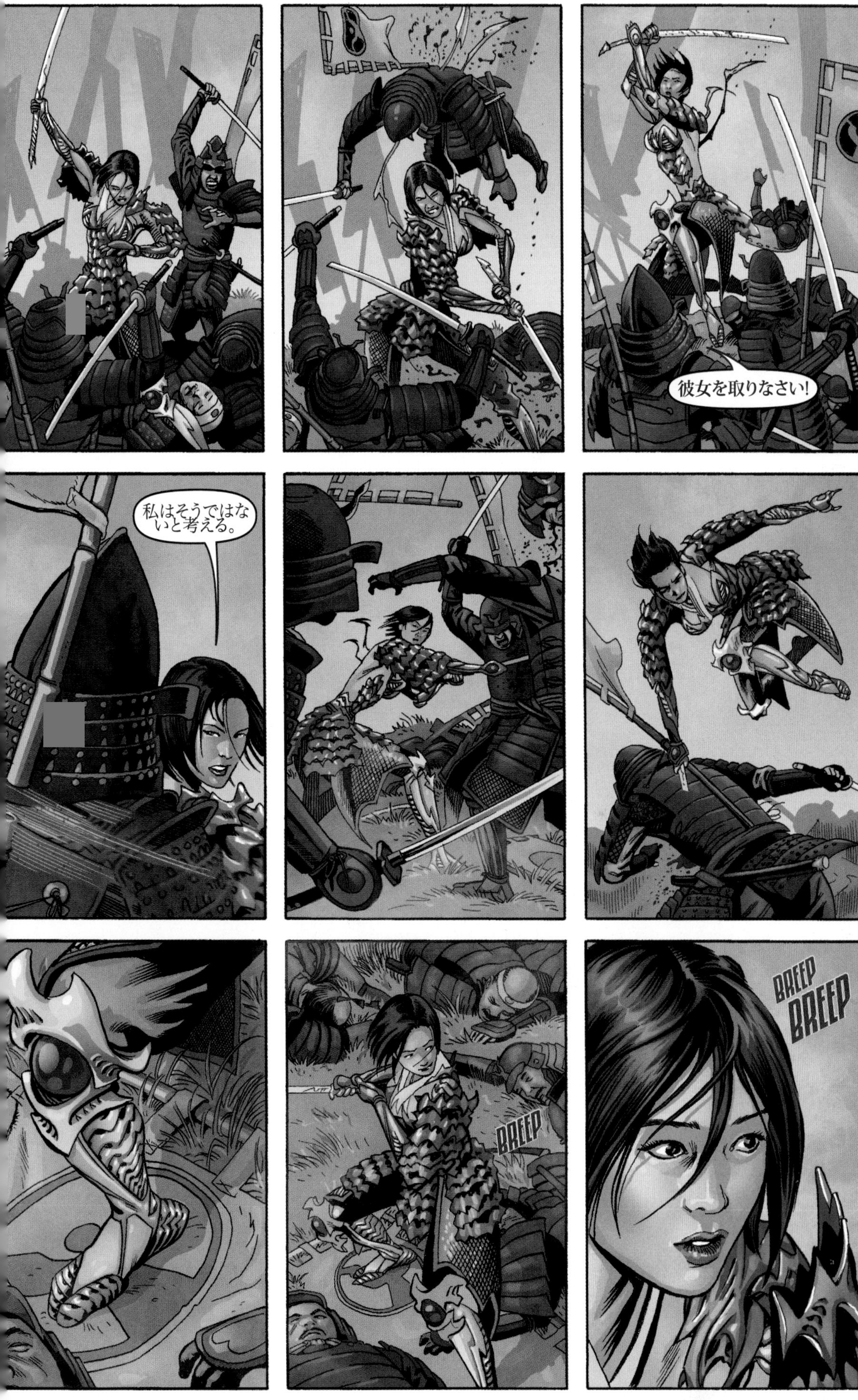
彼女を取りなさい!
私はそうではないと考える。
BREEP
BREEP
BREEP

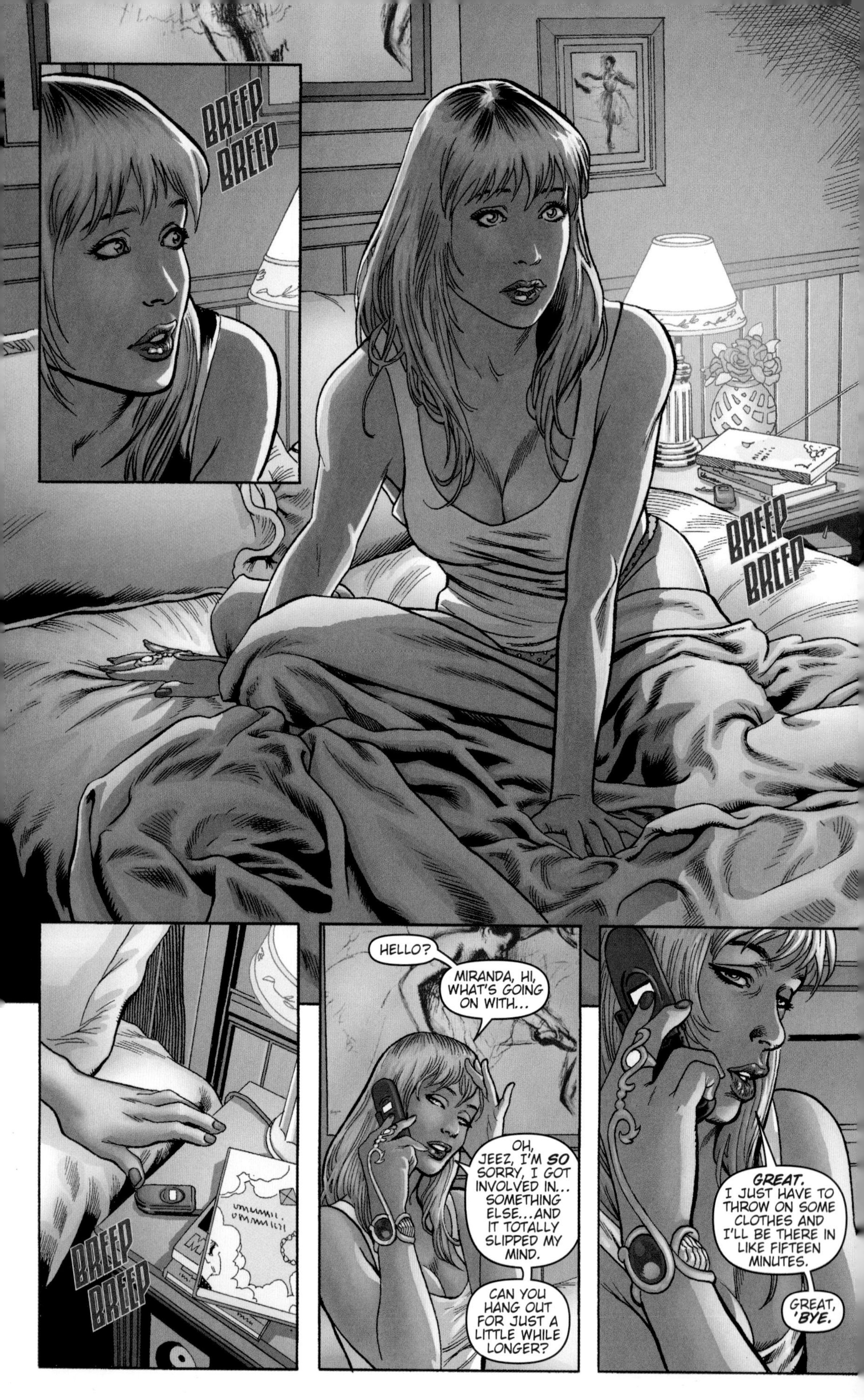
BREEP BREEP
BREEP BREEP
BREEP BREEP
HELLO?
MIRANDA, HI, WHAT'S GOING ON WITH...
OH, JEEZ, I'M **SO** SORRY, I GOT INVOLVED IN... SOMETHING ELSE...AND IT TOTALLY SLIPPED MY MIND.
CAN YOU HANG OUT FOR JUST A LITTLE WHILE LONGER?
GREAT. I JUST HAVE TO THROW ON SOME CLOTHES AND I'LL BE THERE IN LIKE FIFTEEN MINUTES.
GREAT, **'BYE.**

WAY TO GO, DANI.

GOT LOST IN MEMORIES, AND THEY'RE NOT EVEN *MY* MEMORIES.

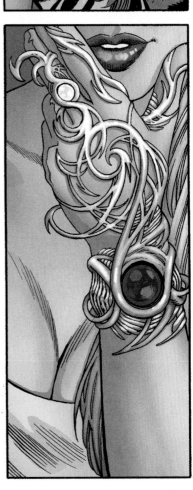

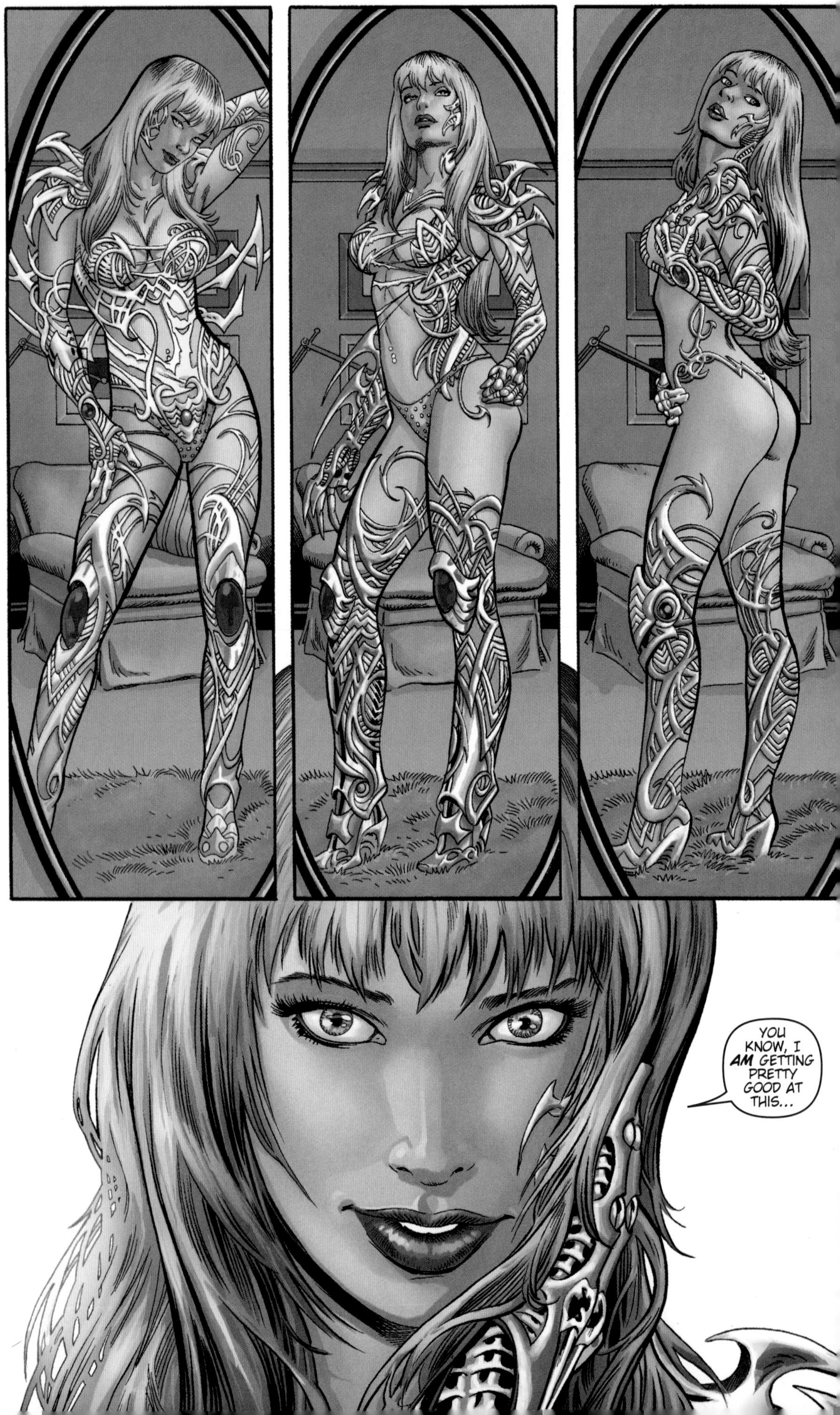
YOU KNOW, I AM GETTING PRETTY GOOD AT THIS...

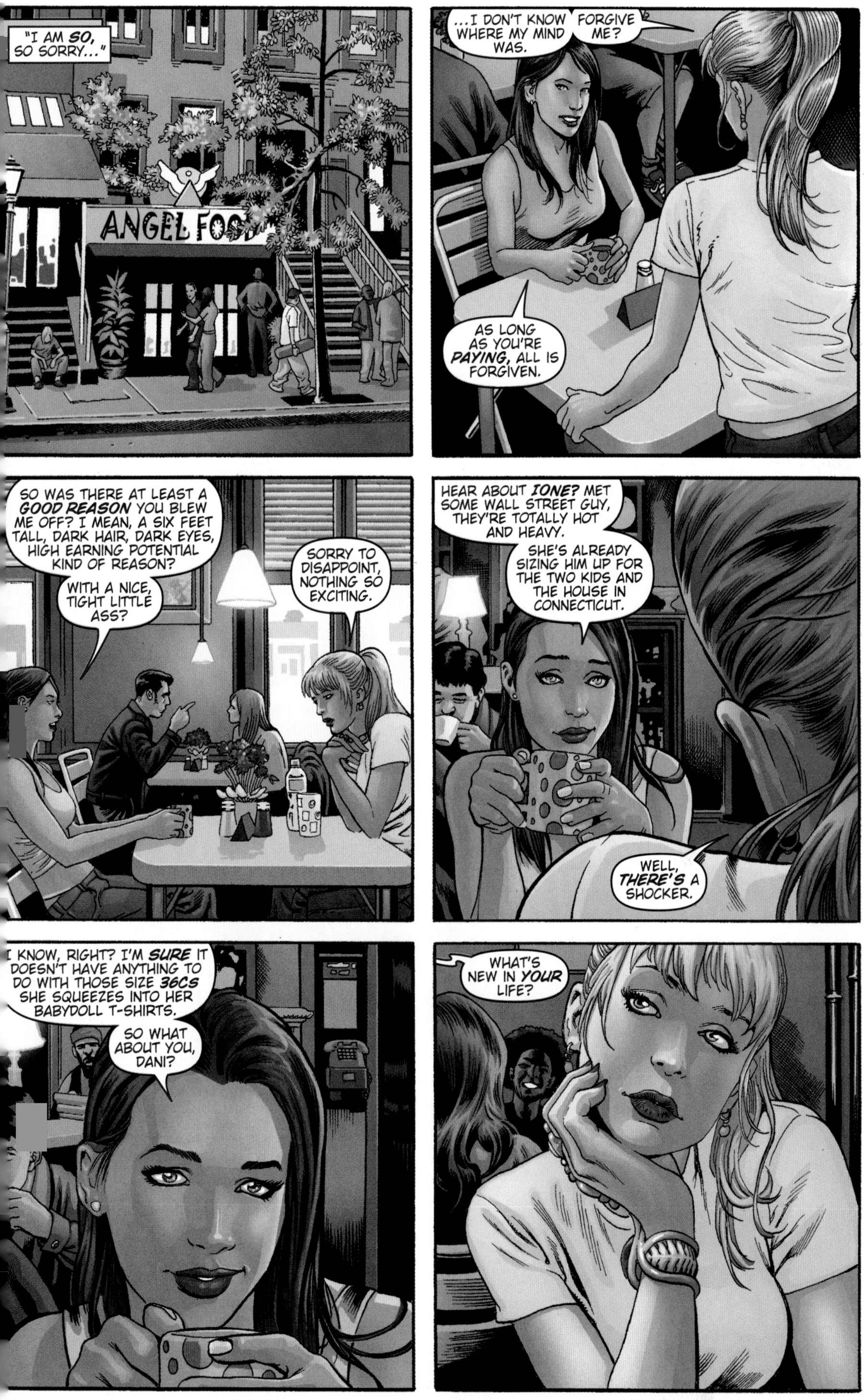
"I AM SO, SO SORRY..."
ANGEL FOO
...I DON'T KNOW WHERE MY MIND WAS.
FORGIVE ME?
AS LONG AS YOU'RE PAYING, ALL IS FORGIVEN.
SO WAS THERE AT LEAST A GOOD REASON YOU BLEW ME OFF? I MEAN, A SIX FEET TALL, DARK HAIR, DARK EYES, HIGH EARNING POTENTIAL KIND OF REASON?
WITH A NICE, TIGHT LITTLE ASS?
SORRY TO DISAPPOINT, NOTHING SO EXCITING.
HEAR ABOUT IONE? MET SOME WALL STREET GUY, THEY'RE TOTALLY HOT AND HEAVY.
SHE'S ALREADY SIZING HIM UP FOR THE TWO KIDS AND THE HOUSE IN CONNECTICUT.
WELL, THERE'S A SHOCKER.
I KNOW, RIGHT? I'M SURE IT DOESN'T HAVE ANYTHING TO DO WITH THOSE SIZE 36CS SHE SQUEEZES INTO HER BABYDOLL T-SHIRTS.
SO WHAT ABOUT YOU, DANI?
WHAT'S NEW IN YOUR LIFE?

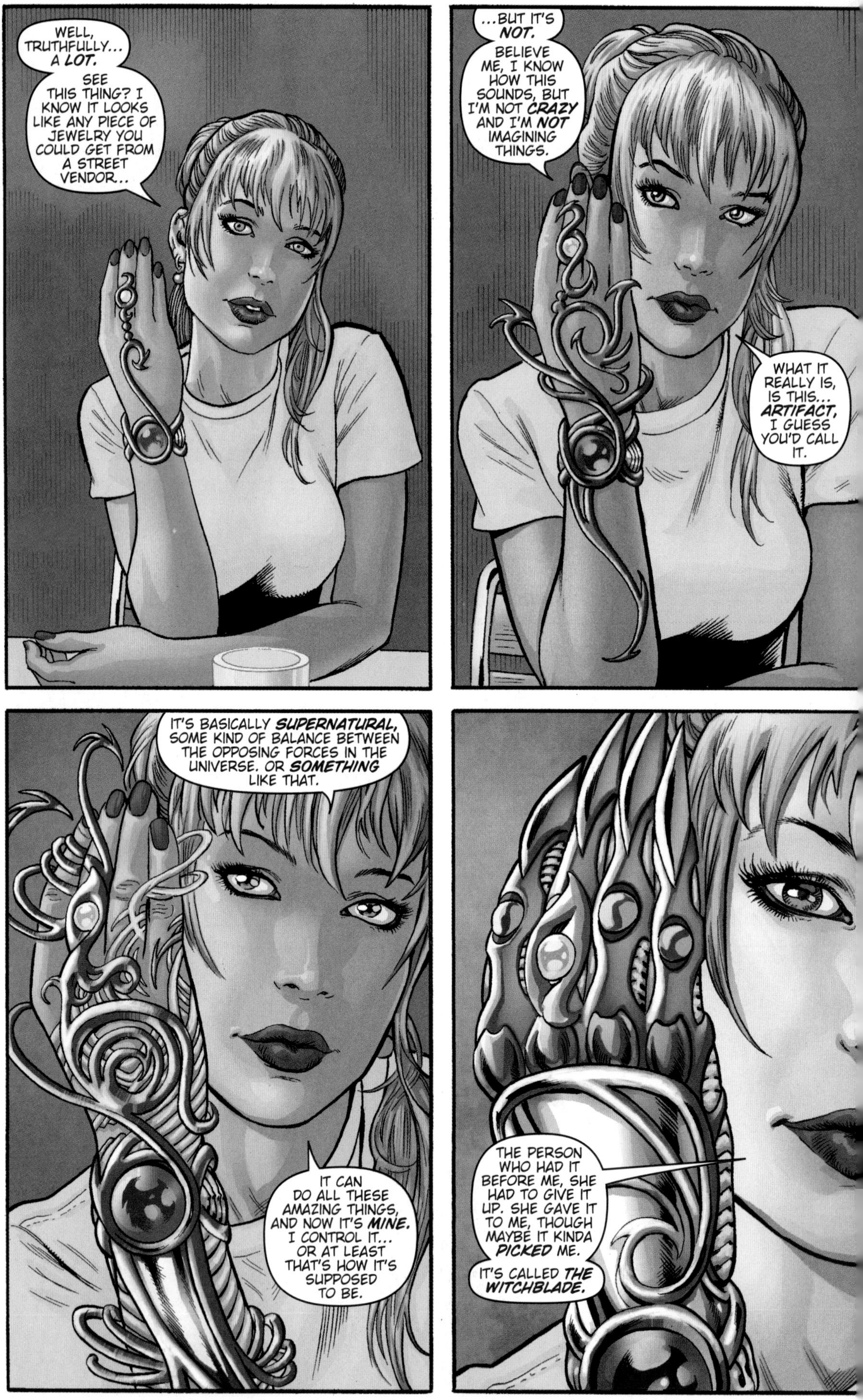
WELL, TRUTHFULLY... A LOT.
SEE THIS THING? I KNOW IT LOOKS LIKE ANY PIECE OF JEWELRY YOU COULD GET FROM A STREET VENDOR...
...BUT IT'S NOT.
BELIEVE ME, I KNOW HOW THIS SOUNDS, BUT I'M NOT CRAZY AND I'M NOT IMAGINING THINGS.
WHAT IT REALLY IS, IS THIS... ARTIFACT, I GUESS YOU'D CALL IT.
IT'S BASICALLY SUPERNATURAL, SOME KIND OF BALANCE BETWEEN THE OPPOSING FORCES IN THE UNIVERSE. OR SOMETHING LIKE THAT.
IT CAN DO ALL THESE AMAZING THINGS, AND NOW IT'S MINE. I CONTROL IT... OR AT LEAST THAT'S HOW IT'S SUPPOSED TO BE.
THE PERSON WHO HAD IT BEFORE ME, SHE HAD TO GIVE IT UP. SHE GAVE IT TO ME, THOUGH MAYBE IT KINDA PICKED ME.
IT'S CALLED THE WITCHBLADE.

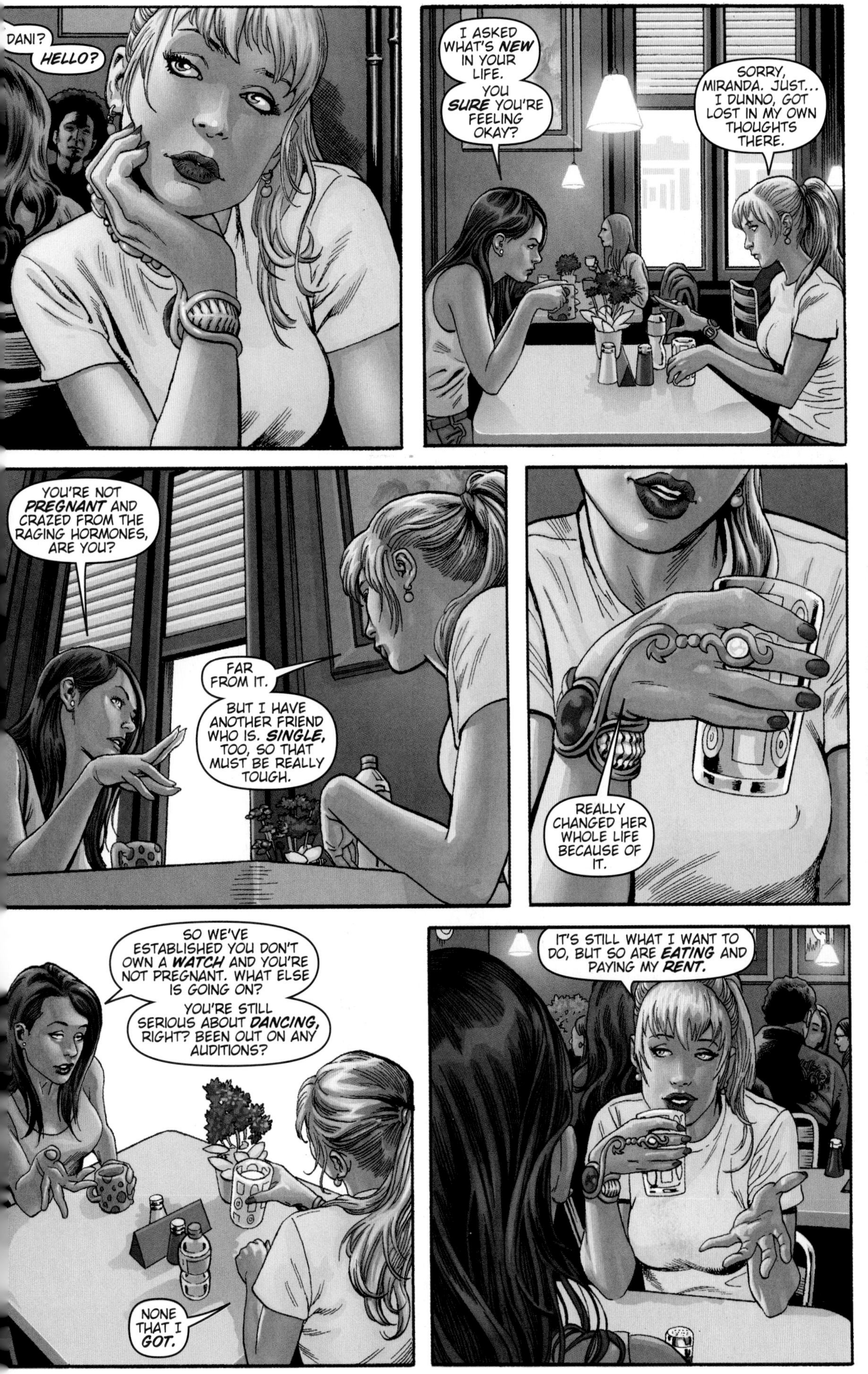
DANI? HELLO?
I ASKED WHAT'S NEW IN YOUR LIFE.
YOU SURE YOU'RE FEELING OKAY?
SORRY, MIRANDA. JUST... I DUNNO, GOT LOST IN MY OWN THOUGHTS THERE.
YOU'RE NOT PREGNANT AND CRAZED FROM THE RAGING HORMONES, ARE YOU?
FAR FROM IT.
BUT I HAVE ANOTHER FRIEND WHO IS. SINGLE, TOO, SO THAT MUST BE REALLY TOUGH.
REALLY CHANGED HER WHOLE LIFE BECAUSE OF IT.
SO WE'VE ESTABLISHED YOU DON'T OWN A WATCH AND YOU'RE NOT PREGNANT. WHAT ELSE IS GOING ON?
YOU'RE STILL SERIOUS ABOUT DANCING, RIGHT? BEEN OUT ON ANY AUDITIONS?
NONE THAT I GOT.
IT'S STILL WHAT I WANT TO DO, BUT SO ARE EATING AND PAYING MY RENT.

ARE'NT EXACTLY A LOT OF OPENINGS FOR CLASSICALLY-TRAINED DANCERS, AND NO LACK OF APPLICANTS WHEN THERE *IS* AN OPENING.

KNOW WHAT I'M SAYING?

YEAH, WELL, *UNTIL* THAT GIG COMES ALONG, THERE ARE PLENTY OF DANCERS MAKING BIG MONEY, EVEN IF THEY'RE NOT WEARING TOE SHOES AND TUTUS...

...OR MUCH OF ANYTHIN' ELSE.

KNOW WHAT I'M SAYING?

NO WAY, I AM *NOT* STRIPPING.

NOT ENOUGH MONEY IN THE *WORLD* FOR ME TO GET PAWED BY DRUNK CONSTRUCTION WORKERS.

ARE YOU KIDDING? IT'S *TAX FREE!*

AND IT'S *TOTALLY* ABOUT FEMALE EMPOWERMENT NOW.

SO WHY NOT? YOU'VE GOT THE *BODY* FOR IT, AND YOU'D PROBABLY BE THE ONLY *NATURAL* BLOND IN THE PLACE.

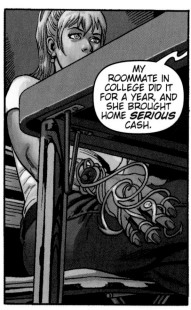

MY ROOMMATE IN COLLEGE DID IT FOR A YEAR, AND SHE BROUGHT HOME *SERIOUS* CASH.

AND IT WASN'T EVEN A NUDE PLACE, JUST TOPLESS. AT LEAST GIVE IT SOME--

UM... DANI? *YOU OKAY?*

I'M JUST...

...I'M JUST FEELING A LITTLE QUEASY ALL OF A SUDDEN.

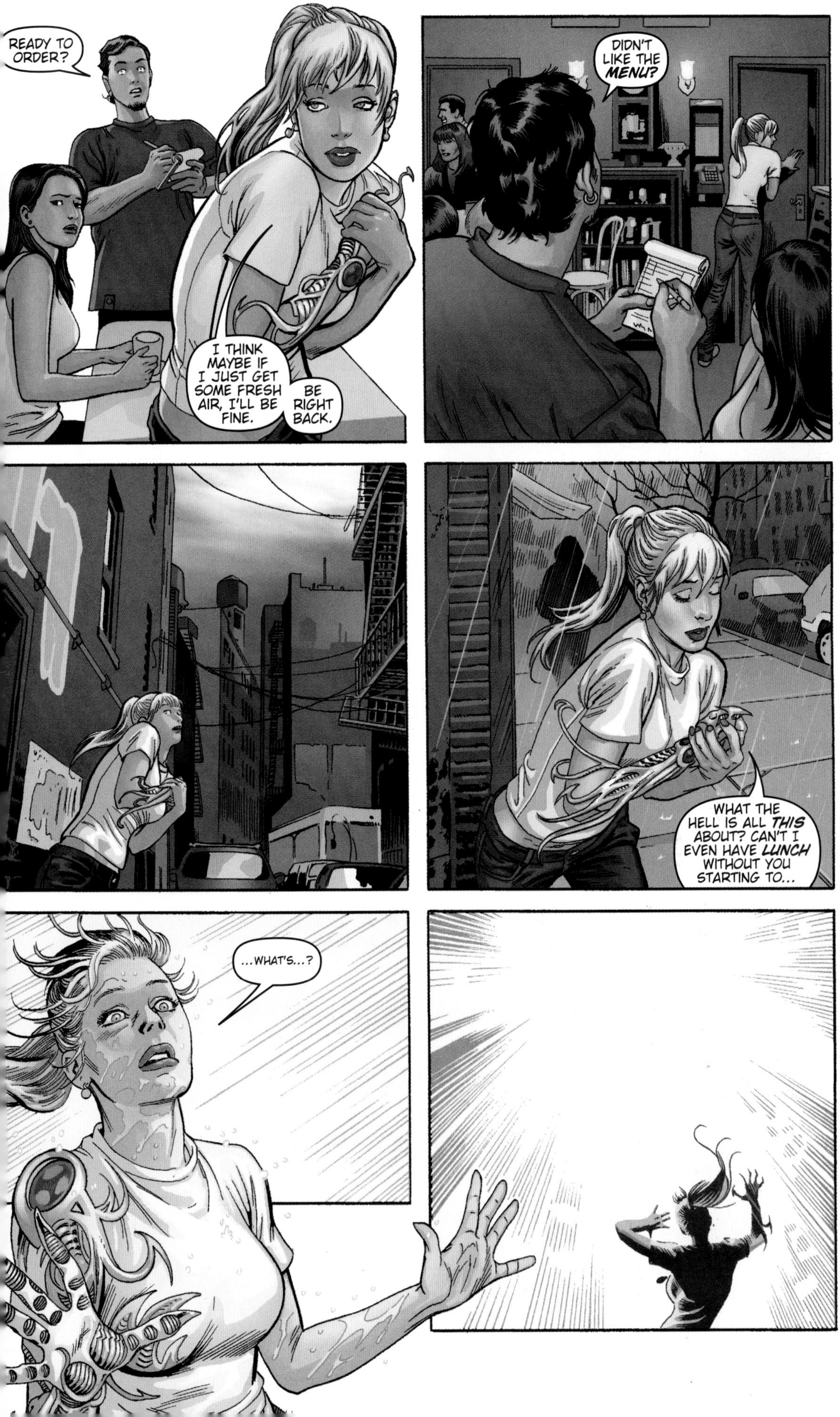
READY TO ORDER?
I THINK MAYBE IF I JUST GET SOME FRESH AIR, I'LL BE FINE.
BE RIGHT BACK.
DIDN'T LIKE THE MENU?
WHAT THE HELL IS ALL THIS ABOUT? CAN'T I EVEN HAVE LUNCH WITHOUT YOU STARTING TO...
...WHAT'S...?

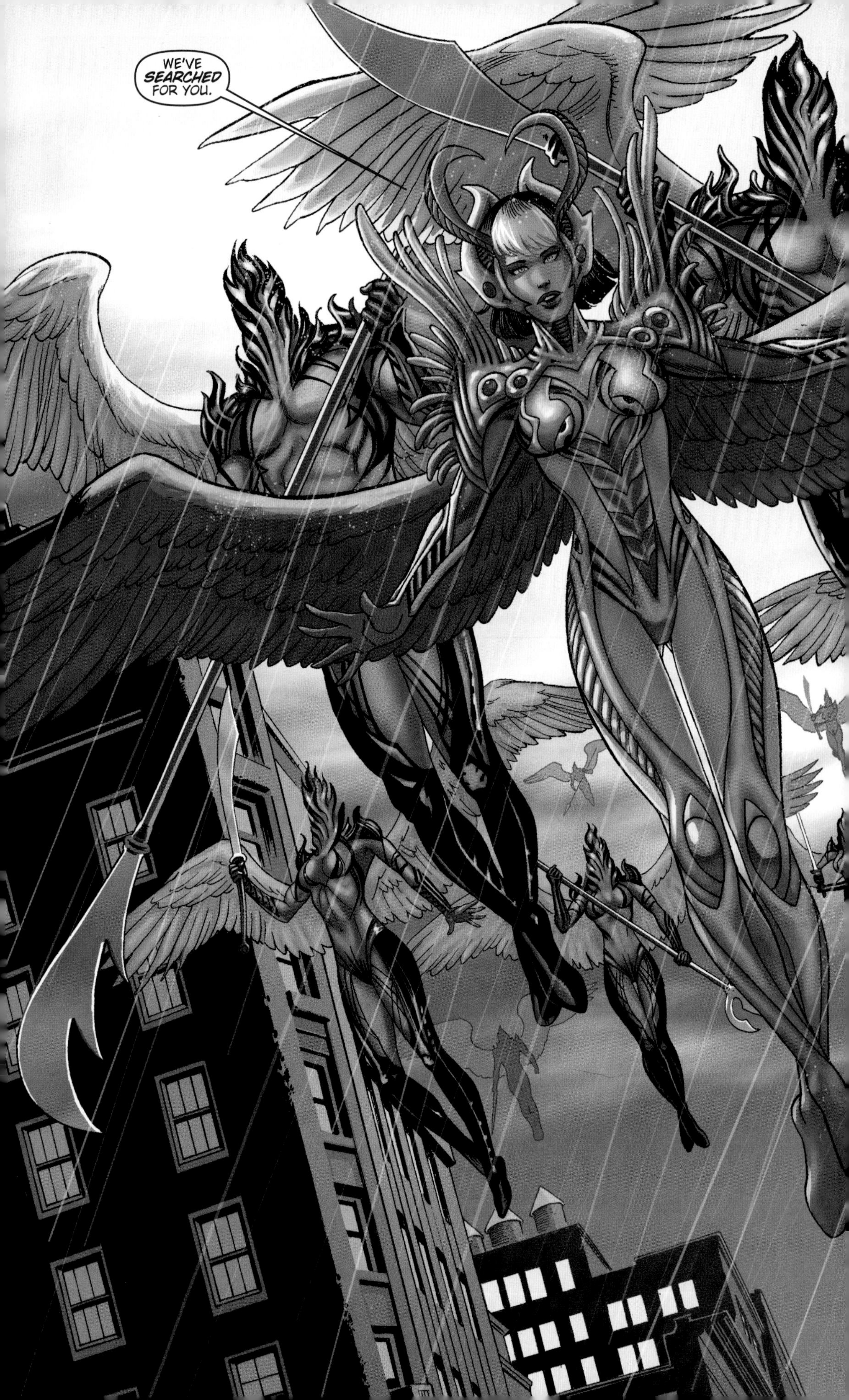
WE'VE *SEARCHED* FOR YOU.

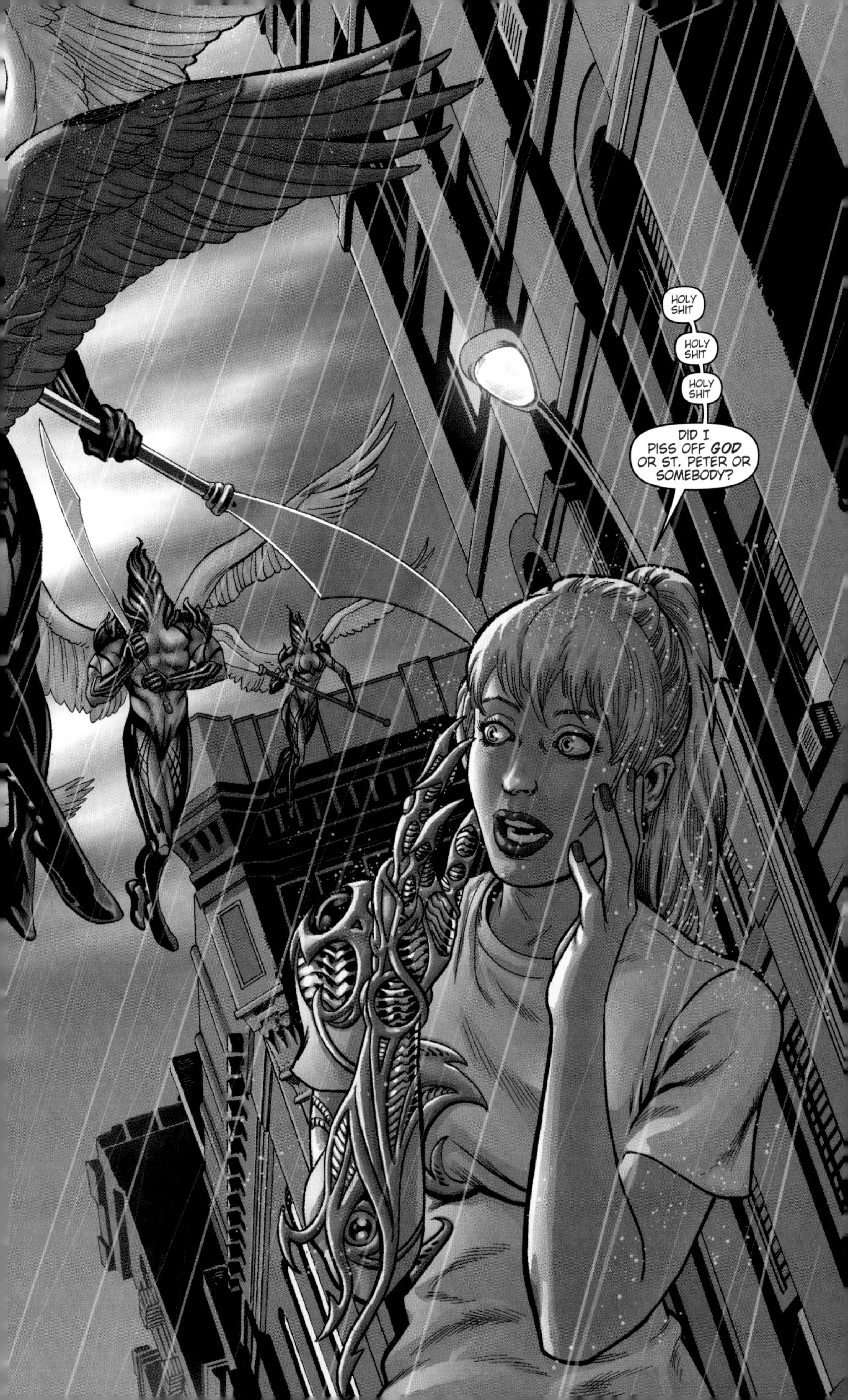
HOLY SHIT
HOLY SHIT
HOLY SHIT
DID I PISS OFF GOD OR ST. PETER OR SOMEBODY?

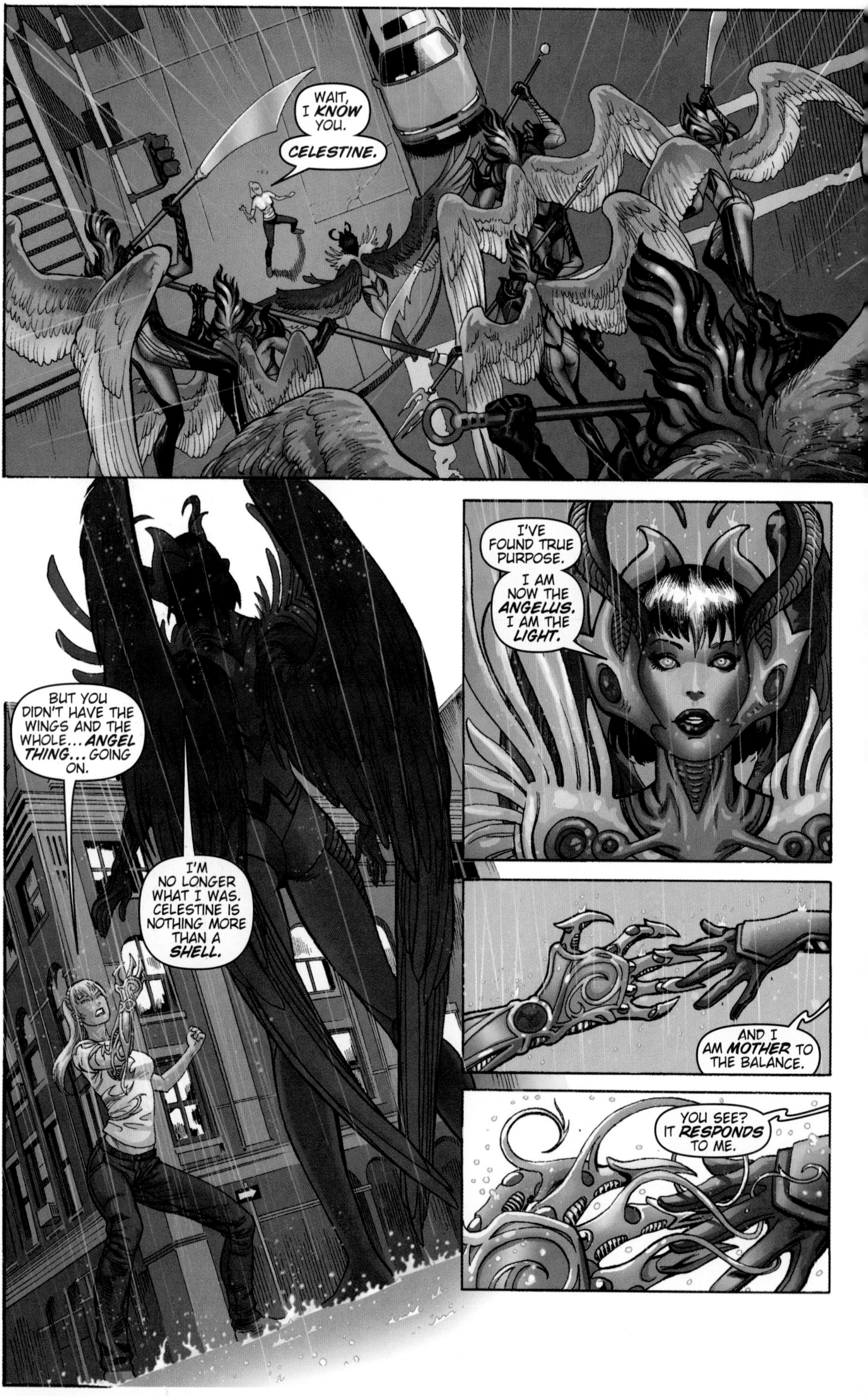
WAIT, I KNOW YOU. CELESTINE.
I'VE FOUND TRUE PURPOSE.
I AM NOW THE ANGELUS. I AM THE LIGHT.
BUT YOU DIDN'T HAVE THE WINGS AND THE WHOLE... ANGEL THING... GOING ON.
I'M NO LONGER WHAT I WAS. CELESTINE IS NOTHING MORE THAN A SHELL.
AND I AM MOTHER TO THE BALANCE.
YOU SEE? IT RESPONDS TO ME.

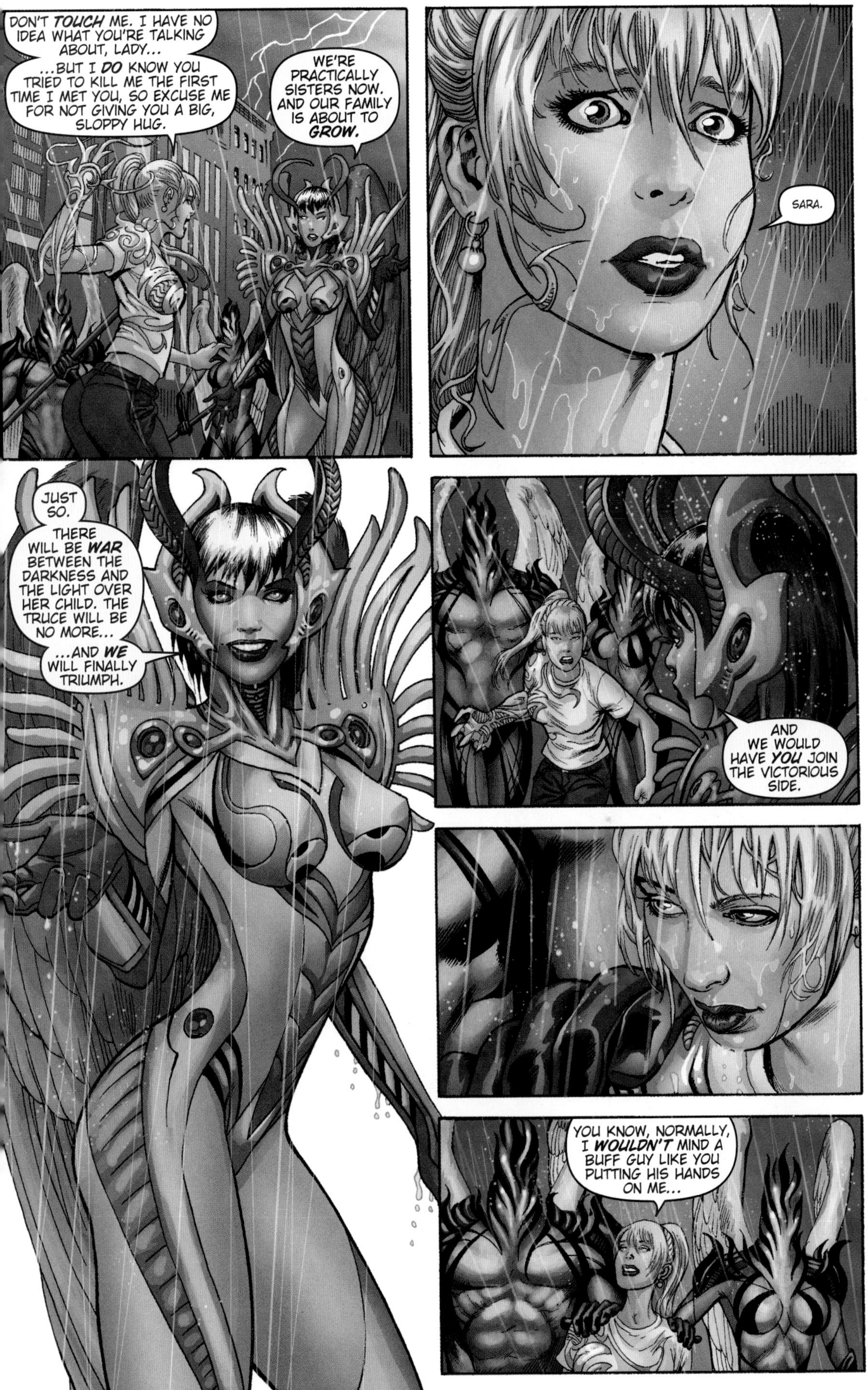
DON'T TOUCH ME. I HAVE NO IDEA WHAT YOU'RE TALKING ABOUT, LADY...
...BUT I DO KNOW YOU TRIED TO KILL ME THE FIRST TIME I MET YOU, SO EXCUSE ME FOR NOT GIVING YOU A BIG, SLOPPY HUG.
WE'RE PRACTICALLY SISTERS NOW. AND OUR FAMILY IS ABOUT TO GROW.
SARA.
JUST SO.
THERE WILL BE WAR BETWEEN THE DARKNESS AND THE LIGHT OVER HER CHILD. THE TRUCE WILL BE NO MORE...
...AND WE WILL FINALLY TRIUMPH.
AND WE WOULD HAVE YOU JOIN THE VICTORIOUS SIDE.
YOU KNOW, NORMALLY, I WOULDN'T MIND A BUFF GUY LIKE YOU PUTTING HIS HANDS ON ME...

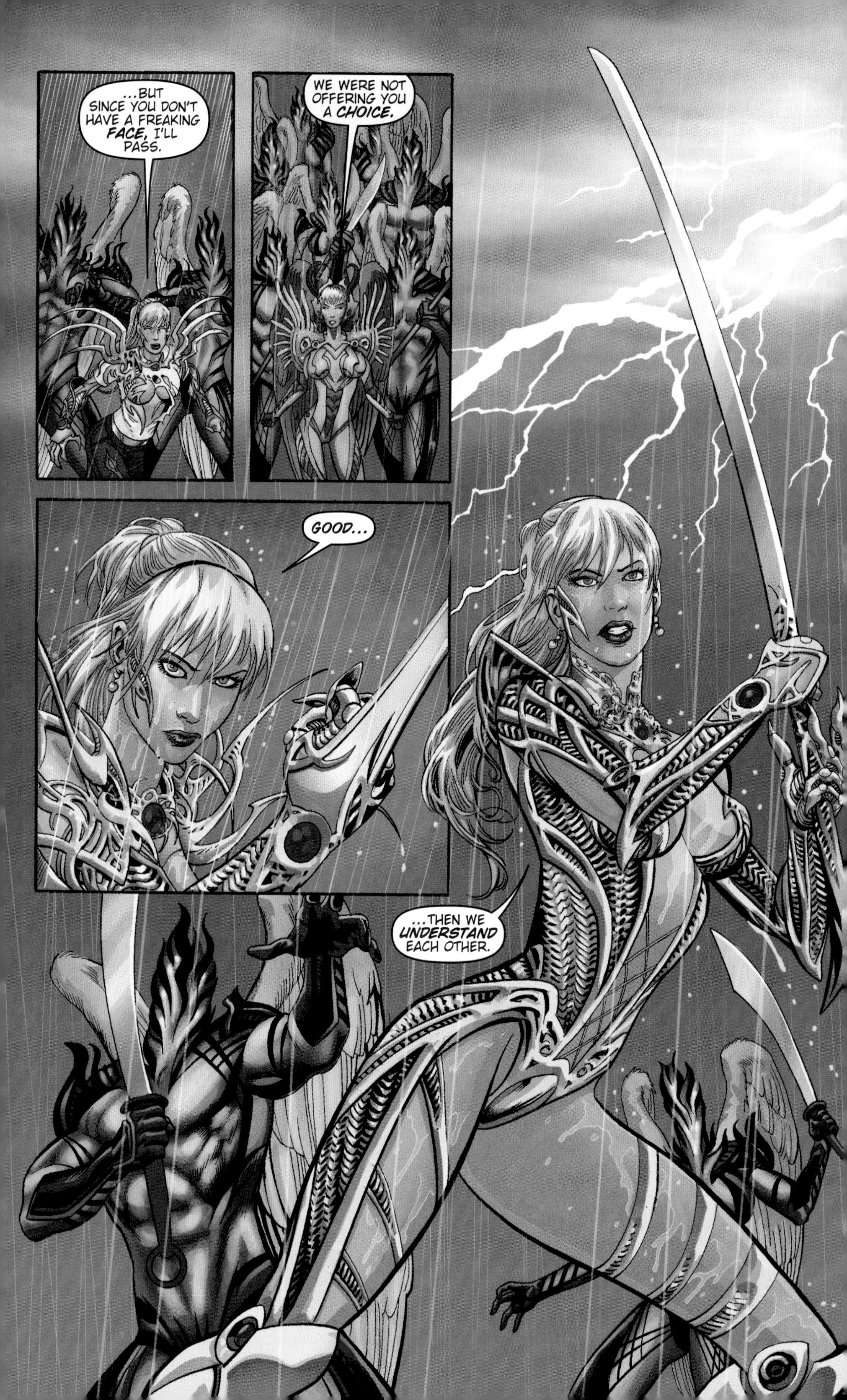

...BUT SINCE YOU DON'T HAVE A FREAKING FACE, I'LL PASS.
WE WERE NOT OFFERING YOU A CHOICE.
GOOD...
...THEN WE UNDERSTAND EACH OTHER.

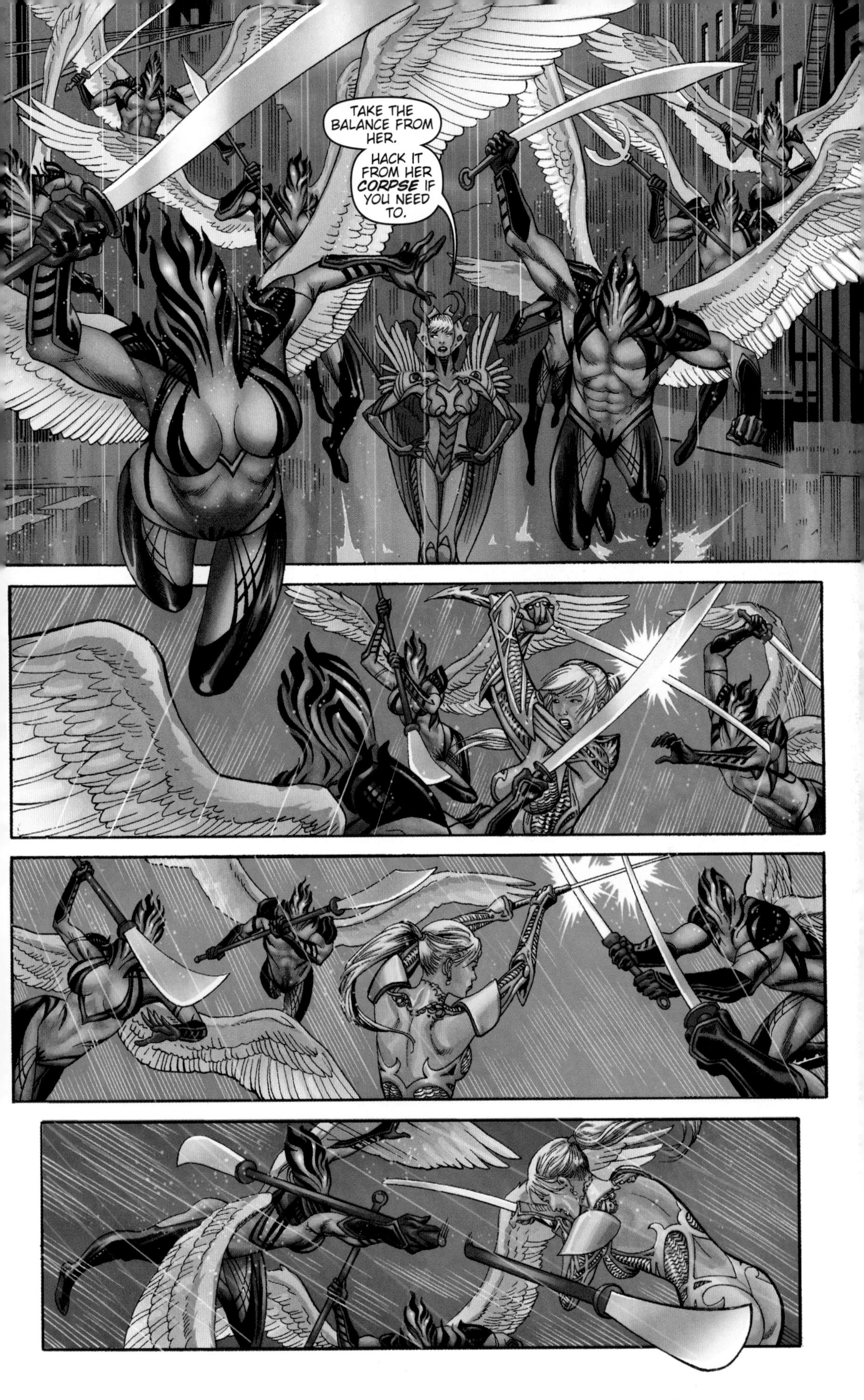
TAKE THE BALANCE FROM HER.
HACK IT FROM HER CORPSE IF YOU NEED TO.

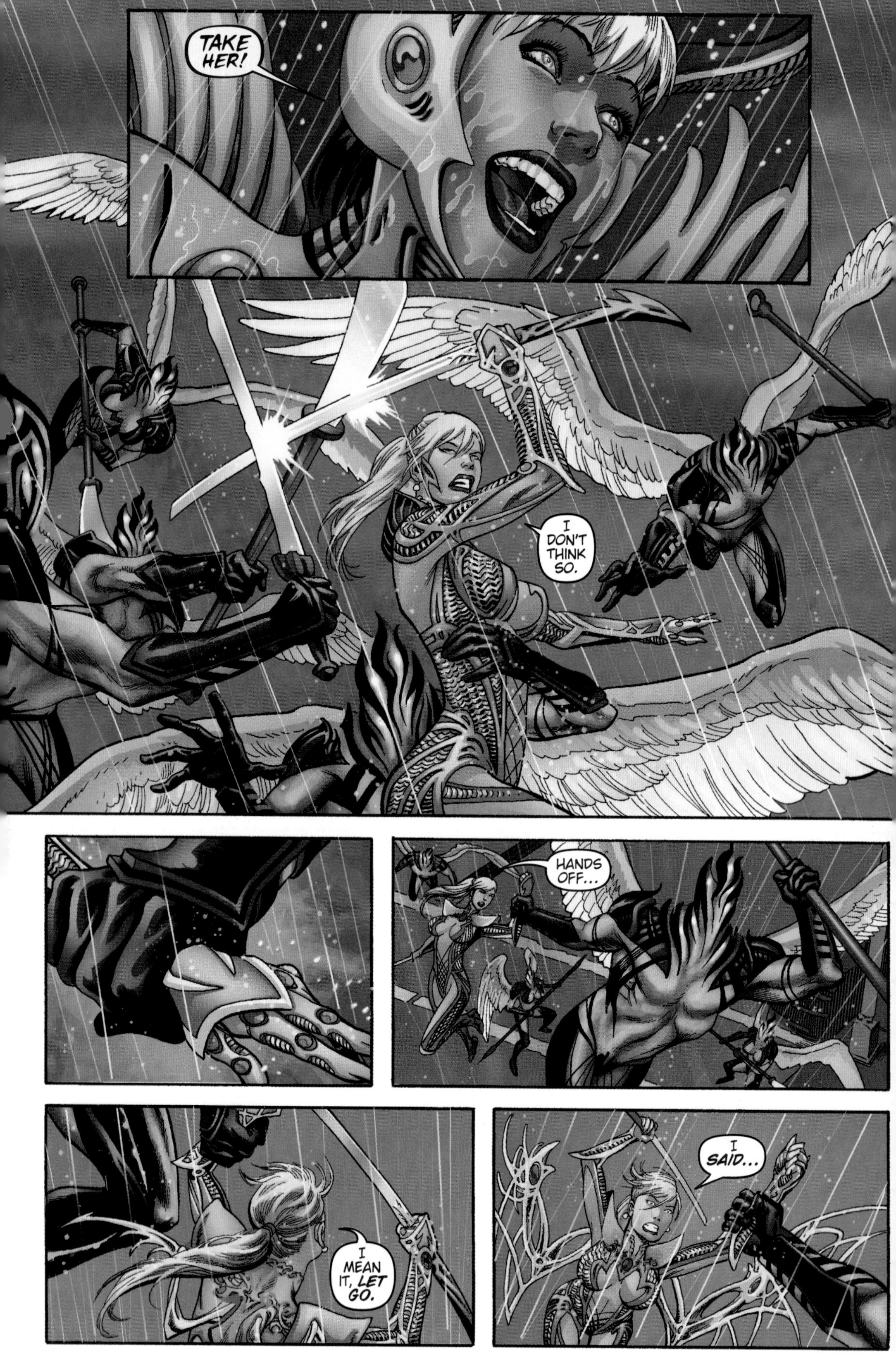
TAKE HER!
I DON'T THINK SO.
HANDS OFF...
I MEAN IT, LET GO.
I SAID...

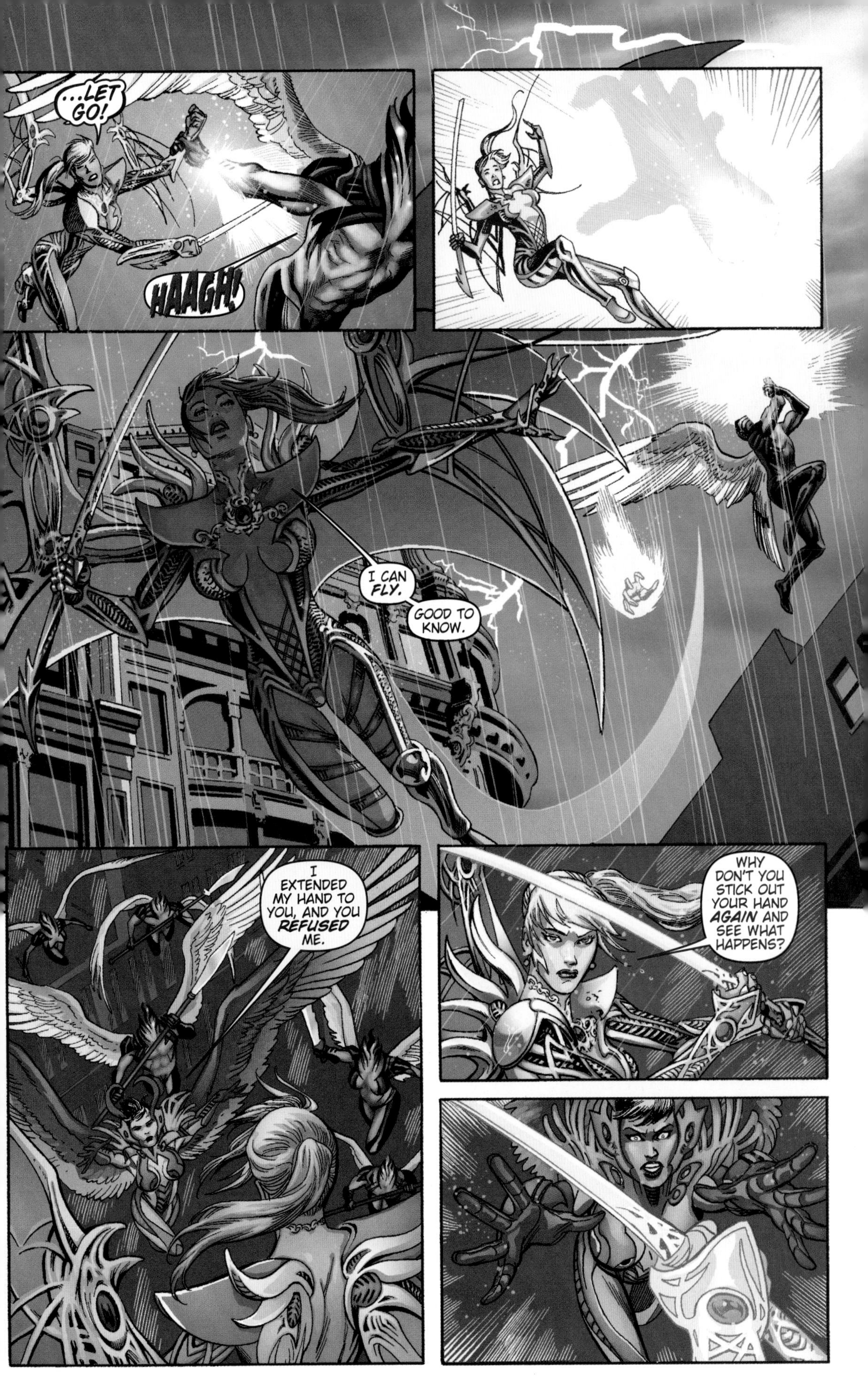
...LET GO!
HAAGH!
I CAN FLY.
GOOD TO KNOW.
I EXTENDED MY HAND TO YOU, AND YOU REFUSED ME.
WHY DON'T YOU STICK OUT YOUR HAND AGAIN AND SEE WHAT HAPPENS?

GONE...

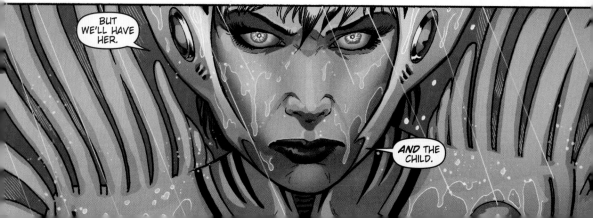

BUT WE'LL HAVE HER.

AND THE CHILD.

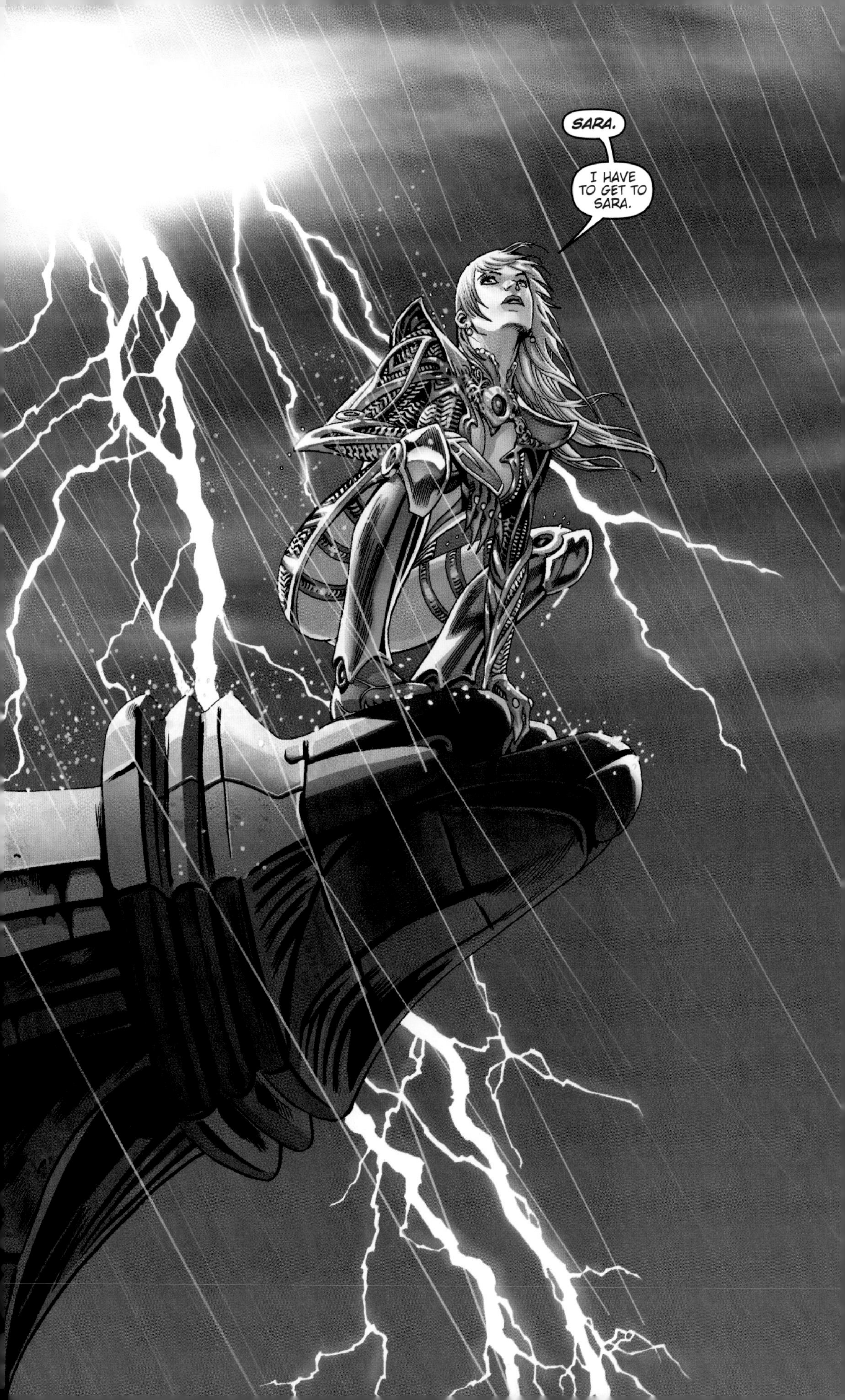
SARA.
I HAVE TO GET TO SARA.

FIRST BORN™

ISSUE #2

written by: **Ron Marz**
art by: **Stjepan Sejic**
letters by: **Troy Peteri**

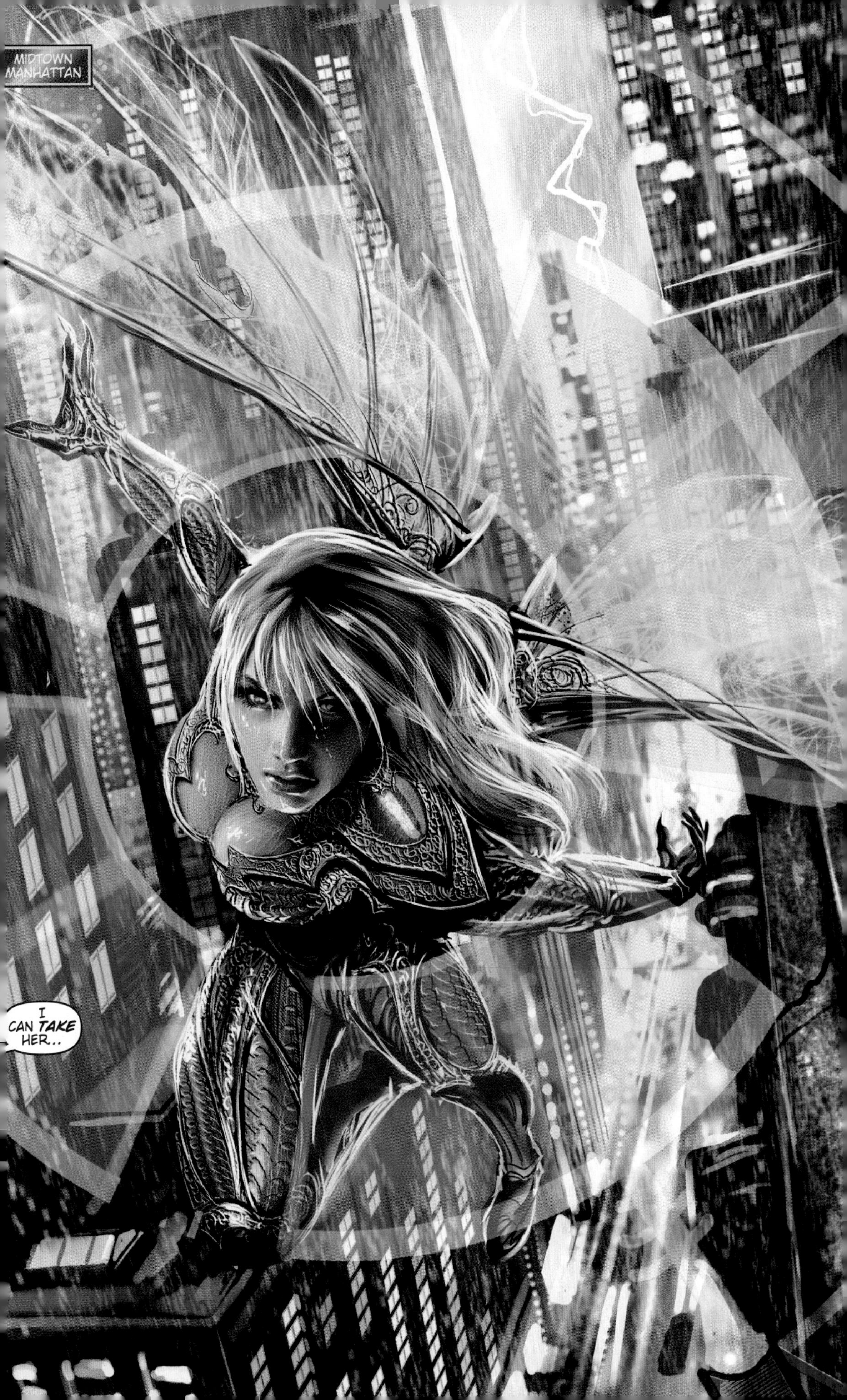
MIDTOWN MANHATTAN
I CAN TAKE HER...

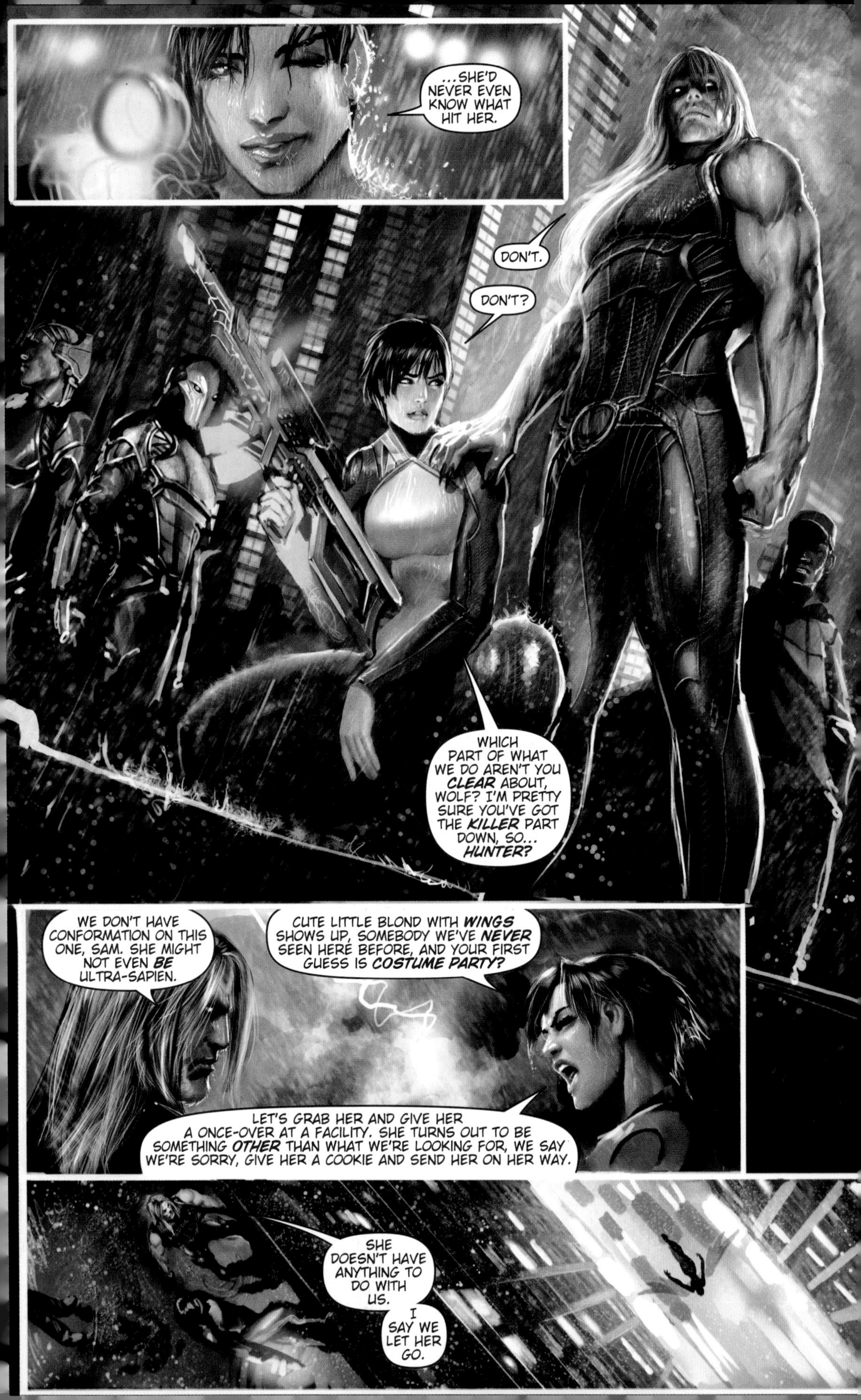
...SHE'D NEVER EVEN KNOW WHAT HIT HER.
DON'T.
DON'T?
WHICH PART OF WHAT WE DO AREN'T YOU CLEAR ABOUT, WOLF? I'M PRETTY SURE YOU'VE GOT THE KILLER PART DOWN, SO... HUNTER?
WE DON'T HAVE CONFORMATION ON THIS ONE, SAM. SHE MIGHT NOT EVEN BE ULTRA-SAPIEN.
CUTE LITTLE BLOND WITH WINGS SHOWS UP, SOMEBODY WE'VE NEVER SEEN HERE BEFORE, AND YOUR FIRST GUESS IS COSTUME PARTY?
LET'S GRAB HER AND GIVE HER A ONCE-OVER AT A FACILITY. SHE TURNS OUT TO BE SOMETHING OTHER THAN WHAT WE'RE LOOKING FOR, WE SAY WE'RE SORRY, GIVE HER A COOKIE AND SEND HER ON HER WAY.
SHE DOESN'T HAVE ANYTHING TO DO WITH US.
I SAY WE LET HER GO.

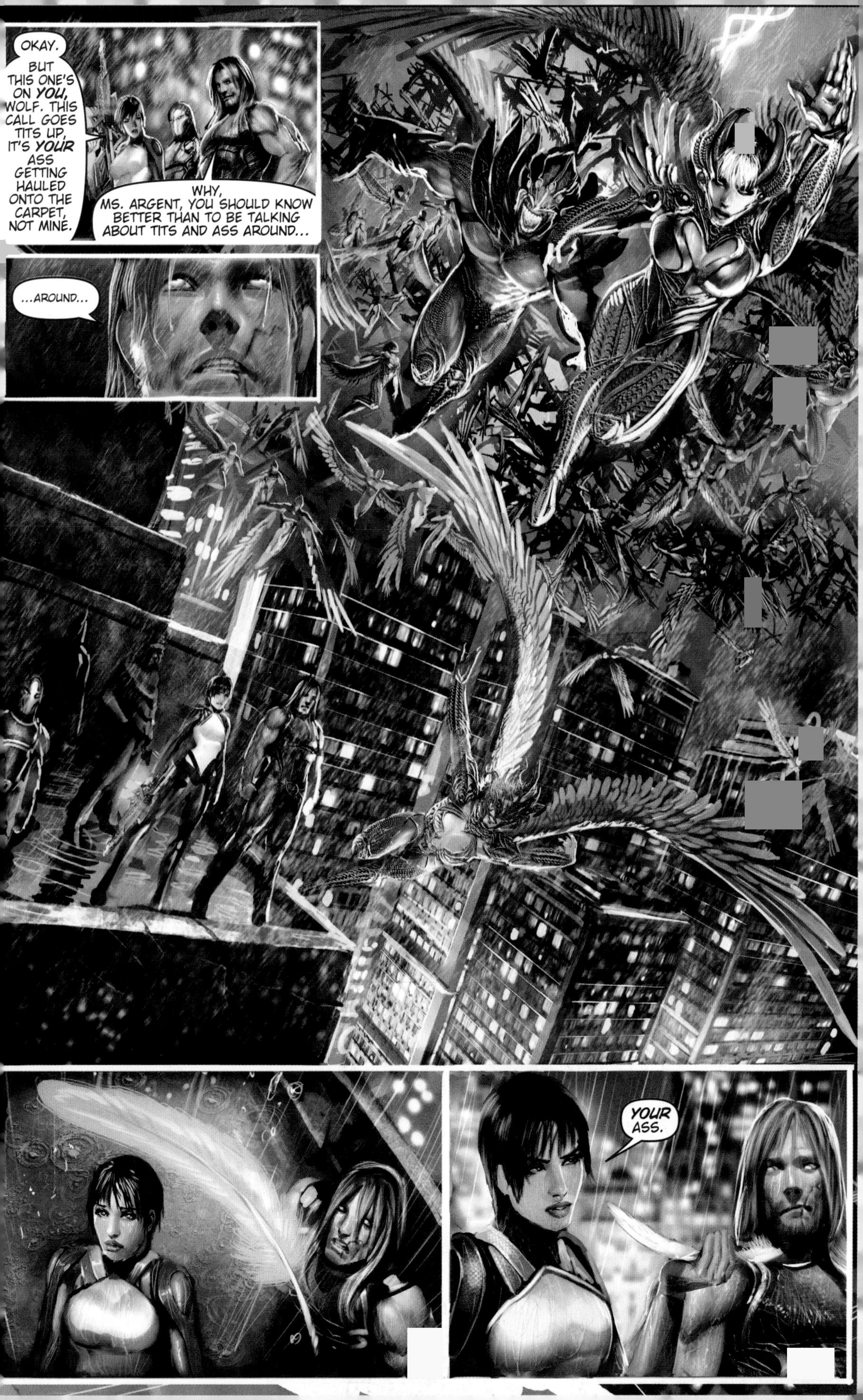

OKAY.
BUT THIS ONE'S ON YOU, WOLF. THIS CALL GOES TITS UP, IT'S YOUR ASS GETTING HAULED ONTO THE CARPET, NOT MINE.
WHY, MS. ARGENT, YOU SHOULD KNOW BETTER THAN TO BE TALKING ABOUT TITS AND ASS AROUND...
...AROUND...
YOUR ASS.

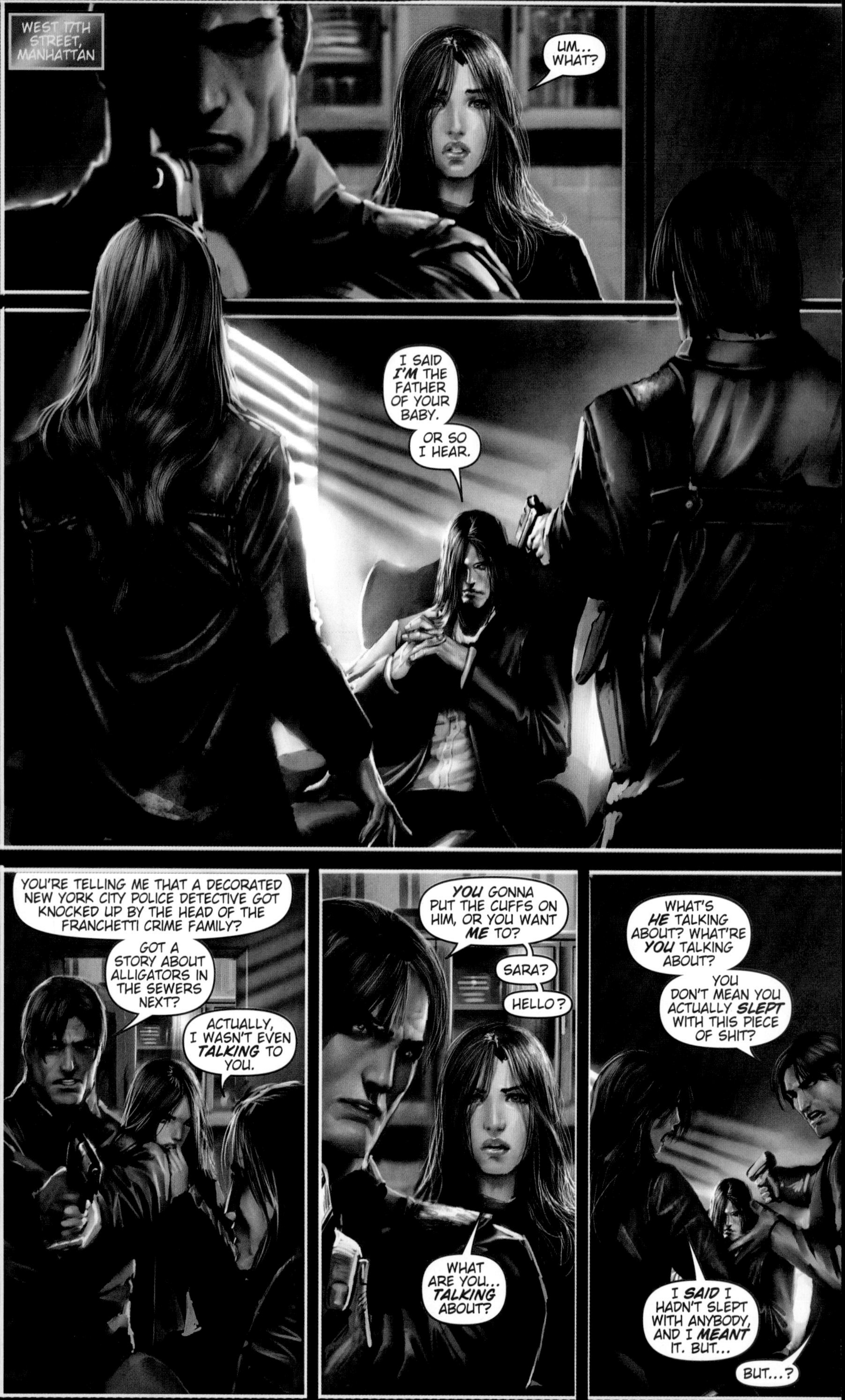
WEST 17TH STREET, MANHATTAN
UM... WHAT?
I SAID I'M THE FATHER OF YOUR BABY.
OR SO I HEAR.
YOU'RE TELLING ME THAT A DECORATED NEW YORK CITY POLICE DETECTIVE GOT KNOCKED UP BY THE HEAD OF THE FRANCHETTI CRIME FAMILY?
GOT A STORY ABOUT ALLIGATORS IN THE SEWERS NEXT?
ACTUALLY, I WASN'T EVEN TALKING TO YOU.
YOU GONNA PUT THE CUFFS ON HIM, OR YOU WANT ME TO?
SARA?
HELLO?
WHAT ARE YOU... TALKING ABOUT?
WHAT'S HE TALKING ABOUT? WHAT'RE YOU TALKING ABOUT?
YOU DON'T MEAN YOU ACTUALLY SLEPT WITH THIS PIECE OF SHIT?
I SAID I HADN'T SLEPT WITH ANYBODY, AND I MEANT IT. BUT...
BUT...?

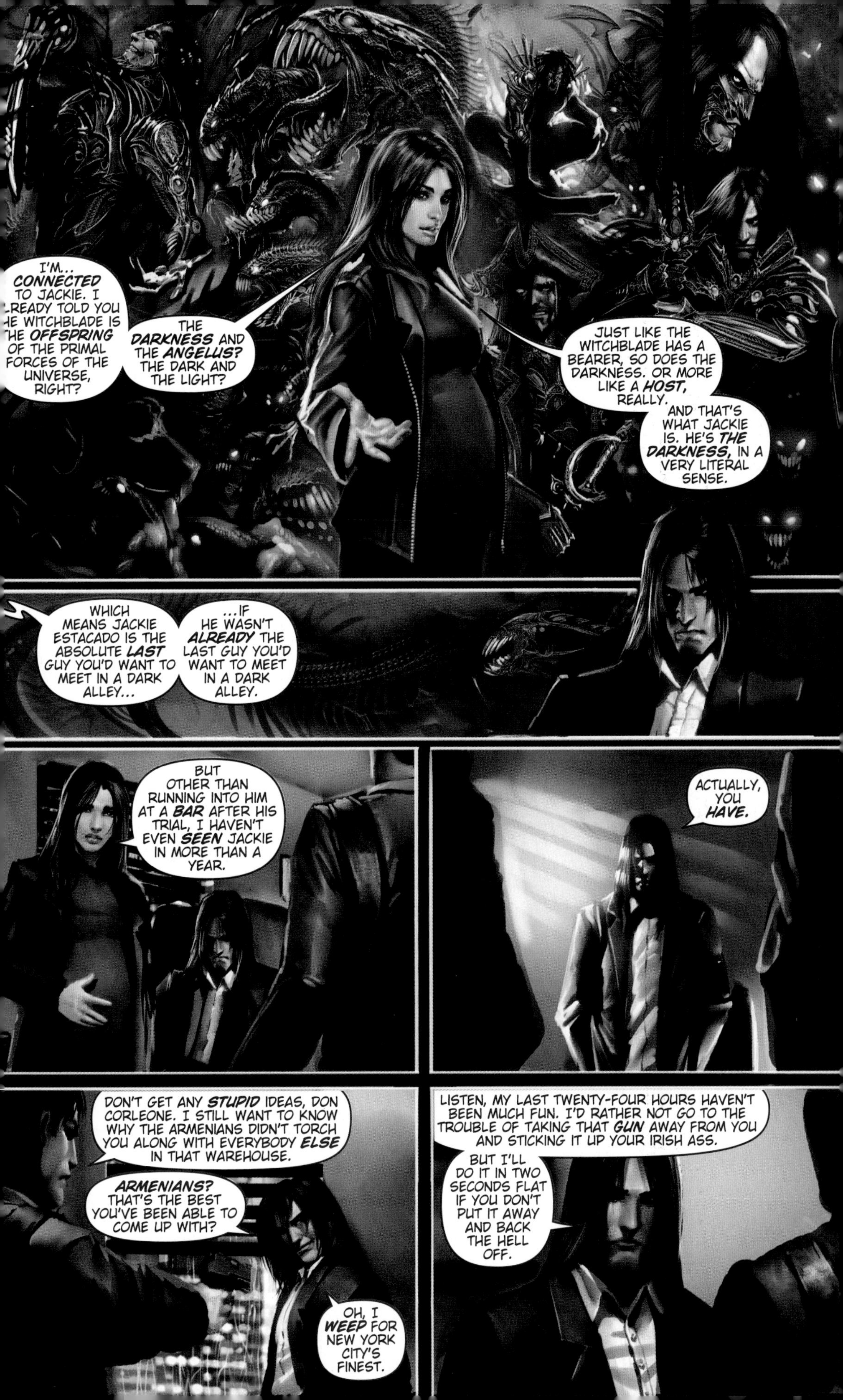
I'M... CONNECTED TO JACKIE. I LREADY TOLD YOU HE WITCHBLADE IS HE OFFSPRING OF THE PRIMAL FORCES OF THE UNIVERSE, RIGHT?
THE DARKNESS AND THE ANGELUS? THE DARK AND THE LIGHT?
JUST LIKE THE WITCHBLADE HAS A BEARER, SO DOES THE DARKNESS. OR MORE LIKE A HOST, REALLY.
AND THAT'S WHAT JACKIE IS. HE'S THE DARKNESS, IN A VERY LITERAL SENSE.
WHICH MEANS JACKIE ESTACADO IS THE ABSOLUTE LAST GUY YOU'D WANT TO MEET IN A DARK ALLEY...
...IF HE WASN'T ALREADY THE LAST GUY YOU'D WANT TO MEET IN A DARK ALLEY.
BUT OTHER THAN RUNNING INTO HIM AT A BAR AFTER HIS TRIAL, I HAVEN'T EVEN SEEN JACKIE IN MORE THAN A YEAR.
ACTUALLY, YOU HAVE.
DON'T GET ANY STUPID IDEAS, DON CORLEONE. I STILL WANT TO KNOW WHY THE ARMENIANS DIDN'T TORCH YOU ALONG WITH EVERYBODY ELSE IN THAT WAREHOUSE.
ARMENIANS? THAT'S THE BEST YOU'VE BEEN ABLE TO COME UP WITH?
OH, I WEEP FOR NEW YORK CITY'S FINEST.
LISTEN, MY LAST TWENTY-FOUR HOURS HAVEN'T BEEN MUCH FUN. I'D RATHER NOT GO TO THE TROUBLE OF TAKING THAT GUN AWAY FROM YOU AND STICKING IT UP YOUR IRISH ASS.
BUT I'LL DO IT IN TWO SECONDS FLAT IF YOU DON'T PUT IT AWAY AND BACK THE HELL OFF.

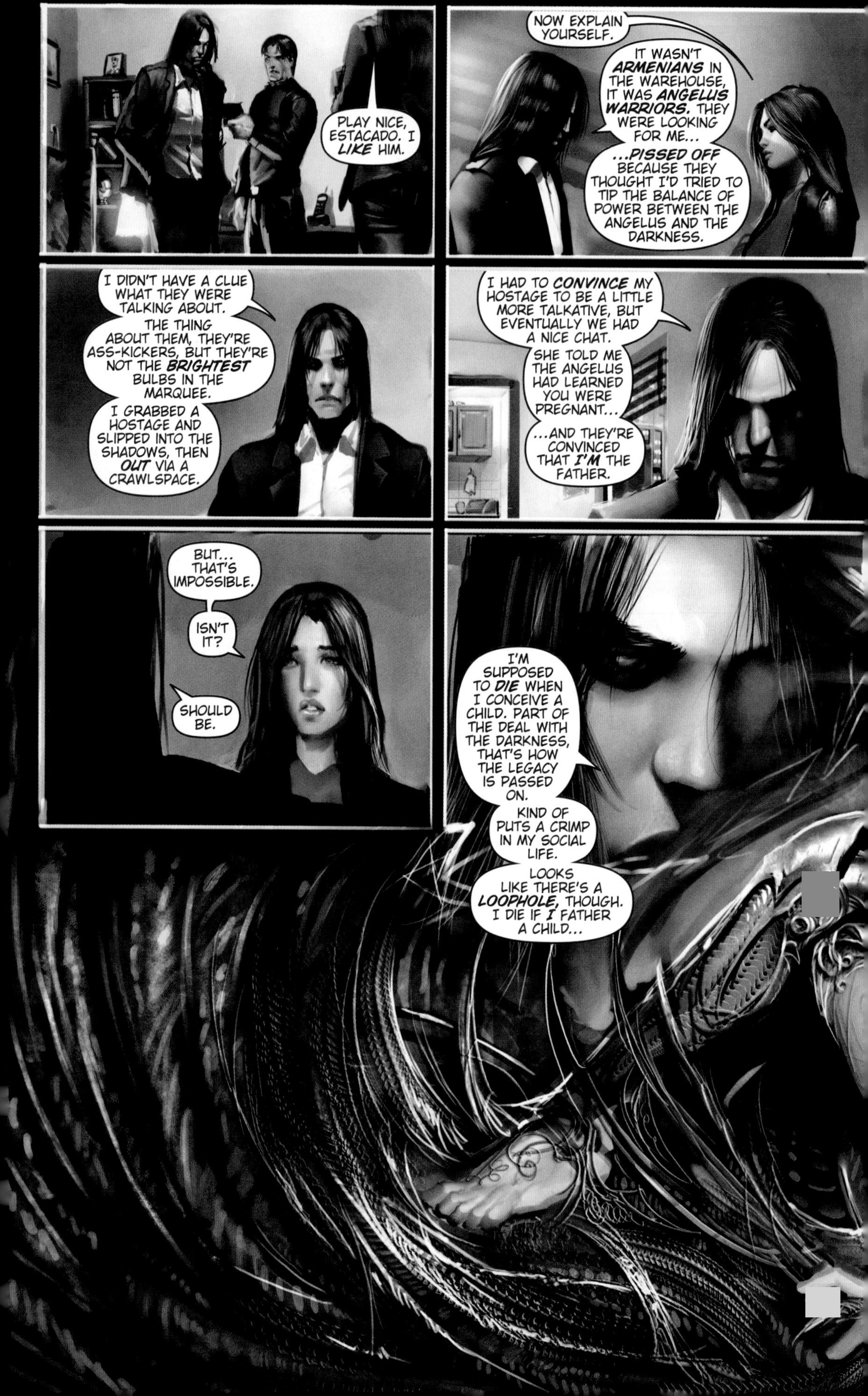
PLAY NICE, ESTACADO. I LIKE HIM.
NOW EXPLAIN YOURSELF.
IT WASN'T ARMENIANS IN THE WAREHOUSE, IT WAS ANGELUS WARRIORS. THEY WERE LOOKING FOR ME...
...PISSED OFF BECAUSE THEY THOUGHT I'D TRIED TO TIP THE BALANCE OF POWER BETWEEN THE ANGELUS AND THE DARKNESS.
I DIDN'T HAVE A CLUE WHAT THEY WERE TALKING ABOUT.
THE THING ABOUT THEM, THEY'RE ASS-KICKERS, BUT THEY'RE NOT THE BRIGHTEST BULBS IN THE MARQUEE.
I GRABBED A HOSTAGE AND SLIPPED INTO THE SHADOWS, THEN OUT VIA A CRAWLSPACE.
I HAD TO CONVINCE MY HOSTAGE TO BE A LITTLE MORE TALKATIVE, BUT EVENTUALLY WE HAD A NICE CHAT.
SHE TOLD ME THE ANGELUS HAD LEARNED YOU WERE PREGNANT...
...AND THEY'RE CONVINCED THAT I'M THE FATHER.
BUT... THAT'S IMPOSSIBLE.
ISN'T IT?
SHOULD BE.
I'M SUPPOSED TO DIE WHEN I CONCEIVE A CHILD. PART OF THE DEAL WITH THE DARKNESS, THAT'S HOW THE LEGACY IS PASSED ON.
KIND OF PUTS A CRIMP IN MY SOCIAL LIFE.
LOOKS LIKE THERE'S A LOOPHOLE, THOUGH. I DIE IF I FATHER A CHILD...

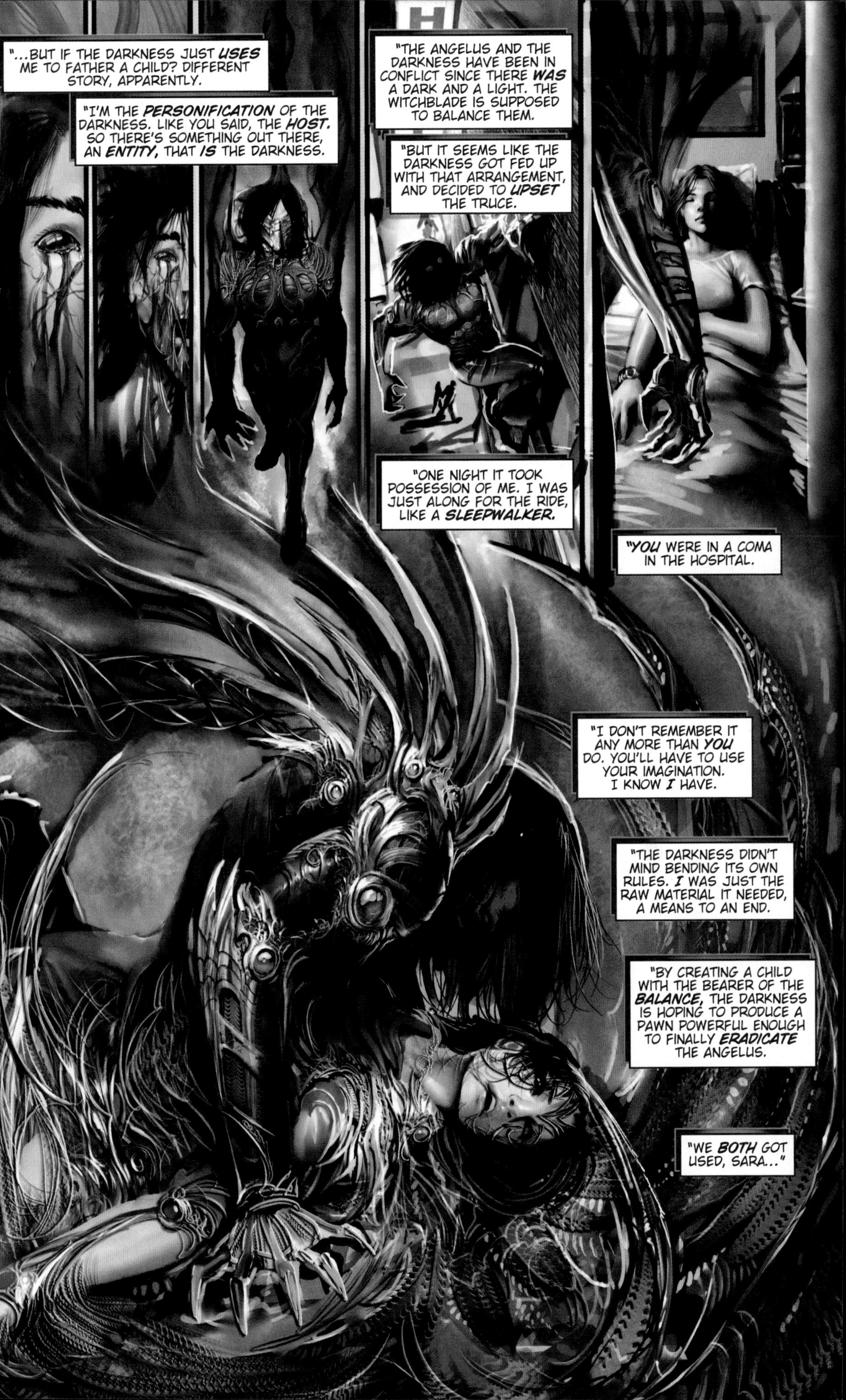
"...BUT IF THE DARKNESS JUST USES ME TO FATHER A CHILD? DIFFERENT STORY, APPARENTLY.
"I'M THE PERSONIFICATION OF THE DARKNESS. LIKE YOU SAID, THE HOST. SO THERE'S SOMETHING OUT THERE, AN ENTITY, THAT IS THE DARKNESS.
"THE ANGELUS AND THE DARKNESS HAVE BEEN IN CONFLICT SINCE THERE WAS A DARK AND A LIGHT. THE WITCHBLADE IS SUPPOSED TO BALANCE THEM.
"BUT IT SEEMS LIKE THE DARKNESS GOT FED UP WITH THAT ARRANGEMENT, AND DECIDED TO UPSET THE TRUCE.
"ONE NIGHT IT TOOK POSSESSION OF ME. I WAS JUST ALONG FOR THE RIDE, LIKE A SLEEPWALKER.
"YOU WERE IN A COMA IN THE HOSPITAL.
"I DON'T REMEMBER IT ANY MORE THAN YOU DO. YOU'LL HAVE TO USE YOUR IMAGINATION. I KNOW I HAVE.
"THE DARKNESS DIDN'T MIND BENDING ITS OWN RULES. I WAS JUST THE RAW MATERIAL IT NEEDED, A MEANS TO AN END.
"BY CREATING A CHILD WITH THE BEARER OF THE BALANCE, THE DARKNESS IS HOPING TO PRODUCE A PAWN POWERFUL ENOUGH TO FINALLY ERADICATE THE ANGELUS.
"WE BOTH GOT USED, SARA..."

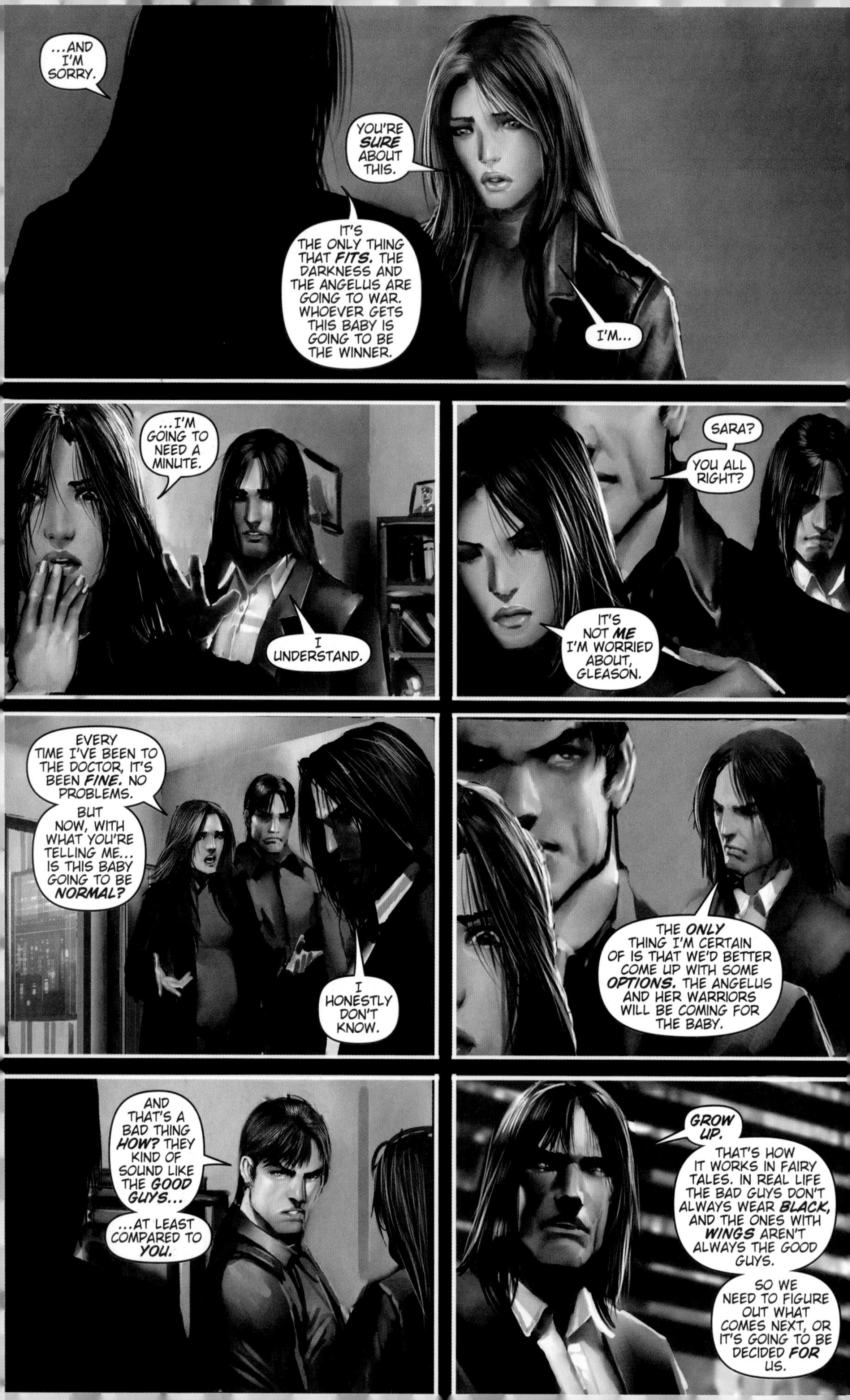
...AND I'M SORRY.
YOU'RE SURE ABOUT THIS.
IT'S THE ONLY THING THAT FITS. THE DARKNESS AND THE ANGELUS ARE GOING TO WAR. WHOEVER GETS THIS BABY IS GOING TO BE THE WINNER.
I'M...
...I'M GOING TO NEED A MINUTE.
I UNDERSTAND.
SARA?
YOU ALL RIGHT?
IT'S NOT ME I'M WORRIED ABOUT, GLEASON.
EVERY TIME I'VE BEEN TO THE DOCTOR, IT'S BEEN FINE. NO PROBLEMS.
BUT NOW, WITH WHAT YOU'RE TELLING ME... IS THIS BABY GOING TO BE NORMAL?
I HONESTLY DON'T KNOW.
THE ONLY THING I'M CERTAIN OF IS THAT WE'D BETTER COME UP WITH SOME OPTIONS. THE ANGELUS AND HER WARRIORS WILL BE COMING FOR THE BABY.
AND THAT'S A BAD THING HOW? THEY KIND OF SOUND LIKE THE GOOD GUYS...
...AT LEAST COMPARED TO YOU.
GROW UP.
THAT'S HOW IT WORKS IN FAIRY TALES. IN REAL LIFE THE BAD GUYS DON'T ALWAYS WEAR BLACK, AND THE ONES WITH WINGS AREN'T ALWAYS THE GOOD GUYS.
SO WE NEED TO FIGURE OUT WHAT COMES NEXT, OR IT'S GOING TO BE DECIDED FOR US.

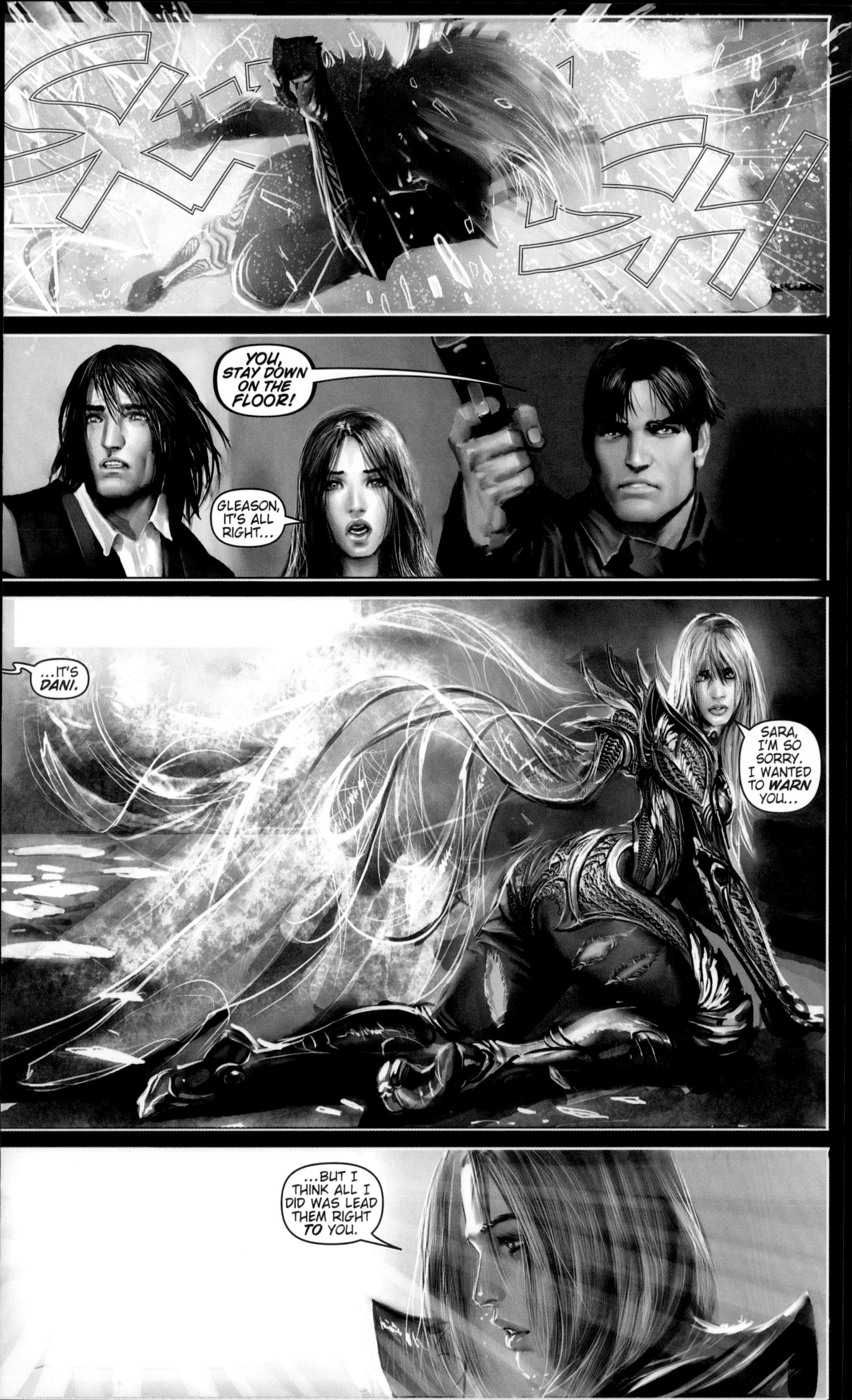
YOU, STAY DOWN ON THE FLOOR!
GLEASON, IT'S ALL RIGHT...
...IT'S DANI.
SARA, I'M SO SORRY. I WANTED TO WARN YOU...
...BUT I THINK ALL I DID WAS LEAD THEM RIGHT TO YOU.

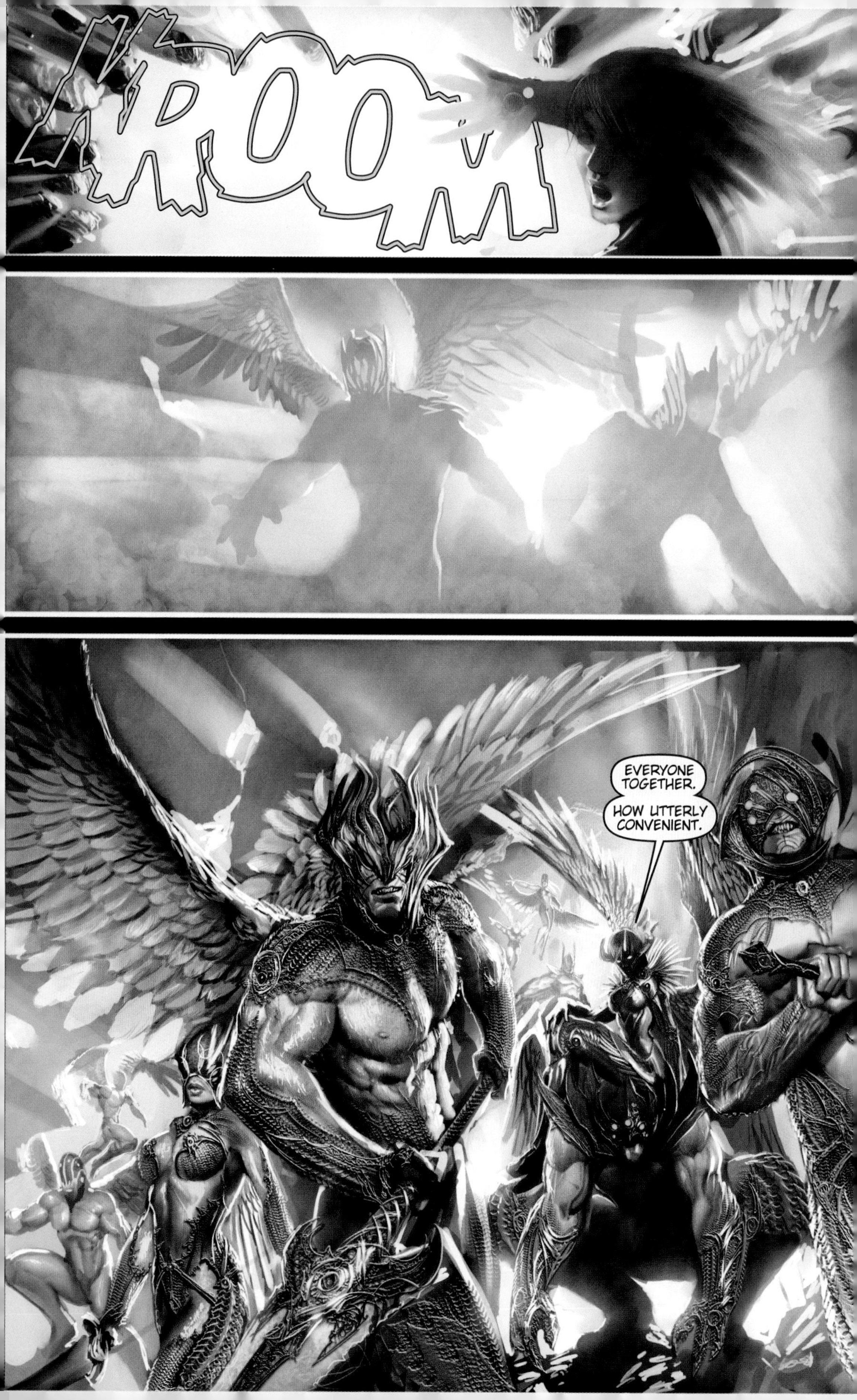
VROOOM
EVERYONE TOGETHER.
HOW UTTERLY CONVENIENT.

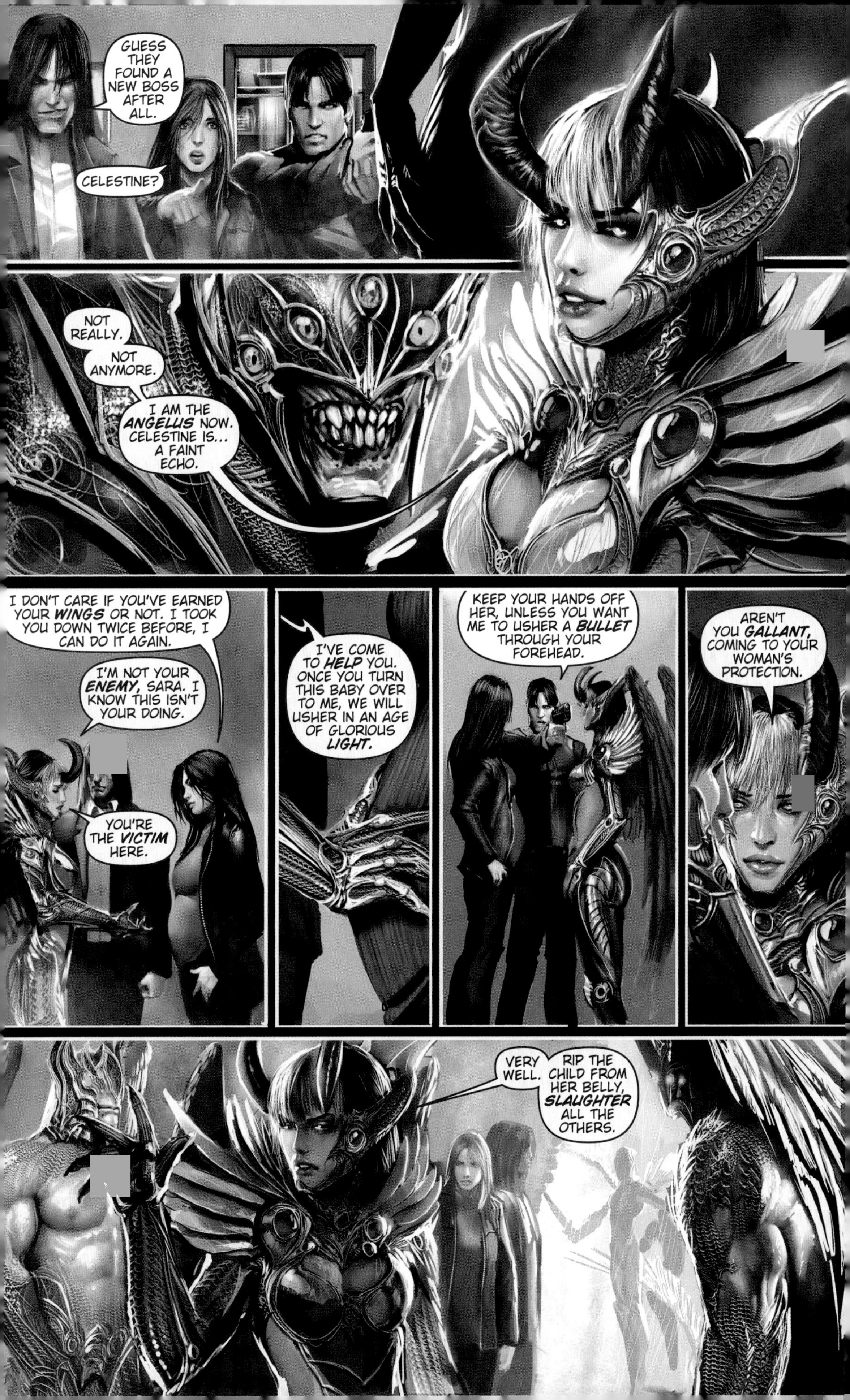
GUESS THEY FOUND A NEW BOSS AFTER ALL.
CELESTINE?
NOT REALLY.
NOT ANYMORE.
I AM THE ANGELUS NOW. CELESTINE IS... A FAINT ECHO.
I DON'T CARE IF YOU'VE EARNED YOUR WINGS OR NOT. I TOOK YOU DOWN TWICE BEFORE, I CAN DO IT AGAIN.
I'M NOT YOUR ENEMY, SARA. I KNOW THIS ISN'T YOUR DOING.
YOU'RE THE VICTIM HERE.
I'VE COME TO HELP YOU. ONCE YOU TURN THIS BABY OVER TO ME, WE WILL USHER IN AN AGE OF GLORIOUS LIGHT.
KEEP YOUR HANDS OFF HER, UNLESS YOU WANT ME TO USHER A BULLET THROUGH YOUR FOREHEAD.
AREN'T YOU GALLANT, COMING TO YOUR WOMAN'S PROTECTION.
VERY WELL.
RIP THE CHILD FROM HER BELLY, SLAUGHTER ALL THE OTHERS.

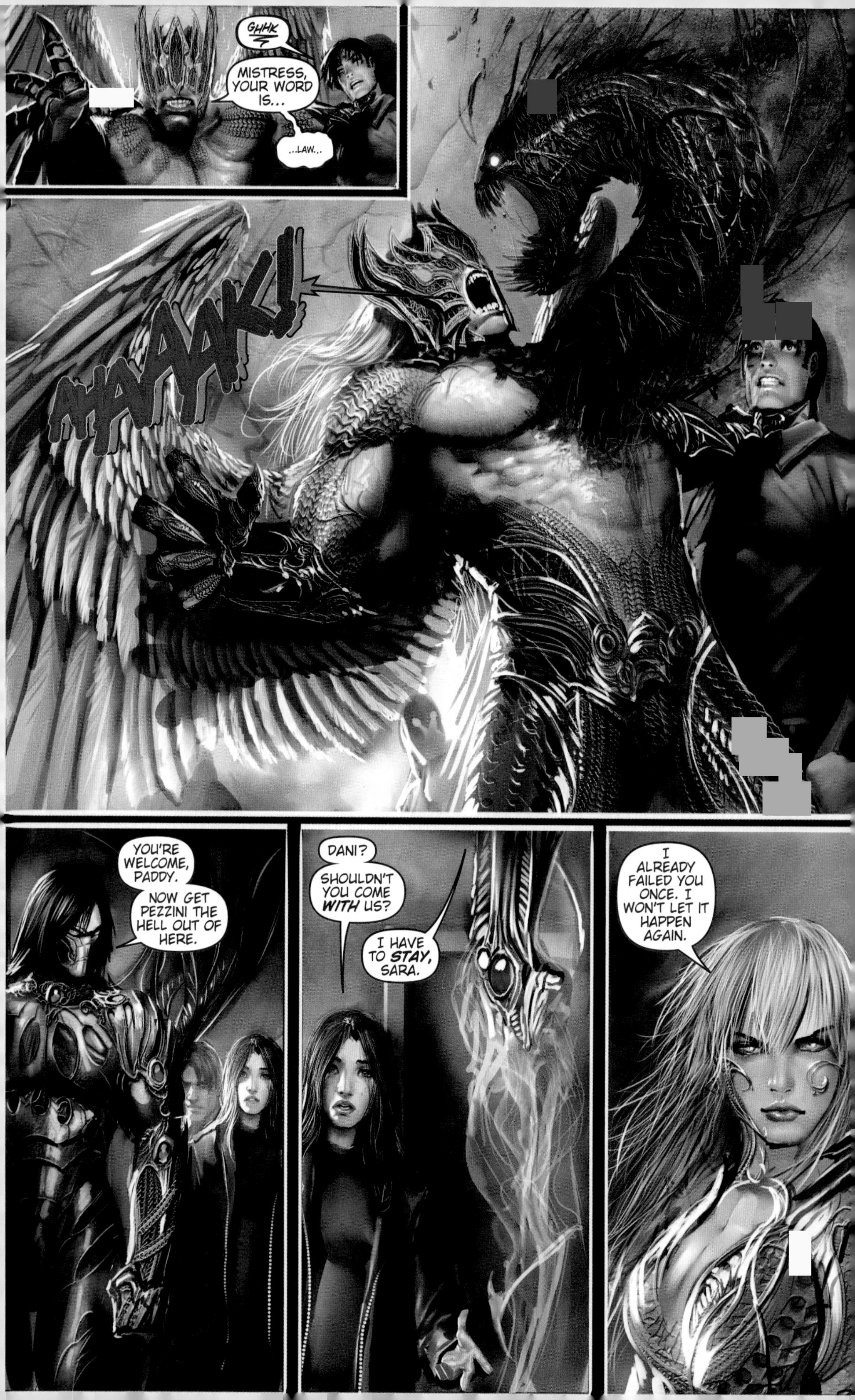
GHHK
MISTRESS, YOUR WORD IS...
...LAW...
AHAAAK!!
YOU'RE WELCOME, PADDY.
NOW GET PEZZINI THE HELL OUT OF HERE.
DANI?
SHOULDN'T YOU COME *WITH* US?
I HAVE TO *STAY*, SARA.
I ALREADY FAILED YOU ONCE. I WON'T LET IT HAPPEN AGAIN.

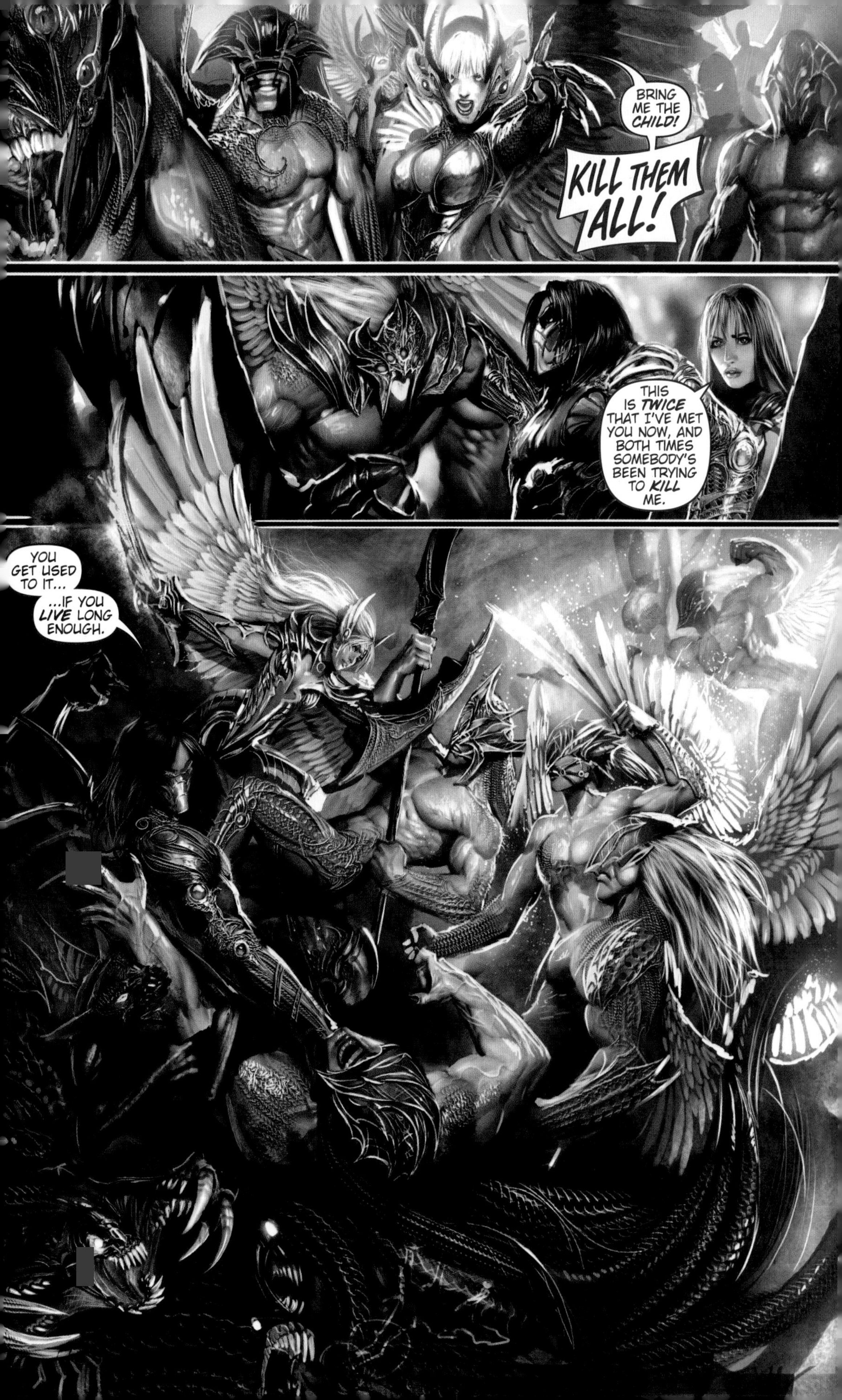
BRING ME THE CHILD!
KILL THEM ALL!
THIS IS TWICE THAT I'VE MET YOU NOW, AND BOTH TIMES SOMEBODY'S BEEN TRYING TO KILL ME.
YOU GET USED TO IT...
...IF YOU LIVE LONG ENOUGH.

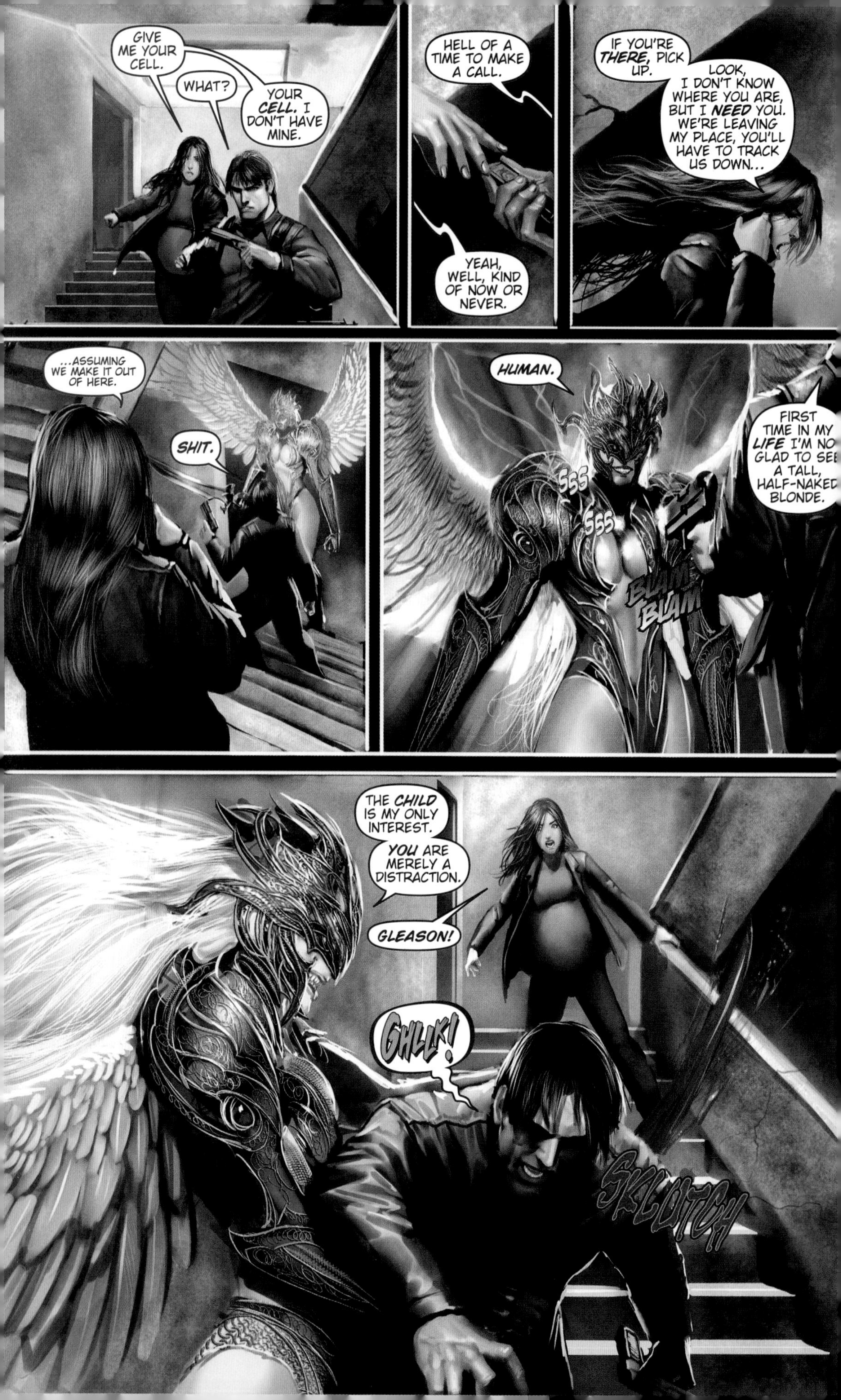
GIVE ME YOUR CELL.
WHAT?
YOUR CELL. I DON'T HAVE MINE.
HELL OF A TIME TO MAKE A CALL.
YEAH, WELL, KIND OF NOW OR NEVER.
IF YOU'RE THERE, PICK UP.
LOOK, I DON'T KNOW WHERE YOU ARE, BUT I NEED YOU. WE'RE LEAVING MY PLACE, YOU'LL HAVE TO TRACK US DOWN...
...ASSUMING WE MAKE IT OUT OF HERE.
SHIT.
HUMAN.
SSS
SSS
BLAM BLAM
FIRST TIME IN MY LIFE I'M NO GLAD TO SEE A TALL, HALF-NAKED BLONDE.
THE CHILD IS MY ONLY INTEREST.
YOU ARE MERELY A DISTRACTION.
GLEASON!
GHLLK!
SKLUTCH

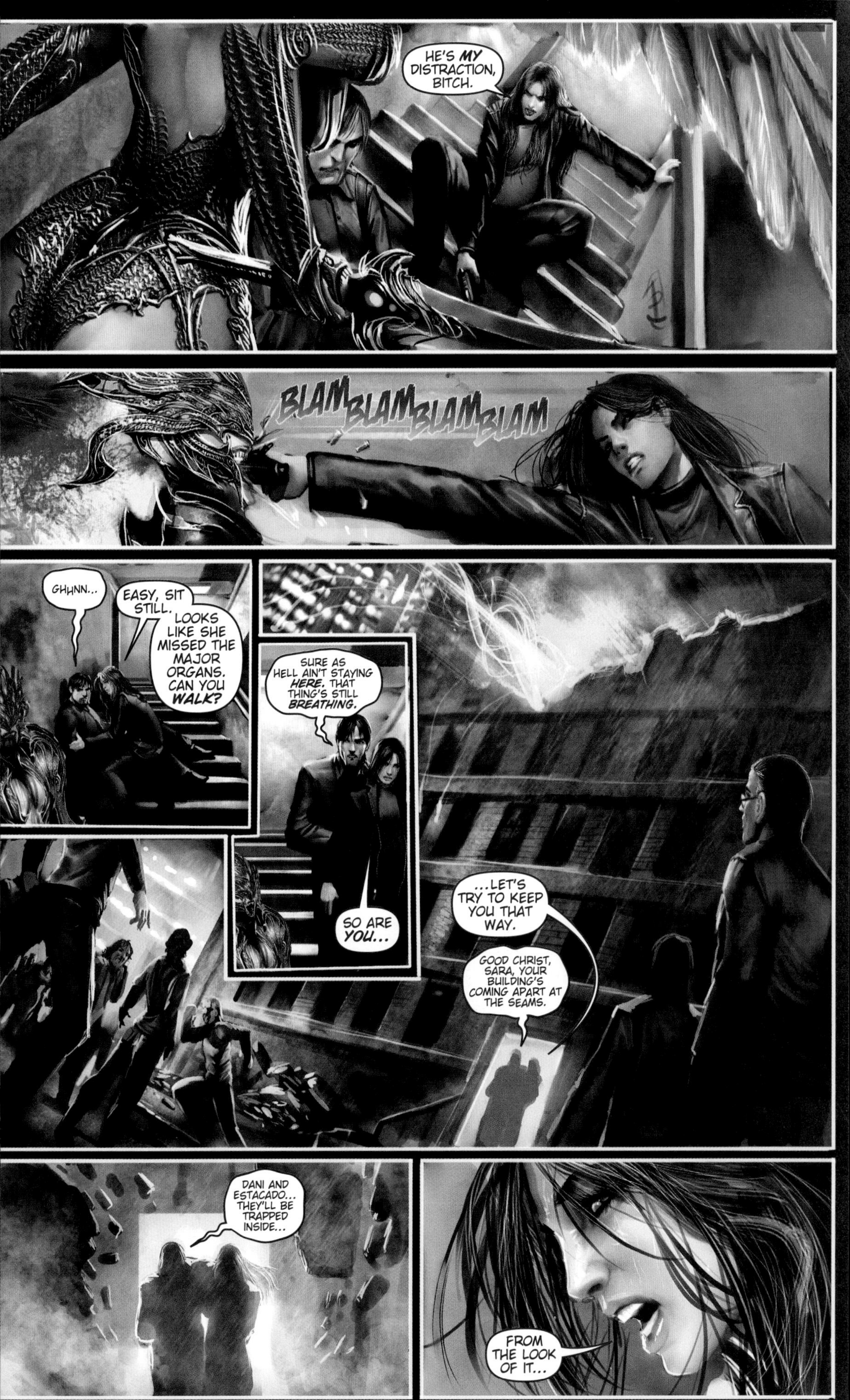
HE'S MY DISTRACTION, BITCH.
BLAM BLAM BLAM BLAM
GHUNN...
EASY, SIT STILL.
LOOKS LIKE SHE MISSED THE MAJOR ORGANS. CAN YOU WALK?
SURE AS HELL AIN'T STAYING HERE. THAT THING'S STILL BREATHING.
SO ARE YOU...
...LET'S TRY TO KEEP YOU THAT WAY.
GOOD CHRIST, SARA, YOUR BUILDING'S COMING APART AT THE SEAMS.
DANI AND ESTACADO... THEY'LL BE TRAPPED INSIDE...
FROM THE LOOK OF IT...

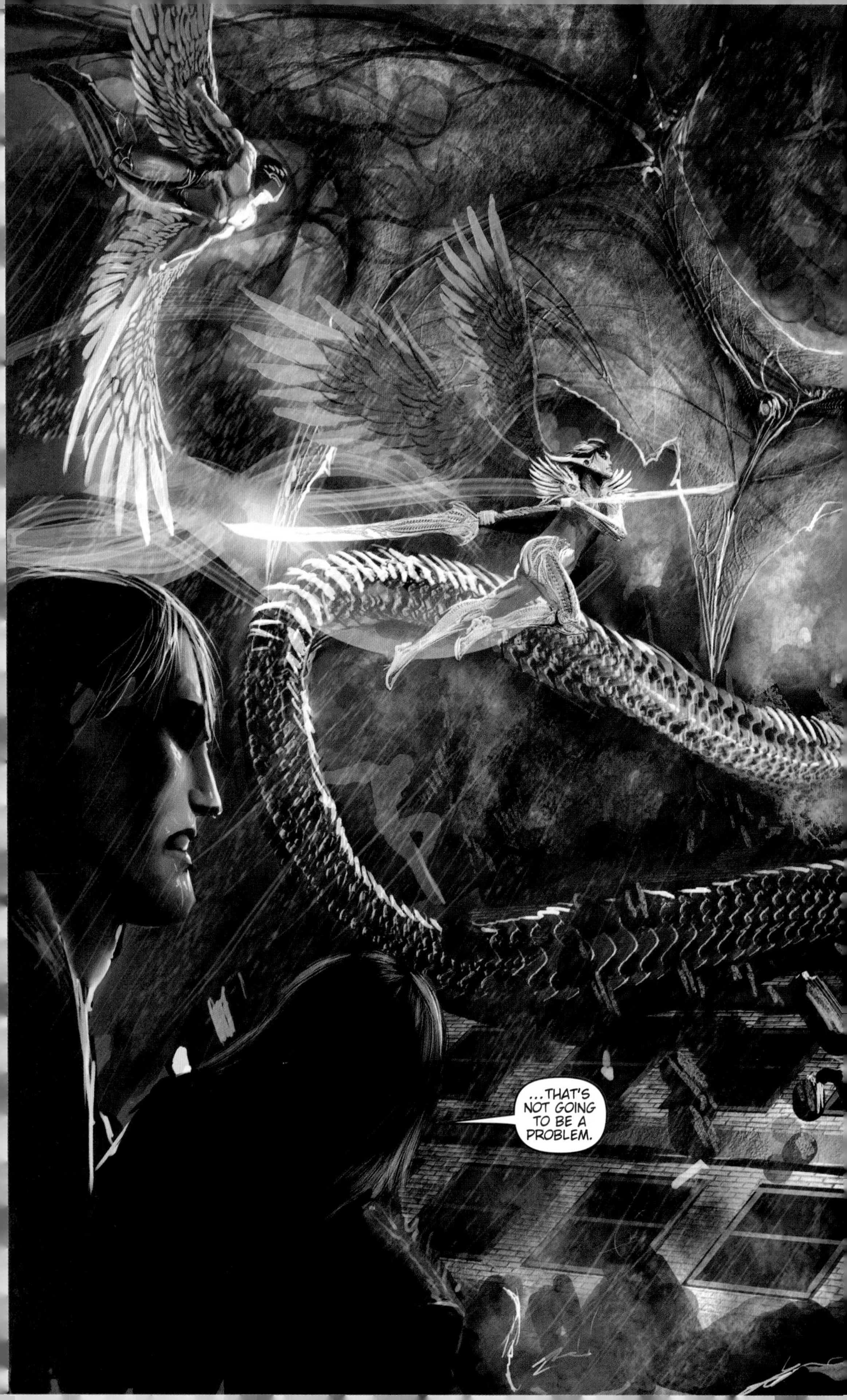
...THAT'S NOT GOING TO BE A PROBLEM.

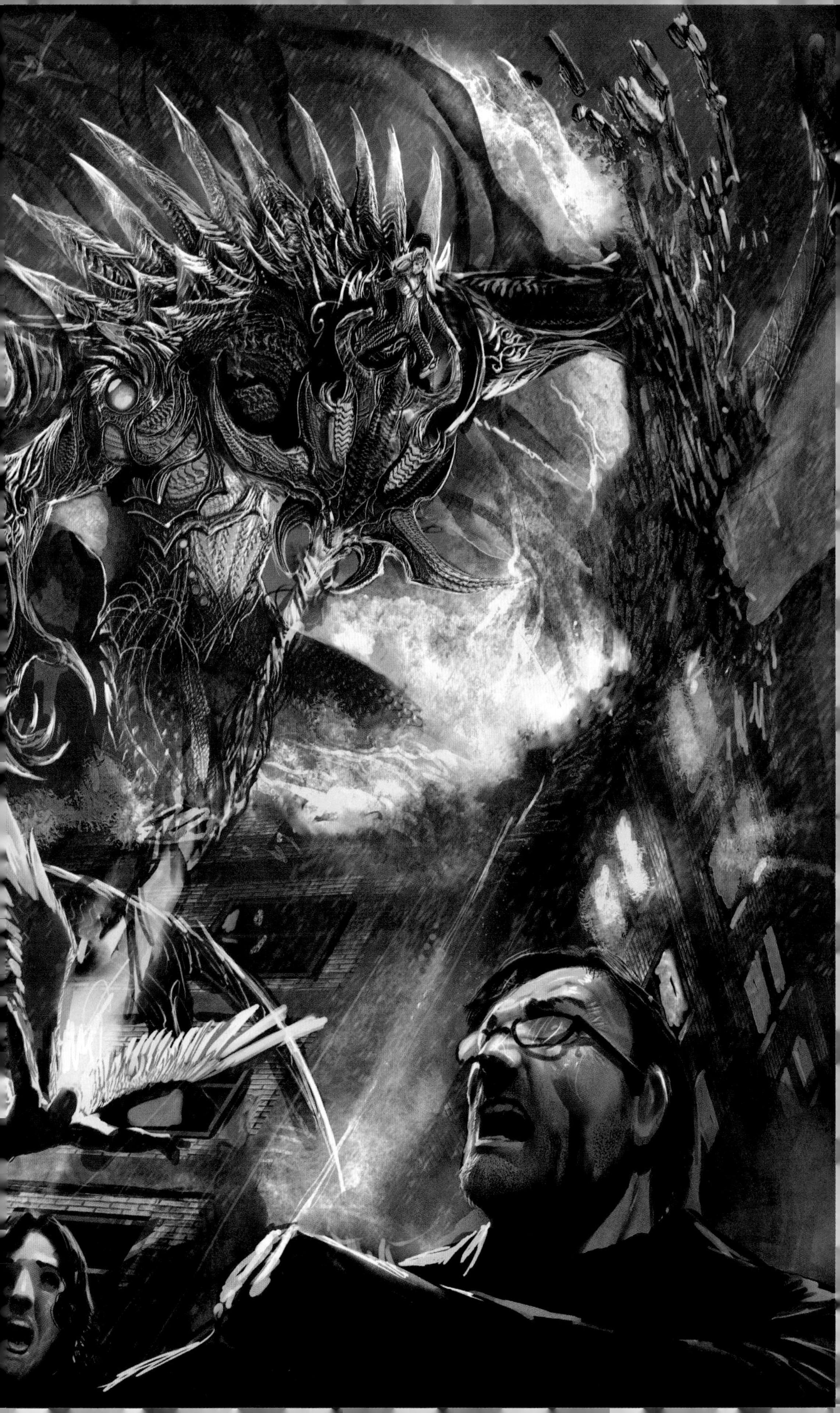

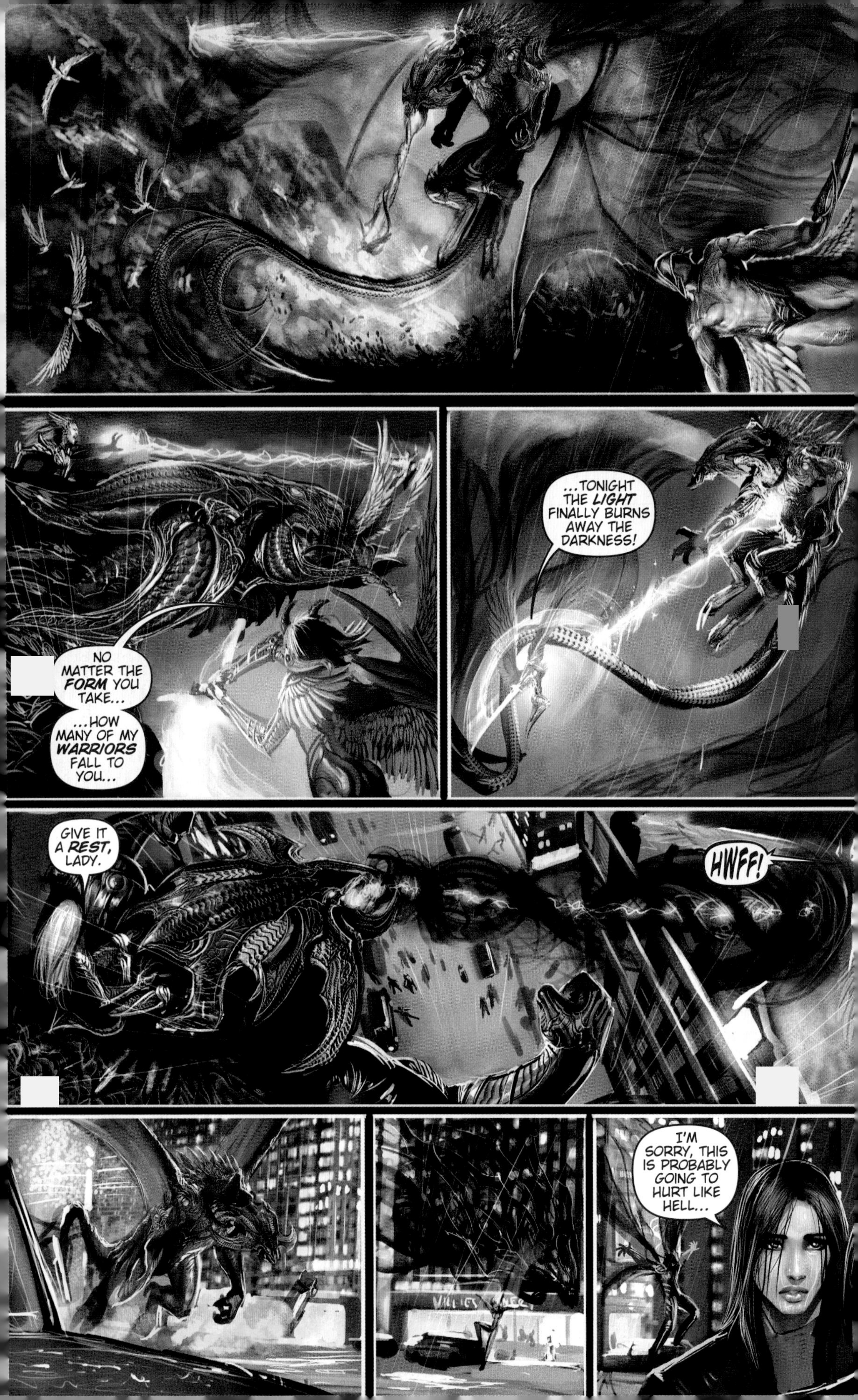
NO MATTER THE FORM YOU TAKE...
...HOW MANY OF MY WARRIORS FALL TO YOU...
...TONIGHT THE LIGHT FINALLY BURNS AWAY THE DARKNESS!
GIVE IT A REST, LADY.
HWFF!
I'M SORRY, THIS IS PROBABLY GOING TO HURT LIKE HELL...

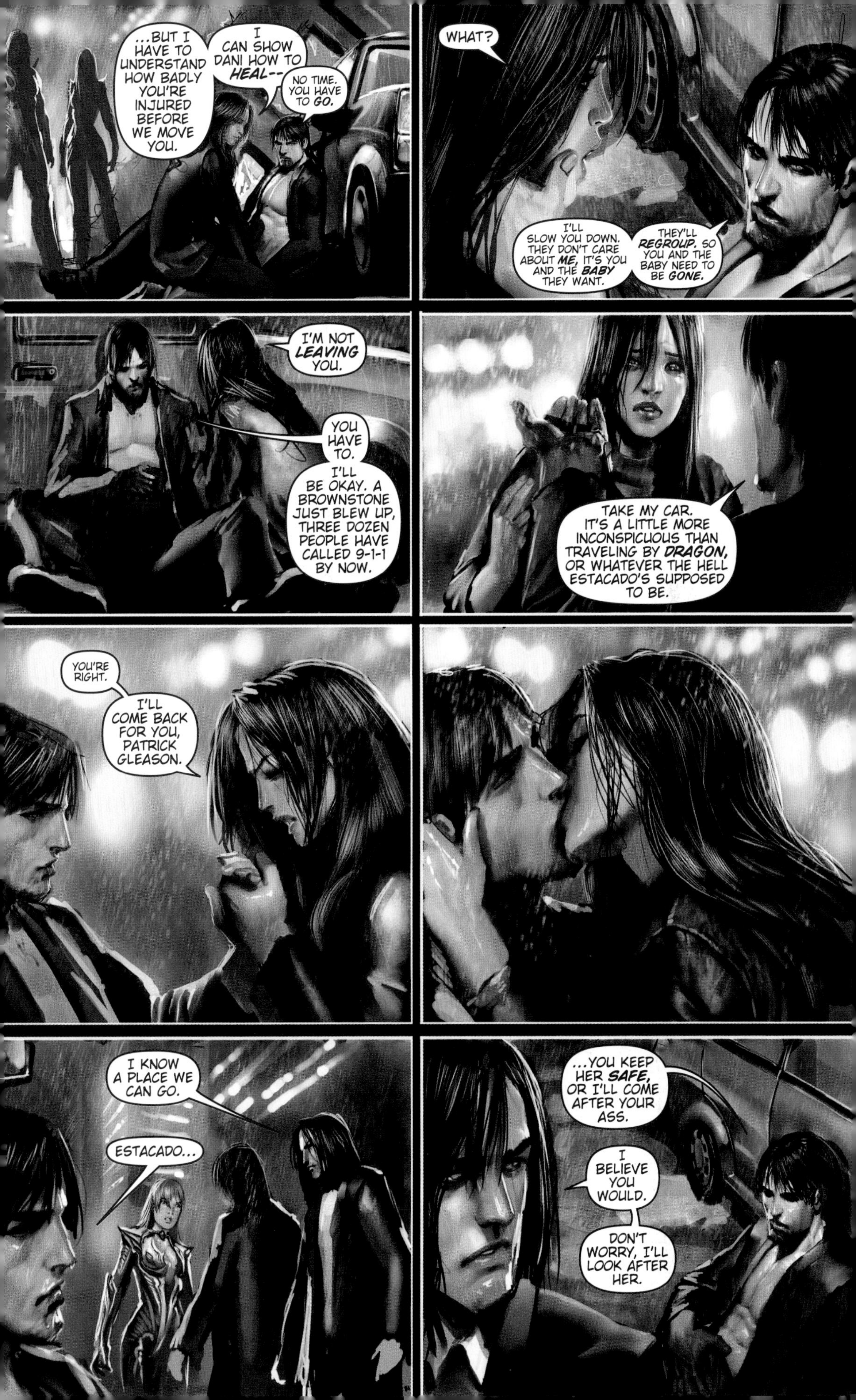
...BUT I HAVE TO UNDERSTAND HOW BADLY YOU'RE INJURED BEFORE WE MOVE YOU.
I CAN SHOW DANI HOW TO HEAL--
NO TIME. YOU HAVE TO GO.
WHAT?
I'LL SLOW YOU DOWN. THEY DON'T CARE ABOUT ME, IT'S YOU AND THE BABY THEY WANT.
THEY'LL REGROUP, SO YOU AND THE BABY NEED TO BE GONE.
I'M NOT LEAVING YOU.
YOU HAVE TO.
I'LL BE OKAY. A BROWNSTONE JUST BLEW UP, THREE DOZEN PEOPLE HAVE CALLED 9-1-1 BY NOW.
TAKE MY CAR. IT'S A LITTLE MORE INCONSPICUOUS THAN TRAVELING BY DRAGON, OR WHATEVER THE HELL ESTACADO'S SUPPOSED TO BE.
YOU'RE RIGHT.
I'LL COME BACK FOR YOU, PATRICK GLEASON.
I KNOW A PLACE WE CAN GO.
ESTACADO...
...YOU KEEP HER SAFE, OR I'LL COME AFTER YOUR ASS.
I BELIEVE YOU WOULD.
DON'T WORRY, I'LL LOOK AFTER HER.

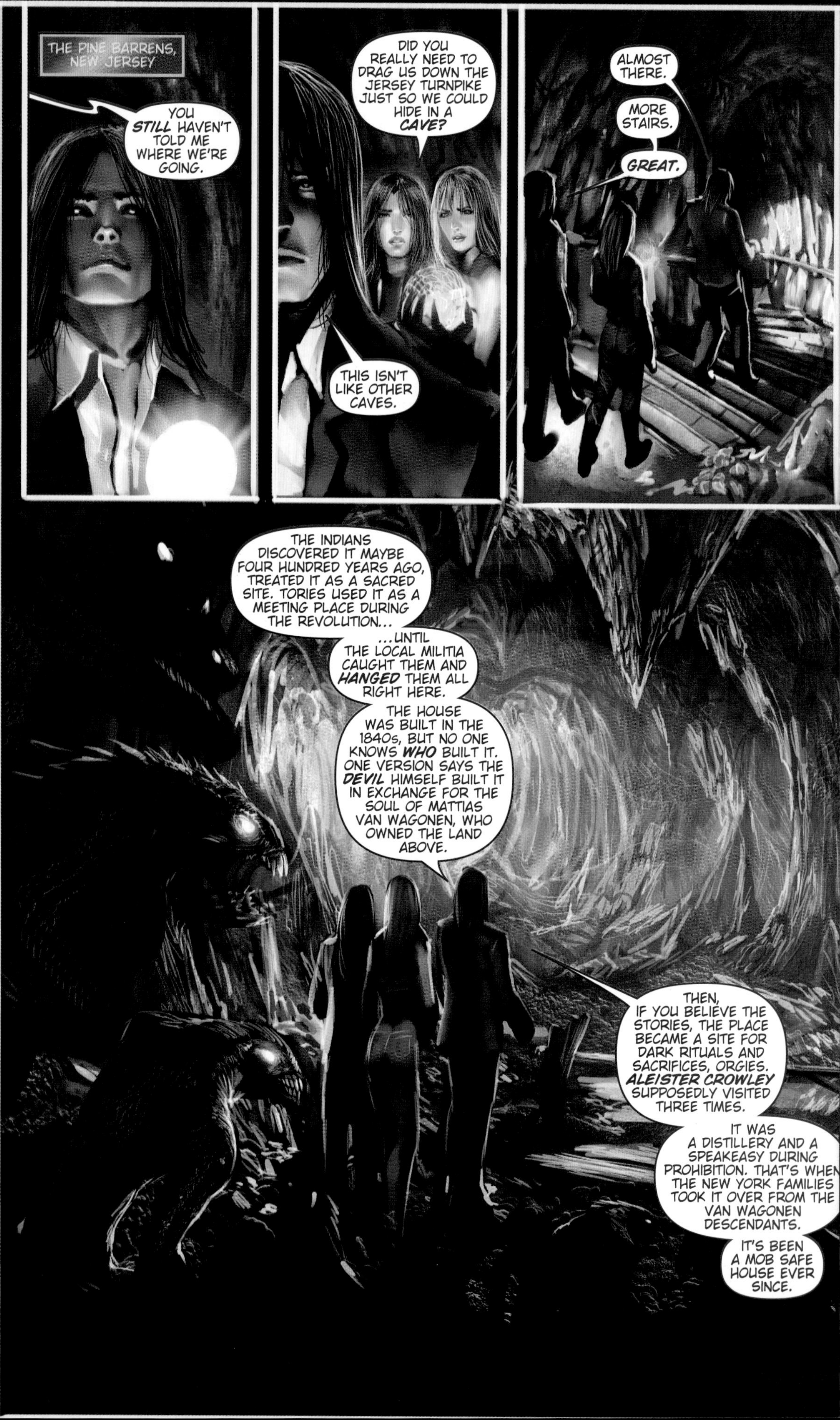
THE PINE BARRENS, NEW JERSEY
YOU STILL HAVEN'T TOLD ME WHERE WE'RE GOING.
DID YOU REALLY NEED TO DRAG US DOWN THE JERSEY TURNPIKE JUST SO WE COULD HIDE IN A CAVE?
THIS ISN'T LIKE OTHER CAVES.
ALMOST THERE.
MORE STAIRS.
GREAT.
THE INDIANS DISCOVERED IT MAYBE FOUR HUNDRED YEARS AGO, TREATED IT AS A SACRED SITE. TORIES USED IT AS A MEETING PLACE DURING THE REVOLUTION...
...UNTIL THE LOCAL MILITIA CAUGHT THEM AND HANGED THEM ALL RIGHT HERE.
THE HOUSE WAS BUILT IN THE 1840s, BUT NO ONE KNOWS WHO BUILT IT. ONE VERSION SAYS THE DEVIL HIMSELF BUILT IT IN EXCHANGE FOR THE SOUL OF MATTIAS VAN WAGONEN, WHO OWNED THE LAND ABOVE.
THEN, IF YOU BELIEVE THE STORIES, THE PLACE BECAME A SITE FOR DARK RITUALS AND SACRIFICES, ORGIES. ALEISTER CROWLEY SUPPOSEDLY VISITED THREE TIMES.
IT WAS A DISTILLERY AND A SPEAKEASY DURING PROHIBITION. THAT'S WHEN THE NEW YORK FAMILIES TOOK IT OVER FROM THE VAN WAGONEN DESCENDANTS.
IT'S BEEN A MOB SAFE HOUSE EVER SINCE.

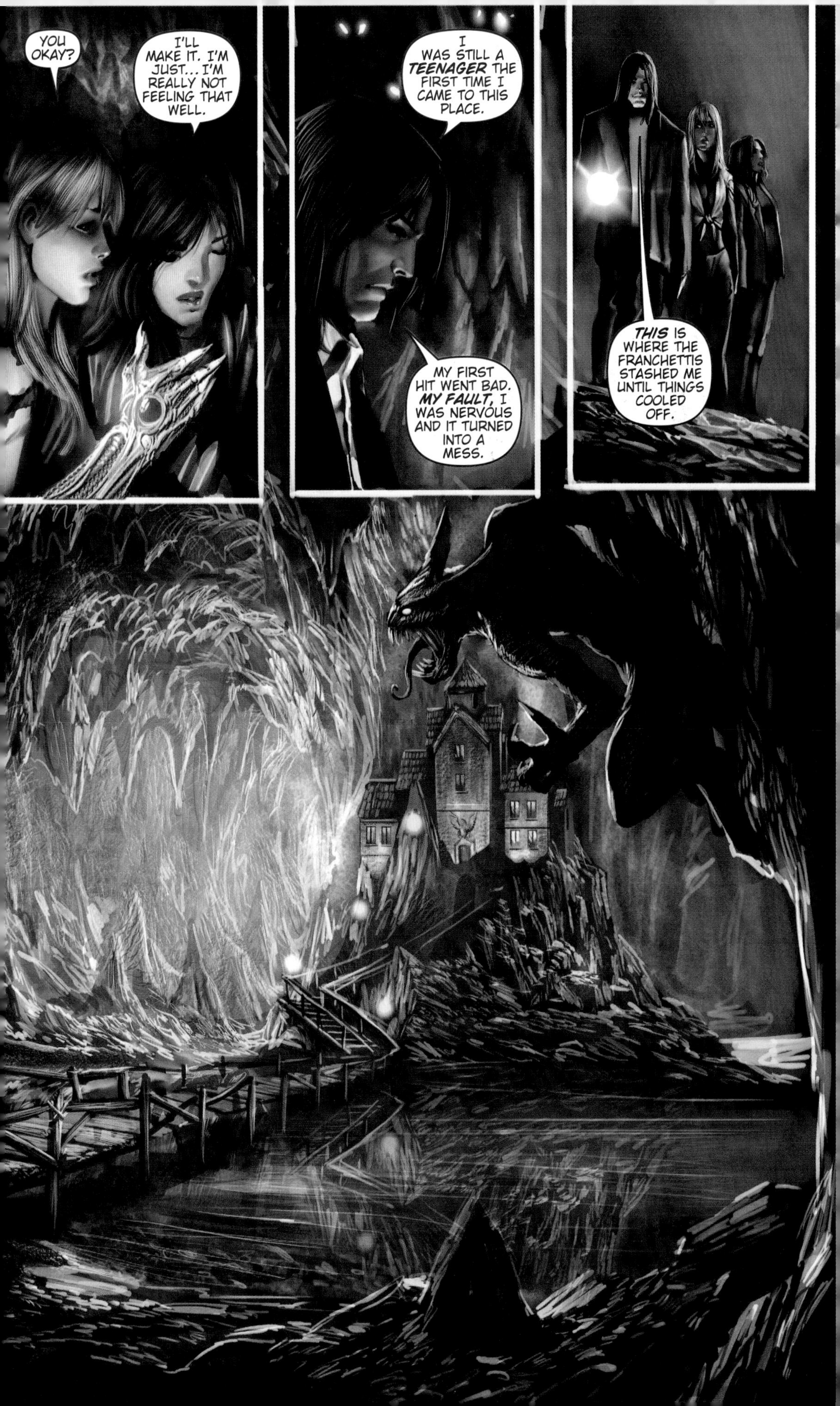

YOU OKAY?
I'LL MAKE IT. I'M JUST... I'M REALLY NOT FEELING THAT WELL.
I WAS STILL A TEENAGER THE FIRST TIME I CAME TO THIS PLACE.
MY FIRST HIT WENT BAD. MY FAULT, I WAS NERVOUS AND IT TURNED INTO A MESS.
THIS IS WHERE THE FRANCHETTIS STASHED ME UNTIL THINGS COOLED OFF.

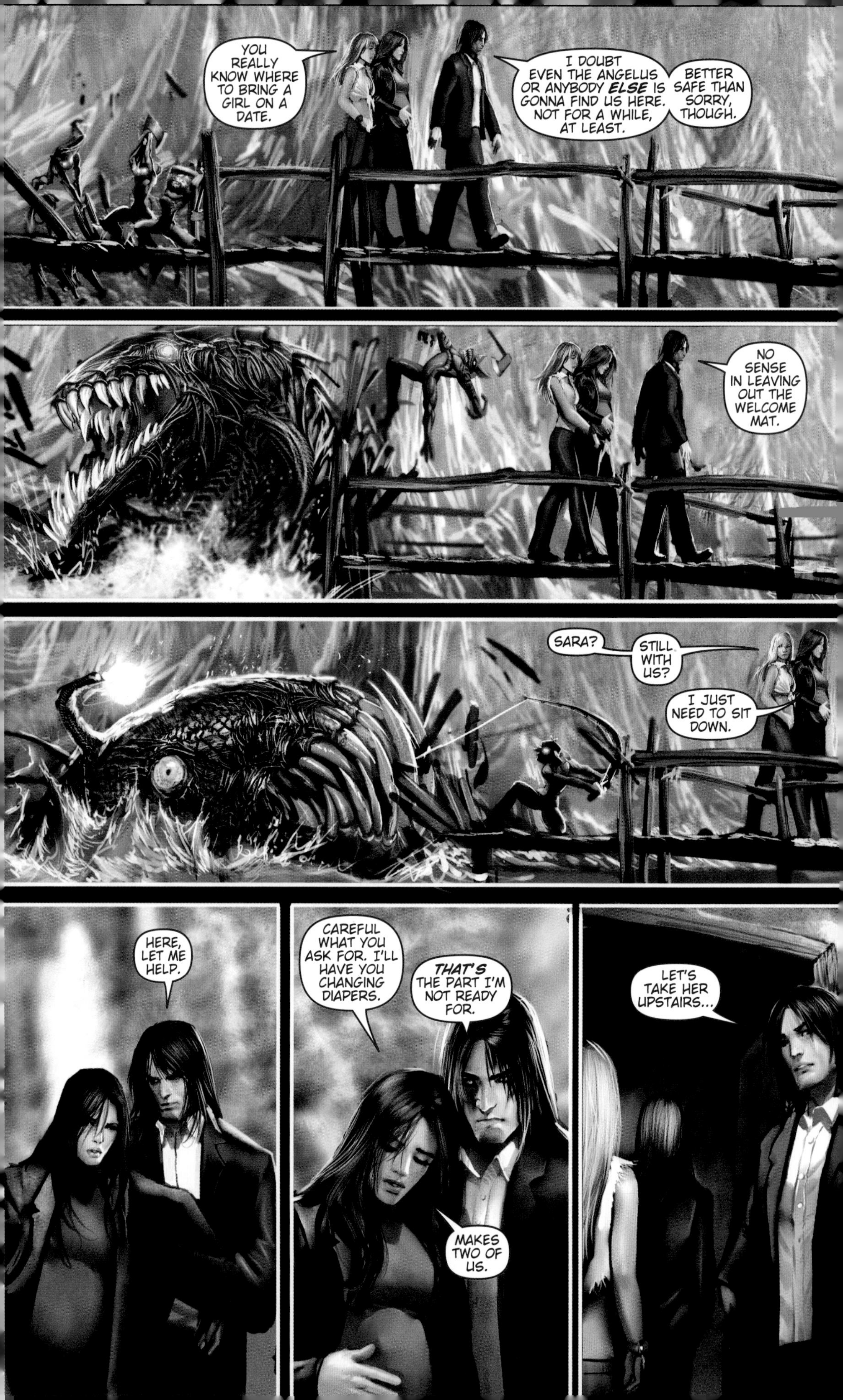
YOU REALLY KNOW WHERE TO BRING A GIRL ON A DATE.
I DOUBT EVEN THE ANGELUS OR ANYBODY ELSE IS GONNA FIND US HERE. NOT FOR A WHILE, AT LEAST.
BETTER SAFE THAN SORRY, THOUGH.
NO SENSE IN LEAVING OUT THE WELCOME MAT.
SARA?
STILL WITH US?
I JUST NEED TO SIT DOWN.
HERE, LET ME HELP.
CAREFUL WHAT YOU ASK FOR. I'LL HAVE YOU CHANGING DIAPERS.
THAT'S THE PART I'M NOT READY FOR.
MAKES TWO OF US.
LET'S TAKE HER UPSTAIRS...

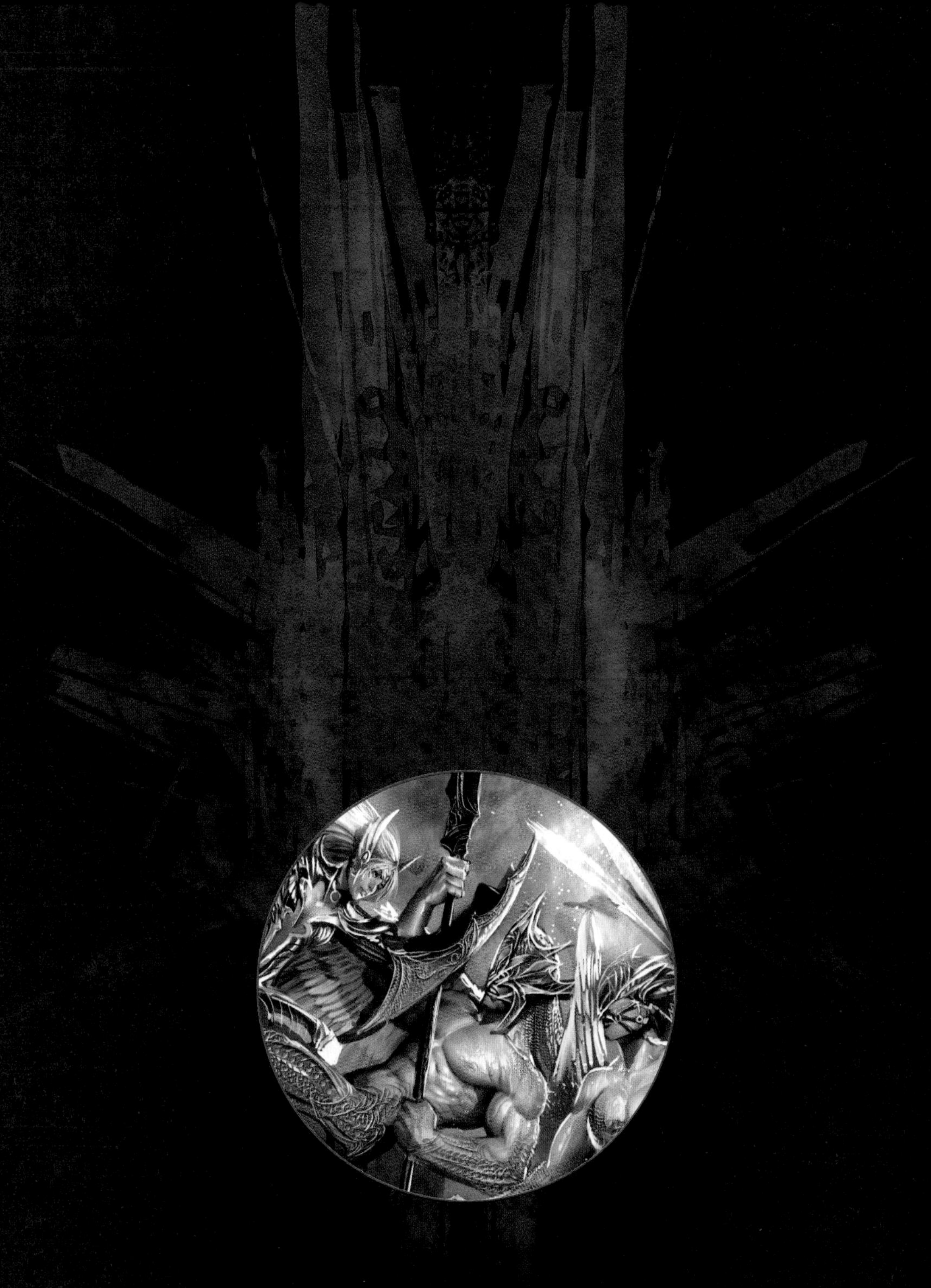

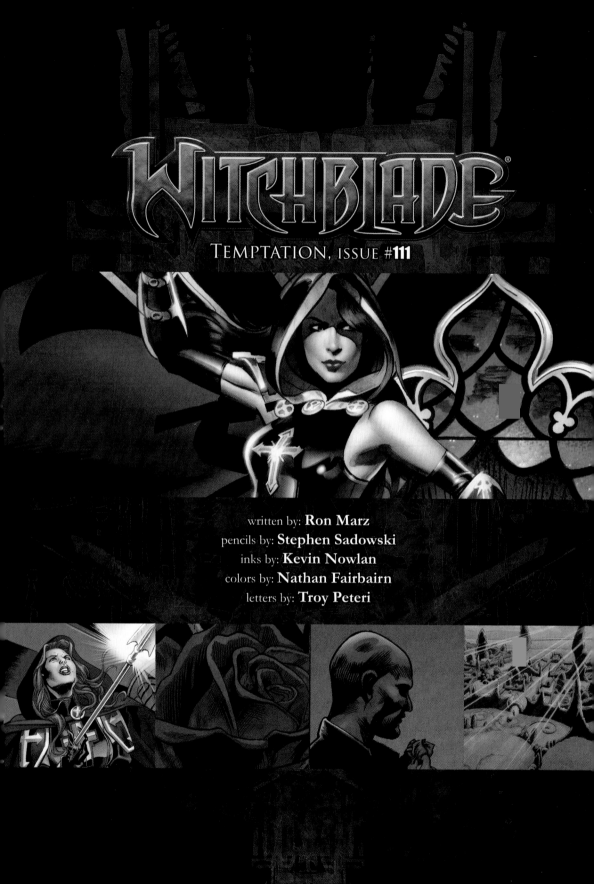

WITCHBLADE

TEMPTATION, ISSUE #111

written by: **Ron Marz**
pencils by: **Stephen Sadowski**
inks by: **Kevin Nowlan**
colors by: **Nathan Fairbairn**
letters by: **Troy Peteri**

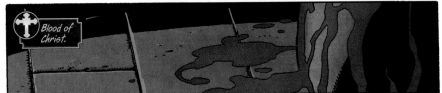

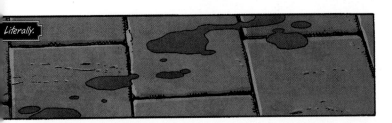

Blood of Christ.

Literally.

I am descended in a straight line from *JESUS OF NAZARETH.* God's only son...

Temptation

...if you believe in that sort of thing.

I'M TIGHT WITH THE *LAST* GUY WHO WAS *RESURRECTED...*

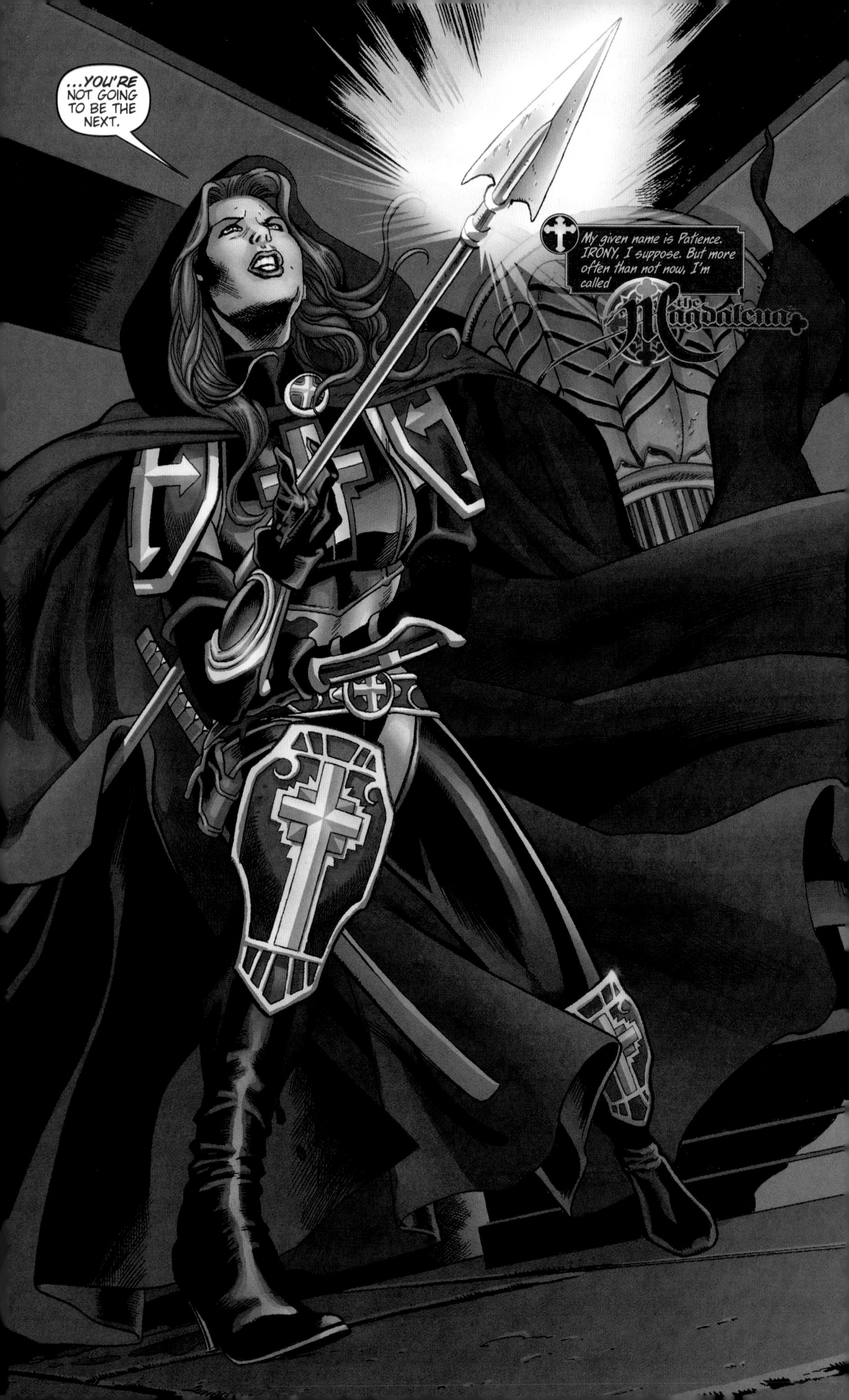
...YOU'RE NOT GOING TO BE THE NEXT.
My given name is Patience. IRONY, I suppose. But more often than not now, I'm called
the Magdalena

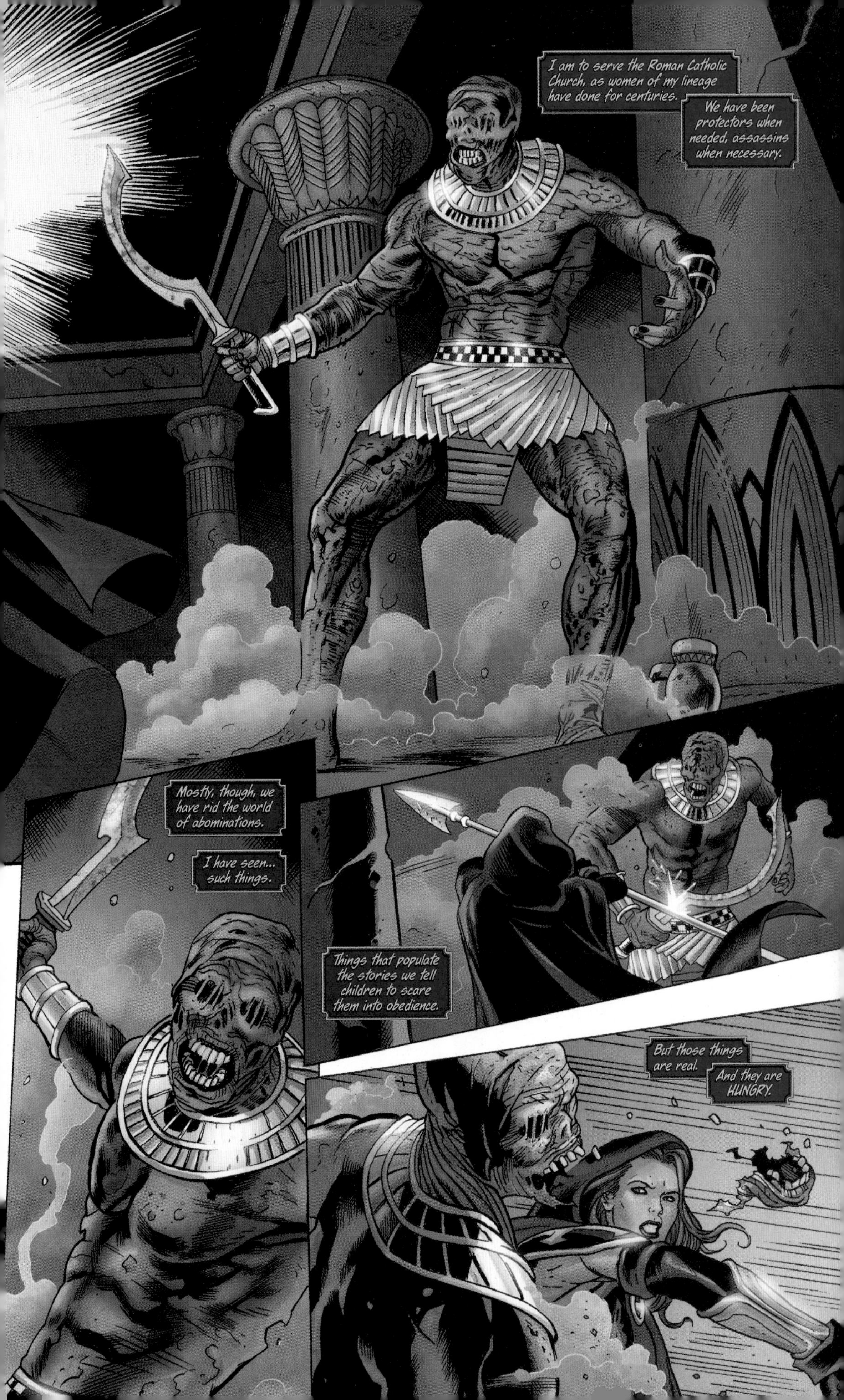
I am to serve the Roman Catholic Church, as women of my lineage have done for centuries.
We have been protectors when needed, assassins when necessary.
Mostly, though, we have rid the world of abominations.
I have seen... such things.
Things that populate the stories we tell children to scare them into obedience.
But those things are real.
And they are HUNGRY.

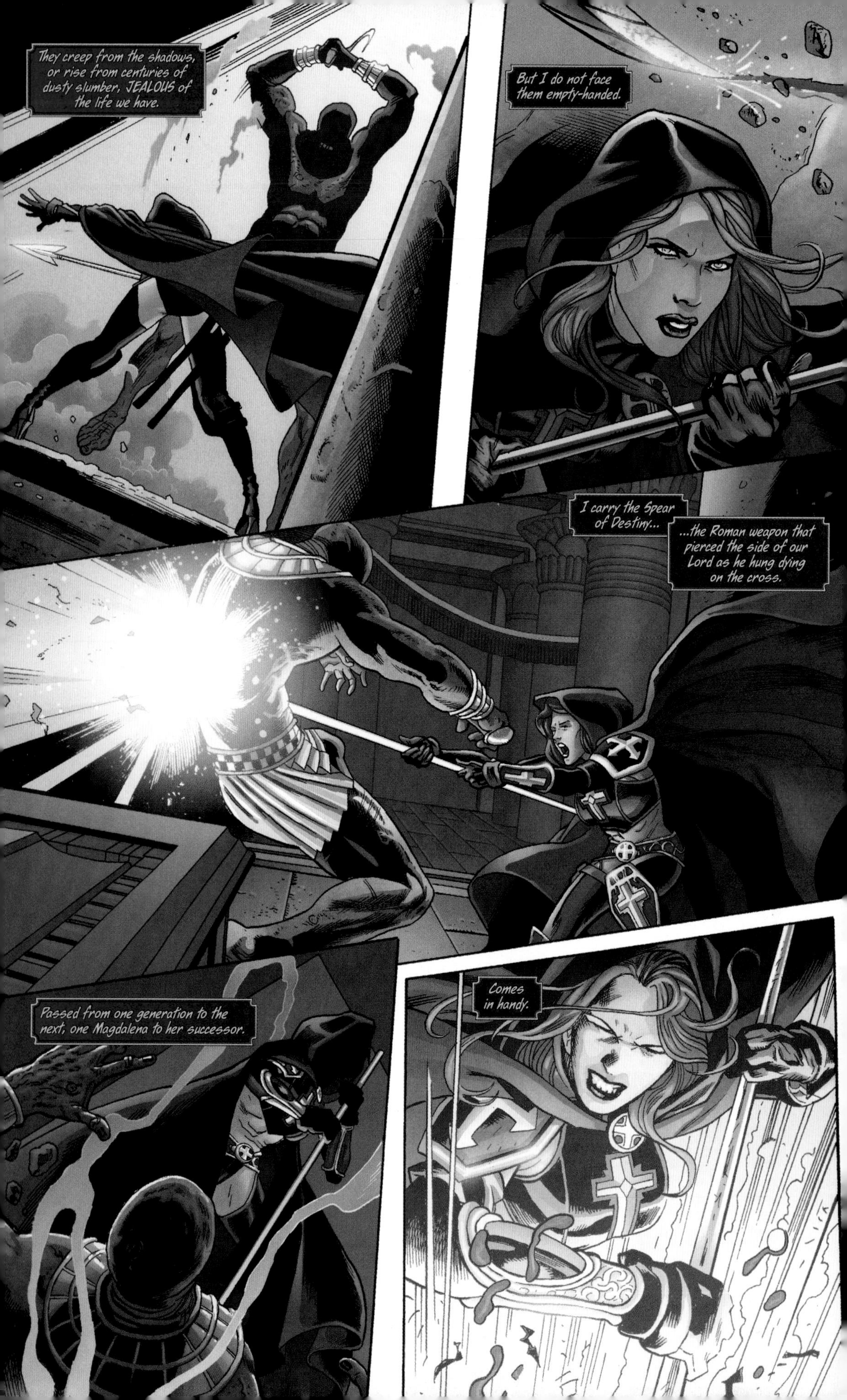
They creep from the shadows, or rise from centuries of dusty slumber, JEALOUS of the life we have.
But I do not face them empty-handed.
I carry the Spear of Destiny...
...the Roman weapon that pierced the side of our Lord as he hung dying on the cross.
Passed from one generation to the next, one Magdalena to her successor.
Comes in handy.

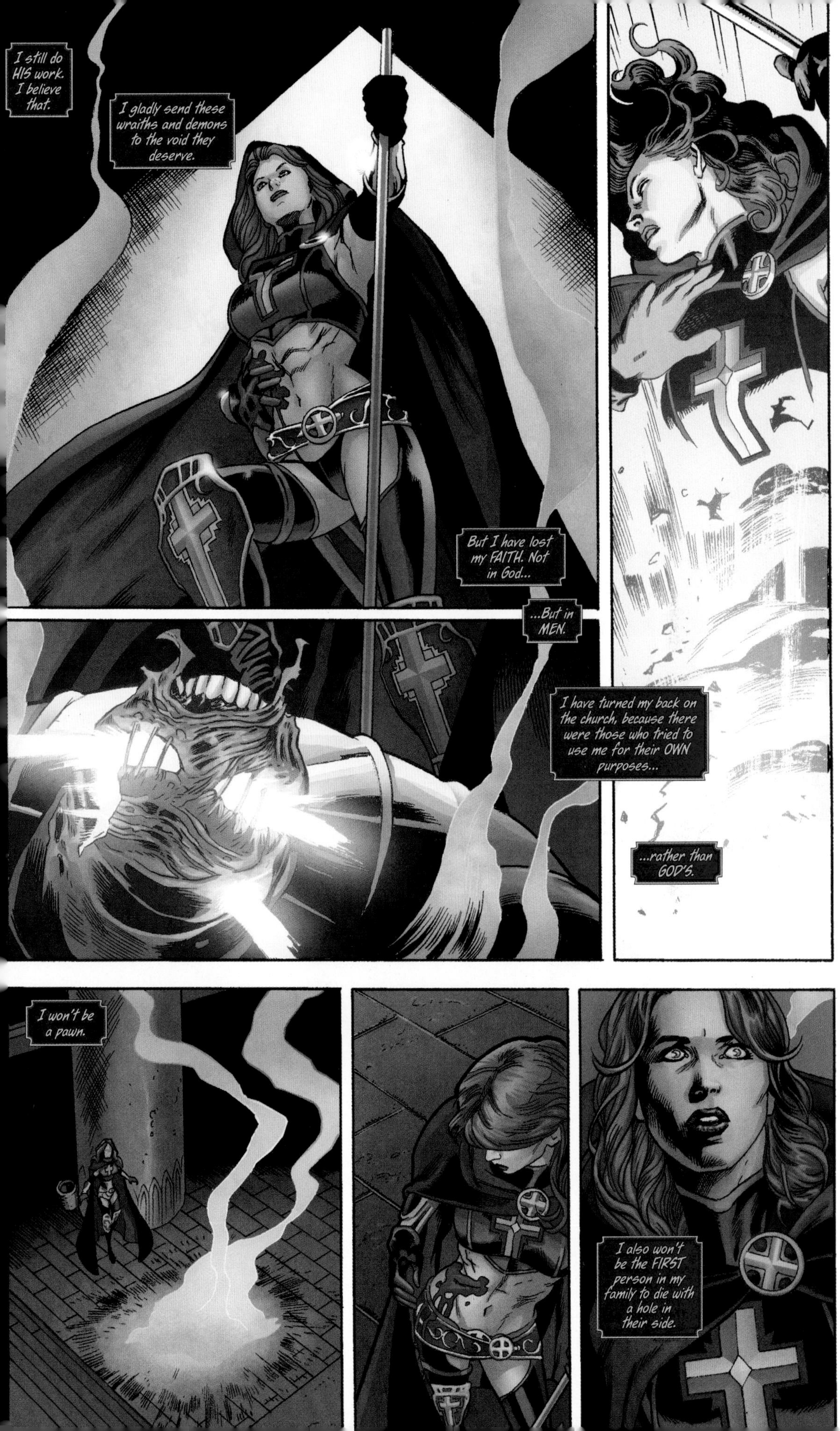
I still do HIS work. I believe that.
I gladly send these wraiths and demons to the void they deserve.
But I have lost my FAITH. Not in God...
...But in MEN.
I have turned my back on the church, because there were those who tried to use me for their OWN purposes...
...rather than GOD'S.
I won't be a pawn.
I also won't be the FIRST person in my family to die with a hole in their side.

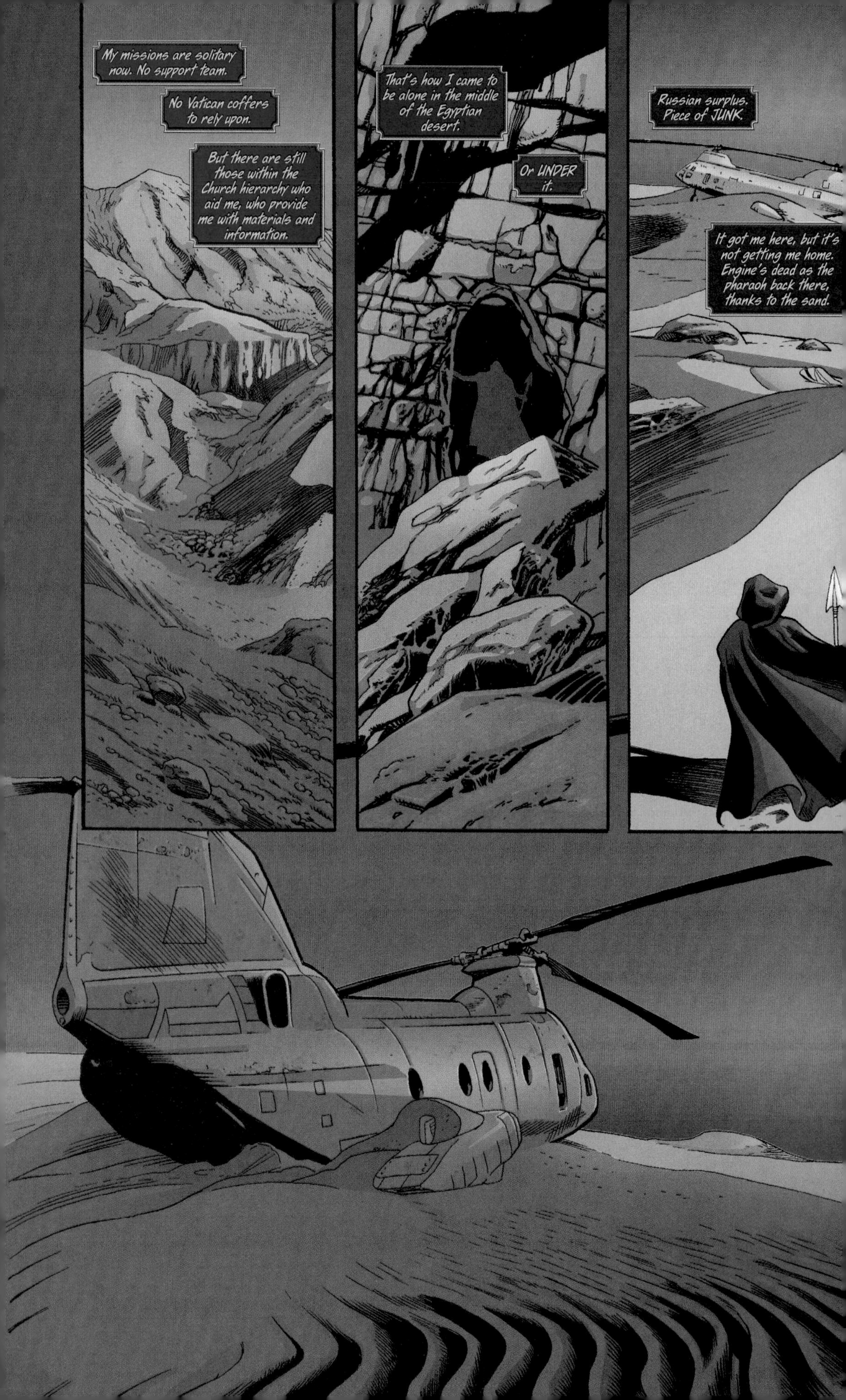
My missions are solitary now. No support team.
No Vatican coffers to rely upon.
But there are still those within the Church hierarchy who aid me, who provide me with materials and information.
That's how I came to be alone in the middle of the Egyptian desert.
Or UNDER it.
Russian surplus. Piece of JUNK.
It got me here, but it's not getting me home. Engine's dead as the pharaoh back there, thanks to the sand.

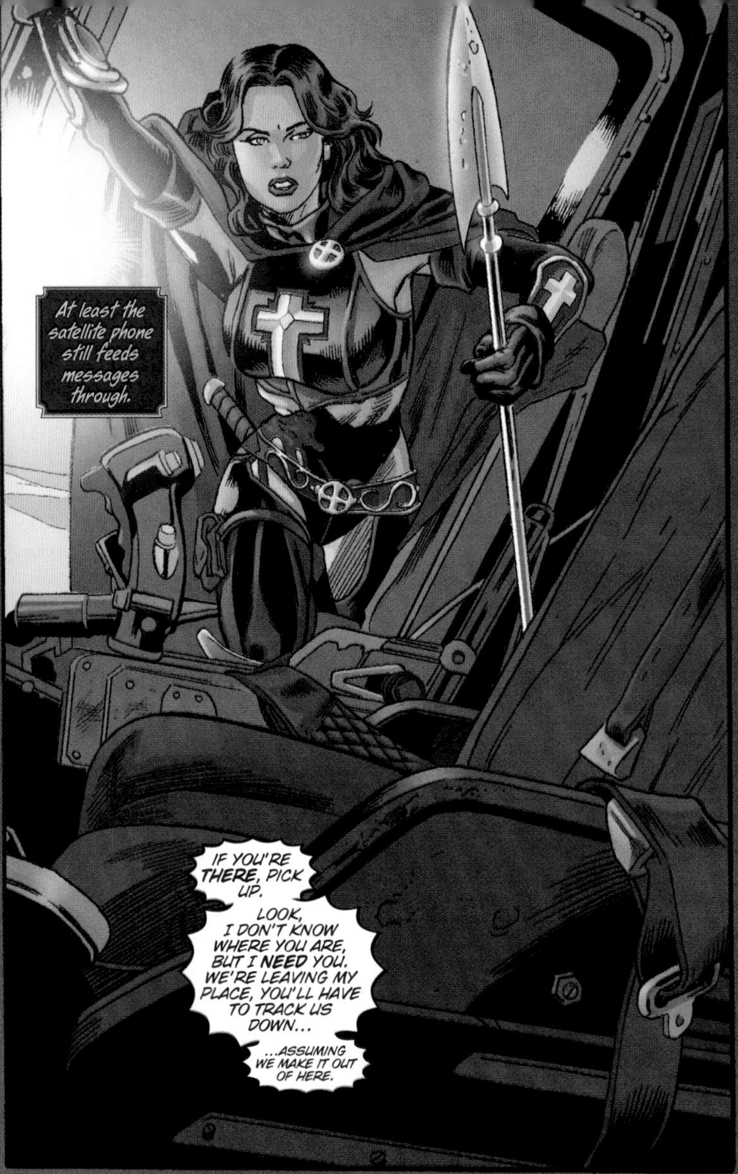
At least the satellite phone still feeds messages through.
IF YOU'RE THERE, PICK UP.
LOOK, I DON'T KNOW WHERE YOU ARE, BUT I NEED YOU. WE'RE LEAVING MY PLACE, YOU'LL HAVE TO TRACK US DOWN...
...ASSUMING WE MAKE IT OUT OF HERE.

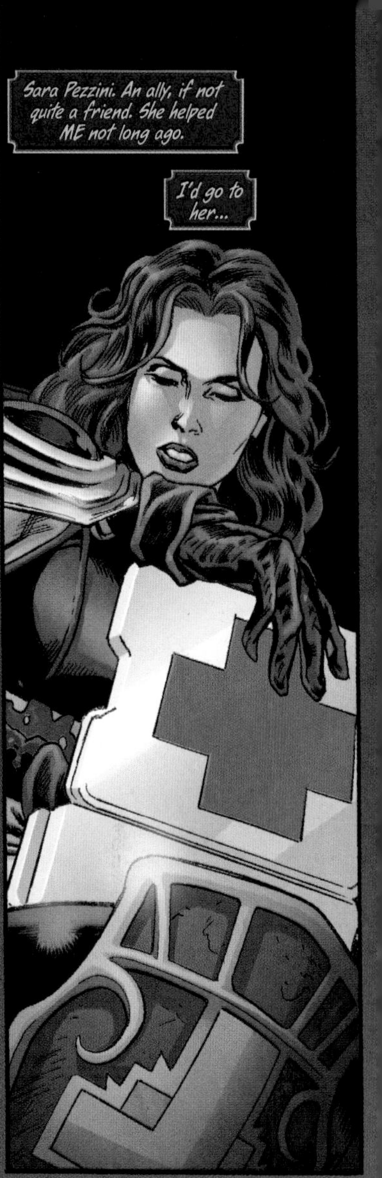
Sara Pezzini. An ally, if not quite a friend. She helped ME not long ago.
I'd go to her...

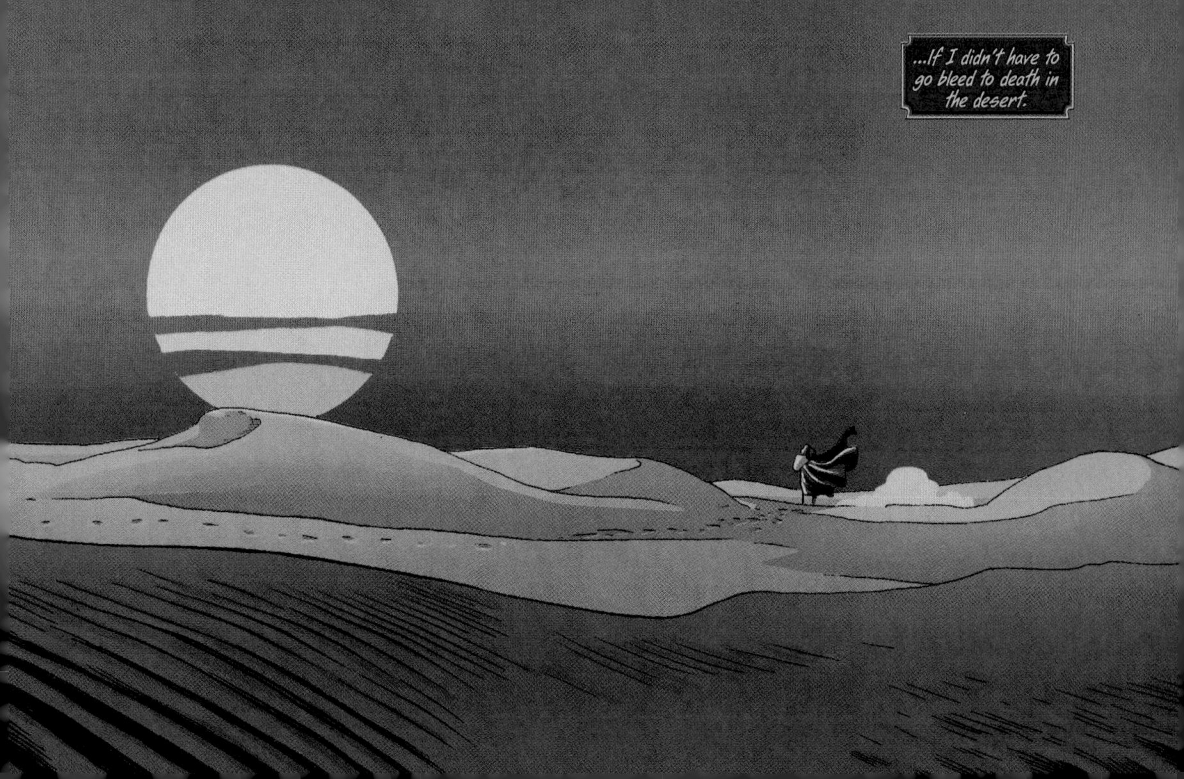
...If I didn't have to go bleed to death in the desert.

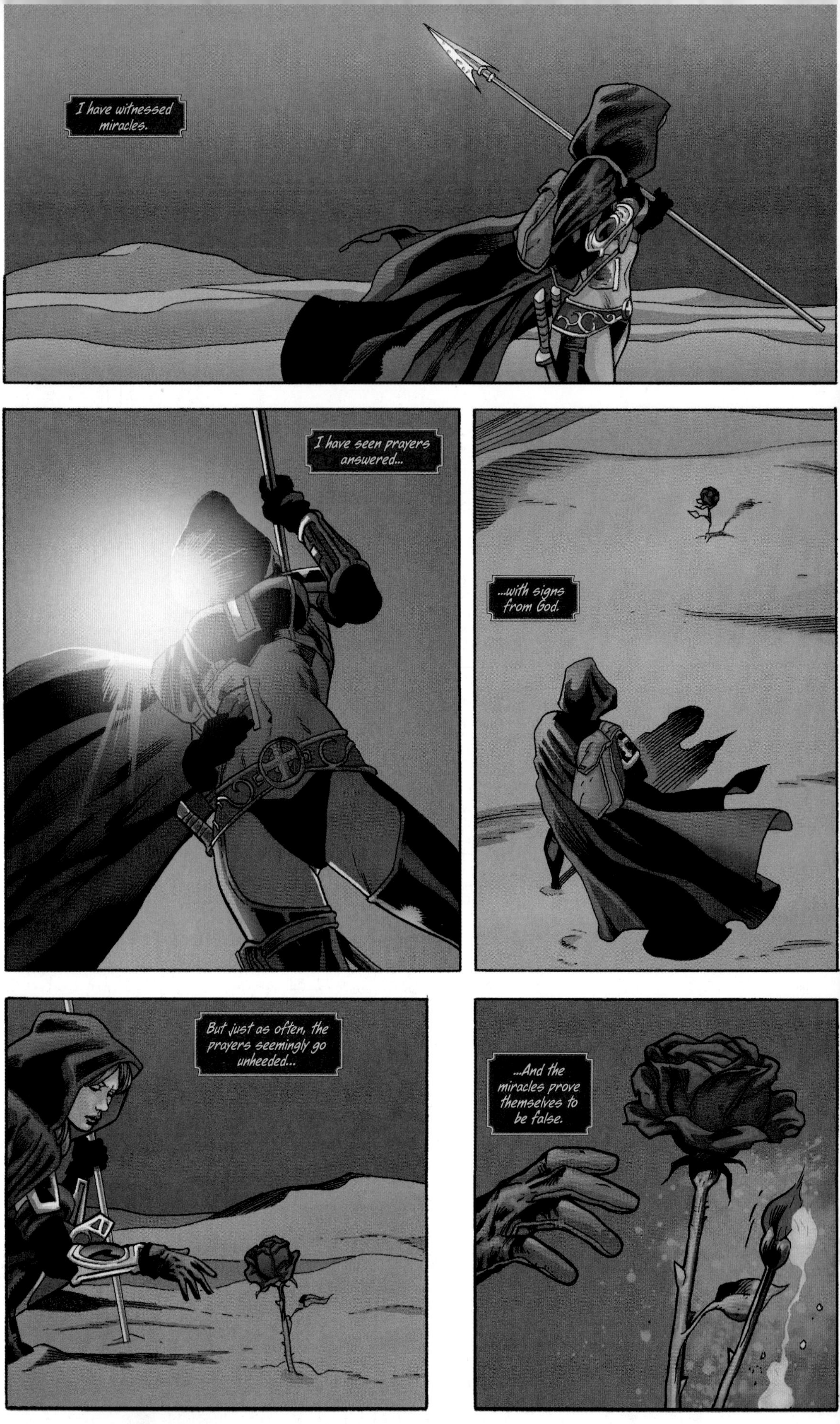
I have witnessed miracles.
I have seen prayers answered...
...with signs from God.
But just as often, the prayers seemingly go unheeded...
...And the miracles prove themselves to be false.

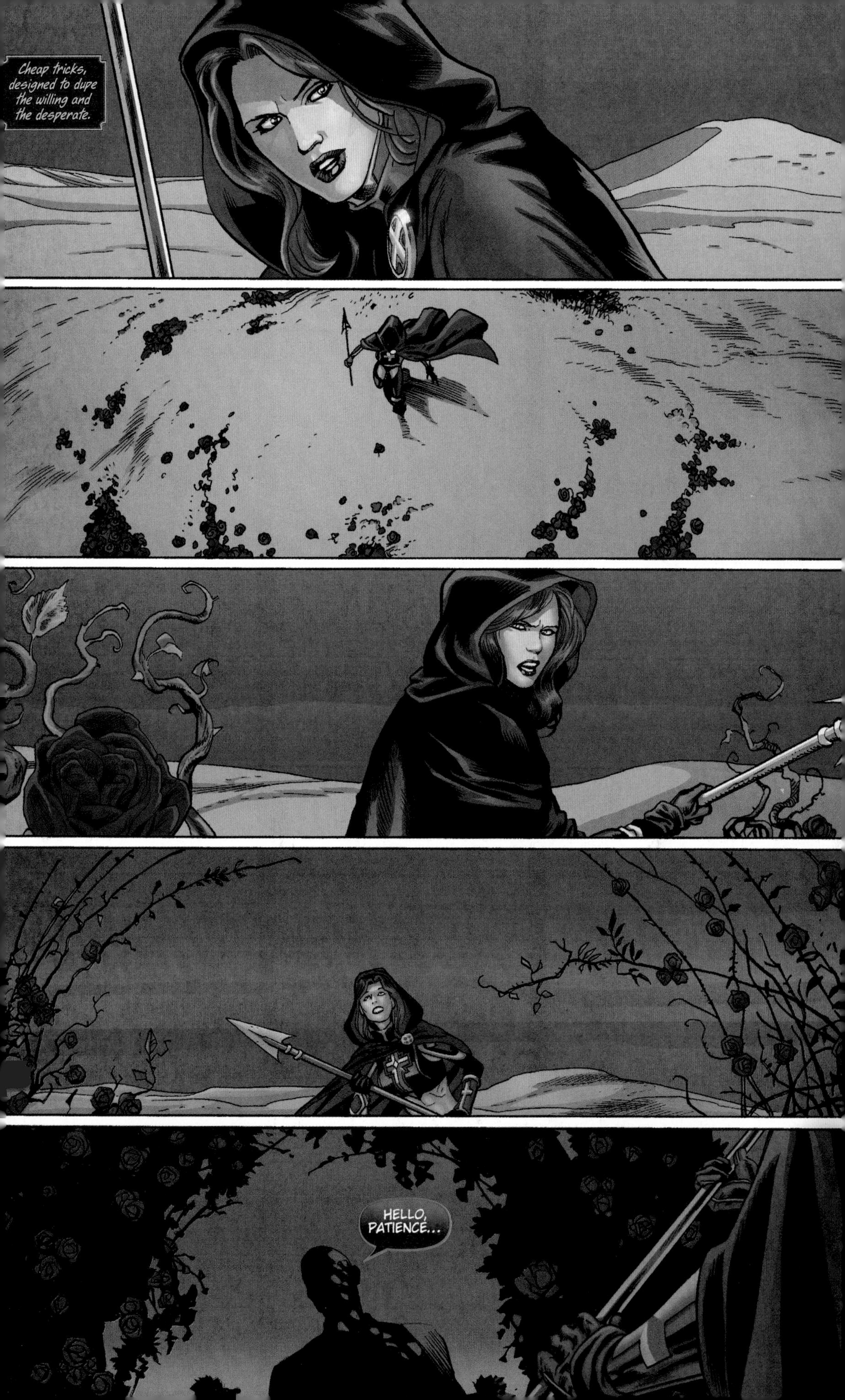
Cheap tricks, designed to dupe the willing and the desperate.
HELLO, PATIENCE...

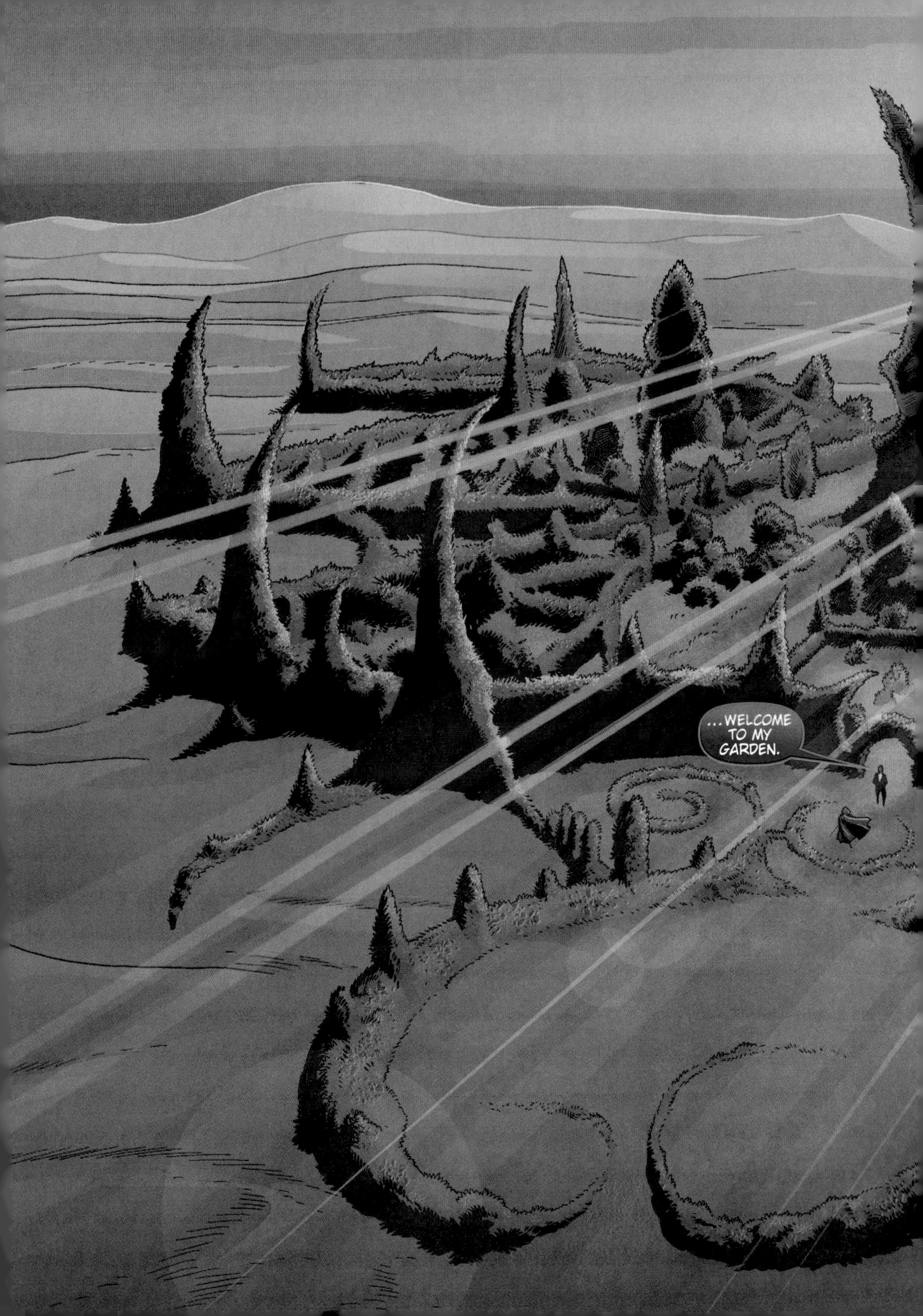
...WELCOME TO MY GARDEN.

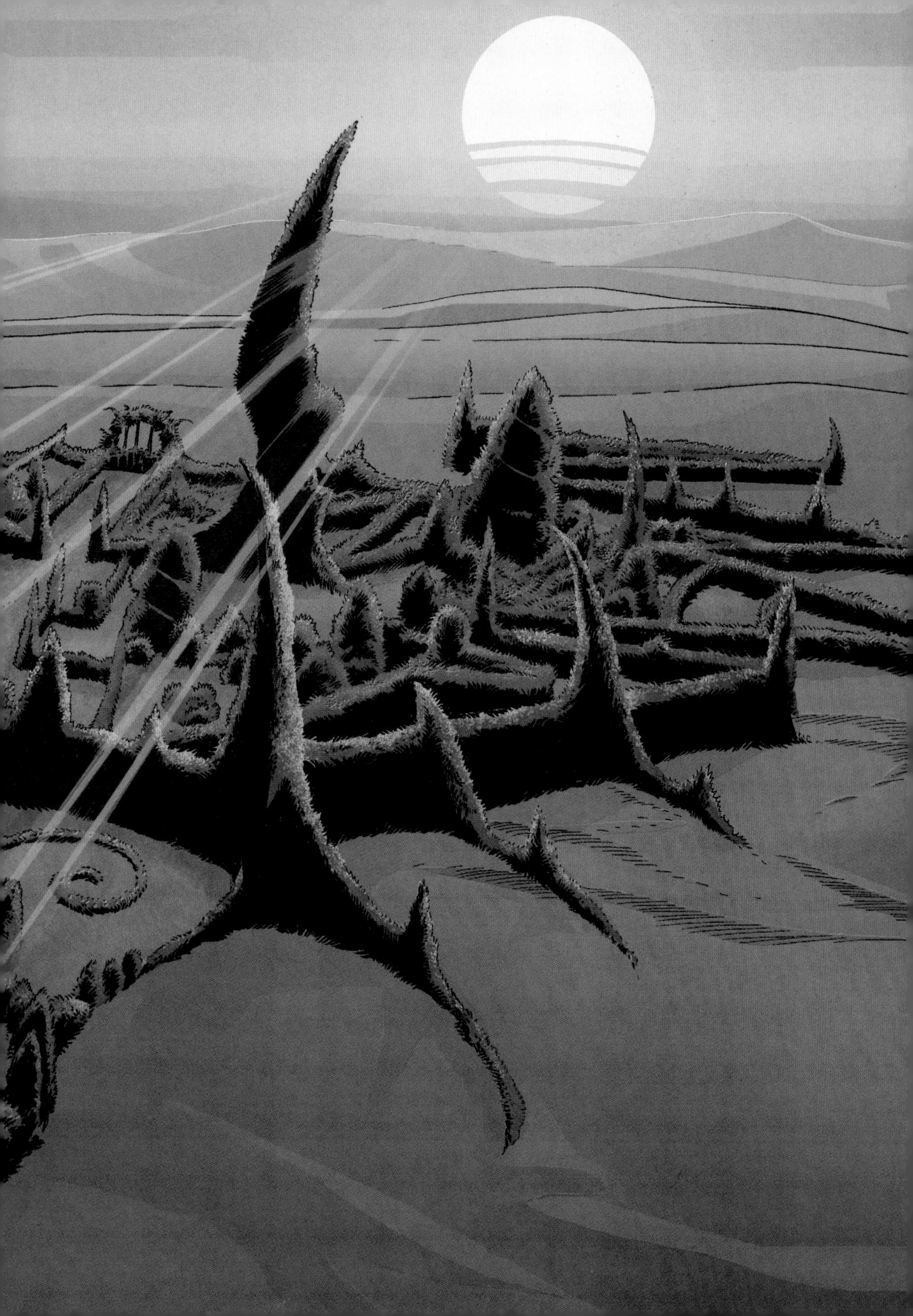

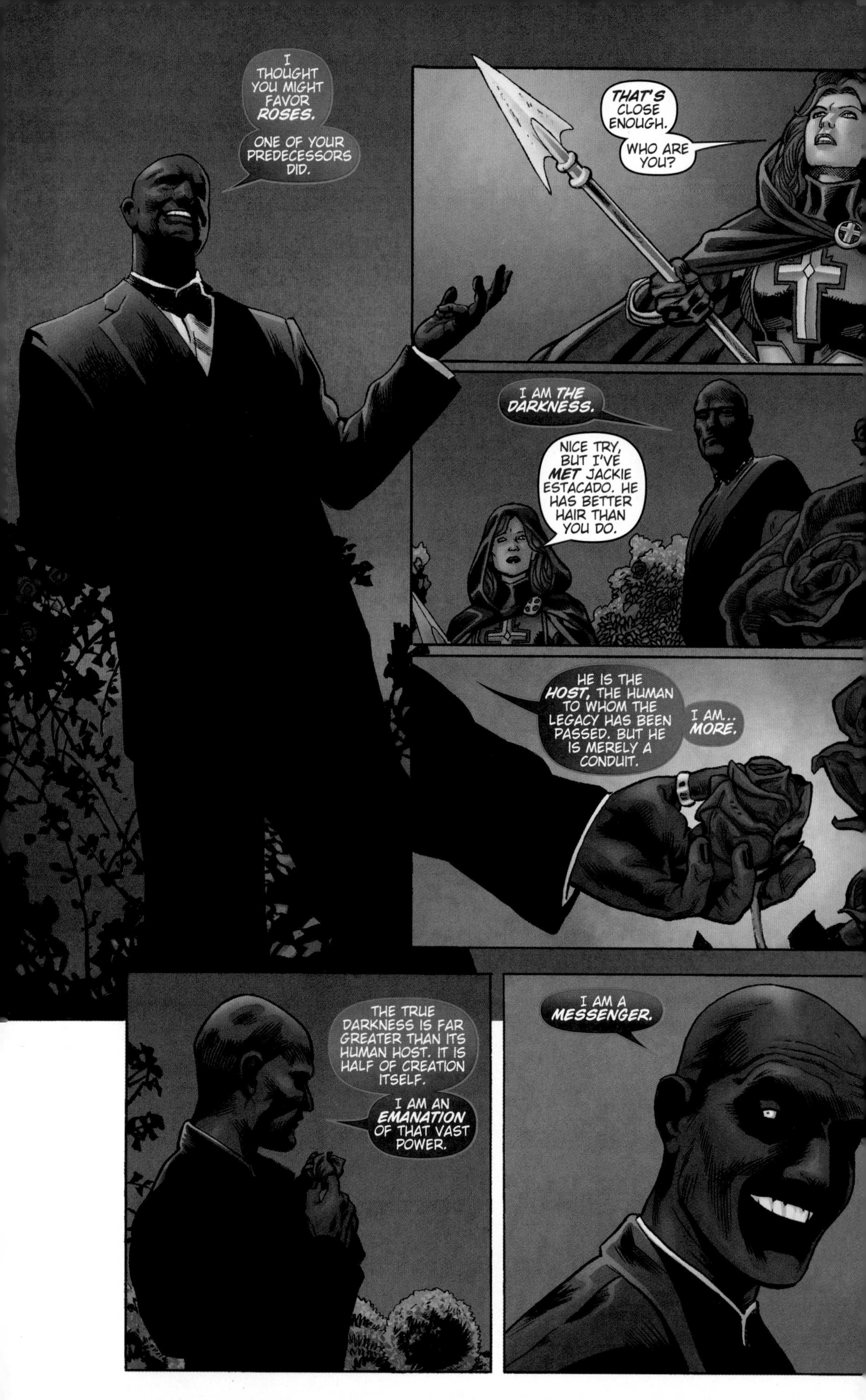
I THOUGHT YOU MIGHT FAVOR ROSES.
ONE OF YOUR PREDECESSORS DID.
THAT'S CLOSE ENOUGH.
WHO ARE YOU?
I AM THE DARKNESS.
NICE TRY, BUT I'VE MET JACKIE ESTACADO. HE HAS BETTER HAIR THAN YOU DO.
HE IS THE HOST, THE HUMAN TO WHOM THE LEGACY HAS BEEN PASSED. BUT HE IS MERELY A CONDUIT.
I AM... MORE.
THE TRUE DARKNESS IS FAR GREATER THAN ITS HUMAN HOST. IT IS HALF OF CREATION ITSELF.
I AM AN EMANATION OF THAT VAST POWER.
I AM A MESSENGER.

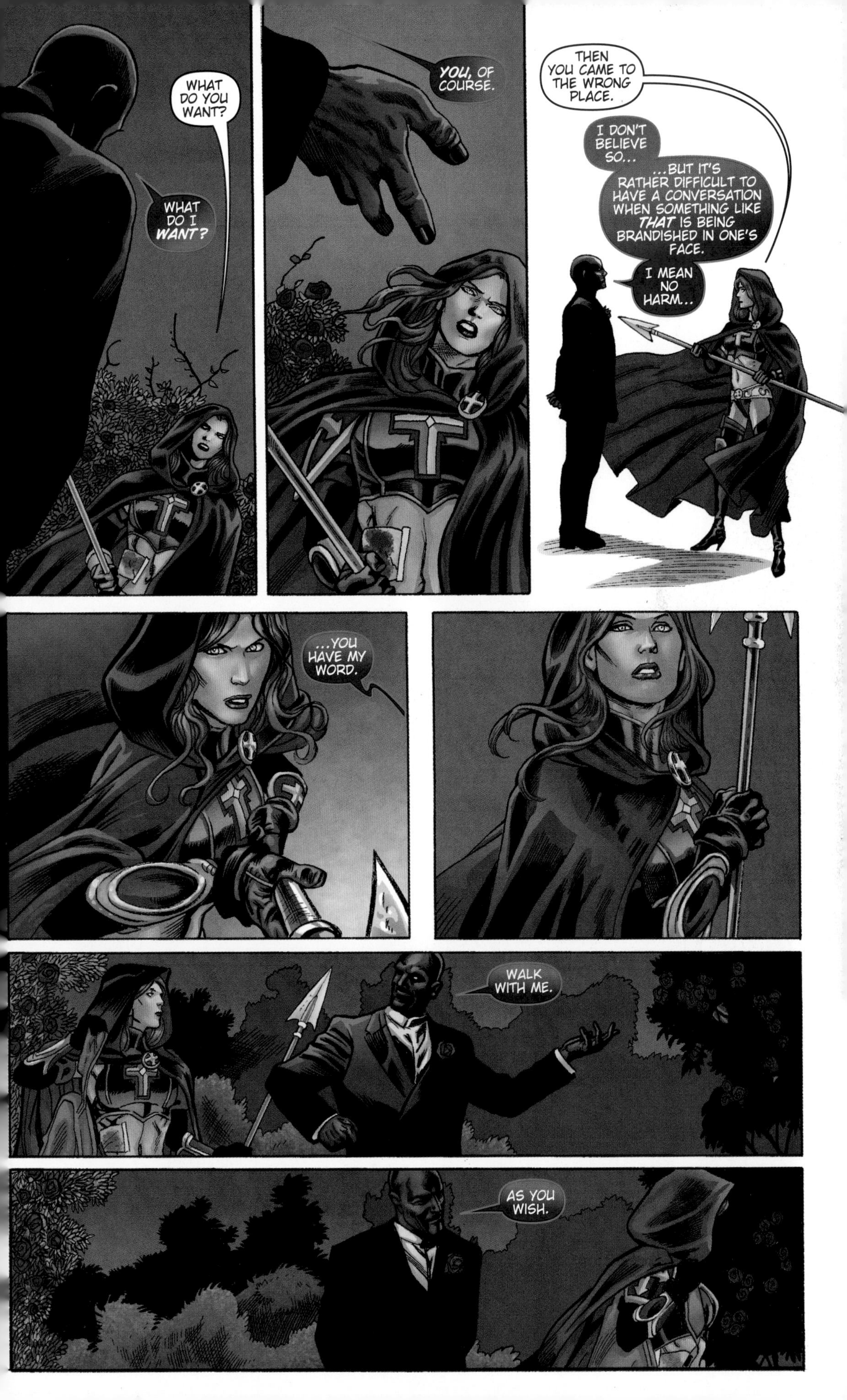
WHAT DO YOU WANT?
WHAT DO I *WANT?*
YOU, OF COURSE.
THEN YOU CAME TO THE WRONG PLACE.
I DON'T BELIEVE SO...
...BUT IT'S RATHER DIFFICULT TO HAVE A CONVERSATION WHEN SOMETHING LIKE *THAT* IS BEING BRANDISHED IN ONE'S FACE.
I MEAN NO HARM...
...YOU HAVE MY WORD.
WALK WITH ME.
AS YOU WISH.

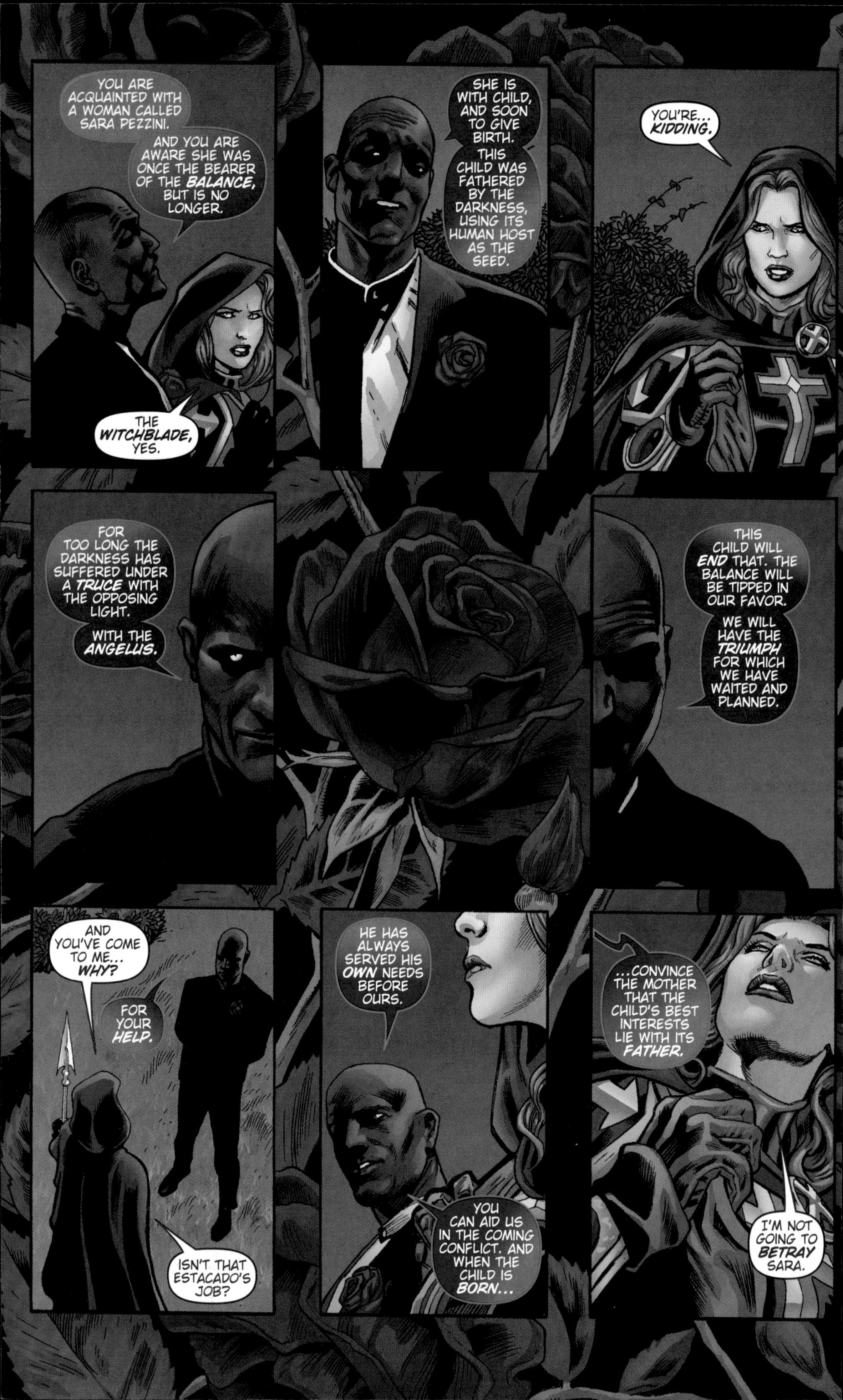

YOU ARE ACQUAINTED WITH A WOMAN CALLED SARA PEZZINI.
AND YOU ARE AWARE SHE WAS ONCE THE BEARER OF THE *BALANCE,* BUT IS NO LONGER.
THE *WITCHBLADE,* YES.
SHE IS WITH CHILD, AND SOON TO GIVE BIRTH.
THIS CHILD WAS FATHERED BY THE DARKNESS, USING ITS HUMAN HOST AS THE SEED.
YOU'RE... *KIDDING.*
FOR TOO LONG THE DARKNESS HAS SUFFERED UNDER A *TRUCE* WITH THE OPPOSING LIGHT.
WITH THE *ANGELUS.*
THIS CHILD WILL *END* THAT. THE BALANCE WILL BE TIPPED IN OUR FAVOR.
WE WILL HAVE THE *TRIUMPH* FOR WHICH WE HAVE WAITED AND PLANNED.
AND YOU'VE COME TO ME... *WHY?*
FOR YOUR *HELP.*
ISN'T THAT ESTACADO'S JOB?
HE HAS ALWAYS SERVED HIS *OWN* NEEDS BEFORE OURS.
YOU CAN AID US IN THE COMING CONFLICT. AND WHEN THE CHILD IS *BORN...*
...CONVINCE THE MOTHER THAT THE CHILD'S BEST INTERESTS LIE WITH ITS *FATHER.*
I'M NOT GOING TO *BETRAY* SARA.

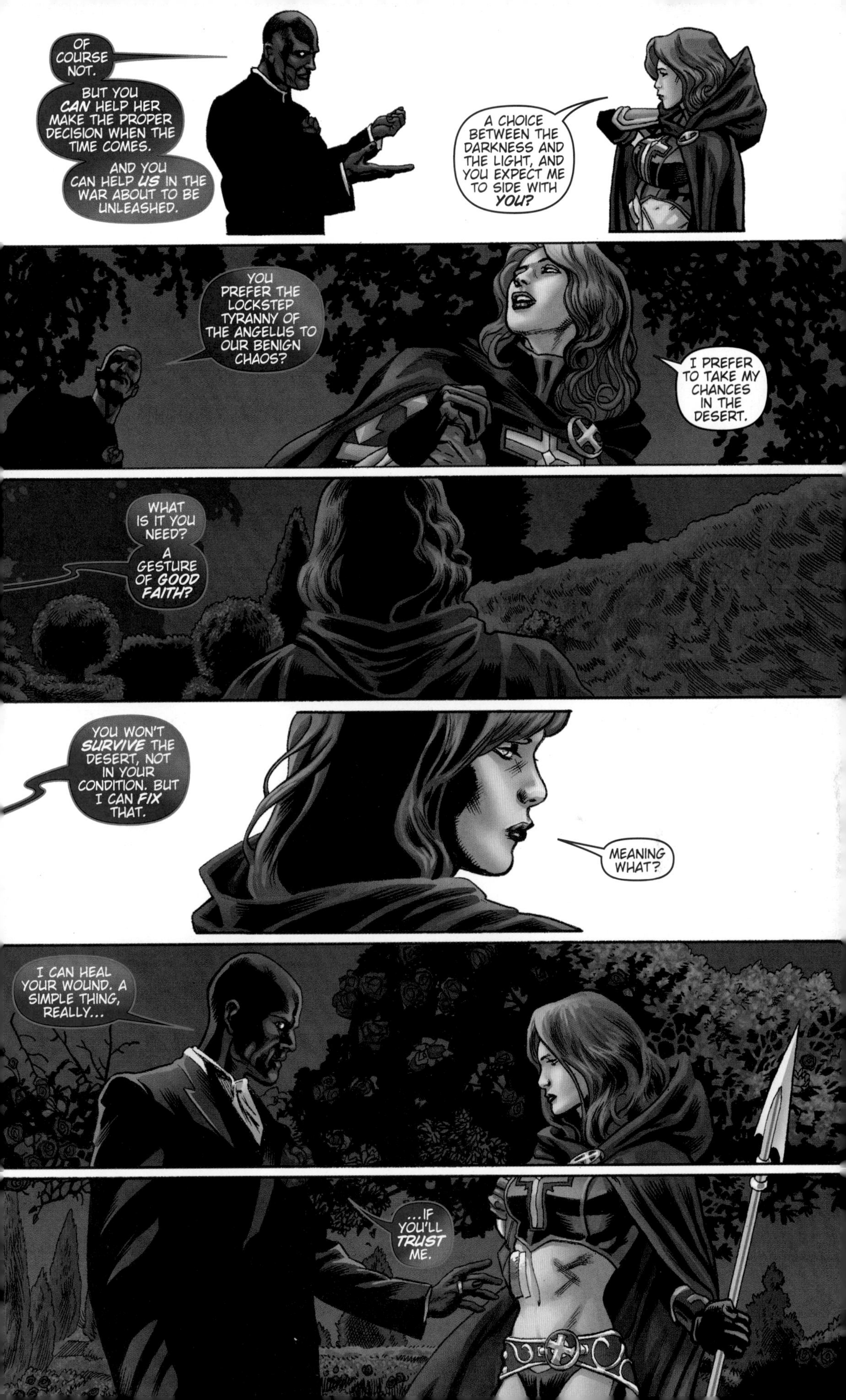
OF COURSE NOT.
BUT YOU CAN HELP HER MAKE THE PROPER DECISION WHEN THE TIME COMES.
AND YOU CAN HELP US IN THE WAR ABOUT TO BE UNLEASHED.
A CHOICE BETWEEN THE DARKNESS AND THE LIGHT, AND YOU EXPECT ME TO SIDE WITH YOU?
YOU PREFER THE LOCKSTEP TYRANNY OF THE ANGELUS TO OUR BENIGN CHAOS?
I PREFER TO TAKE MY CHANCES IN THE DESERT.
WHAT IS IT YOU NEED?
A GESTURE OF GOOD FAITH?
YOU WON'T SURVIVE THE DESERT, NOT IN YOUR CONDITION. BUT I CAN FIX THAT.
MEANING WHAT?
I CAN HEAL YOUR WOUND. A SIMPLE THING, REALLY...
...IF YOU'LL TRUST ME.

AHH!

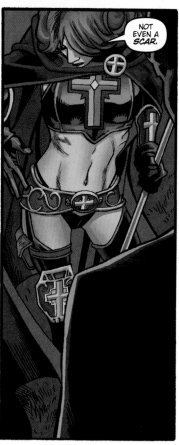

NOT EVEN A SCAR.

DOUBTING THOMAS NEEDED HIS PROOF, YES?

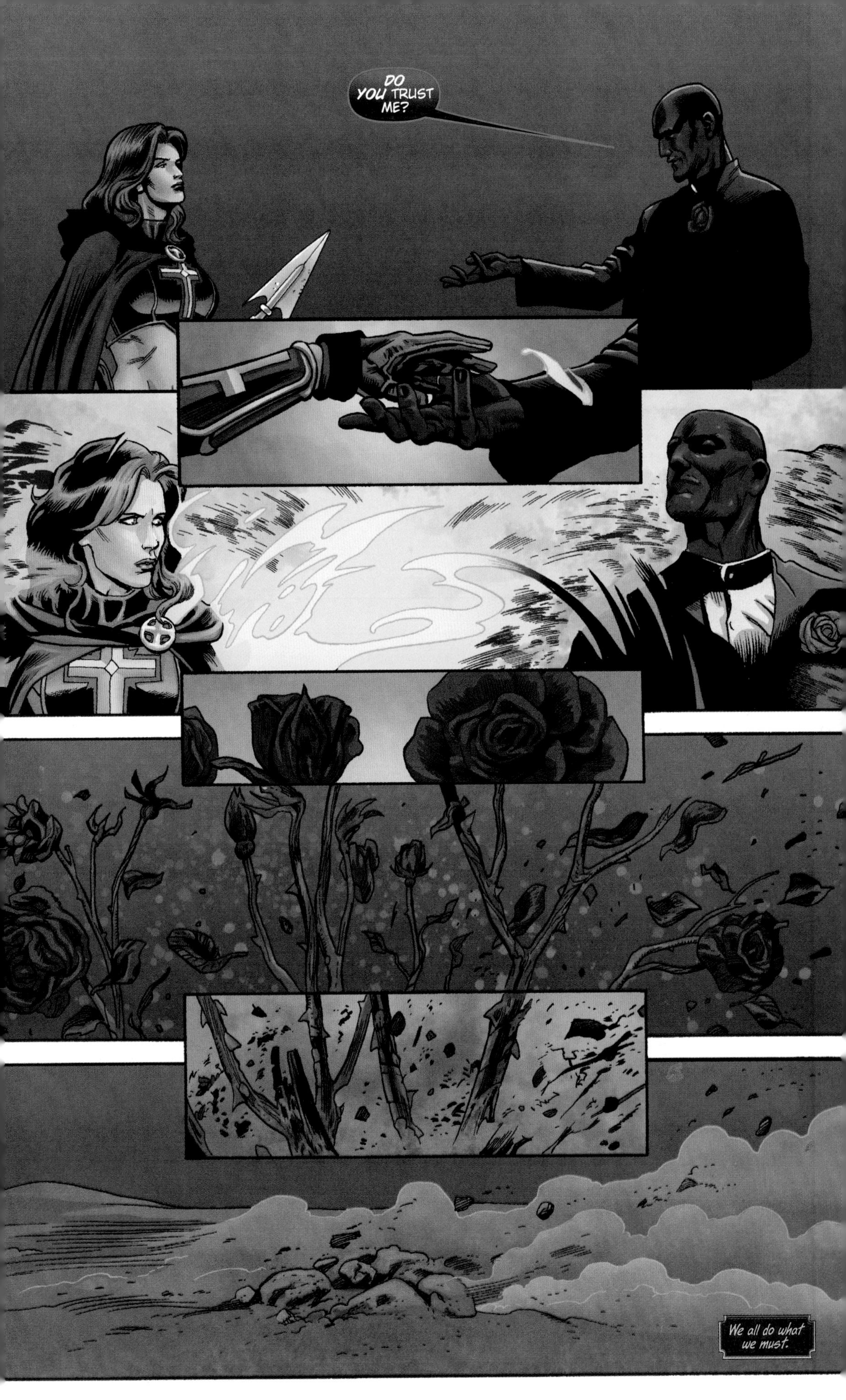
DO YOU TRUST ME?
We all do what we must.

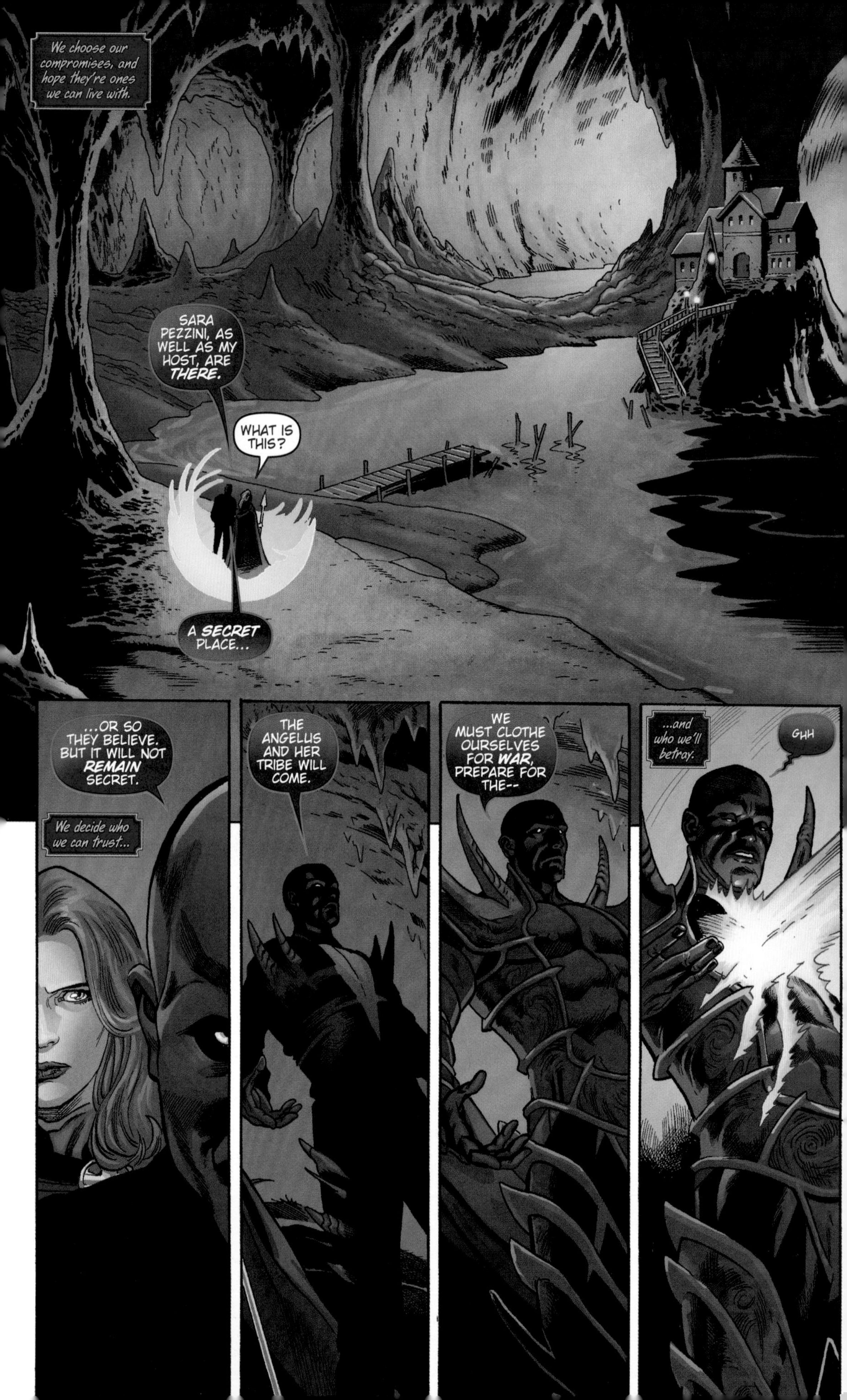
We choose our compromises, and hope they're ones we can live with.
SARA PEZZINI, AS WELL AS MY HOST, ARE THERE.
WHAT IS THIS?
A SECRET PLACE...
...OR SO THEY BELIEVE. BUT IT WILL NOT REMAIN SECRET.
We decide who we can trust...
THE ANGELUS AND HER TRIBE WILL COME.
WE MUST CLOTHE OURSELVES FOR WAR, PREPARE FOR THE--
...and who we'll betray.
GHH

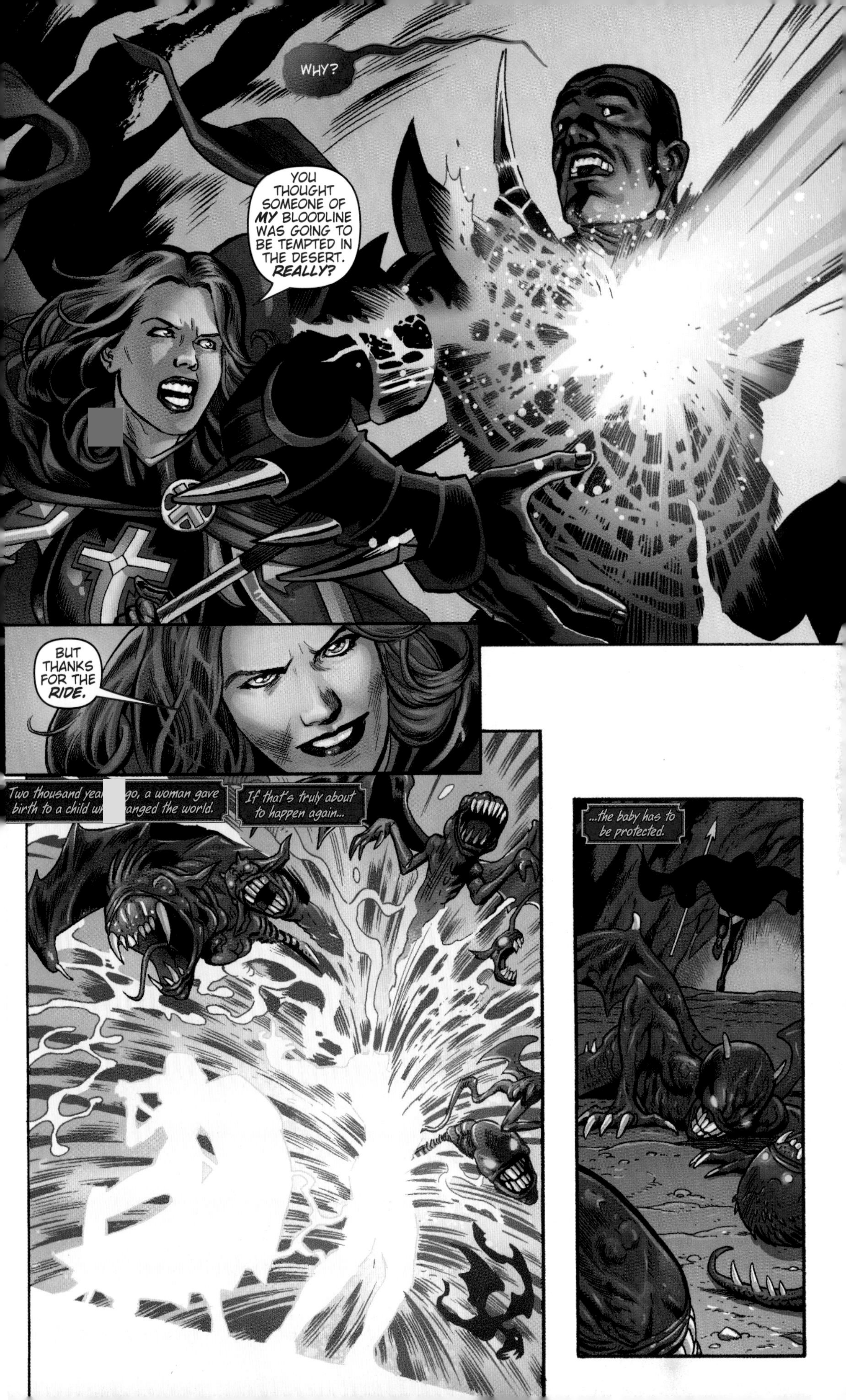
WHY?
YOU THOUGHT SOMEONE OF MY BLOODLINE WAS GOING TO BE TEMPTED IN THE DESERT. REALLY?
BUT THANKS FOR THE RIDE.
Two thousand yea go, a woman gave birth to a child wh anged the world.
If that's truly about to happen again...
...the baby has to be protected.

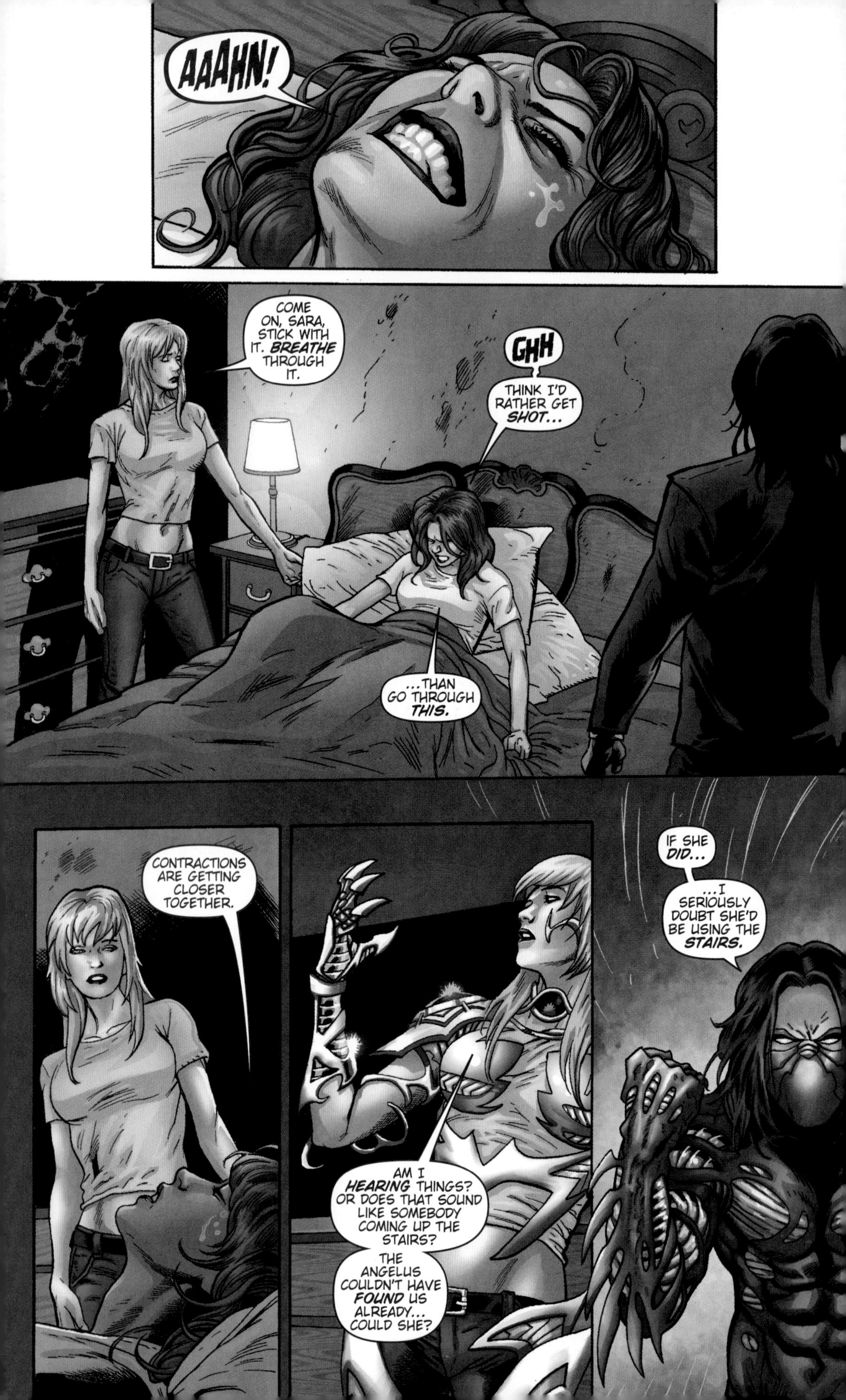
AAAHN!
COME ON, SARA, STICK WITH IT. BREATHE THROUGH IT.
GHH
THINK I'D RATHER GET SHOT...
...THAN GO THROUGH THIS.
CONTRACTIONS ARE GETTING CLOSER TOGETHER.
AM I HEARING THINGS? OR DOES THAT SOUND LIKE SOMEBODY COMING UP THE STAIRS?
THE ANGELUS COULDN'T HAVE FOUND US ALREADY... COULD SHE?
IF SHE DID...
...I SERIOUSLY DOUBT SHE'D BE USING THE STAIRS.

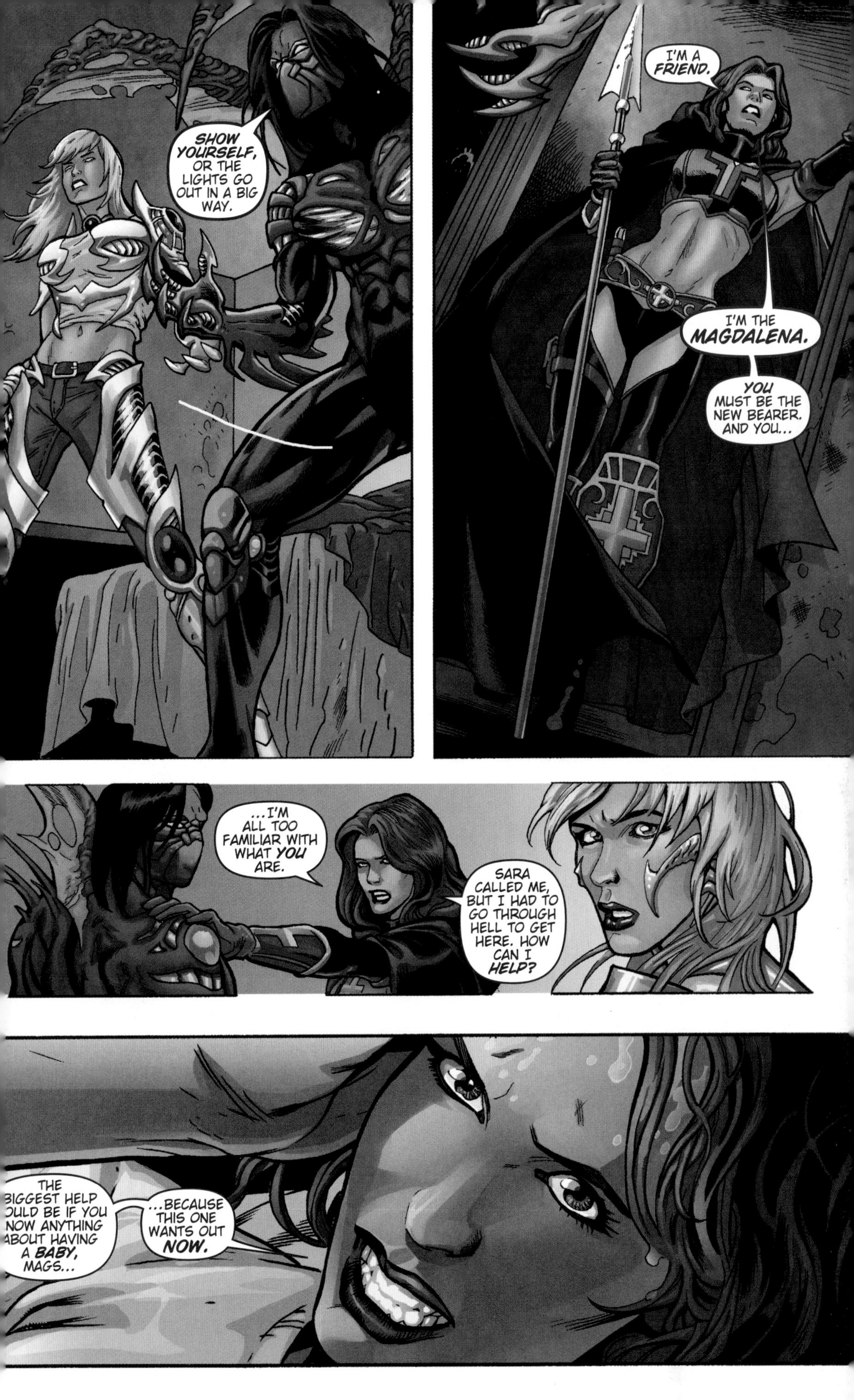
SHOW YOURSELF, OR THE LIGHTS GO OUT IN A BIG WAY.
I'M A FRIEND.
I'M THE MAGDALENA.
YOU MUST BE THE NEW BEARER. AND YOU...
...I'M ALL TOO FAMILIAR WITH WHAT YOU ARE.
SARA CALLED ME, BUT I HAD TO GO THROUGH HELL TO GET HERE. HOW CAN I HELP?
THE BIGGEST HELP OULD BE IF YOU NOW ANYTHING ABOUT HAVING A BABY, MAGS...
...BECAUSE THIS ONE WANTS OUT NOW.

FIRST BORN™

ISSUE **#3**

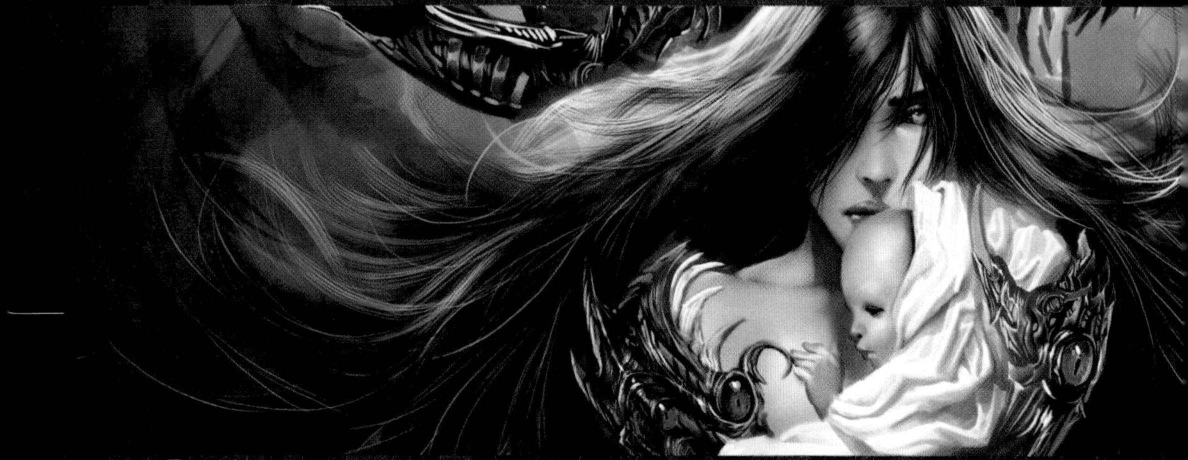

written by: **Ron Marz**
art by: **Stjepan Sejic**
letters by: **Troy Peteri**

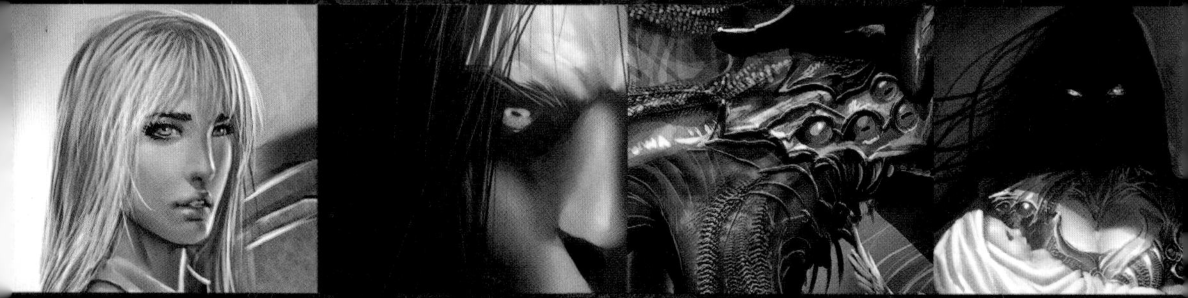

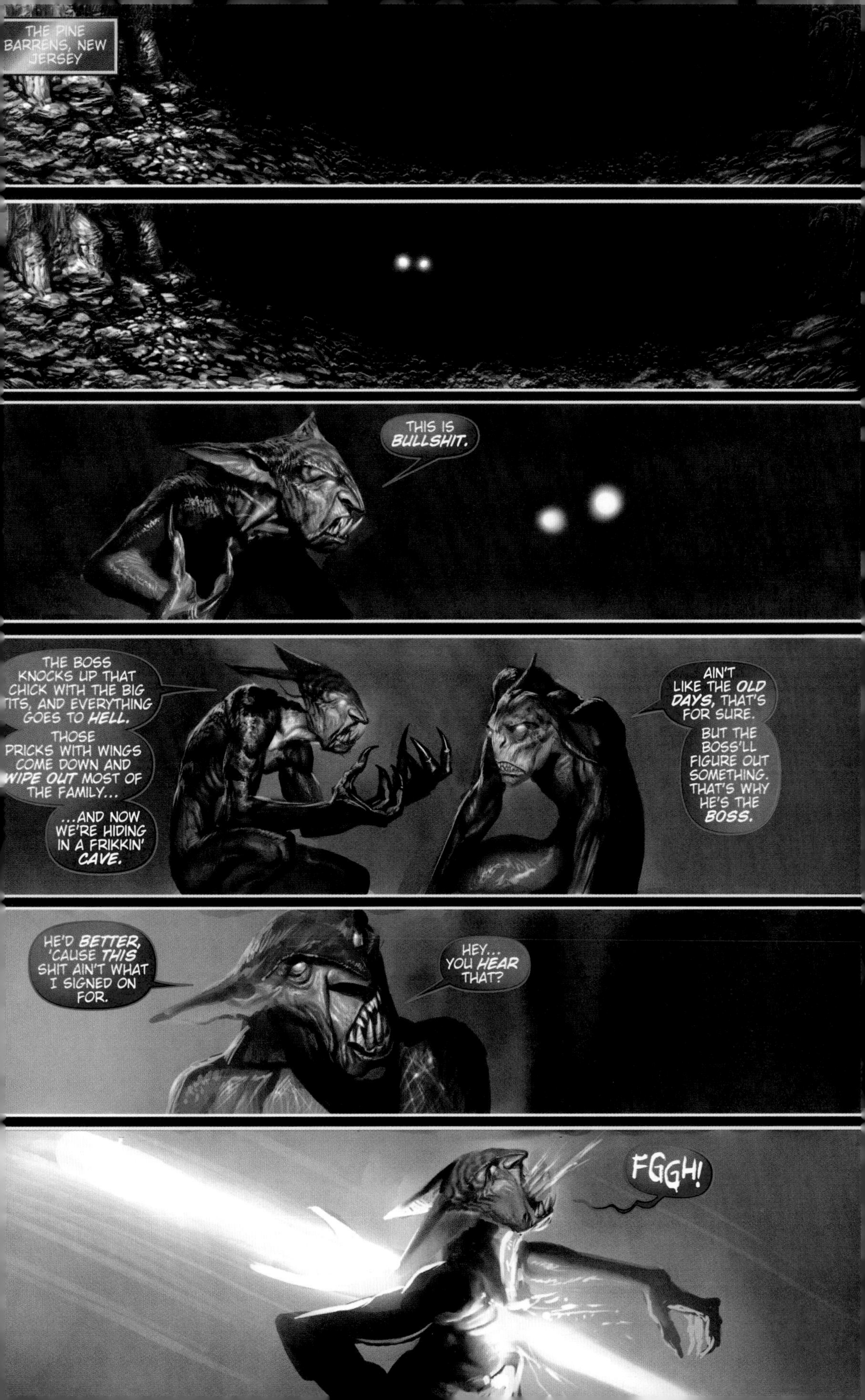
THE PINE BARRENS, NEW JERSEY
THIS IS BULLSHIT.
THE BOSS KNOCKS UP THAT CHICK WITH THE BIG TITS, AND EVERYTHING GOES TO HELL.
THOSE PRICKS WITH WINGS COME DOWN AND WIPE OUT MOST OF THE FAMILY...
...AND NOW WE'RE HIDING IN A FRIKKIN' CAVE.
AIN'T LIKE THE OLD DAYS, THAT'S FOR SURE.
BUT THE BOSS'LL FIGURE OUT SOMETHING. THAT'S WHY HE'S THE BOSS.
HE'D BETTER, 'CAUSE THIS SHIT AIN'T WHAT I SIGNED ON FOR.
HEY... YOU HEAR THAT?
FGGH!

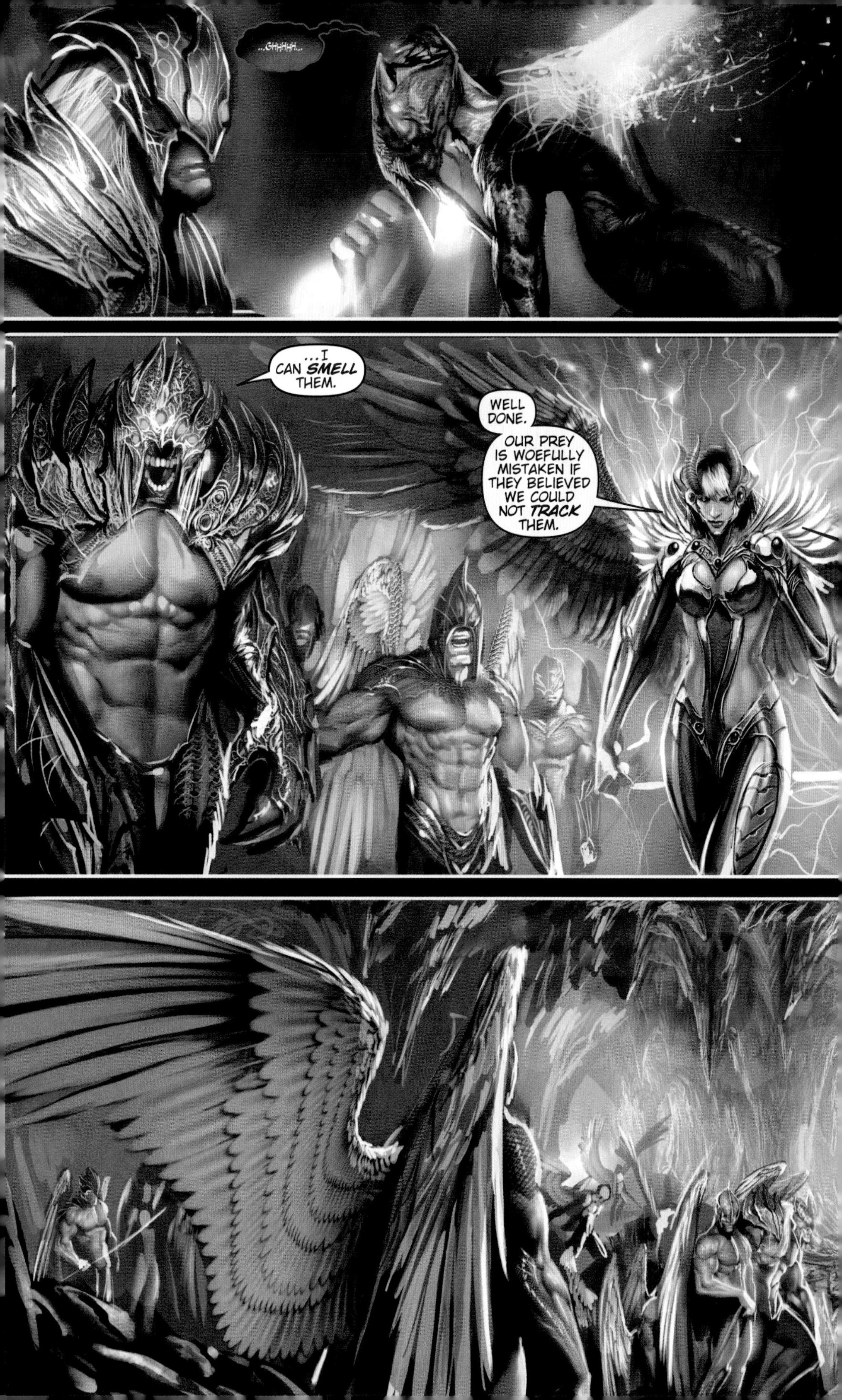
...GHHHHH...
...I CAN *SMELL* THEM.
WELL DONE.
OUR PREY IS WOEFULLY MISTAKEN IF THEY BELIEVED WE COULD NOT *TRACK* THEM.

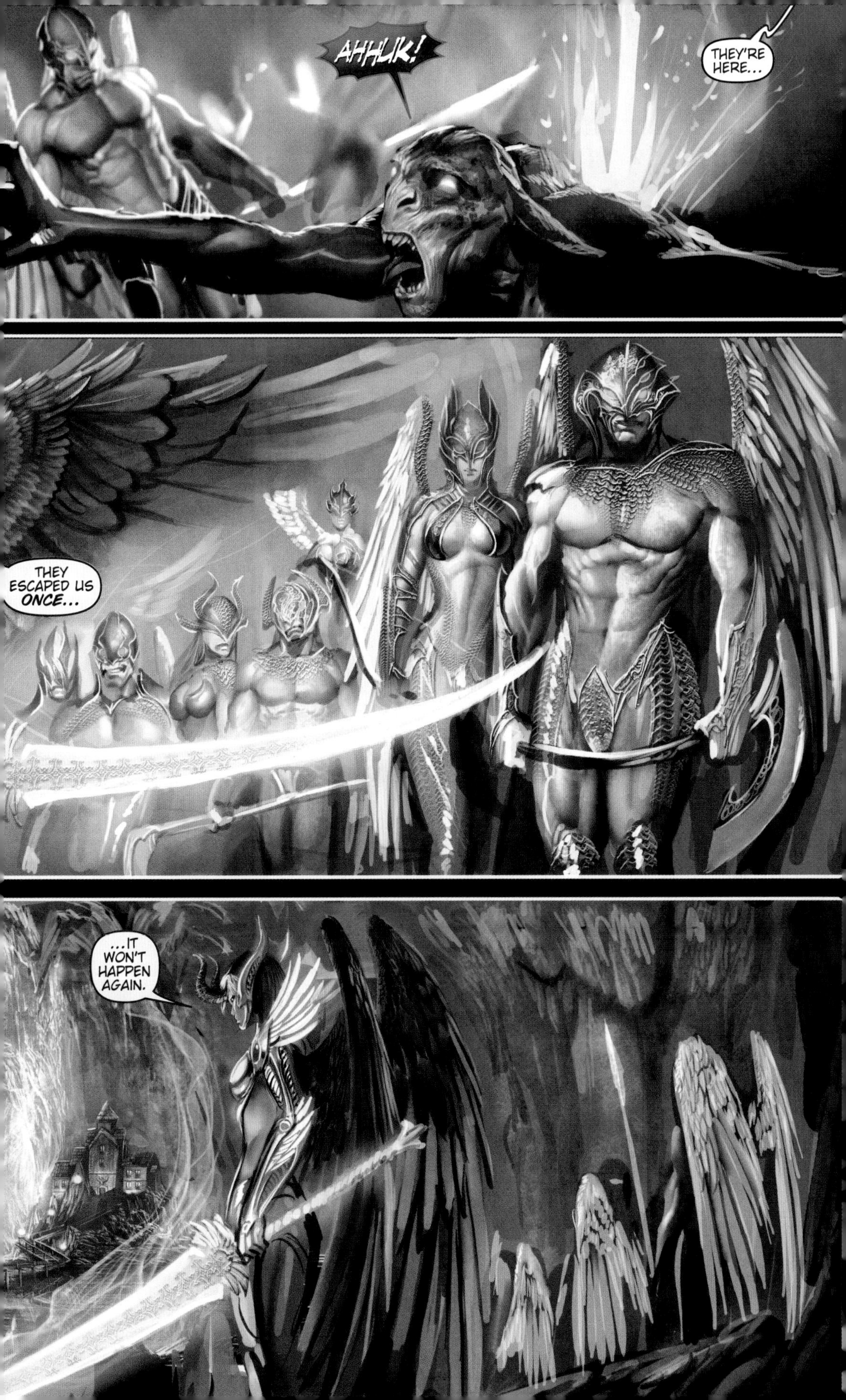
AHHUK!
THEY'RE HERE...
THEY ESCAPED US ONCE...
...IT WON'T HAPPEN AGAIN.

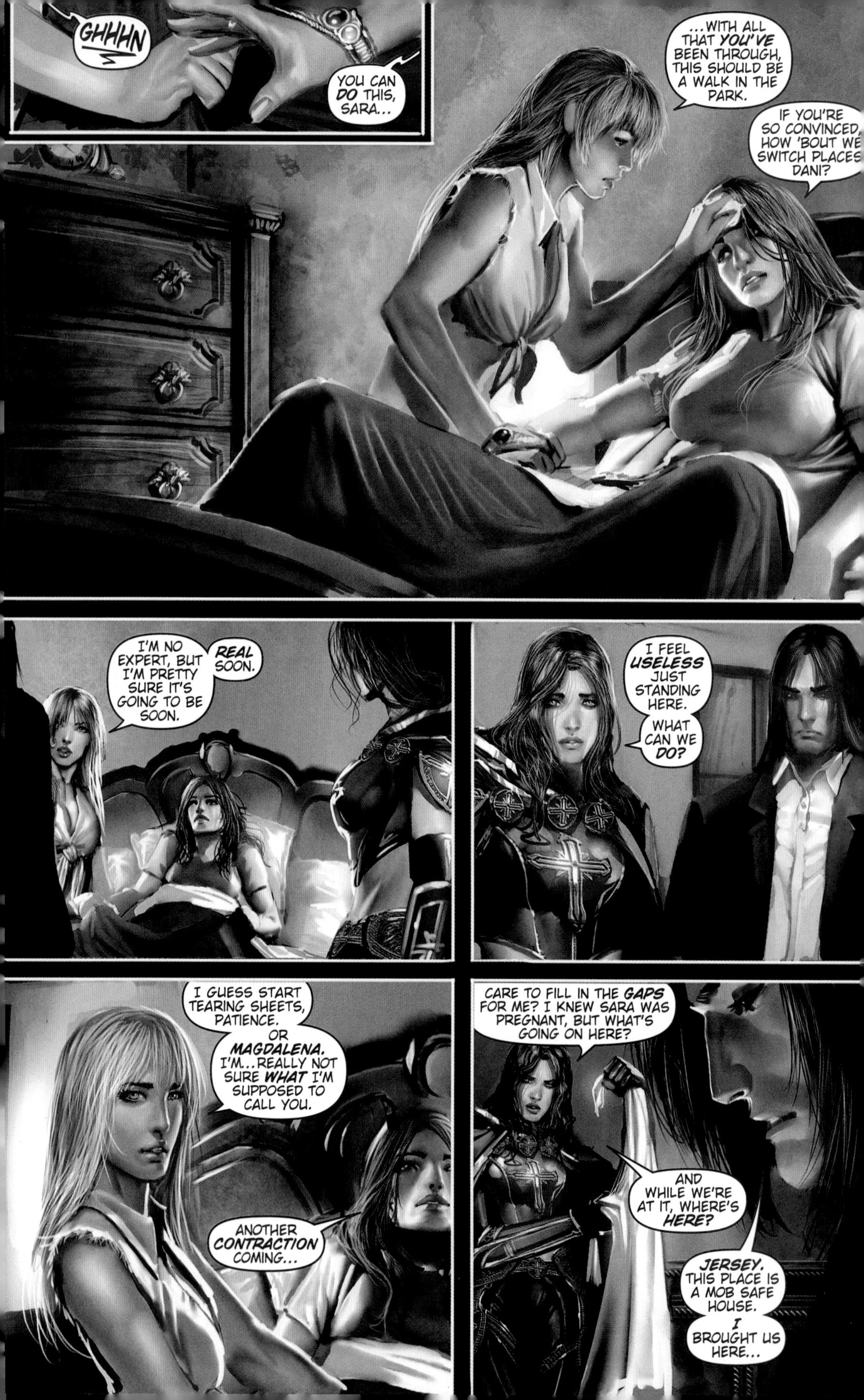
GHHHN
YOU CAN DO THIS, SARA...
...WITH ALL THAT YOU'VE BEEN THROUGH, THIS SHOULD BE A WALK IN THE PARK.
IF YOU'RE SO CONVINCED, HOW 'BOUT WE SWITCH PLACES, DANI?
I'M NO EXPERT, BUT I'M PRETTY SURE IT'S GOING TO BE SOON.
REAL SOON.
I FEEL USELESS JUST STANDING HERE.
WHAT CAN WE DO?
I GUESS START TEARING SHEETS, PATIENCE.
OR MAGDALENA. I'M...REALLY NOT SURE WHAT I'M SUPPOSED TO CALL YOU.
ANOTHER CONTRACTION COMING...
CARE TO FILL IN THE GAPS FOR ME? I KNEW SARA WAS PREGNANT, BUT WHAT'S GOING ON HERE?
AND WHILE WE'RE AT IT, WHERE'S HERE?
JERSEY. THIS PLACE IS A MOB SAFE HOUSE.
I BROUGHT US HERE...

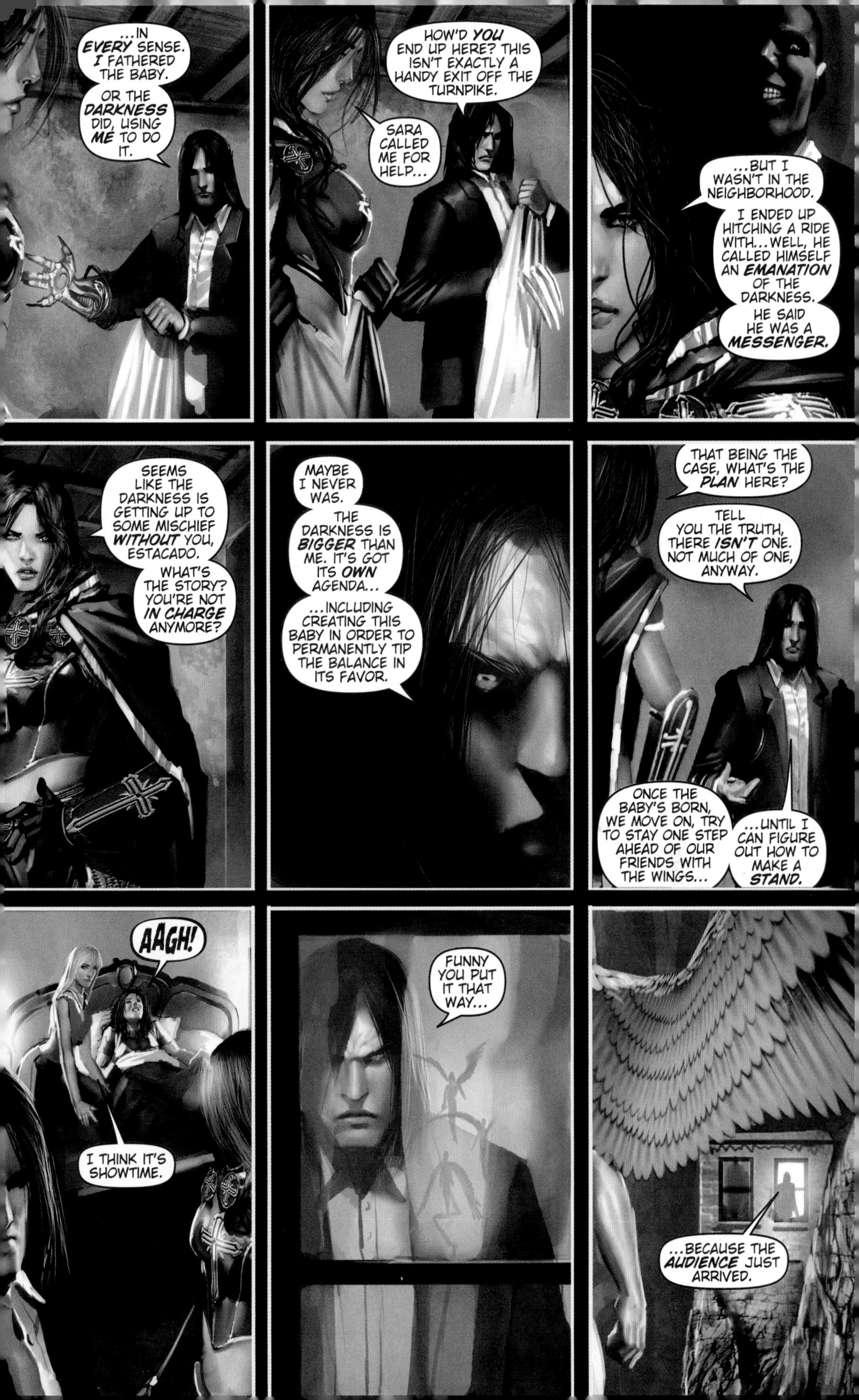
...IN EVERY SENSE. I FATHERED THE BABY.
OR THE DARKNESS DID, USING ME TO DO IT.
HOW'D YOU END UP HERE? THIS ISN'T EXACTLY A HANDY EXIT OFF THE TURNPIKE.
SARA CALLED ME FOR HELP...
...BUT I WASN'T IN THE NEIGHBORHOOD.
I ENDED UP HITCHING A RIDE WITH...WELL, HE CALLED HIMSELF AN EMANATION OF THE DARKNESS.
HE SAID HE WAS A MESSENGER.
SEEMS LIKE THE DARKNESS IS GETTING UP TO SOME MISCHIEF WITHOUT YOU, ESTACADO.
WHAT'S THE STORY? YOU'RE NOT IN CHARGE ANYMORE?
MAYBE I NEVER WAS.
THE DARKNESS IS BIGGER THAN ME. IT'S GOT ITS OWN AGENDA...
...INCLUDING CREATING THIS BABY IN ORDER TO PERMANENTLY TIP THE BALANCE IN ITS FAVOR.
THAT BEING THE CASE, WHAT'S THE PLAN HERE?
TELL YOU THE TRUTH, THERE ISN'T ONE. NOT MUCH OF ONE, ANYWAY.
ONCE THE BABY'S BORN, WE MOVE ON, TRY TO STAY ONE STEP AHEAD OF OUR FRIENDS WITH THE WINGS...
...UNTIL I CAN FIGURE OUT HOW TO MAKE A STAND.
AAGH!
I THINK IT'S SHOWTIME.
FUNNY YOU PUT IT THAT WAY...
...BECAUSE THE AUDIENCE JUST ARRIVED.

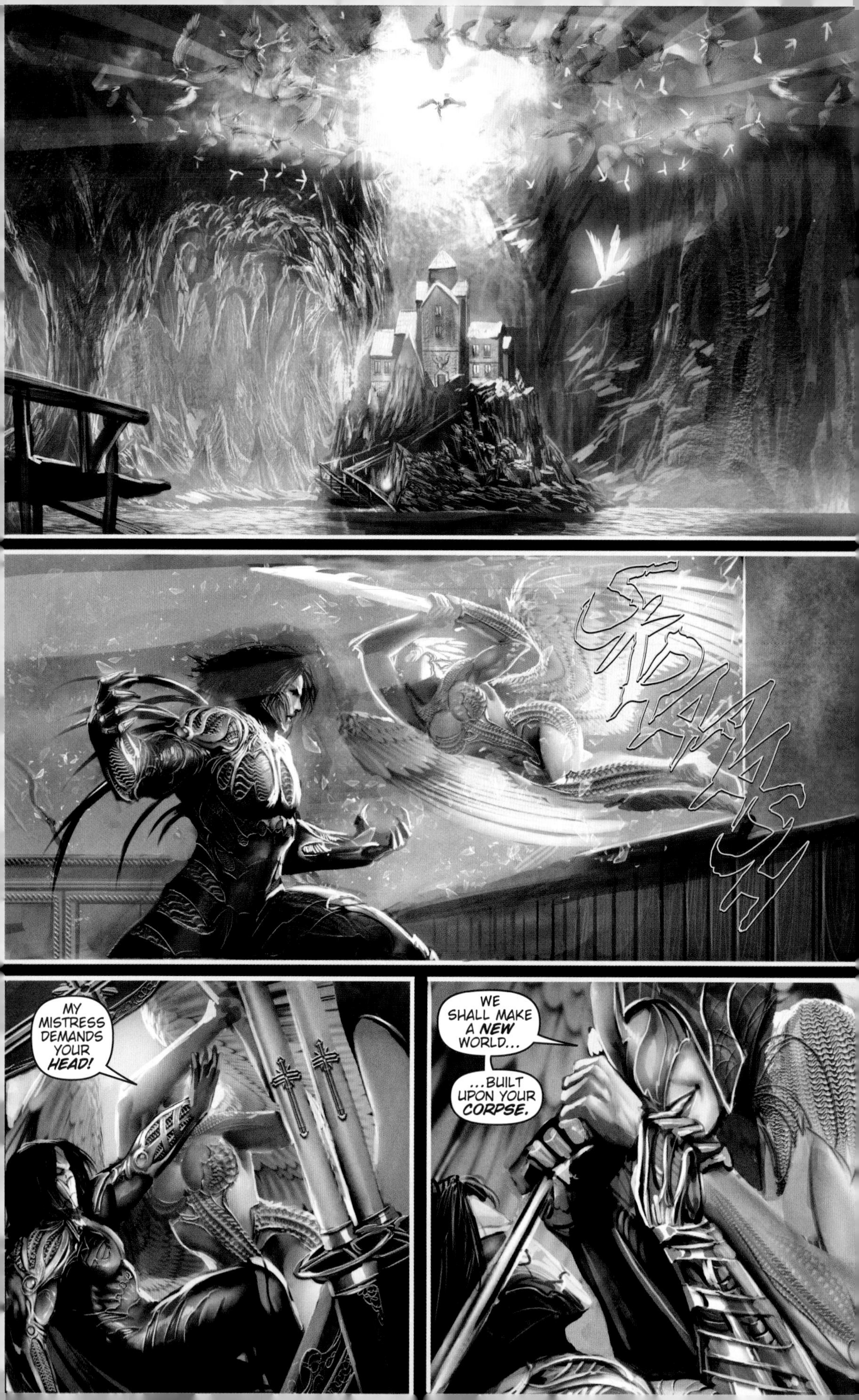
SKRAAASH
MY MISTRESS DEMANDS YOUR HEAD!
WE SHALL MAKE A NEW WORLD...
...BUILT UPON YOUR CORPSE.

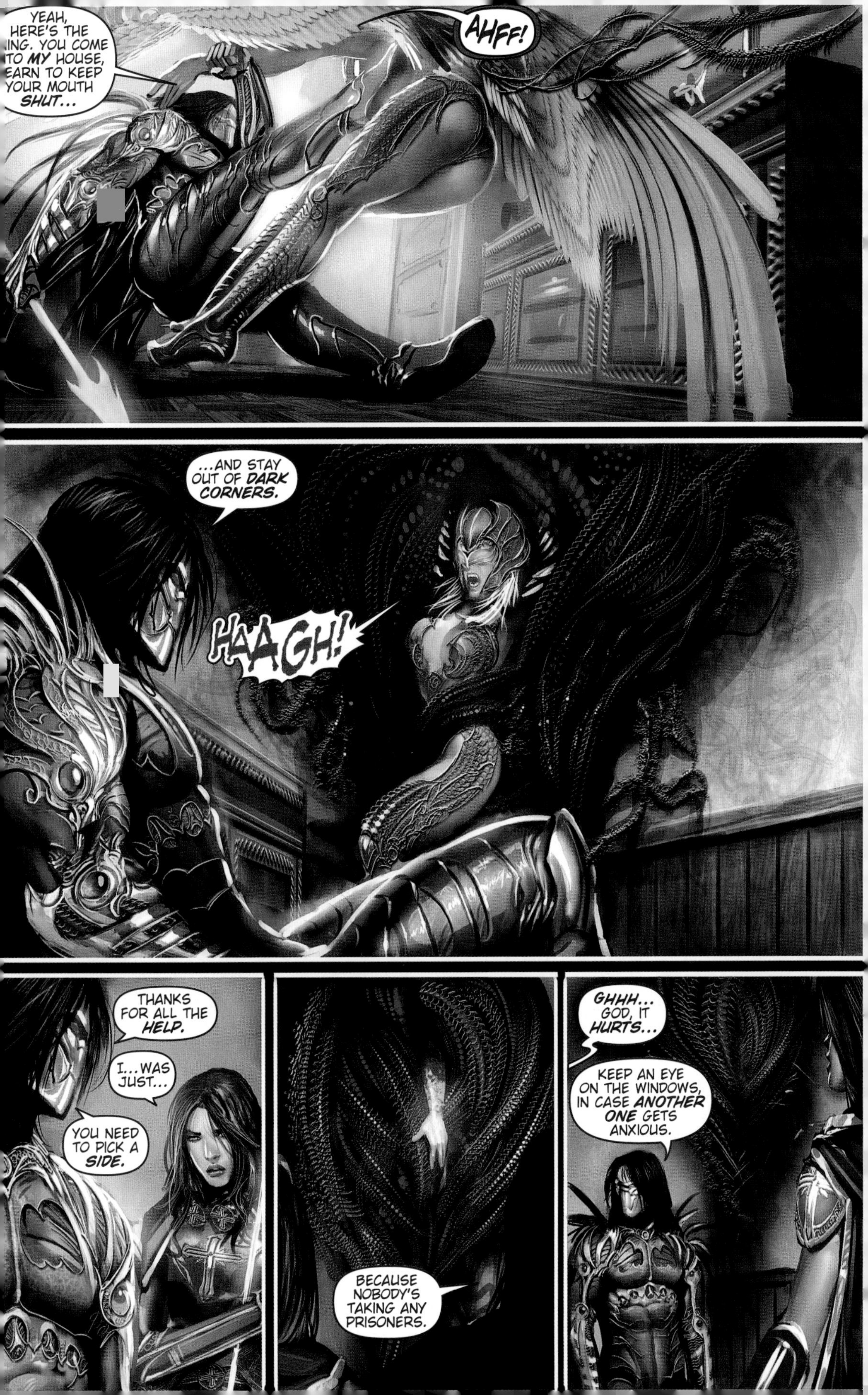
YEAH, HERE'S THE ...ING. YOU COME TO MY HOUSE, ...EARN TO KEEP YOUR MOUTH SHUT...
AHFF!
...AND STAY OUT OF DARK CORNERS.
HAAGH!
THANKS FOR ALL THE HELP.
I...WAS JUST...
YOU NEED TO PICK A SIDE.
BECAUSE NOBODY'S TAKING ANY PRISONERS.
GHHH... GOD, IT HURTS...
KEEP AN EYE ON THE WINDOWS, IN CASE ANOTHER ONE GETS ANXIOUS.

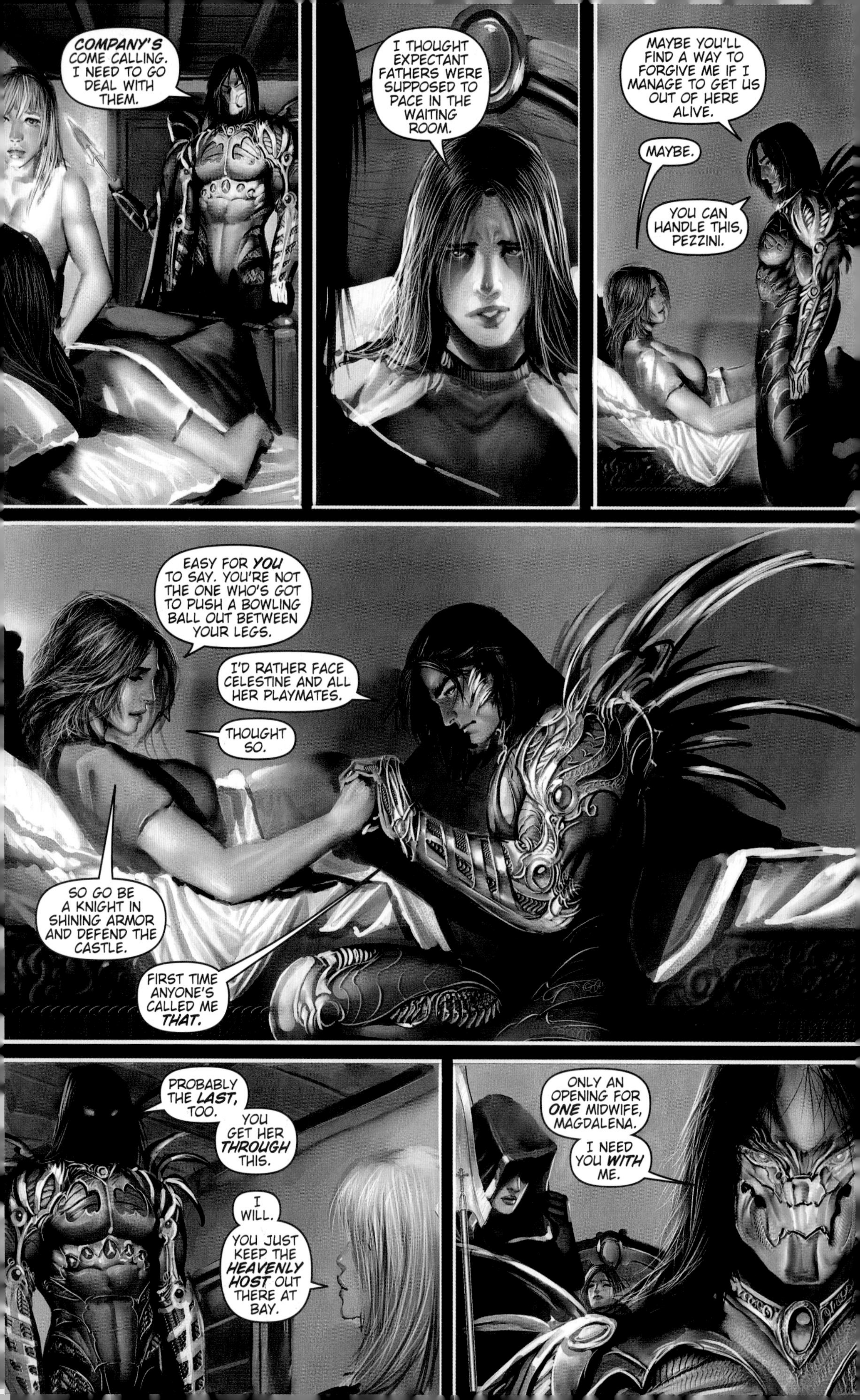
COMPANY'S COME CALLING. I NEED TO GO DEAL WITH THEM.
I THOUGHT EXPECTANT FATHERS WERE SUPPOSED TO PACE IN THE WAITING ROOM.
MAYBE YOU'LL FIND A WAY TO FORGIVE ME IF I MANAGE TO GET US OUT OF HERE ALIVE.
MAYBE.
YOU CAN HANDLE THIS, PEZZINI.
EASY FOR YOU TO SAY. YOU'RE NOT THE ONE WHO'S GOT TO PUSH A BOWLING BALL OUT BETWEEN YOUR LEGS.
I'D RATHER FACE CELESTINE AND ALL HER PLAYMATES.
THOUGHT SO.
SO GO BE A KNIGHT IN SHINING ARMOR AND DEFEND THE CASTLE.
FIRST TIME ANYONE'S CALLED ME THAT.
PROBABLY THE LAST, TOO.
YOU GET HER THROUGH THIS.
I WILL.
YOU JUST KEEP THE HEAVENLY HOST OUT THERE AT BAY.
ONLY AN OPENING FOR ONE MIDWIFE, MAGDALENA.
I NEED YOU WITH ME.

CASTE WARRIORS OF THE ANGELUS...

...HEAR ME!

OUR *TRIUMPH* IS AT HAND. OUR ENEMY HAS *DEFIED* US, AND NOW MUST PAY THE ULTIMATE PRICE.

WE SHALL *PULL APART* THIS HOUSE STONE BY STONE. WE SHALL *SLAUGHTER* ANY WHO WOULD STAND IN OUR WAY.

THE *CHILD* WILL BE OURS...

...AND THEN ALL CREATION WILL BE OURS!

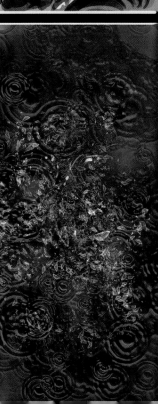

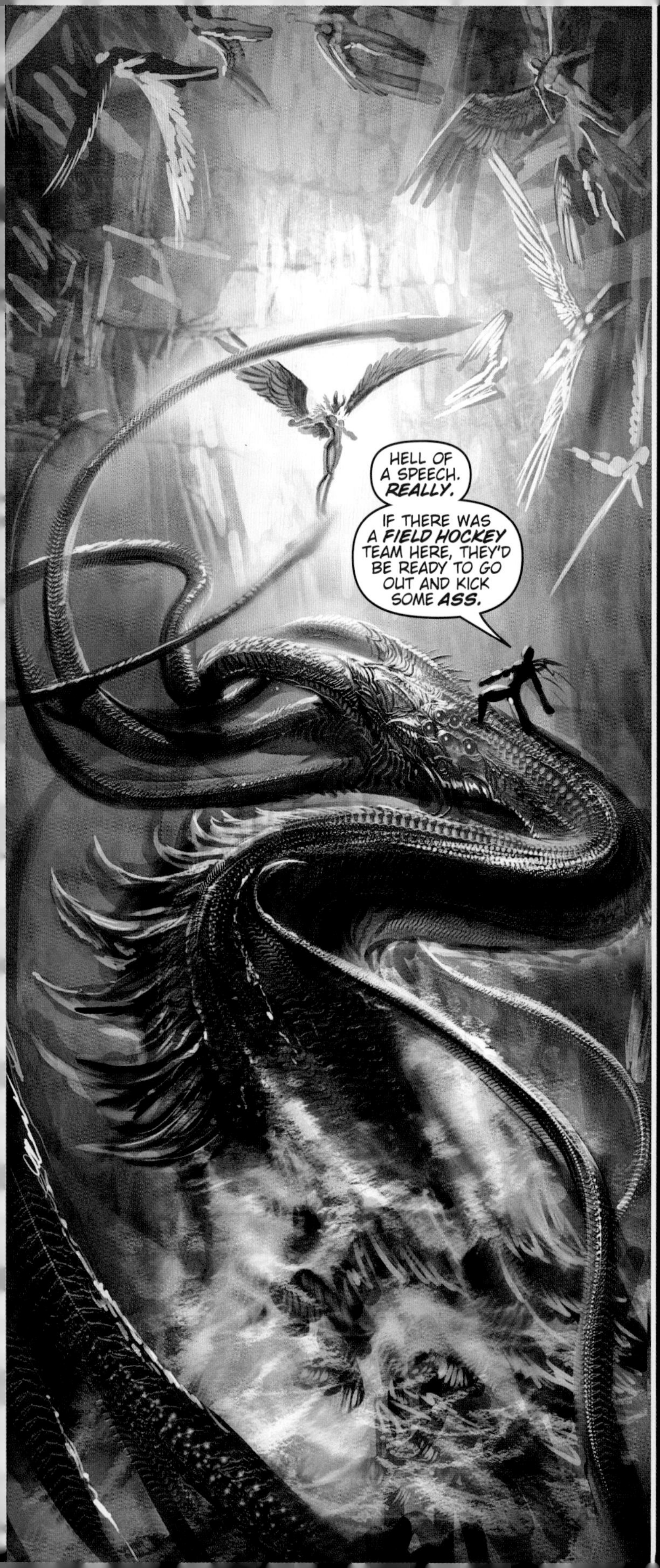
HELL OF A SPEECH. REALLY.
IF THERE WAS A FIELD HOCKEY TEAM HERE, THEY'D BE READY TO GO OUT AND KICK SOME ASS.

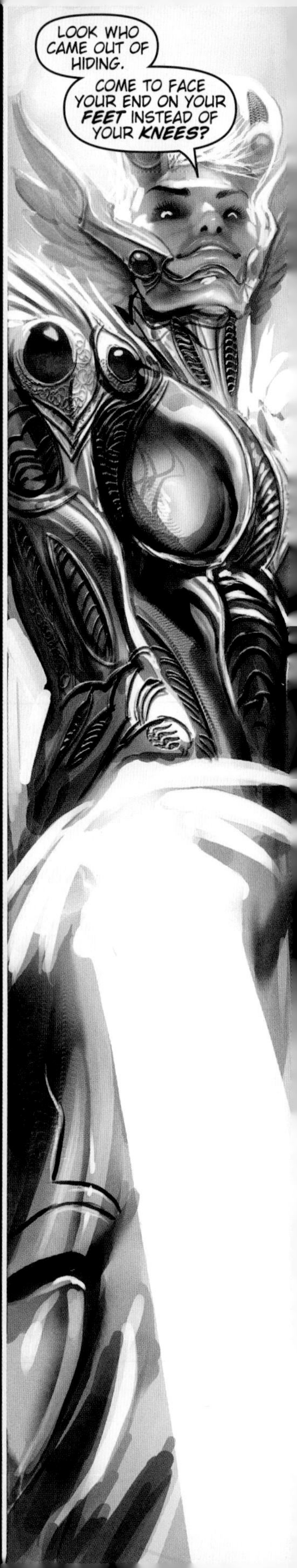
LOOK WHO CAME OUT OF HIDING.
COME TO FACE YOUR END ON YOUR FEET INSTEAD OF YOUR KNEES?

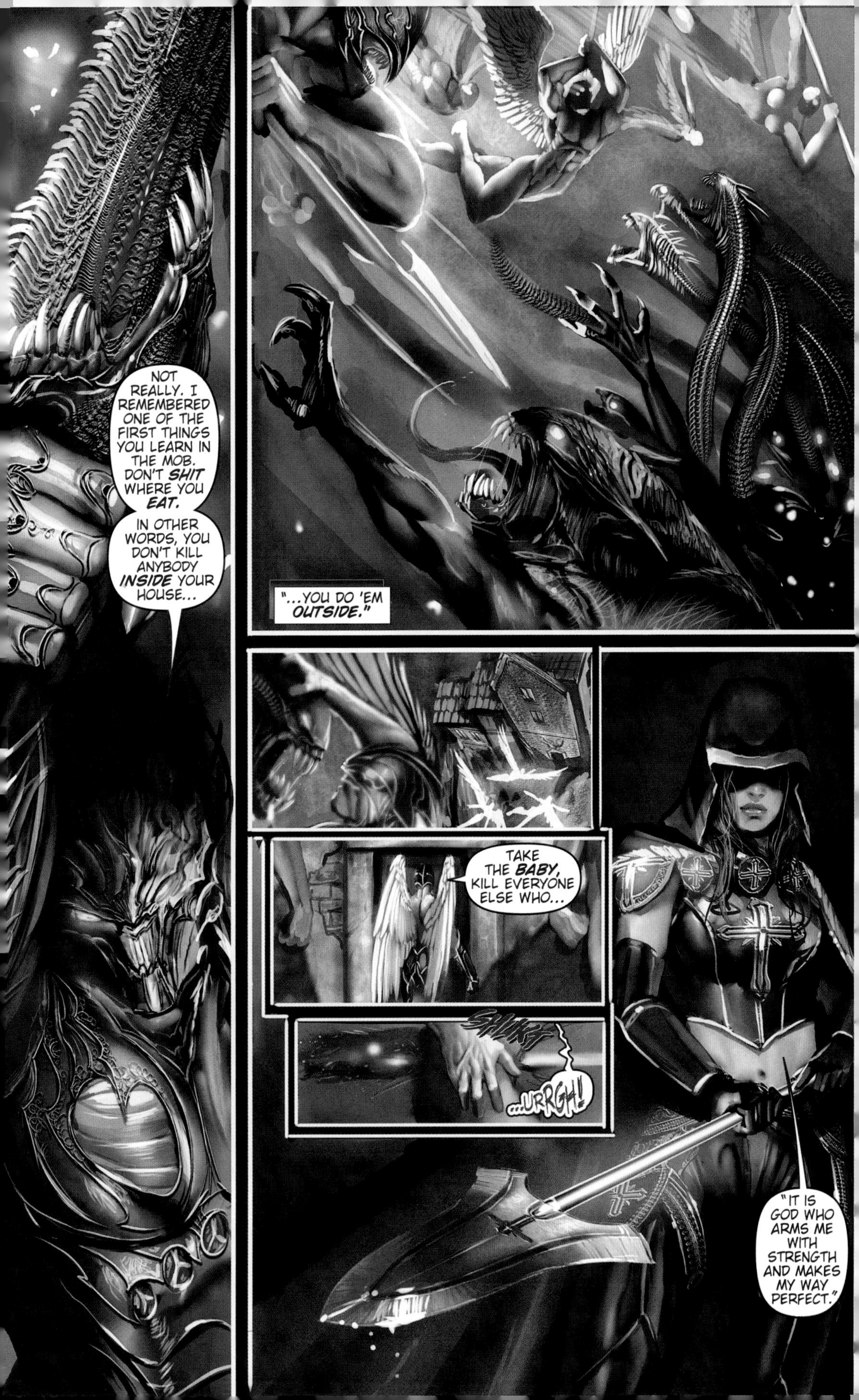
NOT REALLY. I REMEMBERED ONE OF THE FIRST THINGS YOU LEARN IN THE MOB. DON'T SHIT WHERE YOU EAT.
IN OTHER WORDS, YOU DON'T KILL ANYBODY INSIDE YOUR HOUSE...
"...YOU DO 'EM OUTSIDE."
TAKE THE BABY, KILL EVERYONE ELSE WHO...
SHUKT
...URRGH!
"IT IS GOD WHO ARMS ME WITH STRENGTH AND MAKES MY WAY PERFECT."

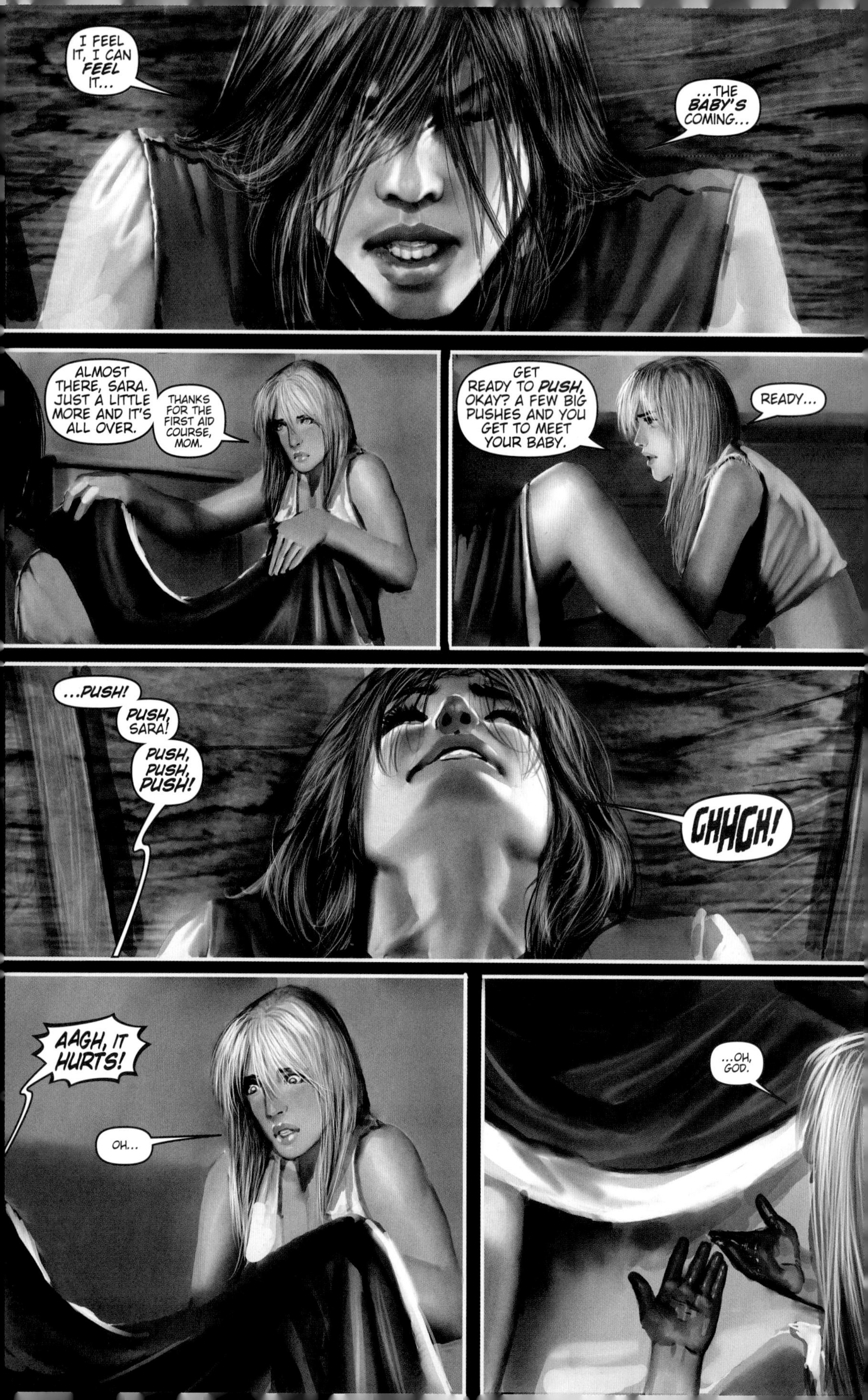
I FEEL IT, I CAN FEEL IT...
...THE BABY'S COMING...
ALMOST THERE, SARA. JUST A LITTLE MORE AND IT'S ALL OVER.
THANKS FOR THE FIRST AID COURSE, MOM.
GET READY TO PUSH, OKAY? A FEW BIG PUSHES AND YOU GET TO MEET YOUR BABY.
READY...
...PUSH!
PUSH, SARA!
PUSH, PUSH, PUSH!
GHHGH!
AAGH, IT HURTS!
OH...
...OH, GOD.

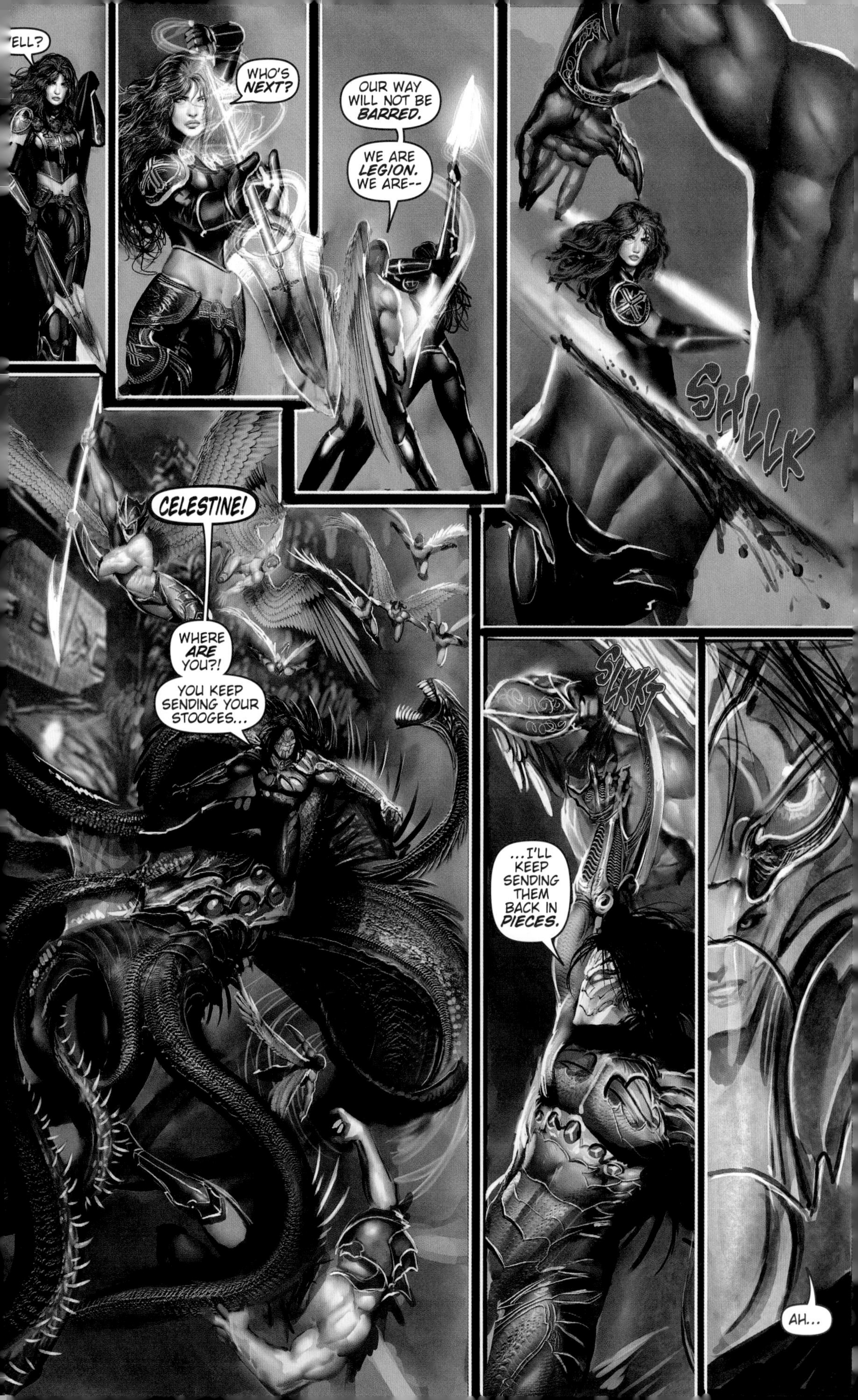

...ELL?
WHO'S NEXT?
OUR WAY WILL NOT BE BARRED.
WE ARE LEGION. WE ARE--
SHLLK
CELESTINE!
WHERE ARE YOU?!
YOU KEEP SENDING YOUR STOOGES...
SLKKT
...I'LL KEEP SENDING THEM BACK IN PIECES.
AH...

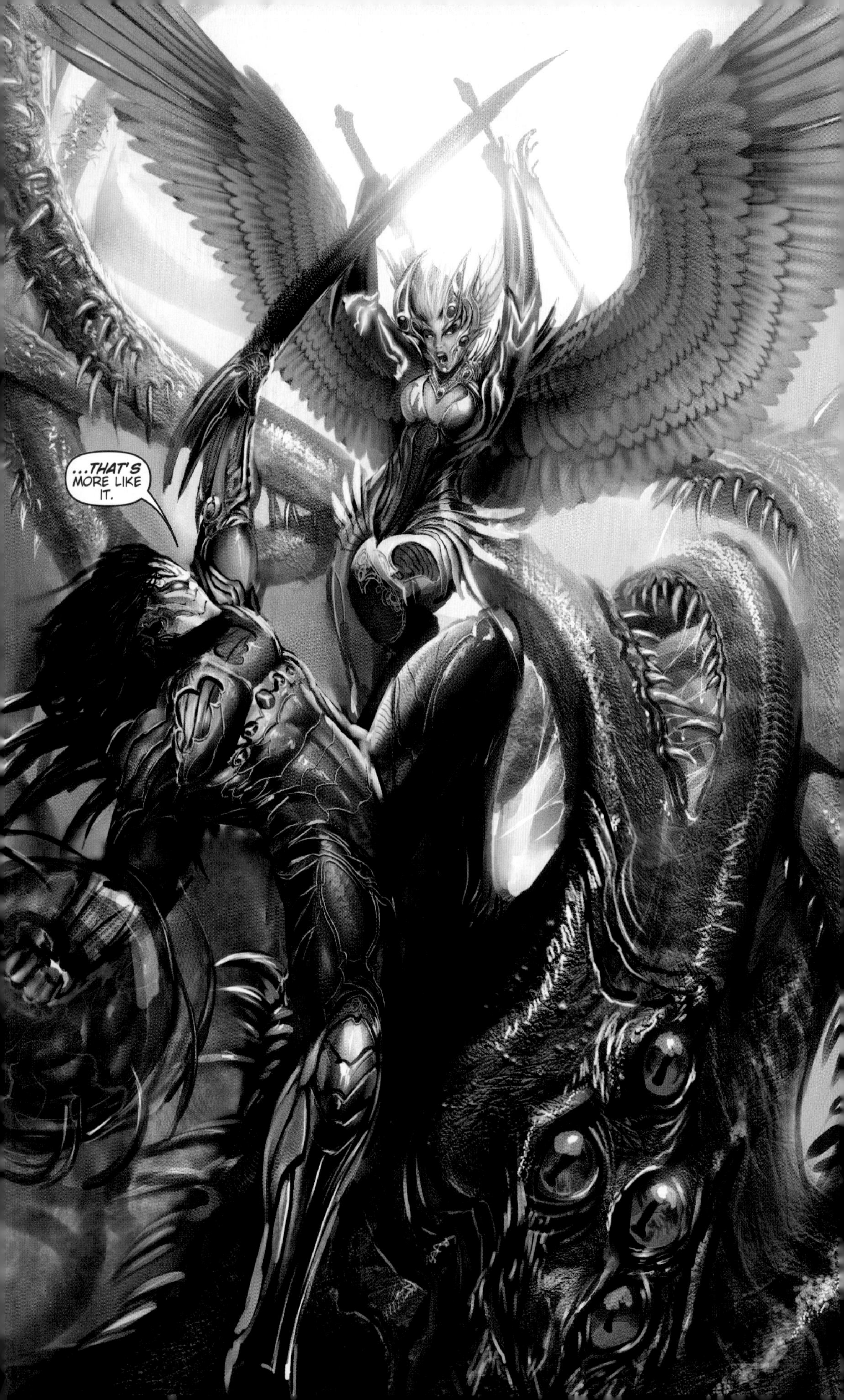
...THAT'S MORE LIKE IT.

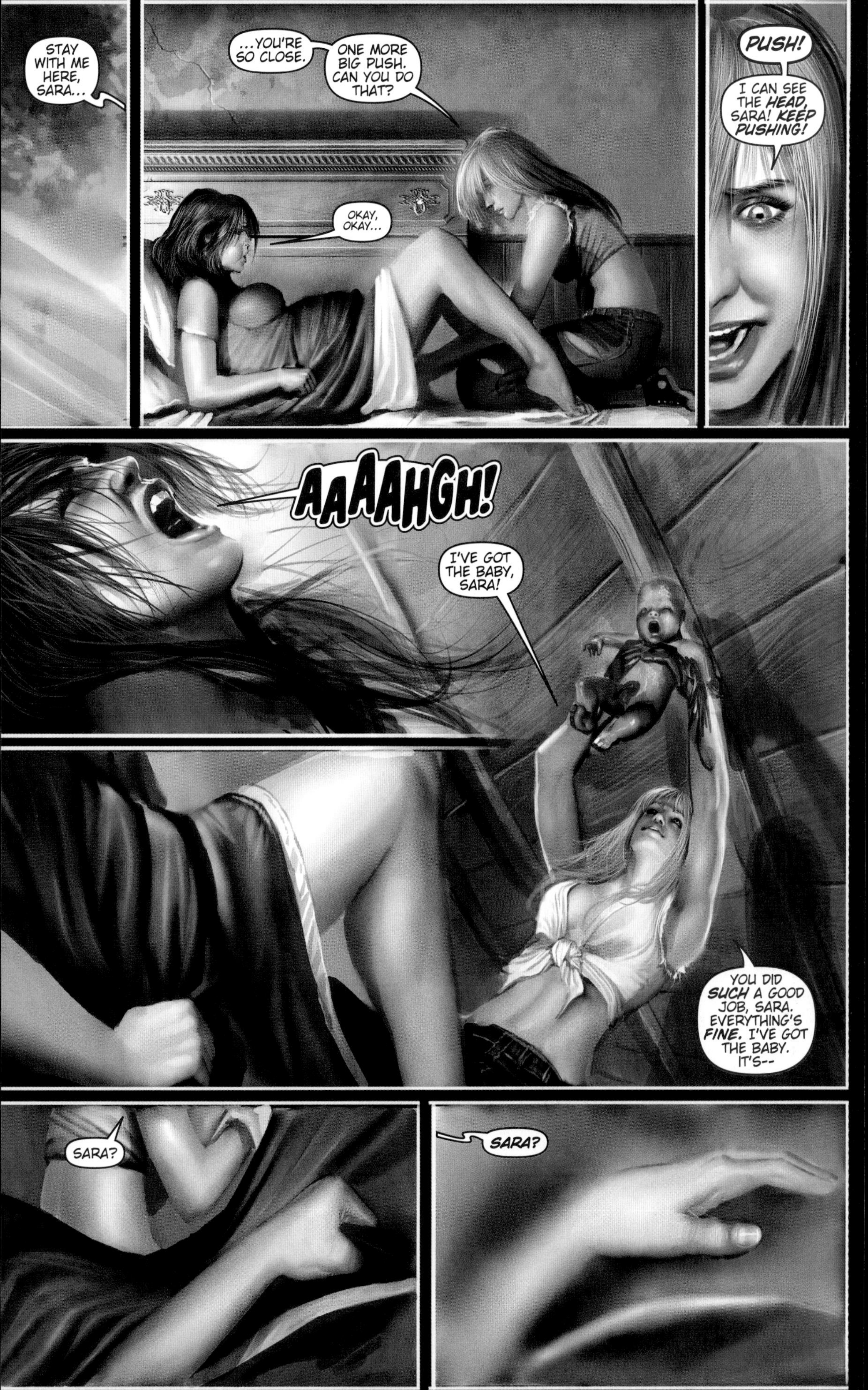
STAY WITH ME HERE, SARA...
...YOU'RE SO CLOSE.
ONE MORE BIG PUSH. CAN YOU DO THAT?
OKAY, OKAY...
PUSH!
I CAN SEE THE HEAD, SARA! KEEP PUSHING!
AAAAHGH!
I'VE GOT THE BABY, SARA!
YOU DID SUCH A GOOD JOB, SARA. EVERYTHING'S FINE. I'VE GOT THE BABY. IT'S--
SARA?
SARA?

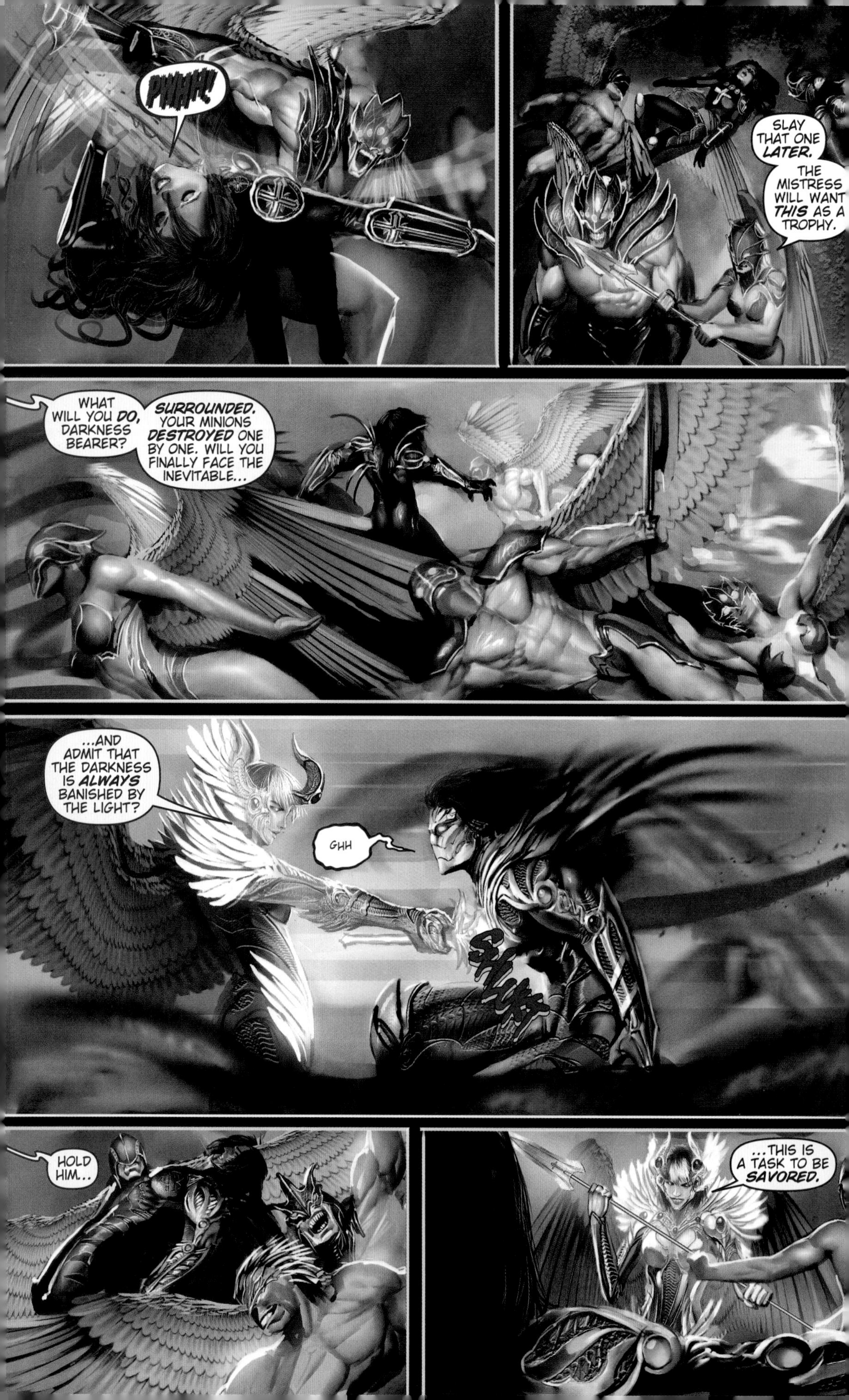
PWHH!
SLAY THAT ONE LATER.
THE MISTRESS WILL WANT THIS AS A TROPHY.
WHAT WILL YOU DO, DARKNESS BEARER?
SURROUNDED. YOUR MINIONS DESTROYED ONE BY ONE. WILL YOU FINALLY FACE THE INEVITABLE...
...AND ADMIT THAT THE DARKNESS IS ALWAYS BANISHED BY THE LIGHT?
GHH
HOLD HIM...
...THIS IS A TASK TO BE SAVORED.

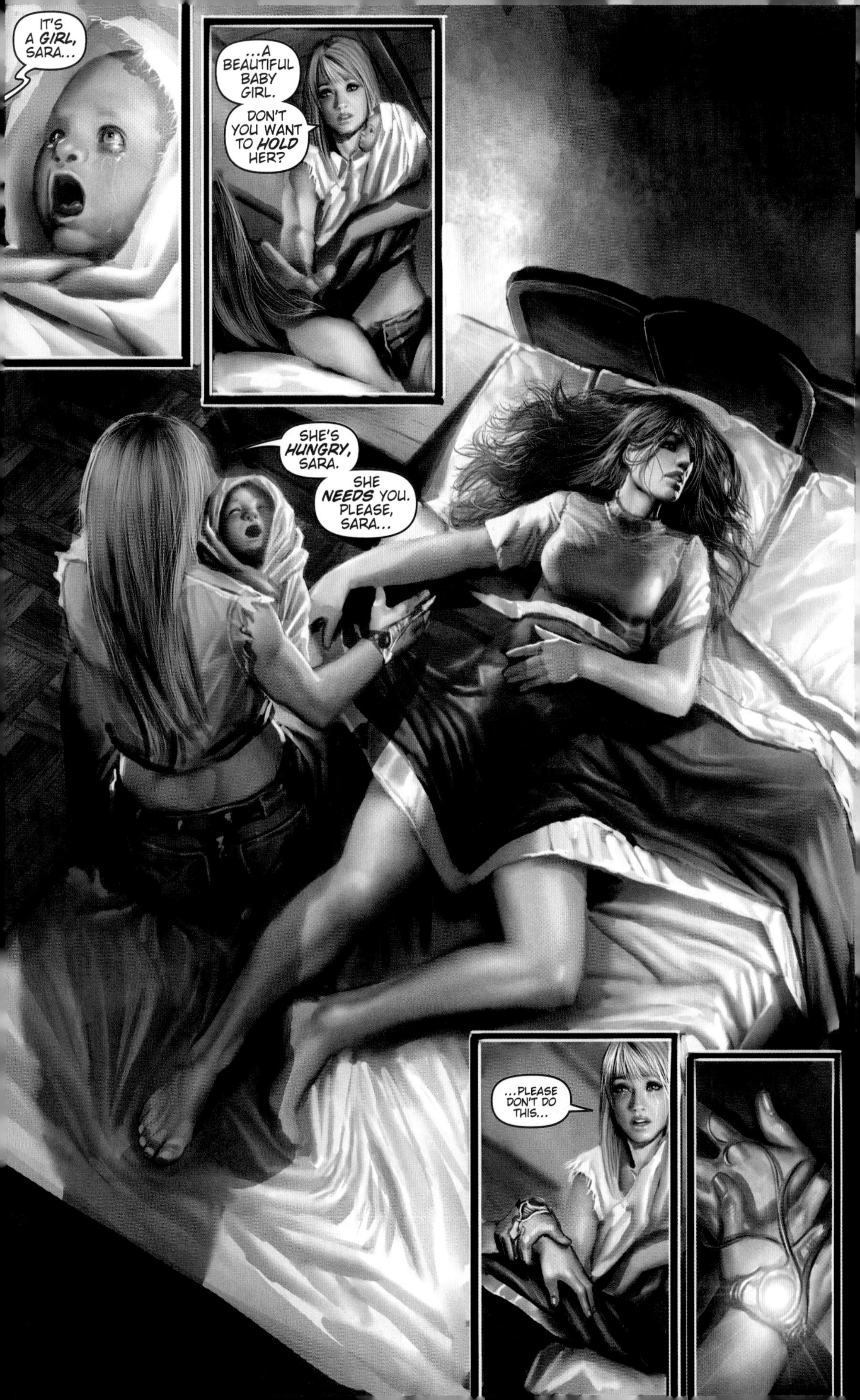
IT'S A GIRL, SARA...
...A BEAUTIFUL BABY GIRL.
DON'T YOU WANT TO HOLD HER?
SHE'S HUNGRY, SARA.
SHE NEEDS YOU. PLEASE, SARA...
...PLEASE DON'T DO THIS...

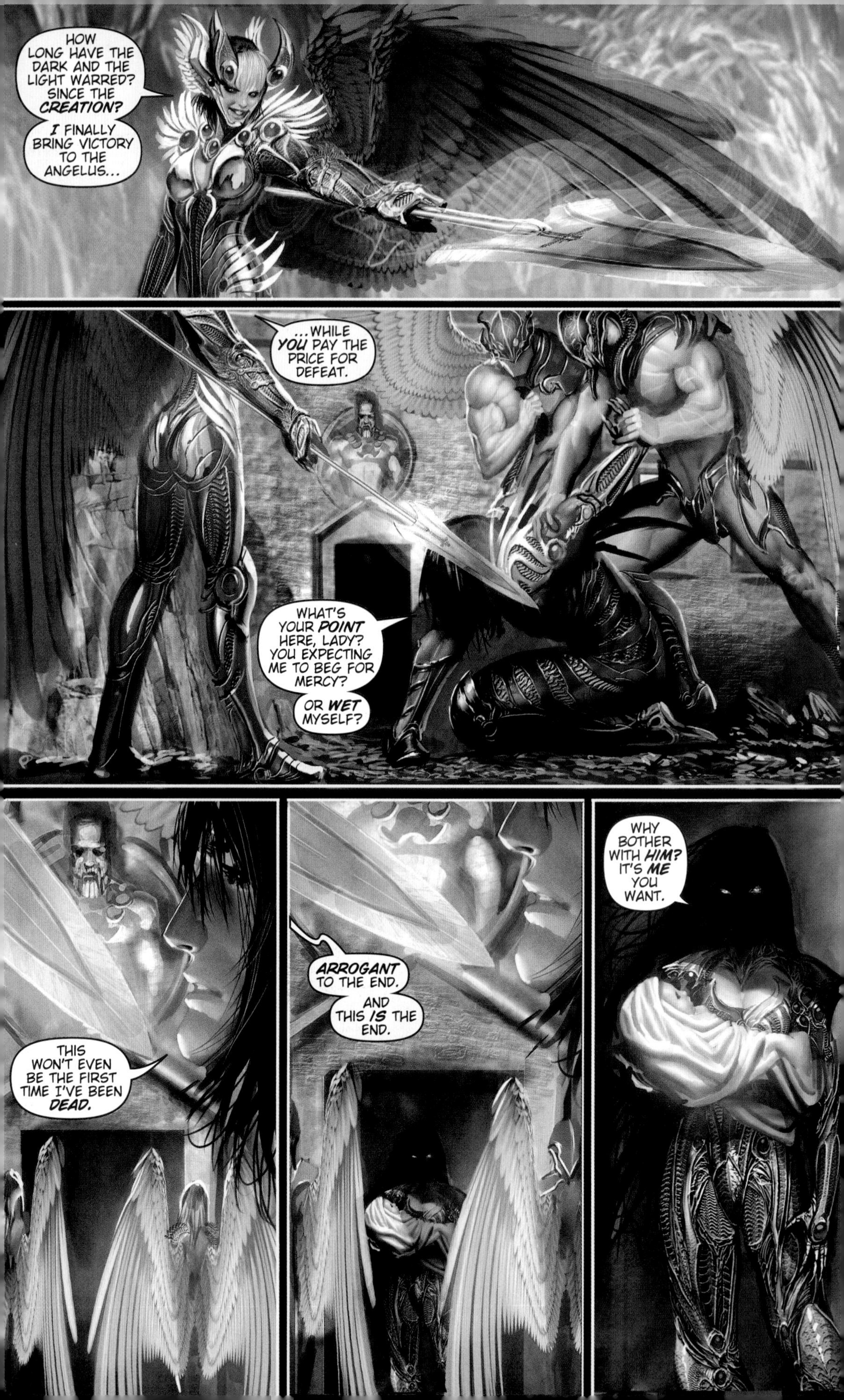
HOW LONG HAVE THE DARK AND THE LIGHT WARRED? SINCE THE ***CREATION?***
I FINALLY BRING VICTORY TO THE ANGELUS...
...WHILE ***YOU*** PAY THE PRICE FOR DEFEAT.
WHAT'S YOUR ***POINT*** HERE, LADY? YOU EXPECTING ME TO BEG FOR MERCY?
OR ***WET*** MYSELF?
THIS WON'T EVEN BE THE FIRST TIME I'VE BEEN ***DEAD.***
ARROGANT TO THE END.
AND THIS ***IS*** THE END.
WHY BOTHER WITH ***HIM?*** IT'S ***ME*** YOU WANT.

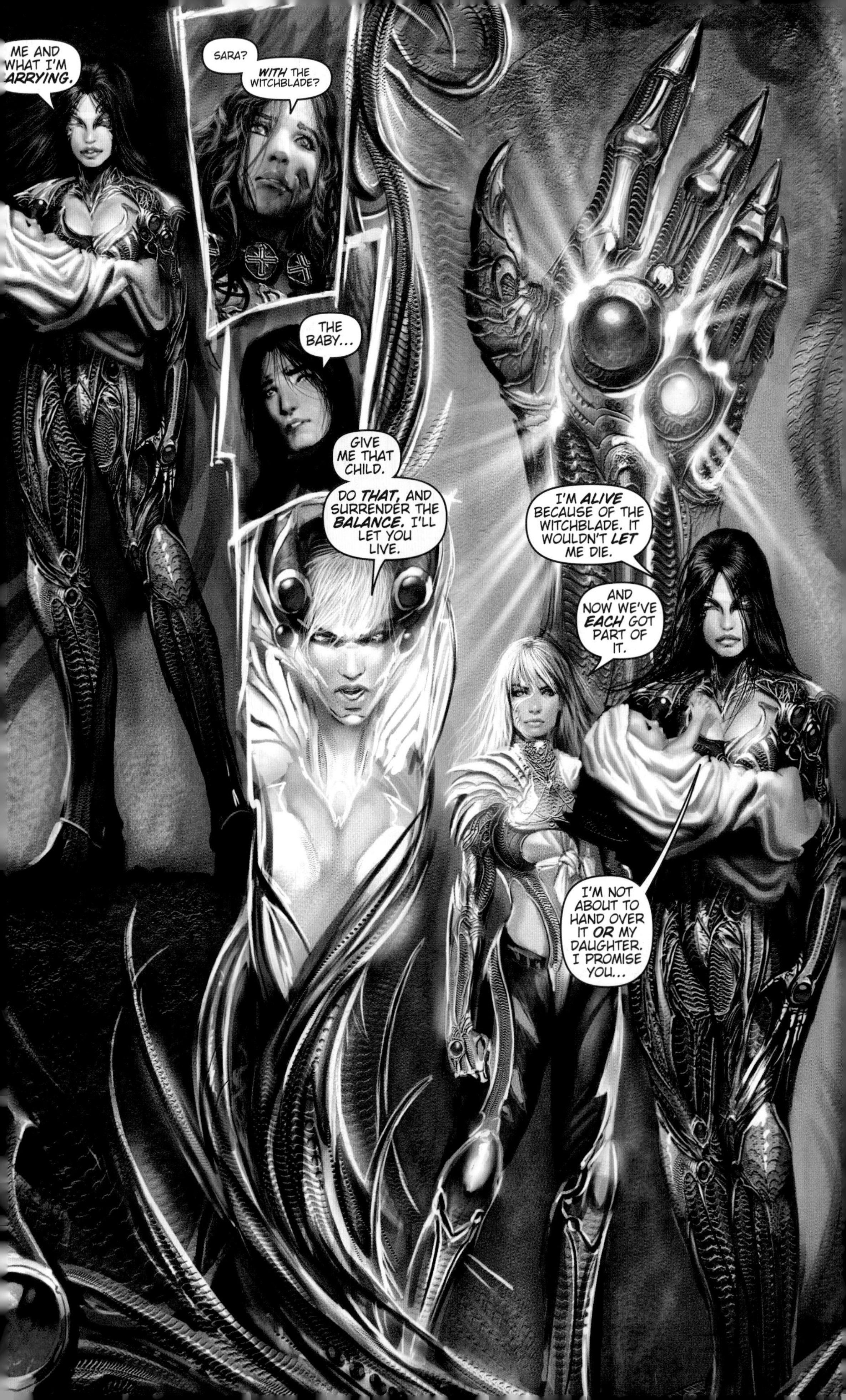
ME AND WHAT I'M ARRYING.
SARA? WITH THE WITCHBLADE?
THE BABY...
GIVE ME THAT CHILD.
DO THAT, AND SURRENDER THE BALANCE. I'LL LET YOU LIVE.
I'M ALIVE BECAUSE OF THE WITCHBLADE. IT WOULDN'T LET ME DIE.
AND NOW WE'VE EACH GOT PART OF IT.
I'M NOT ABOUT TO HAND OVER IT OR MY DAUGHTER. I PROMISE YOU...

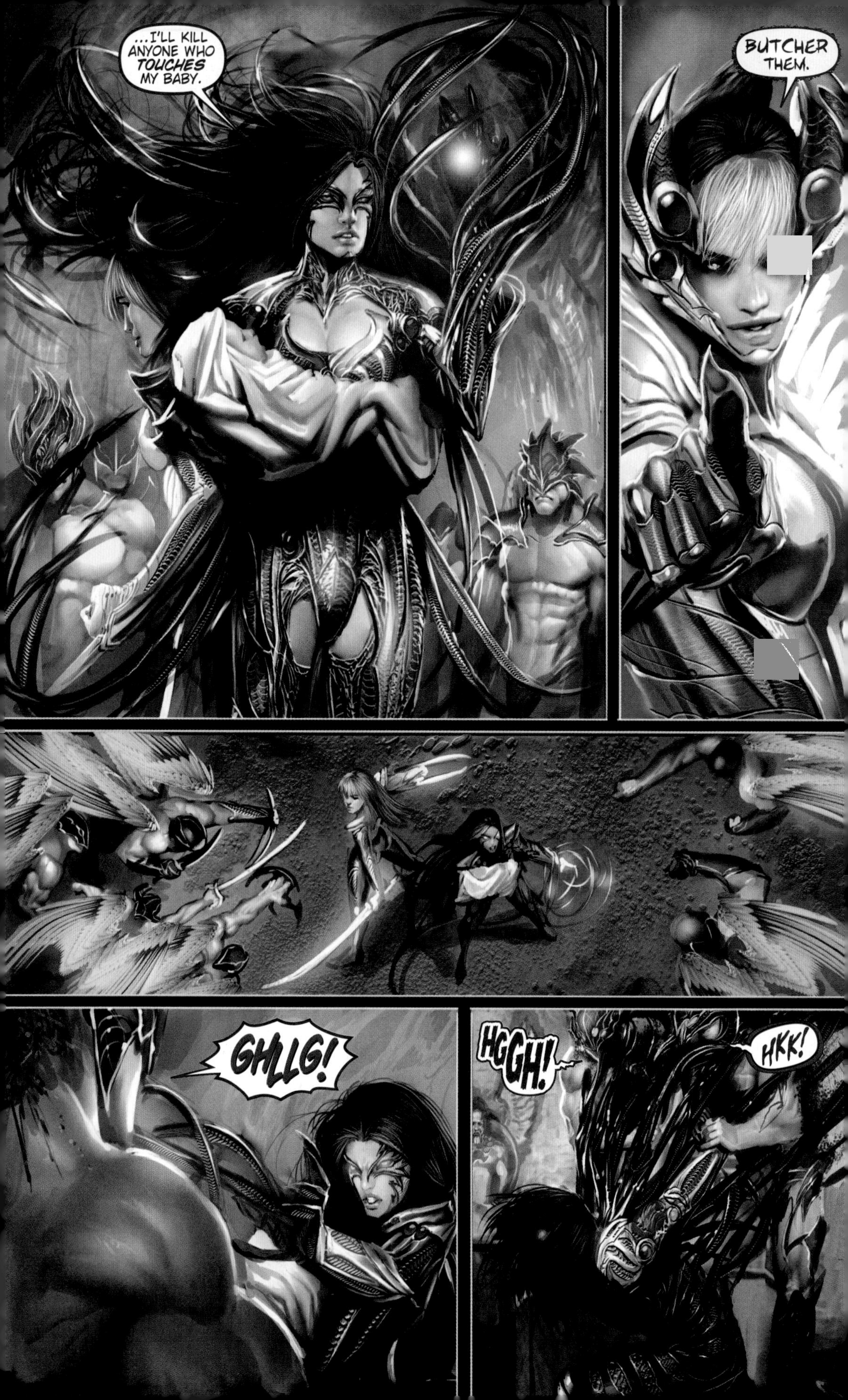
...I'LL KILL ANYONE WHO TOUCHES MY BABY.
BUTCHER THEM.
GHLLG!
HGGH!
HKK!

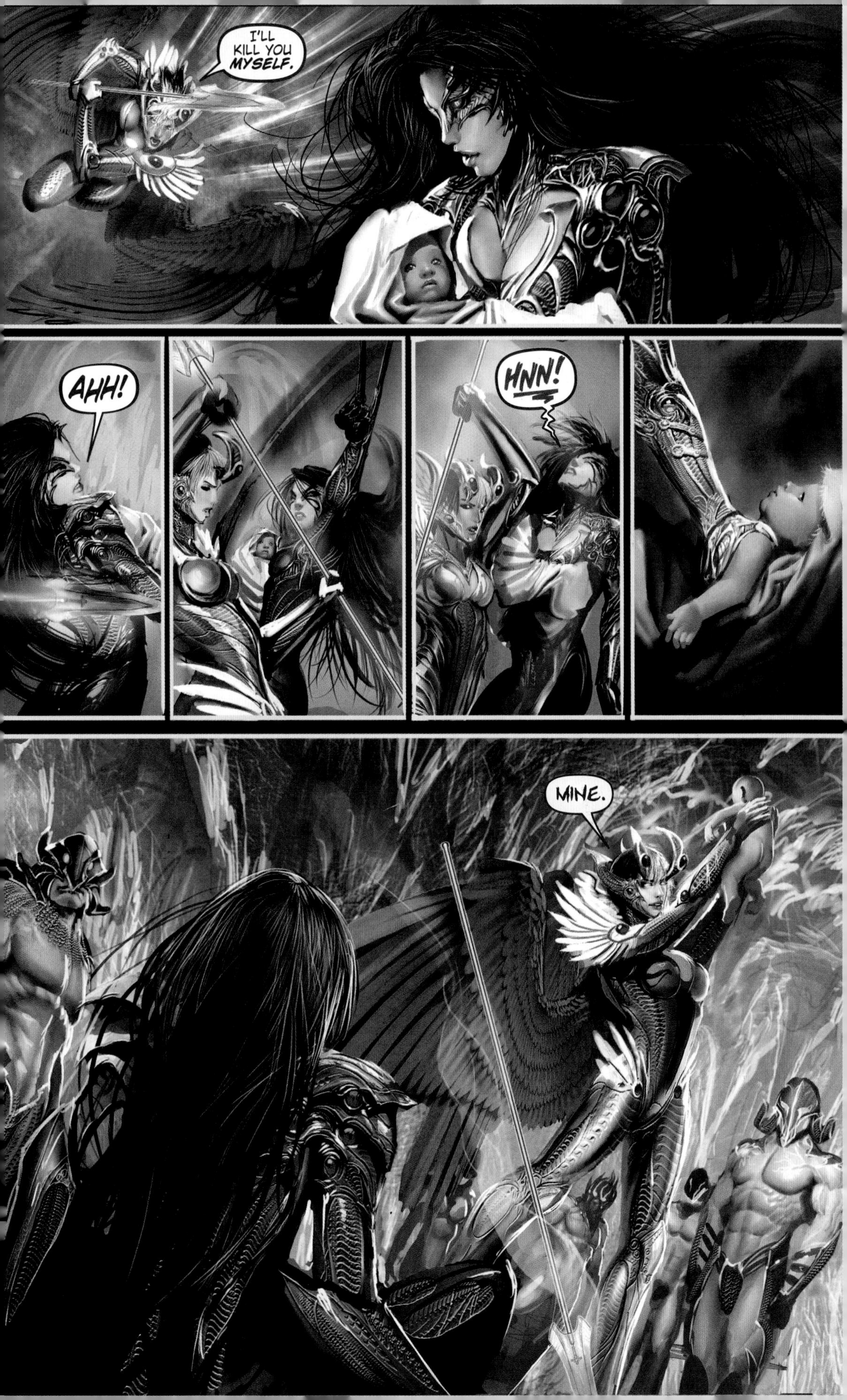
I'LL KILL YOU MYSELF.
AHH!
HNN!
MINE.

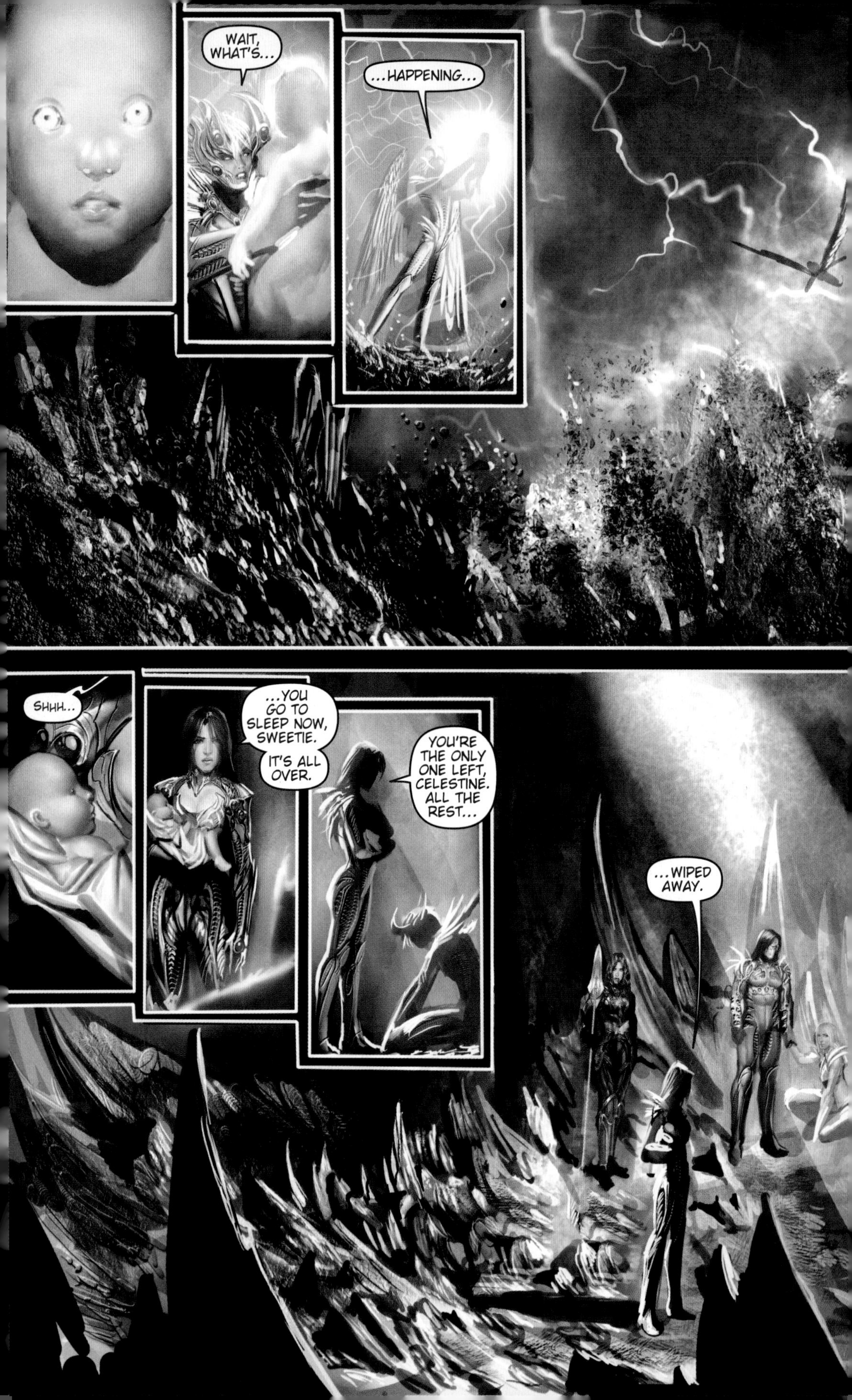
WAIT, WHAT'S...
...HAPPENING...
SHHH...
...YOU GO TO SLEEP NOW, SWEETIE.
IT'S ALL OVER.
YOU'RE THE ONLY ONE LEFT, CELESTINE. ALL THE REST...
...WIPED AWAY.

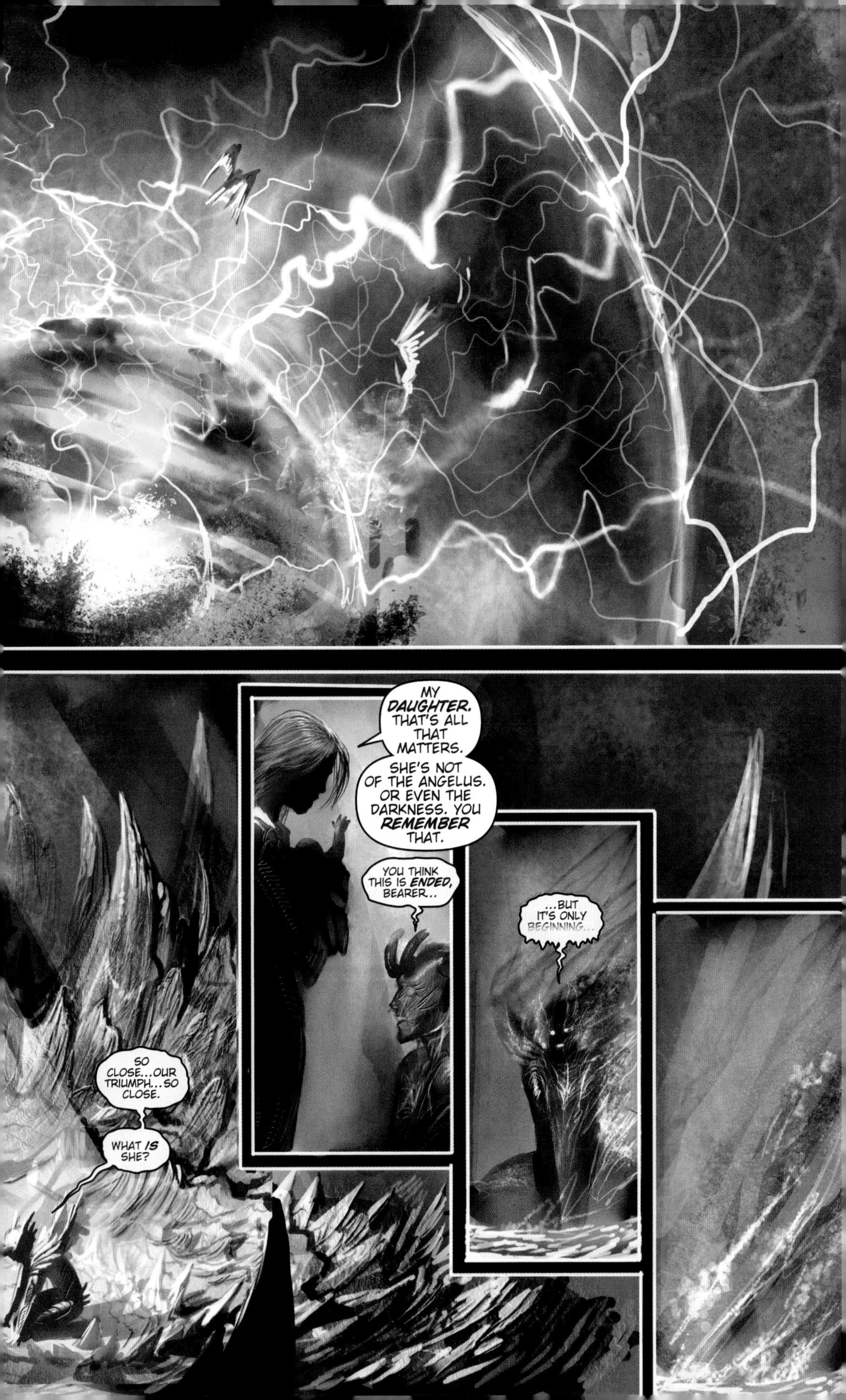
MY DAUGHTER. THAT'S ALL THAT MATTERS.
SHE'S NOT OF THE ANGELUS. OR EVEN THE DARKNESS. YOU REMEMBER THAT.
YOU THINK THIS IS ENDED, BEARER...
...BUT IT'S ONLY BEGINNING...
SO CLOSE...OUR TRIUMPH...SO CLOSE.
WHAT IS SHE?

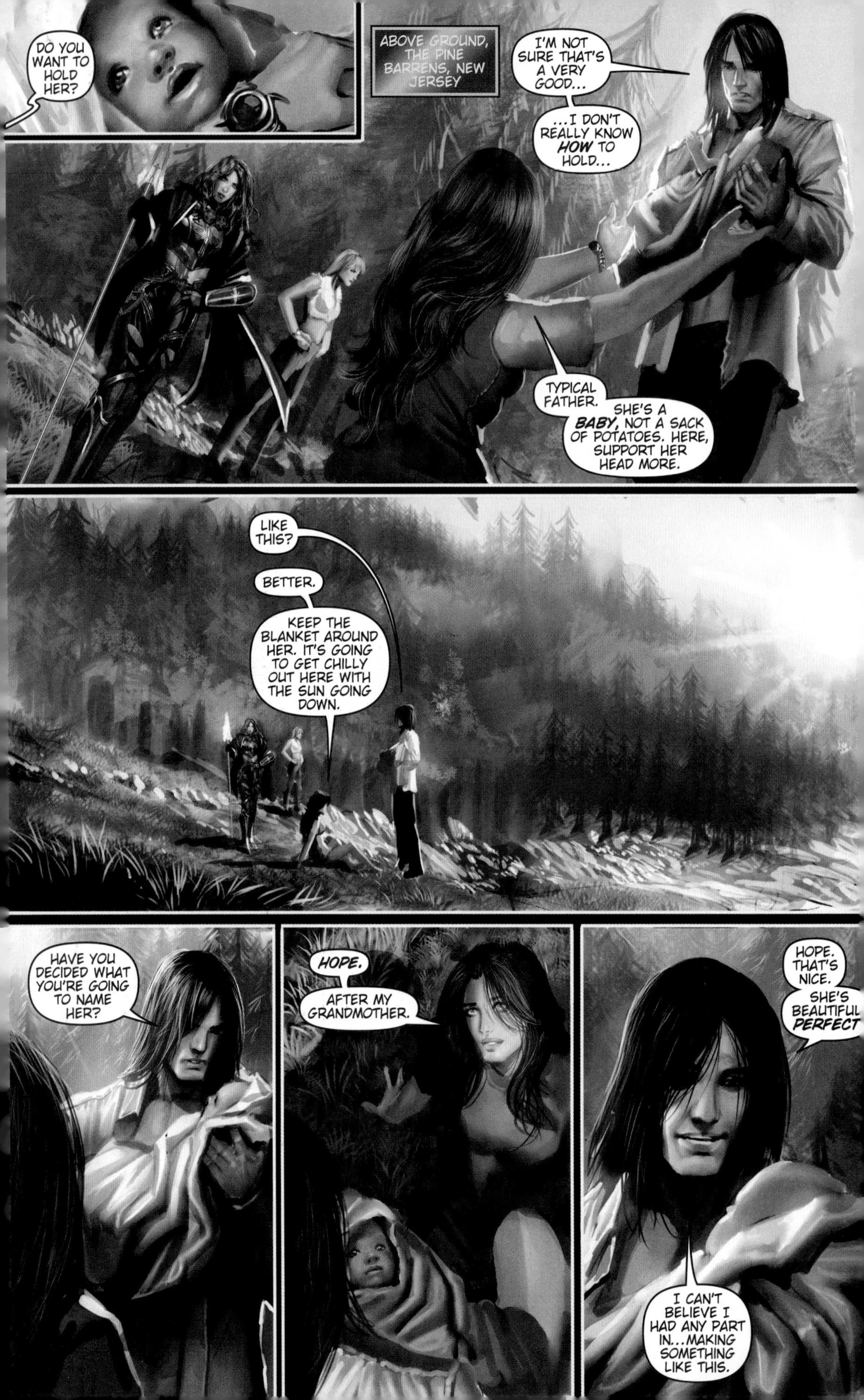
DO YOU WANT TO HOLD HER?
ABOVE GROUND, THE PINE BARRENS, NEW JERSEY
I'M NOT SURE THAT'S A VERY GOOD...
...I DON'T REALLY KNOW HOW TO HOLD...
TYPICAL FATHER.
SHE'S A BABY, NOT A SACK OF POTATOES. HERE, SUPPORT HER HEAD MORE.
LIKE THIS?
BETTER.
KEEP THE BLANKET AROUND HER. IT'S GOING TO GET CHILLY OUT HERE WITH THE SUN GOING DOWN.
HAVE YOU DECIDED WHAT YOU'RE GOING TO NAME HER?
HOPE.
AFTER MY GRANDMOTHER.
HOPE. THAT'S NICE.
SHE'S BEAUTIFUL PERFECT
I CAN'T BELIEVE I HAD ANY PART IN...MAKING SOMETHING LIKE THIS.

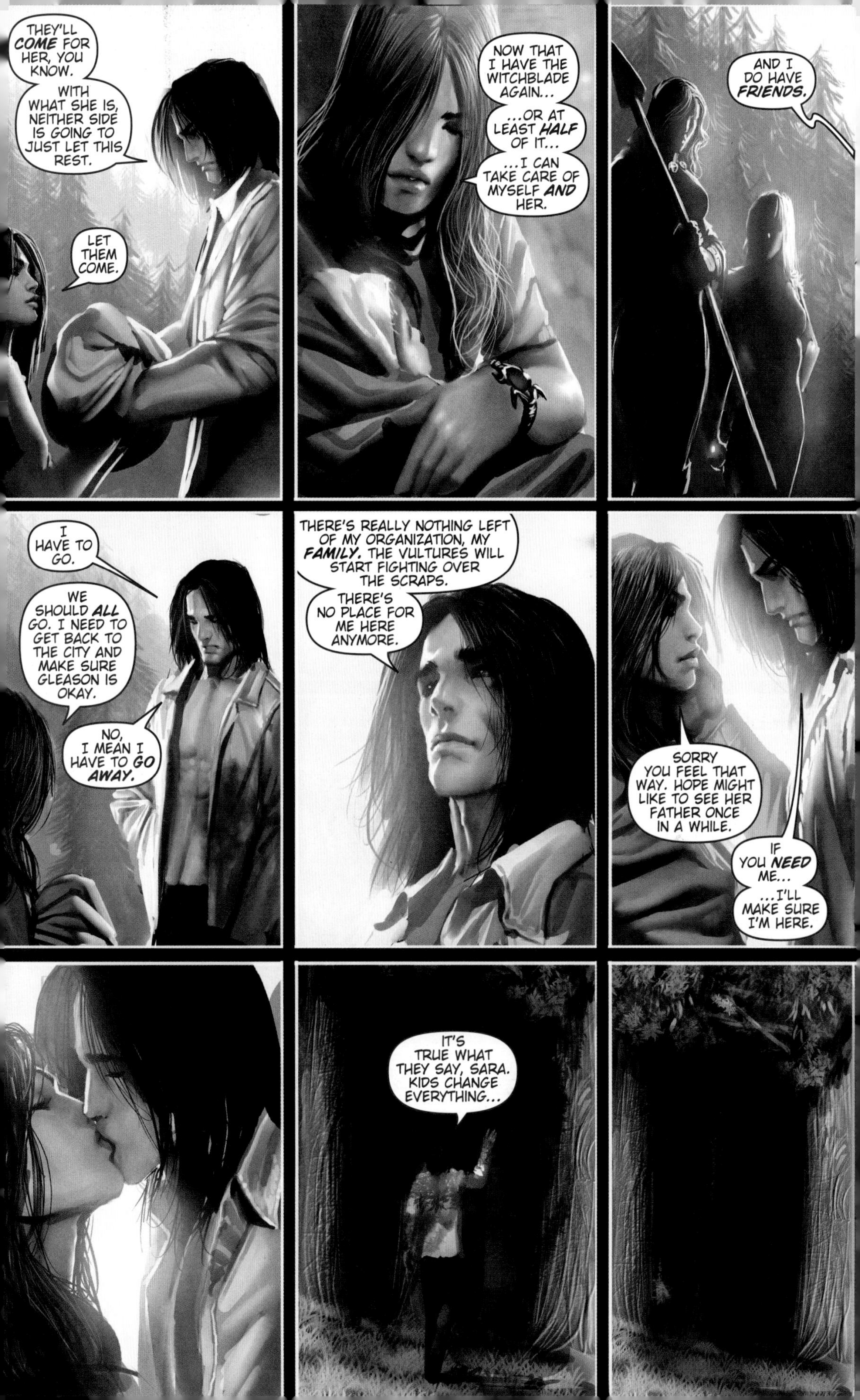
THEY'LL COME FOR HER, YOU KNOW.
WITH WHAT SHE IS, NEITHER SIDE IS GOING TO JUST LET THIS REST.
LET THEM COME.
NOW THAT I HAVE THE WITCHBLADE AGAIN...
...OR AT LEAST HALF OF IT...
...I CAN TAKE CARE OF MYSELF AND HER.
AND I DO HAVE FRIENDS.
I HAVE TO GO.
WE SHOULD ALL GO. I NEED TO GET BACK TO THE CITY AND MAKE SURE GLEASON IS OKAY.
NO, I MEAN I HAVE TO GO AWAY.
THERE'S REALLY NOTHING LEFT OF MY ORGANIZATION, MY FAMILY. THE VULTURES WILL START FIGHTING OVER THE SCRAPS.
THERE'S NO PLACE FOR ME HERE ANYMORE.
SORRY YOU FEEL THAT WAY. HOPE MIGHT LIKE TO SEE HER FATHER ONCE IN A WHILE.
IF YOU NEED ME...
...I'LL MAKE SURE I'M HERE.
IT'S TRUE WHAT THEY SAY, SARA. KIDS CHANGE EVERYTHING...

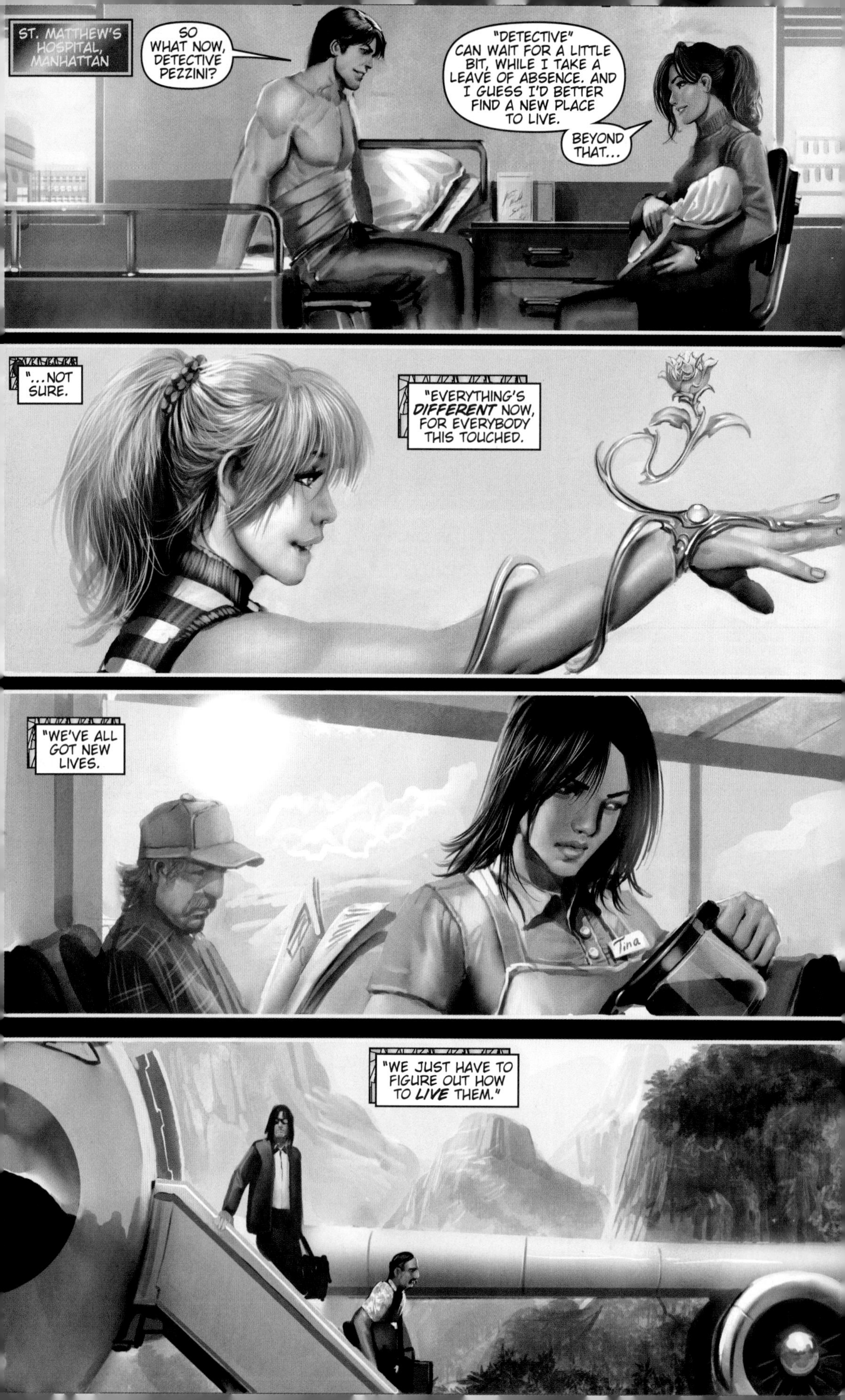

ST. MATTHEW'S HOSPITAL, MANHATTAN
SO WHAT NOW, DETECTIVE PEZZINI?
"DETECTIVE" CAN WAIT FOR A LITTLE BIT, WHILE I TAKE A LEAVE OF ABSENCE. AND I GUESS I'D BETTER FIND A NEW PLACE TO LIVE.
BEYOND THAT...
"...NOT SURE.
"EVERYTHING'S DIFFERENT NOW, FOR EVERYBODY THIS TOUCHED.
"WE'VE ALL GOT NEW LIVES.
Tina
"WE JUST HAVE TO FIGURE OUT HOW TO LIVE THEM."

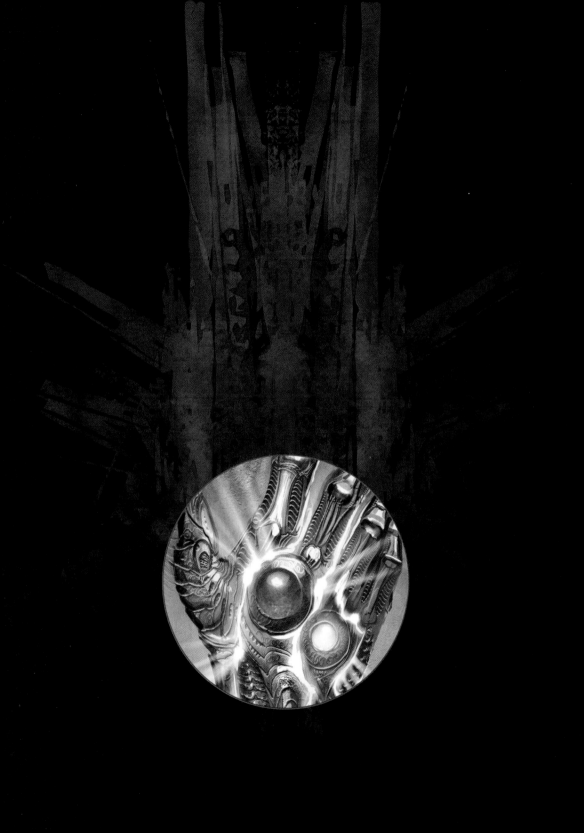

WITCHBLADE®

SHADOWS AND LIGHT, ISSUE #112

written by: **Ron Marz**
pencils by: **Rick Leonardi**
inks by: **Kevin Nowlan**
colors by: **Dave McCaig**
letters by: **Troy Peteri**

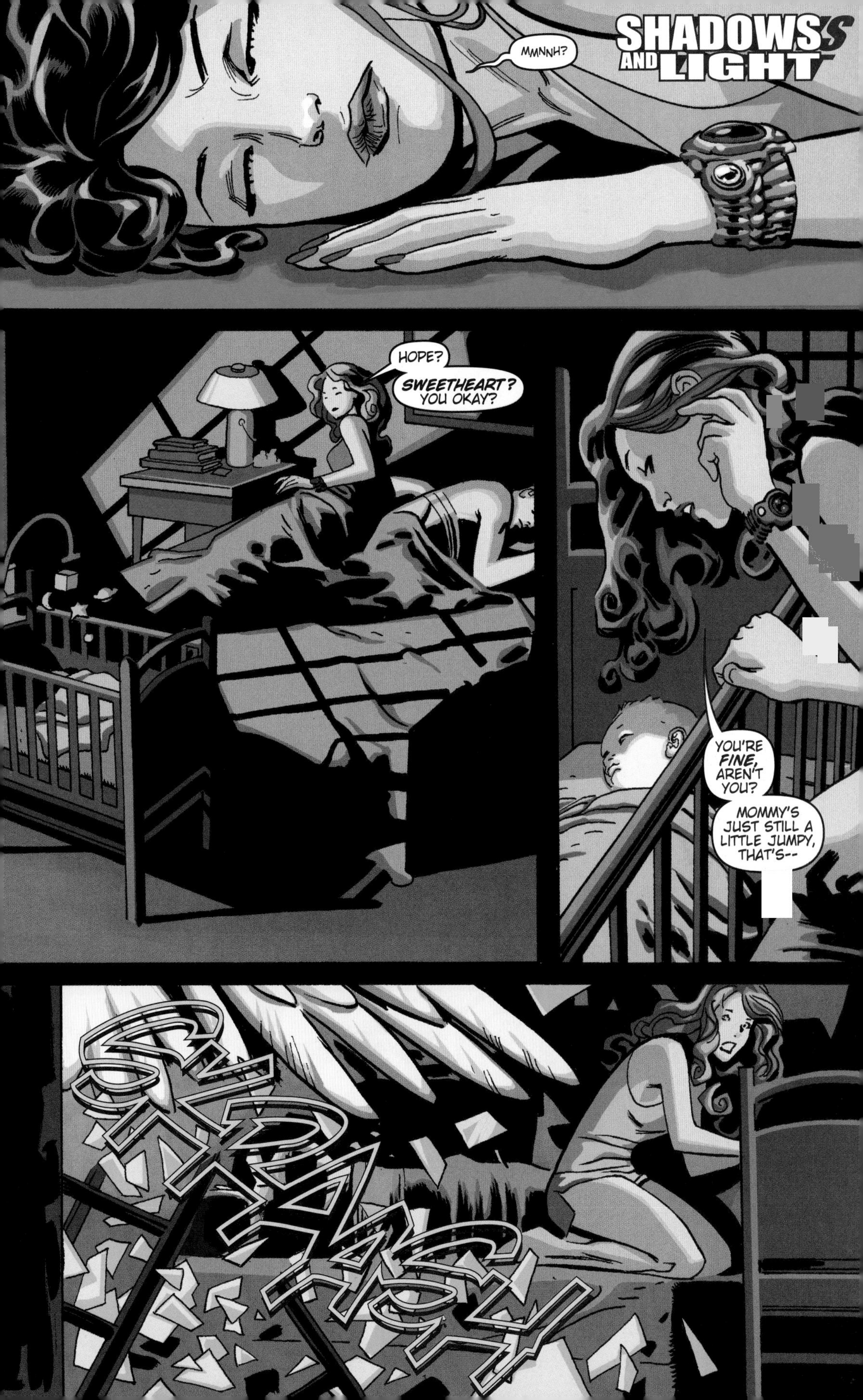
SHADOWS AND LIGHT
MMNNH?
HOPE?
SWEETHEART? YOU OKAY?
YOU'RE FINE, AREN'T YOU?
MOMMY'S JUST STILL A LITTLE JUMPY, THAT'S--

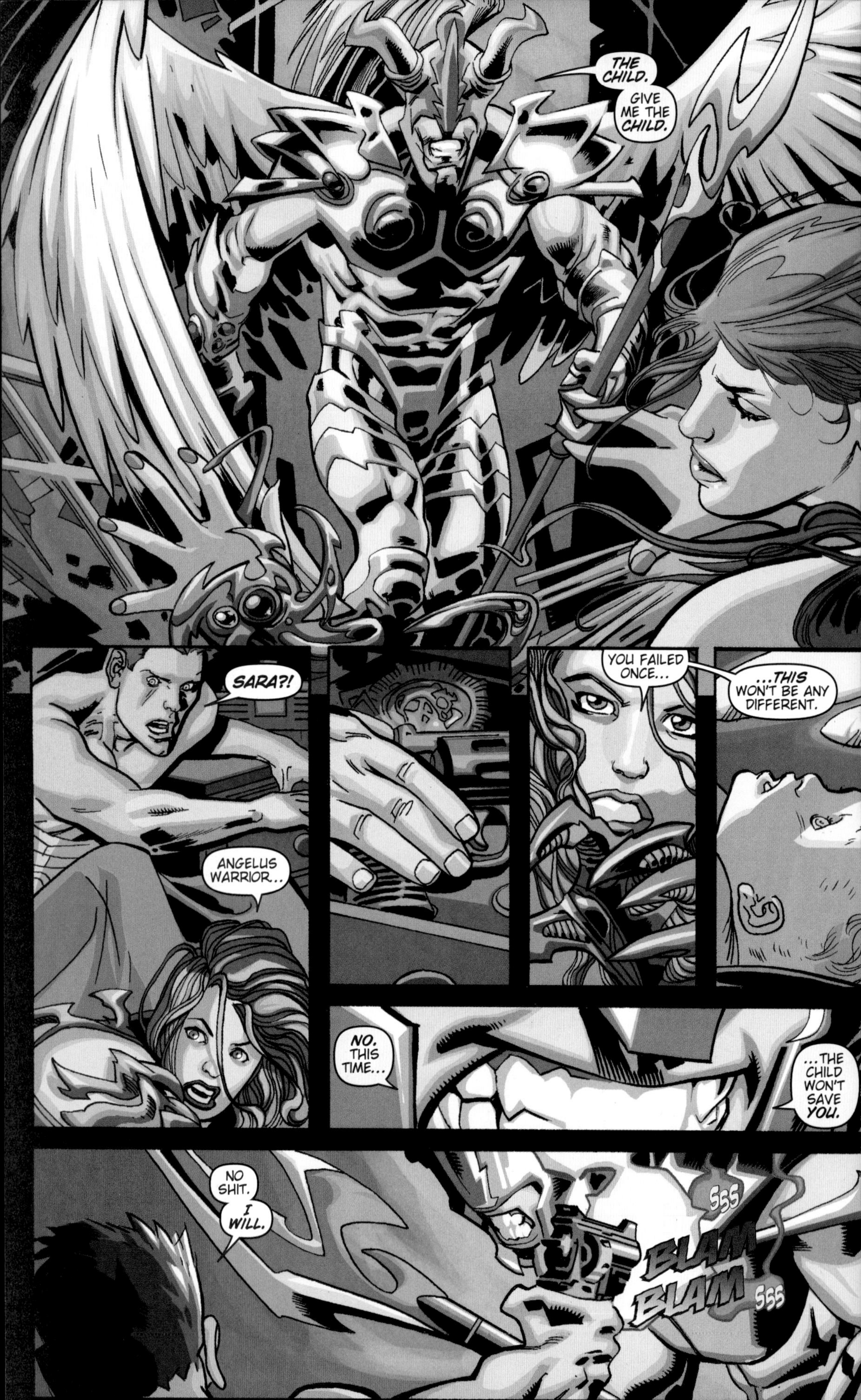
THE CHILD.
GIVE ME THE CHILD.
SARA?!
ANGELUS WARRIOR...
YOU FAILED ONCE...
...THIS WON'T BE ANY DIFFERENT.
NO. THIS TIME...
...THE CHILD WON'T SAVE YOU.
NO SHIT. I WILL.
SSS
BLAM
BLAM
SSS

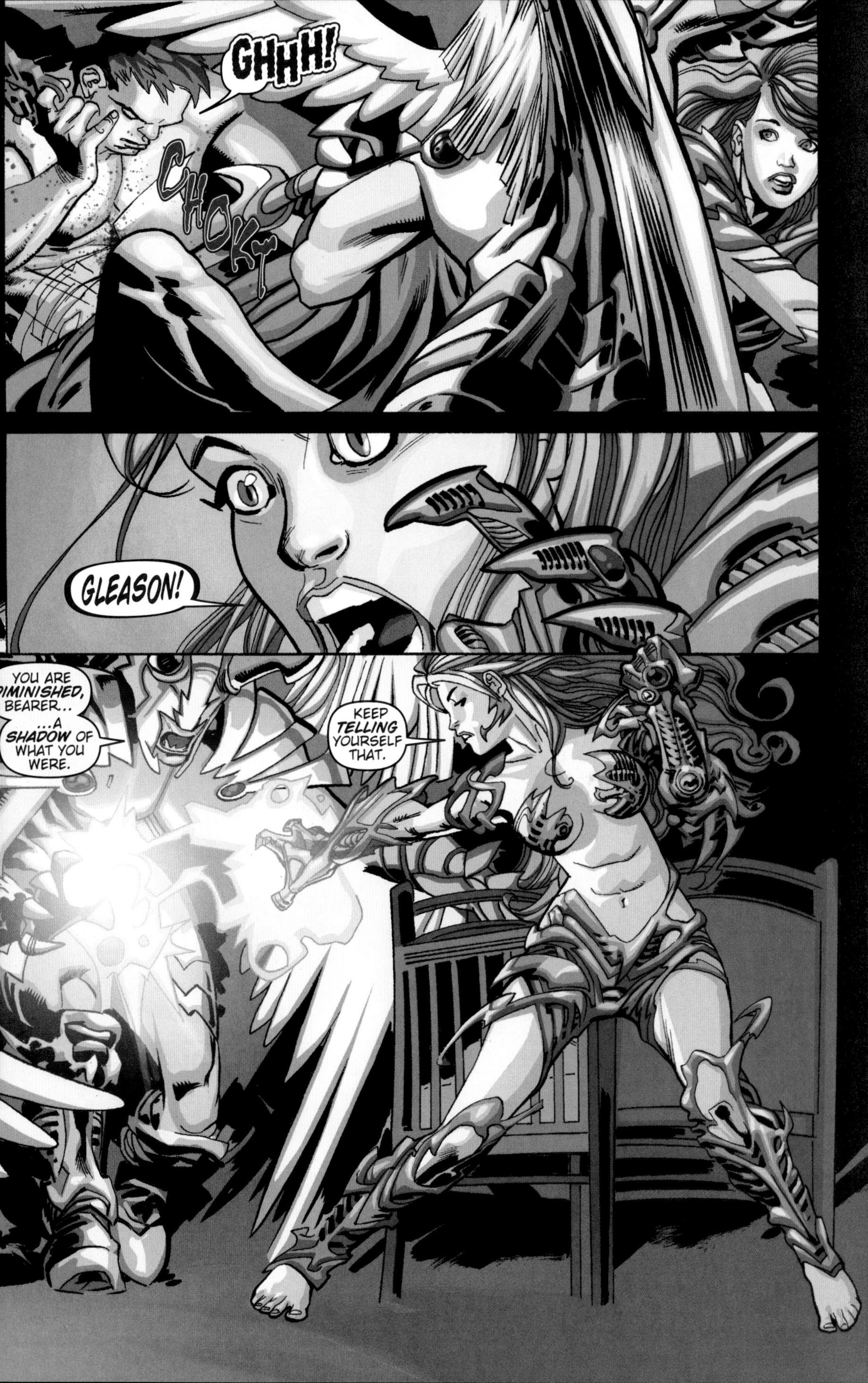
GHHH!
CHOKT
GLEASON!
YOU ARE DIMINISHED, BEARER...
...A SHADOW OF WHAT YOU WERE.
KEEP TELLING YOURSELF THAT.

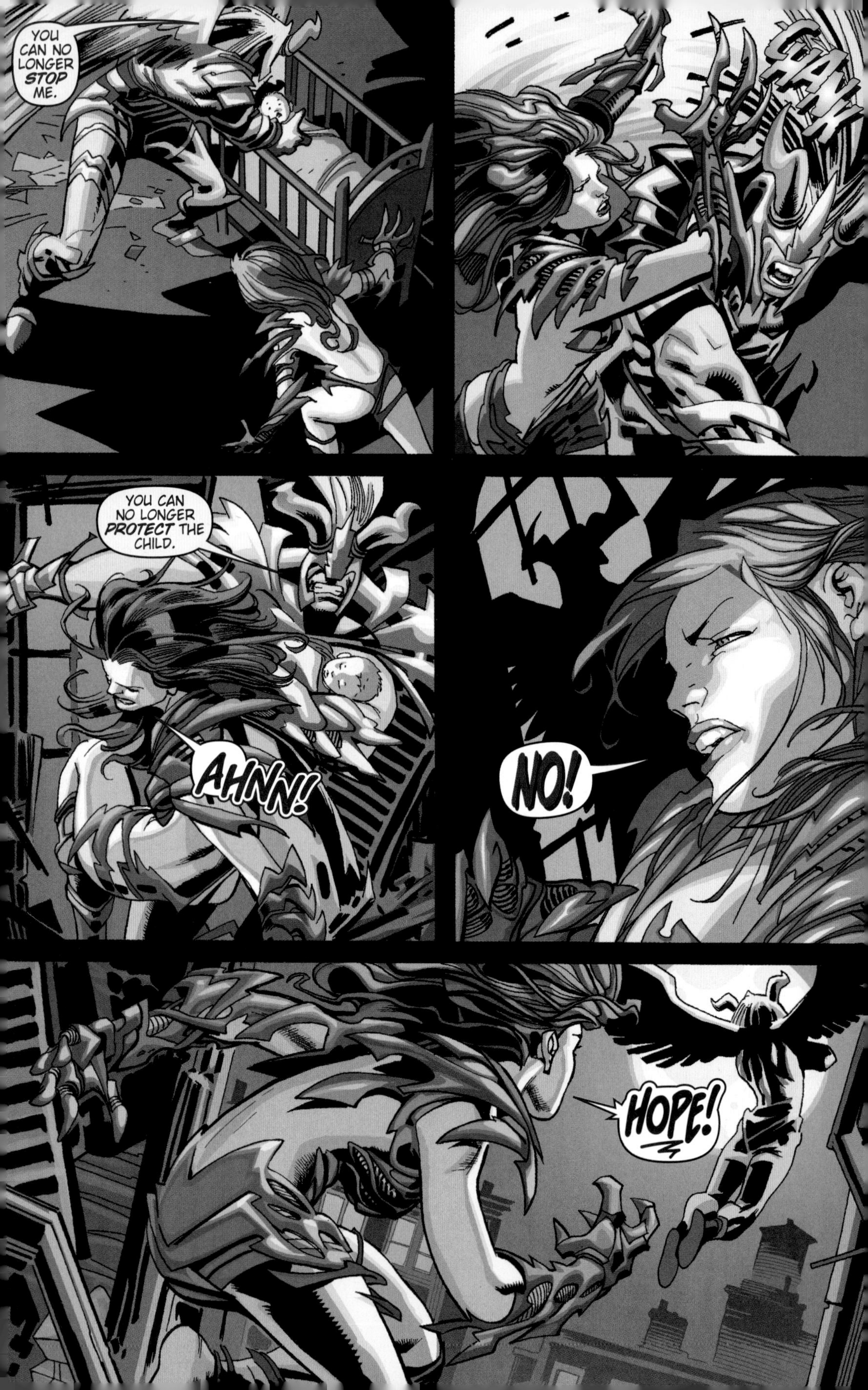
YOU CAN NO LONGER STOP ME.
YOU CAN NO LONGER PROTECT THE CHILD.
AHNN!
NO!
HOPE!

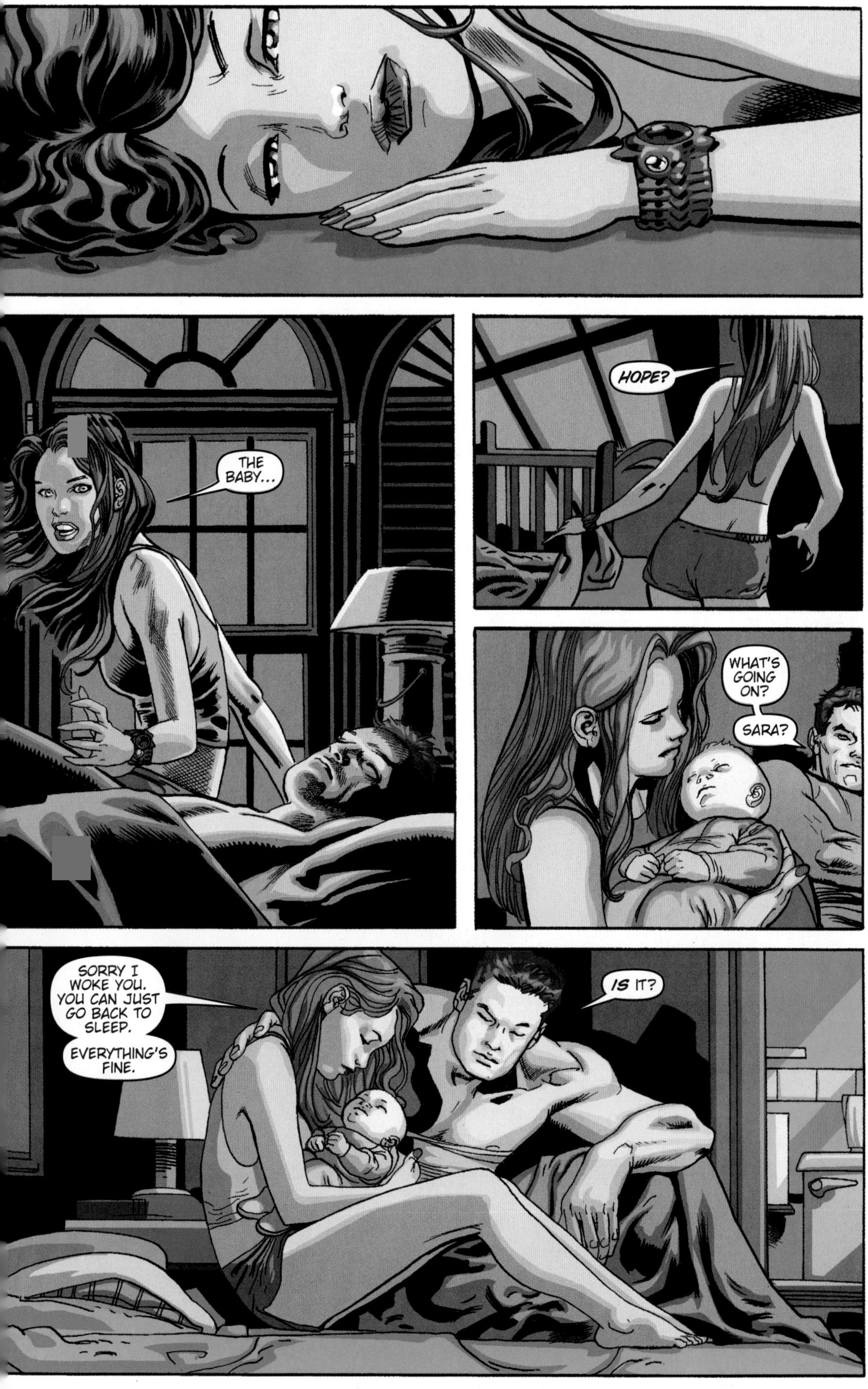
THE BABY...
HOPE?
WHAT'S GOING ON?
SARA?
SORRY I WOKE YOU. YOU CAN JUST GO BACK TO SLEEP.
EVERYTHING'S FINE.
IS IT?

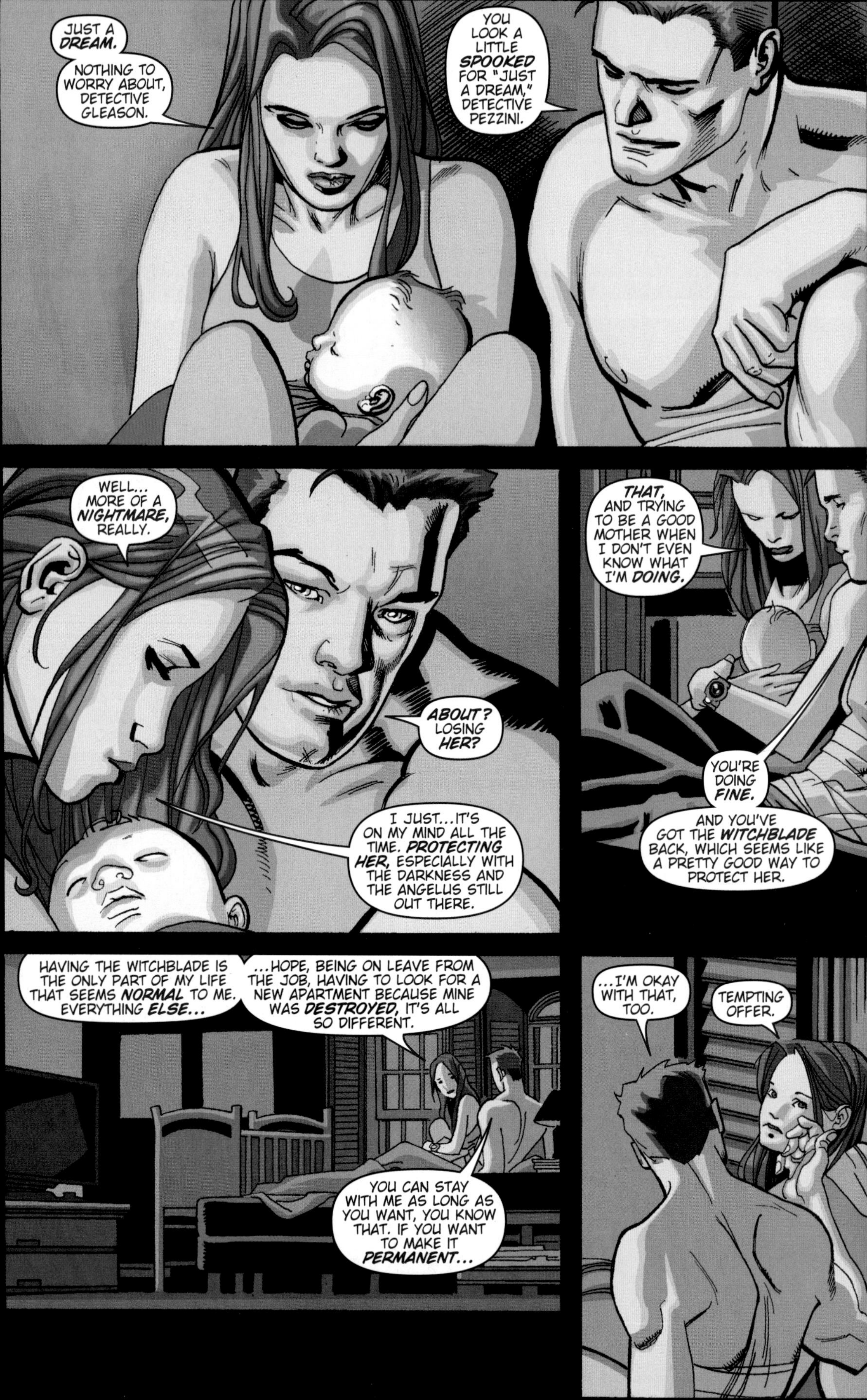
JUST A DREAM.
NOTHING TO WORRY ABOUT, DETECTIVE GLEASON.
YOU LOOK A LITTLE SPOOKED FOR "JUST A DREAM," DETECTIVE PEZZINI.
WELL... MORE OF A NIGHTMARE, REALLY.
ABOUT? LOSING HER?
I JUST...IT'S ON MY MIND ALL THE TIME. PROTECTING HER, ESPECIALLY WITH THE DARKNESS AND THE ANGELUS STILL OUT THERE.
THAT, AND TRYING TO BE A GOOD MOTHER WHEN I DON'T EVEN KNOW WHAT I'M DOING.
YOU'RE DOING FINE.
AND YOU'VE GOT THE WITCHBLADE BACK, WHICH SEEMS LIKE A PRETTY GOOD WAY TO PROTECT HER.
HAVING THE WITCHBLADE IS THE ONLY PART OF MY LIFE THAT SEEMS NORMAL TO ME. EVERYTHING ELSE...
...HOPE, BEING ON LEAVE FROM THE JOB, HAVING TO LOOK FOR A NEW APARTMENT BECAUSE MINE WAS DESTROYED, IT'S ALL SO DIFFERENT.
YOU CAN STAY WITH ME AS LONG AS YOU WANT, YOU KNOW THAT. IF YOU WANT TO MAKE IT PERMANENT...
...I'M OKAY WITH THAT, TOO.
TEMPTING OFFER.

I'M EVEN GETTING USED TO THE *TOILET SEAT* BEING LEFT UP ALL THE TIME.

BUT I FEEL LIKE I NEED MY OWN PLACE, AT LEAST FOR *NOW*. I NEED TO HAVE CONTROL OF MY LIFE AGAIN.

AND THAT MEANS FIGURING OUT MY LIFE WITH *HER* BEFORE ANYTHING ELSE.

I KNOW. NO PRESSURE.

BUT IT *IS* NICE HAVING YOU AROUND...

...HAVING YOU IN THE SAME BED.

EASY, FELLA. NOT QUITE OPEN FOR BUSINESS YET. SOON, THOUGH.

HEY, I'M A PATIENT MAN.

ANY PLANS FOR TOMORROW?

JUST TAKE SLEEPING BEAUTY HERE FOR A WALK...

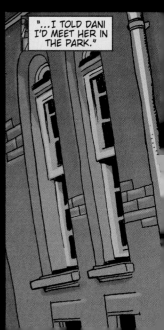

"...I TOLD DANI I'D MEET HER IN THE PARK."

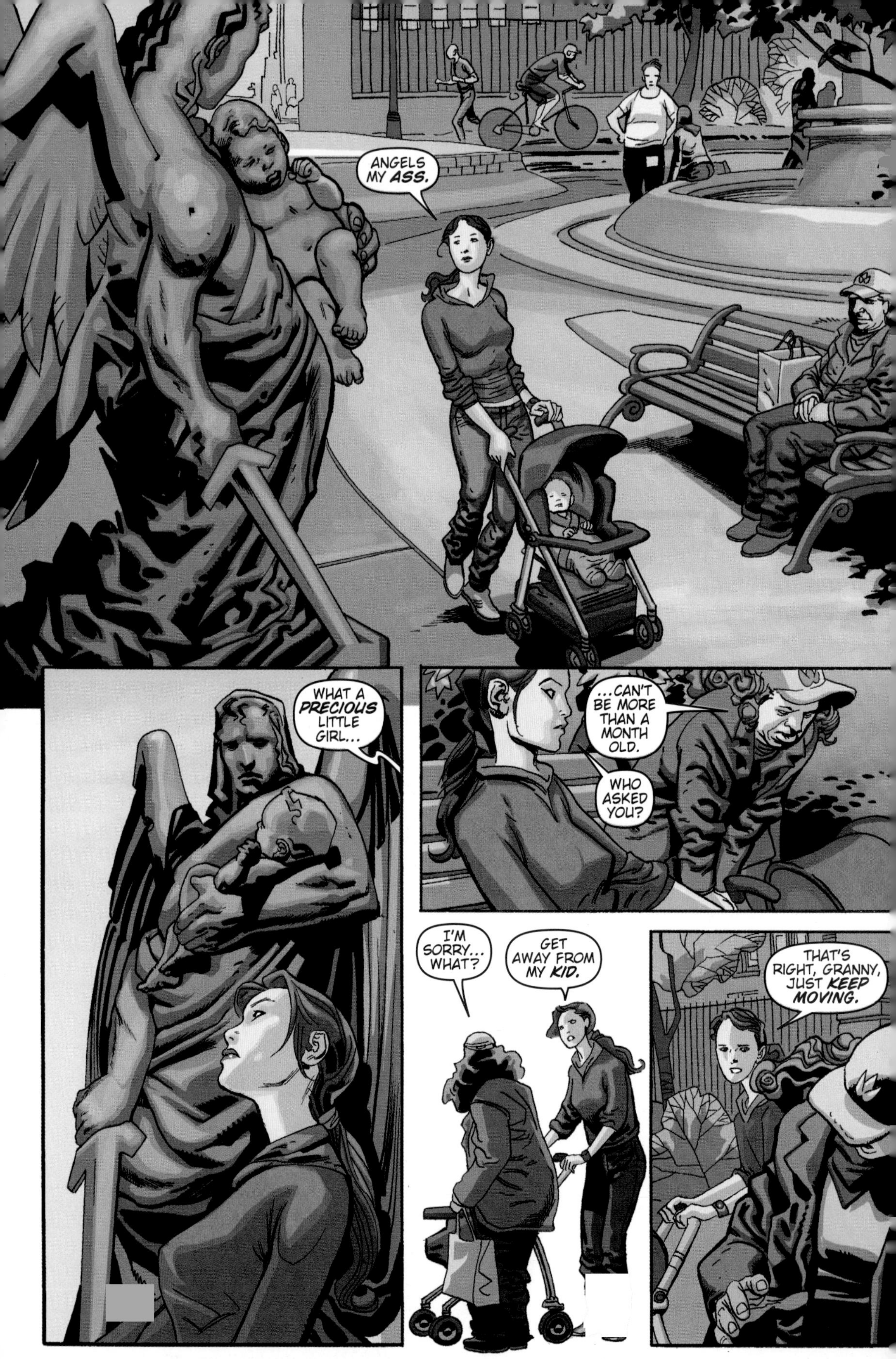
ANGELS MY ASS.
WHAT A PRECIOUS LITTLE GIRL...
...CAN'T BE MORE THAN A MONTH OLD.
WHO ASKED YOU?
I'M SORRY... WHAT?
GET AWAY FROM MY KID.
THAT'S RIGHT, GRANNY, JUST KEEP MOVING.

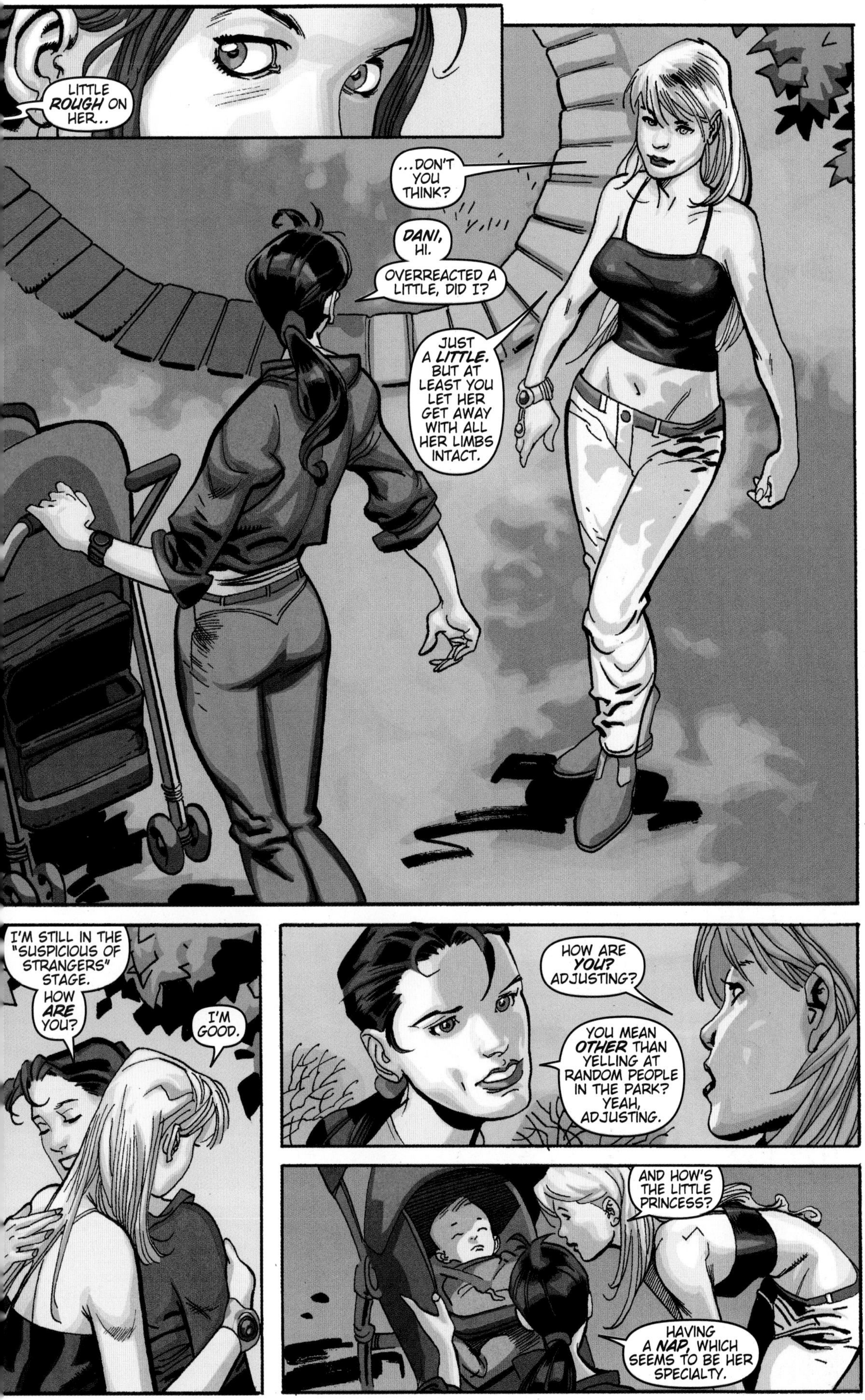
LITTLE ROUGH ON HER...
...DON'T YOU THINK?
DANI, HI.
OVERREACTED A LITTLE, DID I?
JUST A LITTLE. BUT AT LEAST YOU LET HER GET AWAY WITH ALL HER LIMBS INTACT.
I'M STILL IN THE "SUSPICIOUS OF STRANGERS" STAGE.
HOW ARE YOU?
I'M GOOD.
HOW ARE YOU? ADJUSTING?
YOU MEAN OTHER THAN YELLING AT RANDOM PEOPLE IN THE PARK? YEAH, ADJUSTING.
AND HOW'S THE LITTLE PRINCESS?
HAVING A NAP, WHICH SEEMS TO BE HER SPECIALTY.

FOR YOU. WELL, FOR *HOPE*, ACTUALLY, BUT I'LL LET YOU OPEN IT.

YOU HELPED BRING HER *INTO* THE WORLD, YOU DIDN'T HAVE TO DO THIS.

SHUSH, JUST OPEN IT.

OH, DANI, IT'S *BEAUTIFUL.*

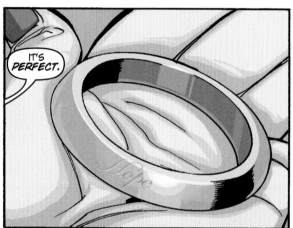

IT'S *PERFECT.*

YOU TELL HER IT'S FROM HER AUNTIE DANI, OKAY?

YOU BET. NOW I FEEL BAD FOR *HATING YOU* WHEN WE FIRST MET.

SO TELL ME *EVERYTHING.*

WELL, I CAN TELL YOU SORE NIPPLES ARE A REAL JOY.

THAT'S LOVELY.

SERIOUSLY, THIS IS THE *HARDEST* THING I'VE EVER DONE. AND THE *BEST,* NO CONTEST.

YOU KNOW HOW EVERYBODY SAYS IT CHANGES YOU? IT DOES, *COMPLETELY.*

YOU DON'T LIVE YOUR LIFE FOR *YOURSELF* ANYMORE, IT'S ALL ABOUT YOUR CHILD. IF I HAD TO STEP OUT IN FRONT OF *BUS* TO MAKE SURE SHE WAS SAFE, I'D DO IT WITHOUT THINKING TWICE.

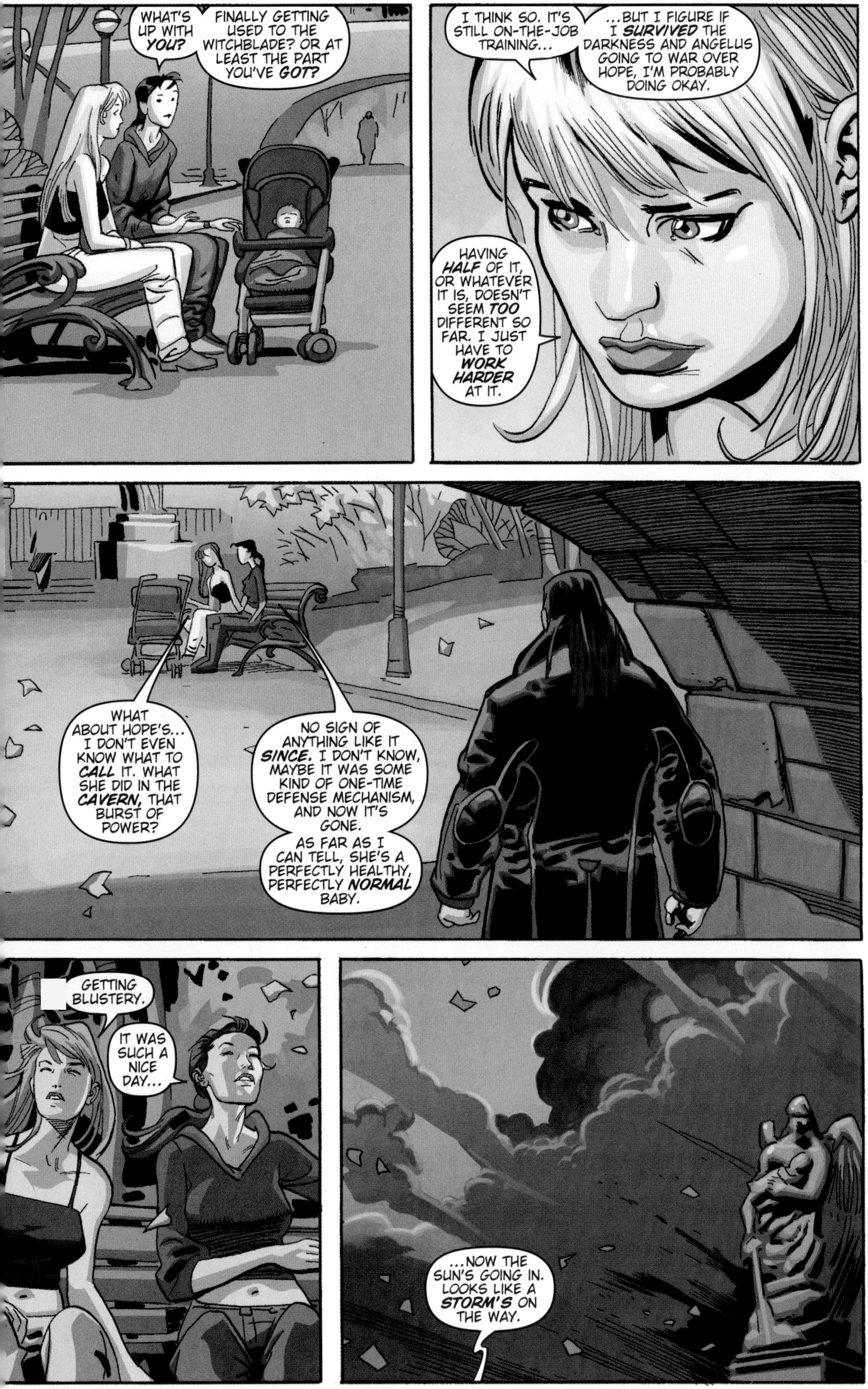
WHAT'S UP WITH YOU?
FINALLY GETTING USED TO THE WITCHBLADE? OR AT LEAST THE PART YOU'VE GOT?
I THINK SO. IT'S STILL ON-THE-JOB TRAINING...
...BUT I FIGURE IF I SURVIVED THE DARKNESS AND ANGELUS GOING TO WAR OVER HOPE, I'M PROBABLY DOING OKAY.
HAVING HALF OF IT, OR WHATEVER IT IS, DOESN'T SEEM TOO DIFFERENT SO FAR. I JUST HAVE TO WORK HARDER AT IT.
WHAT ABOUT HOPE'S... I DON'T EVEN KNOW WHAT TO CALL IT. WHAT SHE DID IN THE CAVERN, THAT BURST OF POWER?
NO SIGN OF ANYTHING LIKE IT SINCE. I DON'T KNOW, MAYBE IT WAS SOME KIND OF ONE-TIME DEFENSE MECHANISM, AND NOW IT'S GONE.
AS FAR AS I CAN TELL, SHE'S A PERFECTLY HEALTHY, PERFECTLY NORMAL BABY.
GETTING BLUSTERY.
IT WAS SUCH A NICE DAY...
...NOW THE SUN'S GOING IN. LOOKS LIKE A STORM'S ON THE WAY.

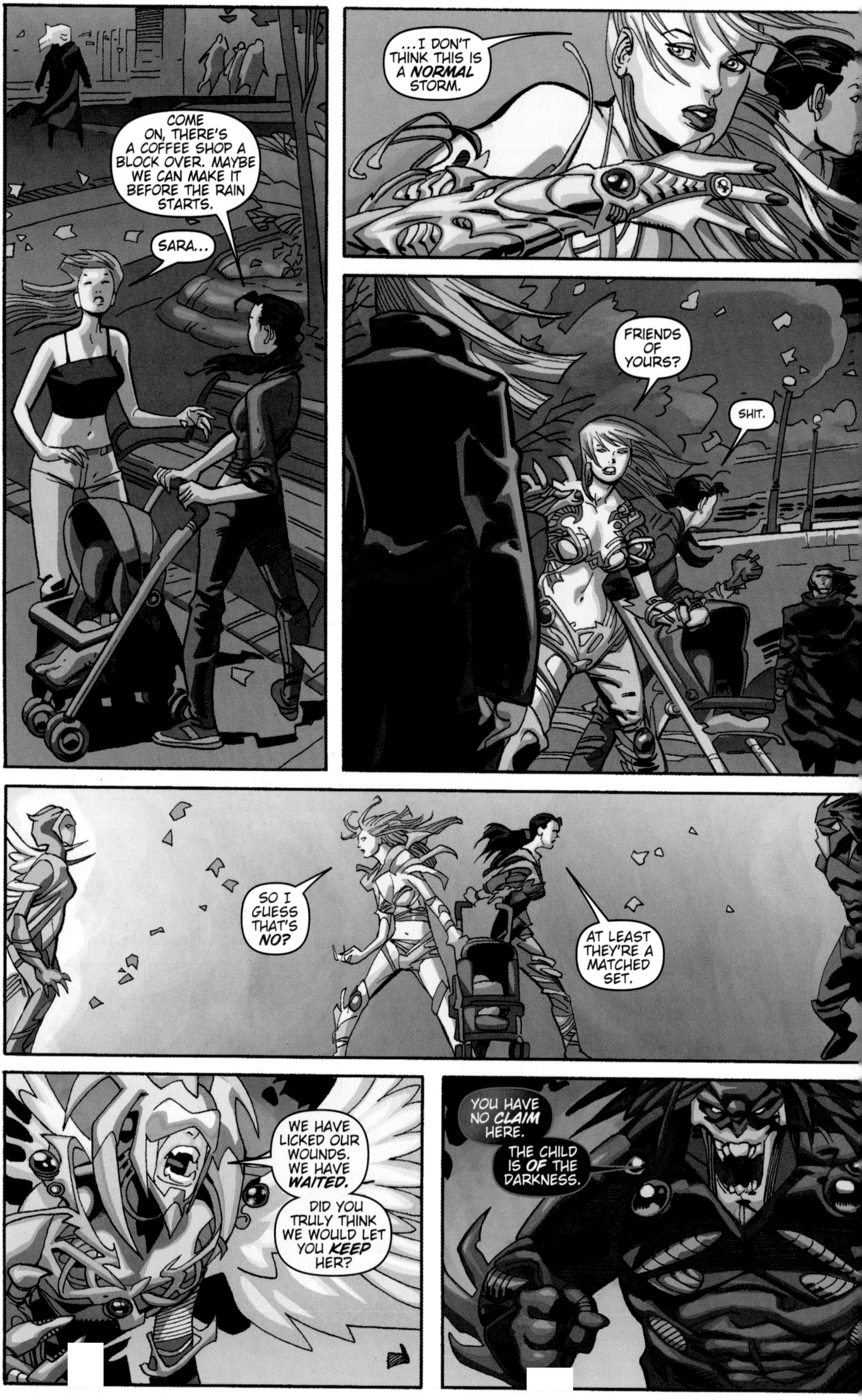
COME ON, THERE'S A COFFEE SHOP A BLOCK OVER. MAYBE WE CAN MAKE IT BEFORE THE RAIN STARTS.
SARA...
...I DON'T THINK THIS IS A NORMAL STORM.
FRIENDS OF YOURS?
SHIT.
SO I GUESS THAT'S NO?
AT LEAST THEY'RE A MATCHED SET.
WE HAVE LICKED OUR WOUNDS. WE HAVE WAITED.
DID YOU TRULY THINK WE WOULD LET YOU KEEP HER?
YOU HAVE NO CLAIM HERE.
THE CHILD IS OF THE DARKNESS.

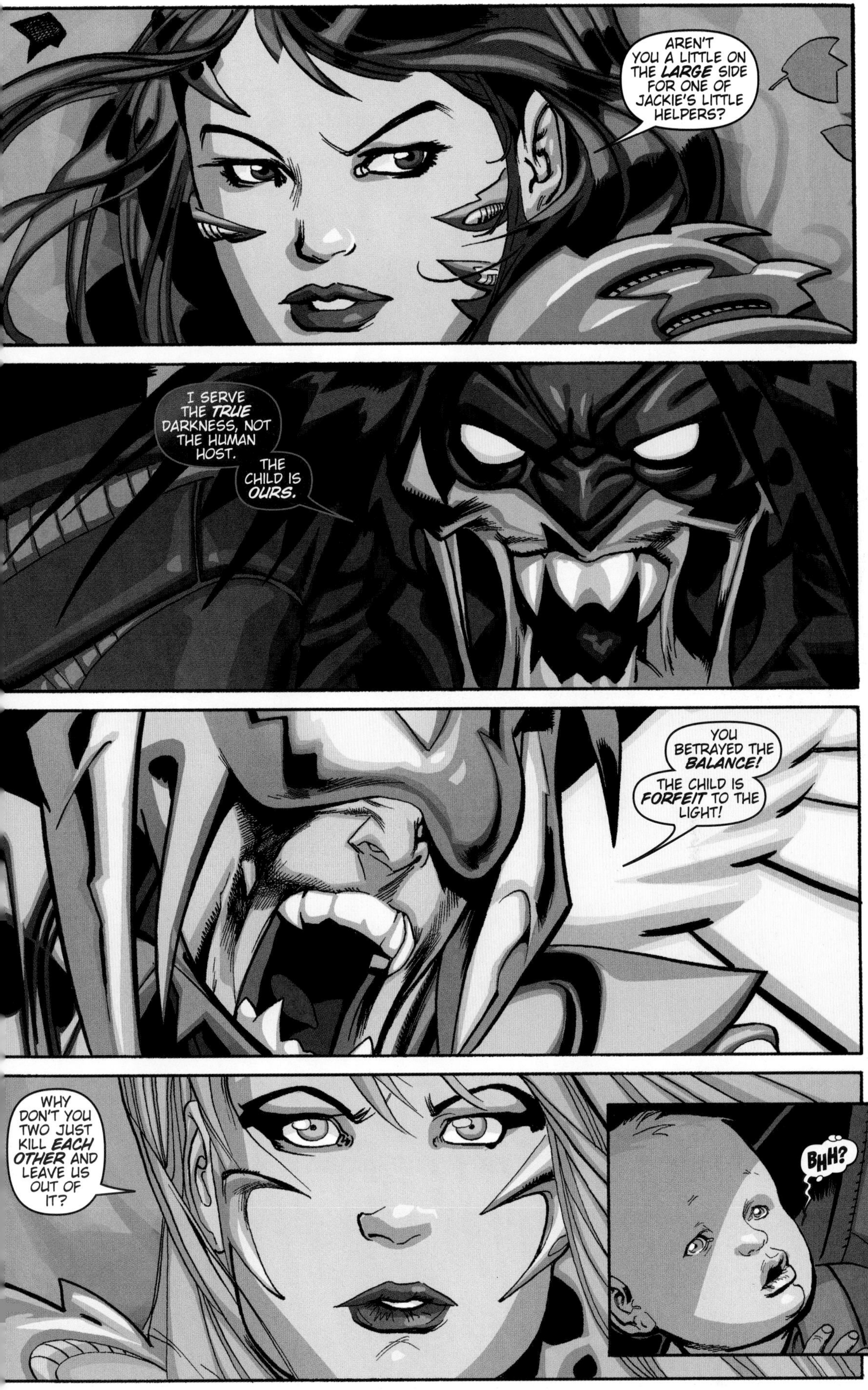
AREN'T YOU A LITTLE ON THE LARGE SIDE FOR ONE OF JACKIE'S LITTLE HELPERS?
I SERVE THE TRUE DARKNESS, NOT THE HUMAN HOST.
THE CHILD IS OURS.
YOU BETRAYED THE BALANCE!
THE CHILD IS FORFEIT TO THE LIGHT!
WHY DON'T YOU TWO JUST KILL EACH OTHER AND LEAVE US OUT OF IT?
BHH?

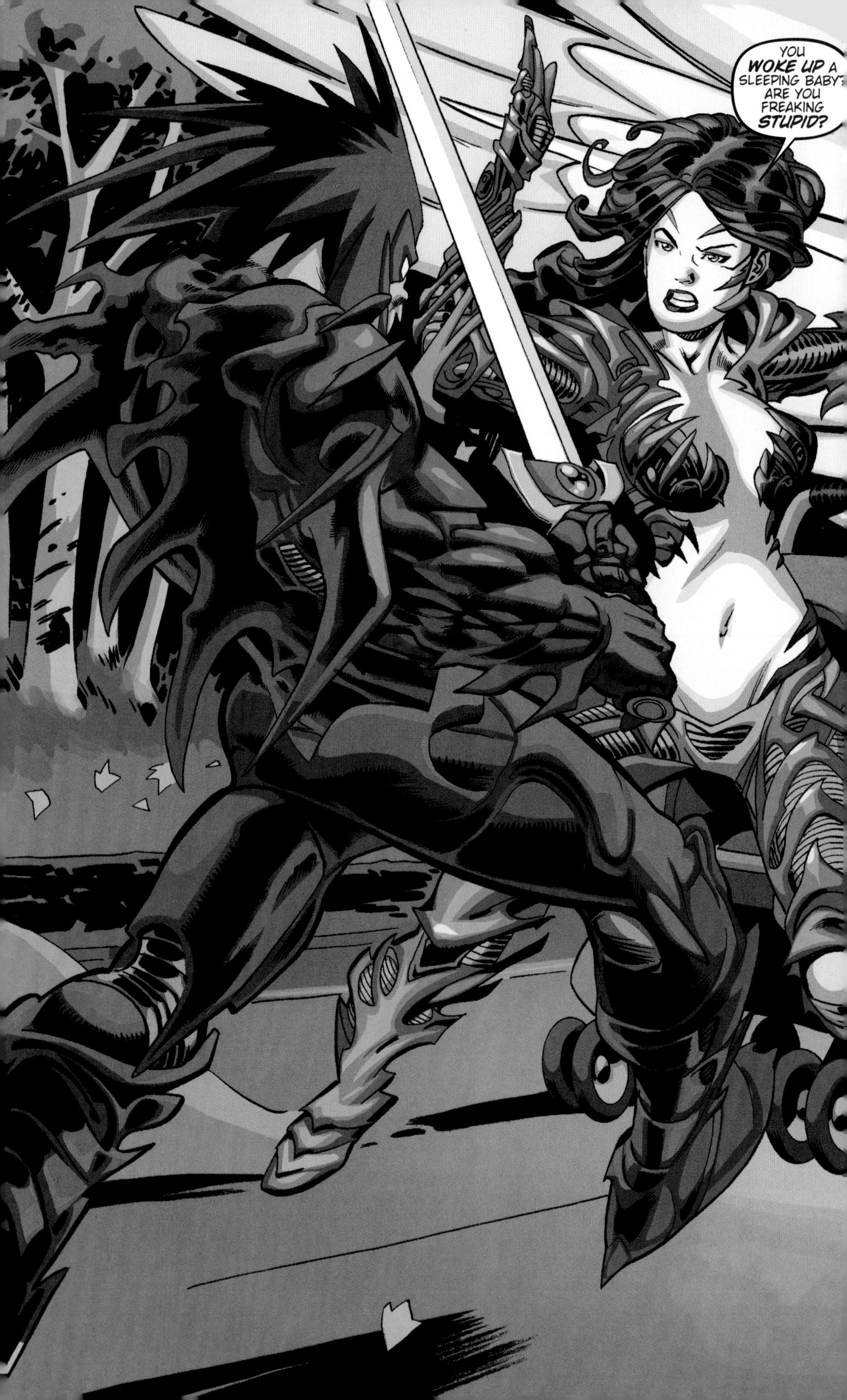
YOU WOKE UP A SLEEPING BABY? ARE YOU FREAKING STUPID?

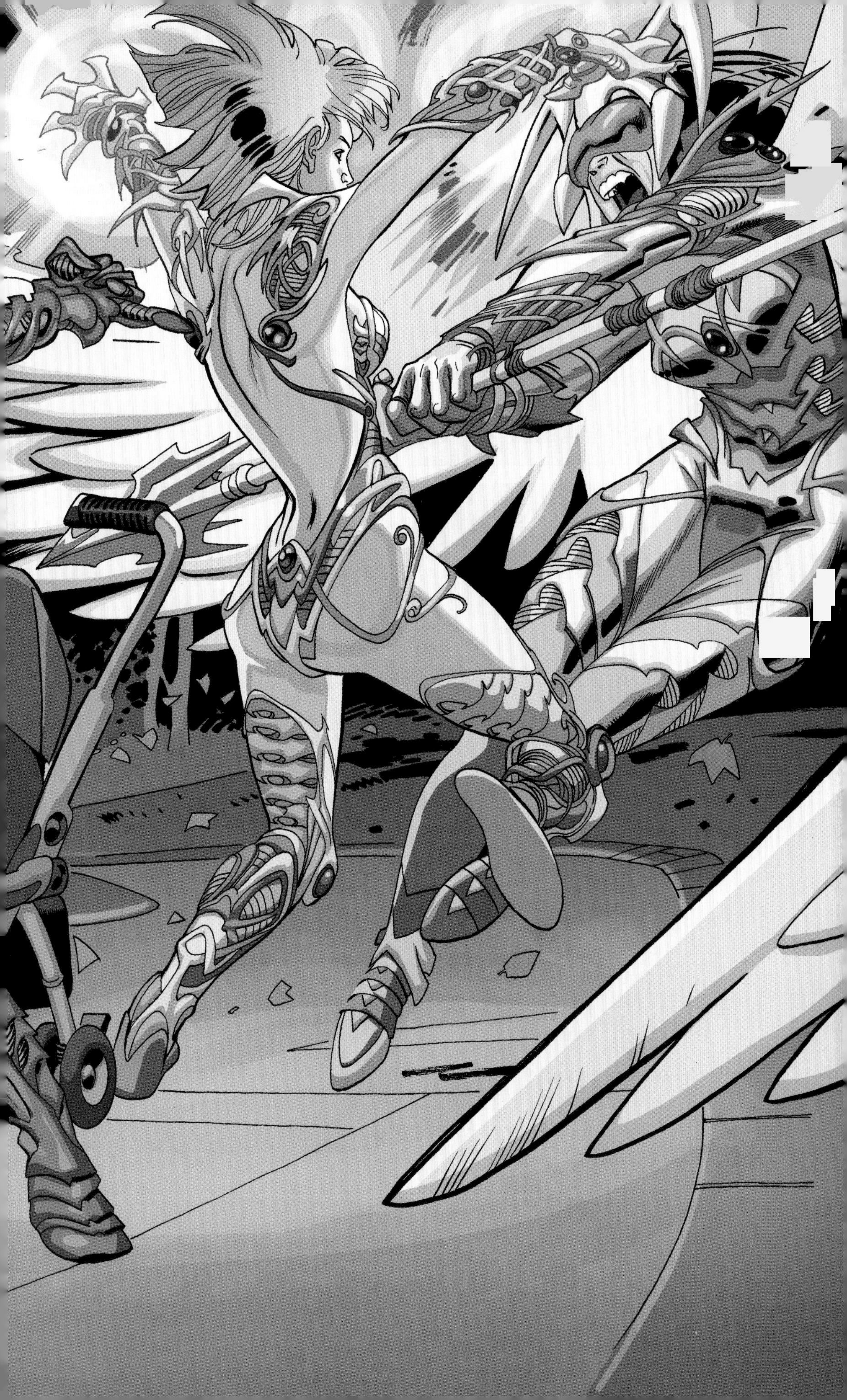

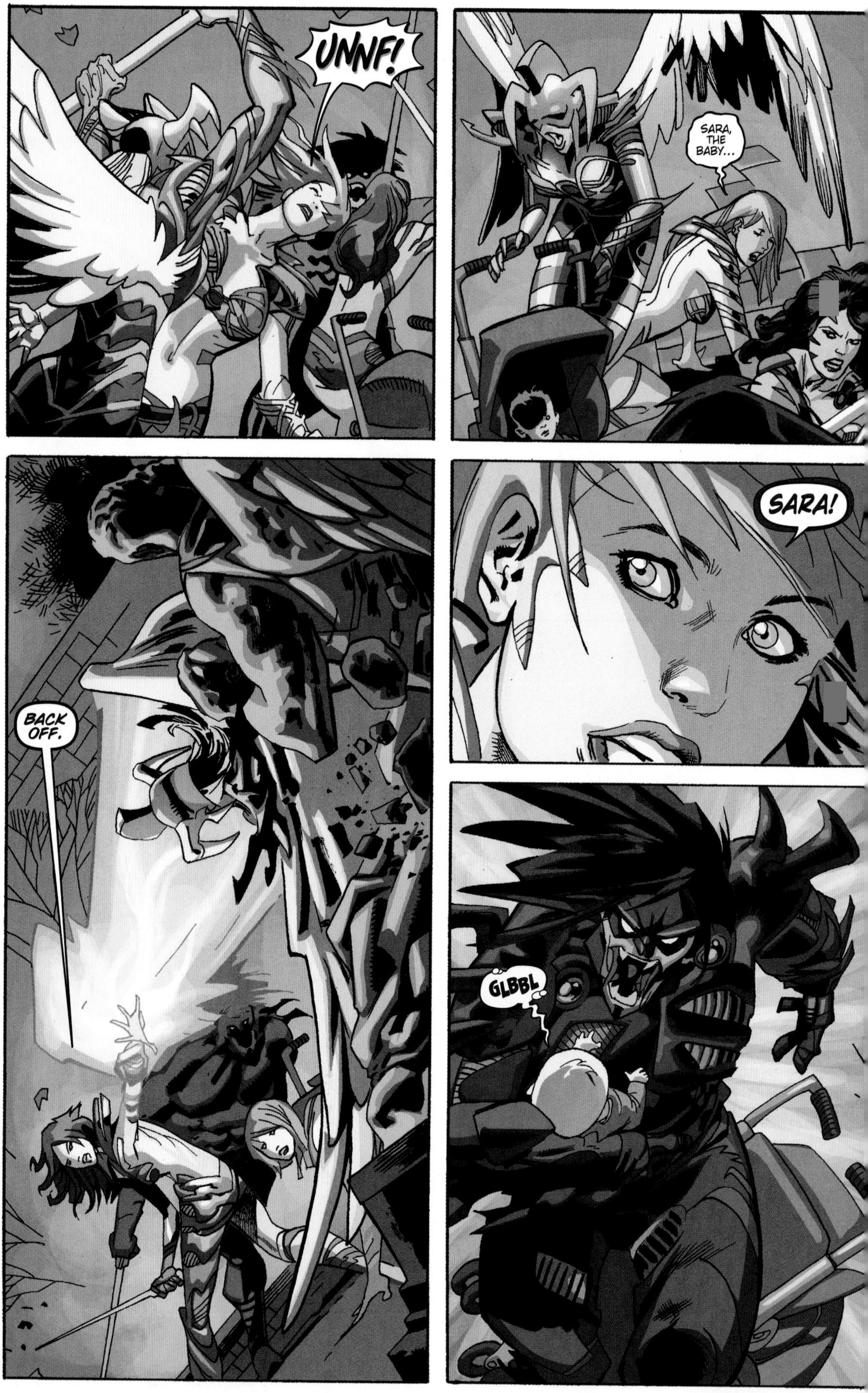
UNNF!
SARA, THE BABY...
BACK OFF.
SARA!
GLBBL

SHE WILL BELONG TO THE *LIGHT!*

NO...

NNH!

C-R-A-A-K-T

...SHE BELONGS TO *ME.*

AAHR!

YOU.

WHNNK

CRAWL BACK INTO WHATEVER *DARK CORNER* YOU CAME FROM.

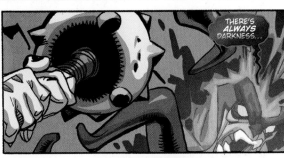

THERE'S *ALWAYS* DARKNESS...

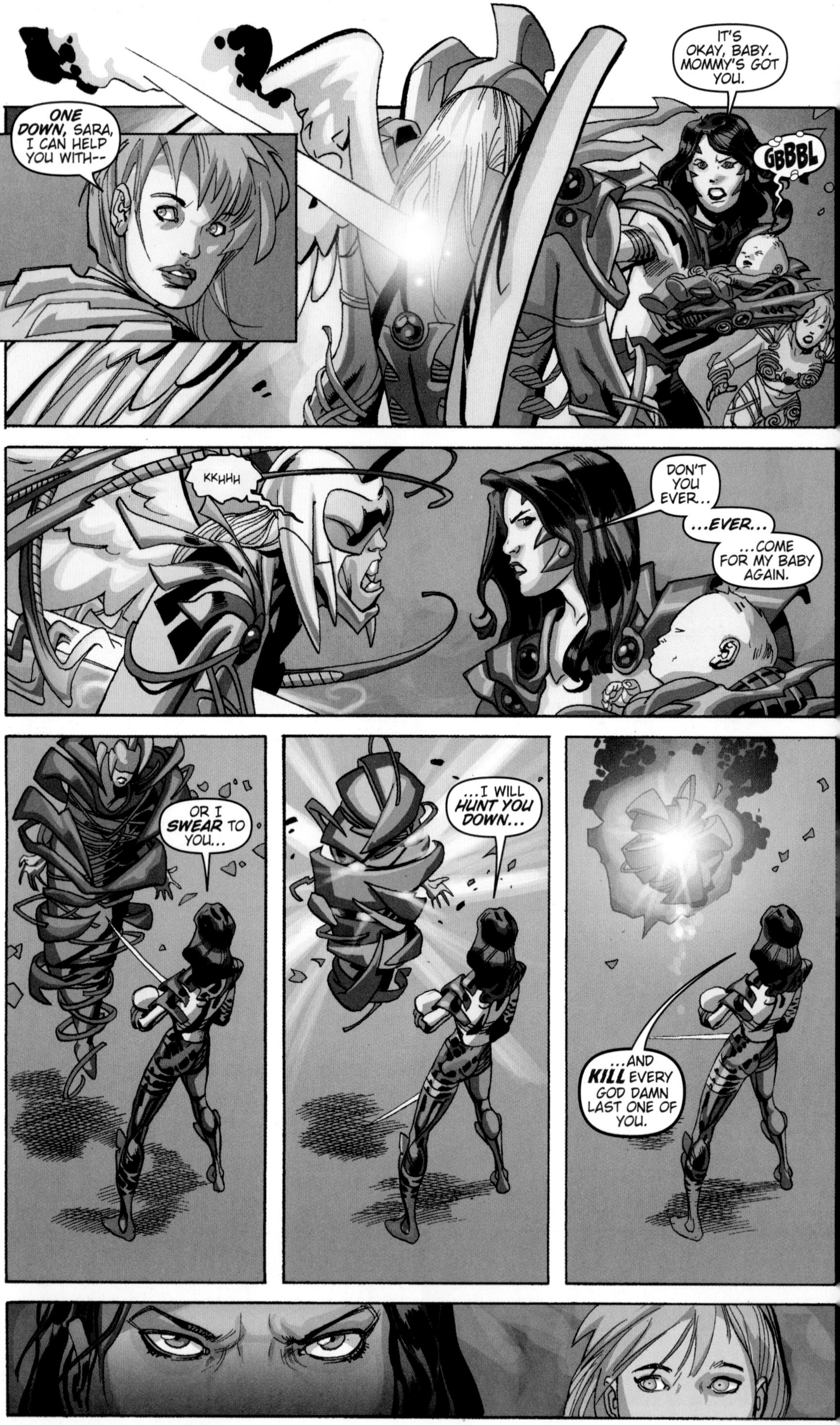
ONE DOWN, SARA, I CAN HELP YOU WITH--
IT'S OKAY, BABY. MOMMY'S GOT YOU.
GBBBL
KKHHH
DON'T YOU EVER...
...EVER...
...COME FOR MY BABY AGAIN.
OR I SWEAR TO YOU...
...I WILL HUNT YOU DOWN...
...AND KILL EVERY GOD DAMN LAST ONE OF YOU.

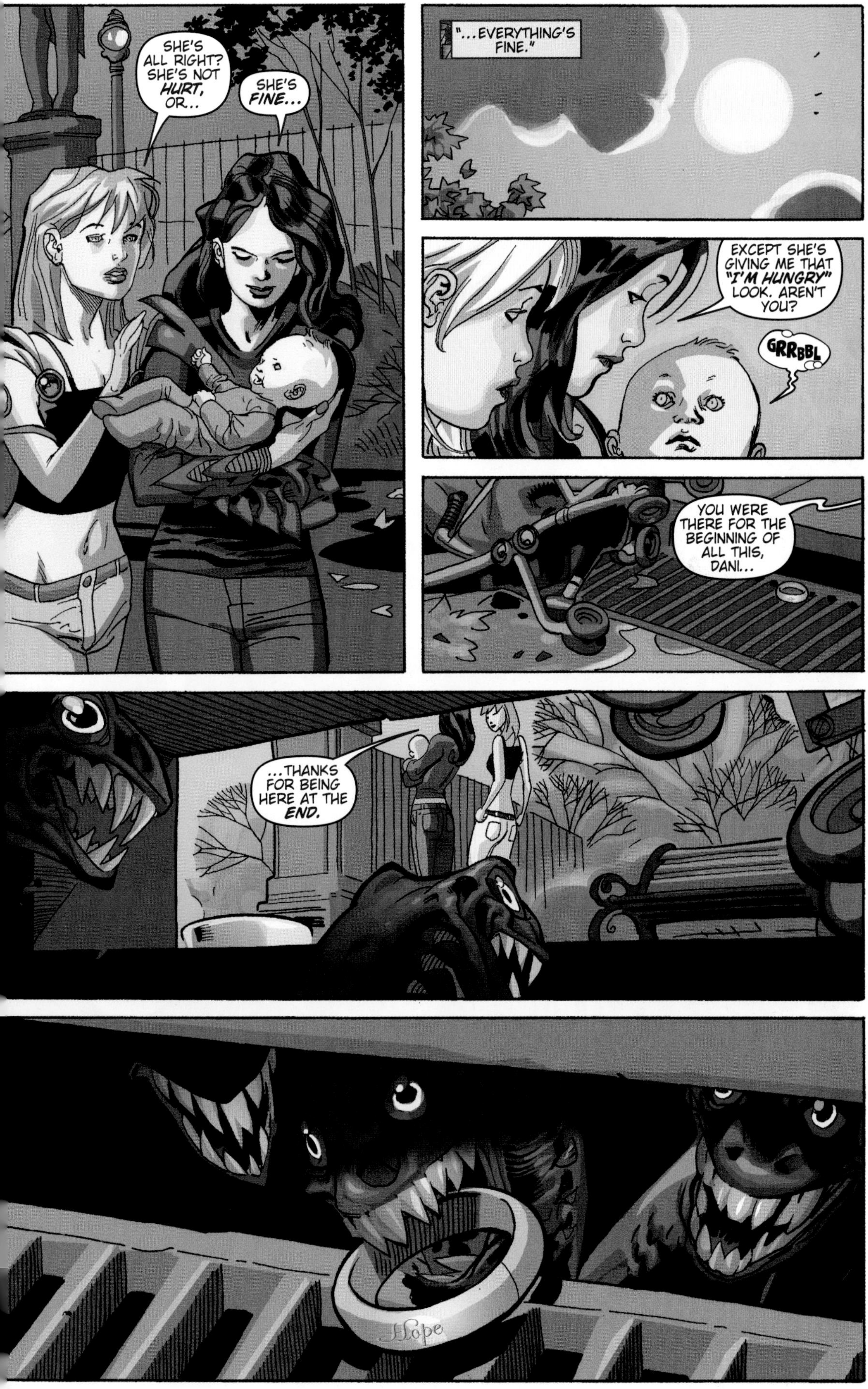
SHE'S ALL RIGHT? SHE'S NOT *HURT,* OR...
SHE'S *FINE...*
"...EVERYTHING'S FINE."
EXCEPT SHE'S GIVING ME THAT *"I'M HUNGRY"* LOOK. AREN'T YOU?
GRRBBL
YOU WERE THERE FOR THE BEGINNING OF ALL THIS, DANI...
...THANKS FOR BEING HERE AT THE *END.*
Hope

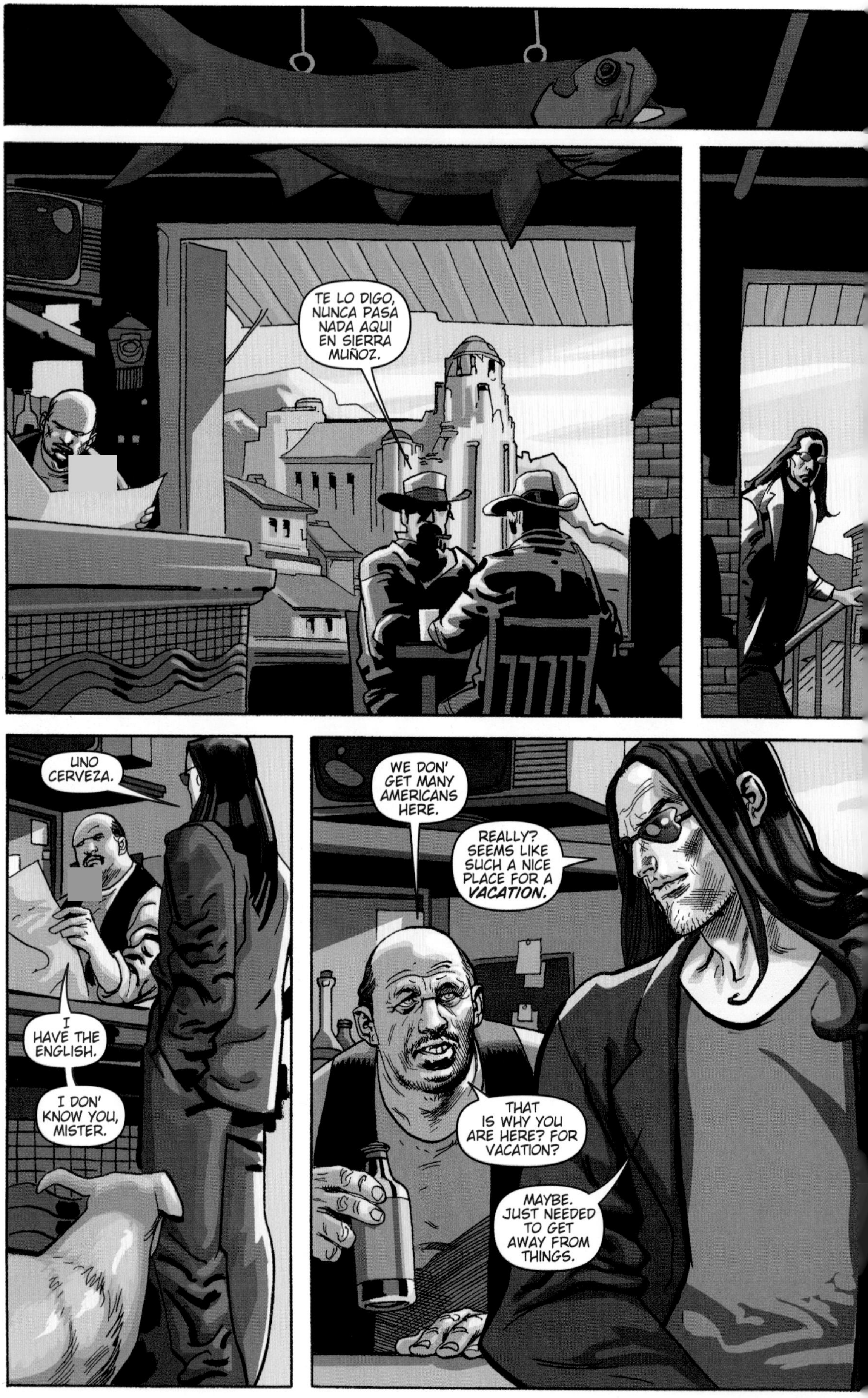
TE LO DIGO, NUNCA PASA NADA AQUI EN SIERRA MUÑOZ.
UNO CERVEZA.
I HAVE THE ENGLISH.
I DON' KNOW YOU, MISTER.
WE DON' GET MANY AMERICANS HERE.
REALLY? SEEMS LIKE SUCH A NICE PLACE FOR A *VACATION.*
THAT IS WHY YOU ARE HERE? FOR VACATION?
MAYBE. JUST NEEDED TO GET AWAY FROM THINGS.

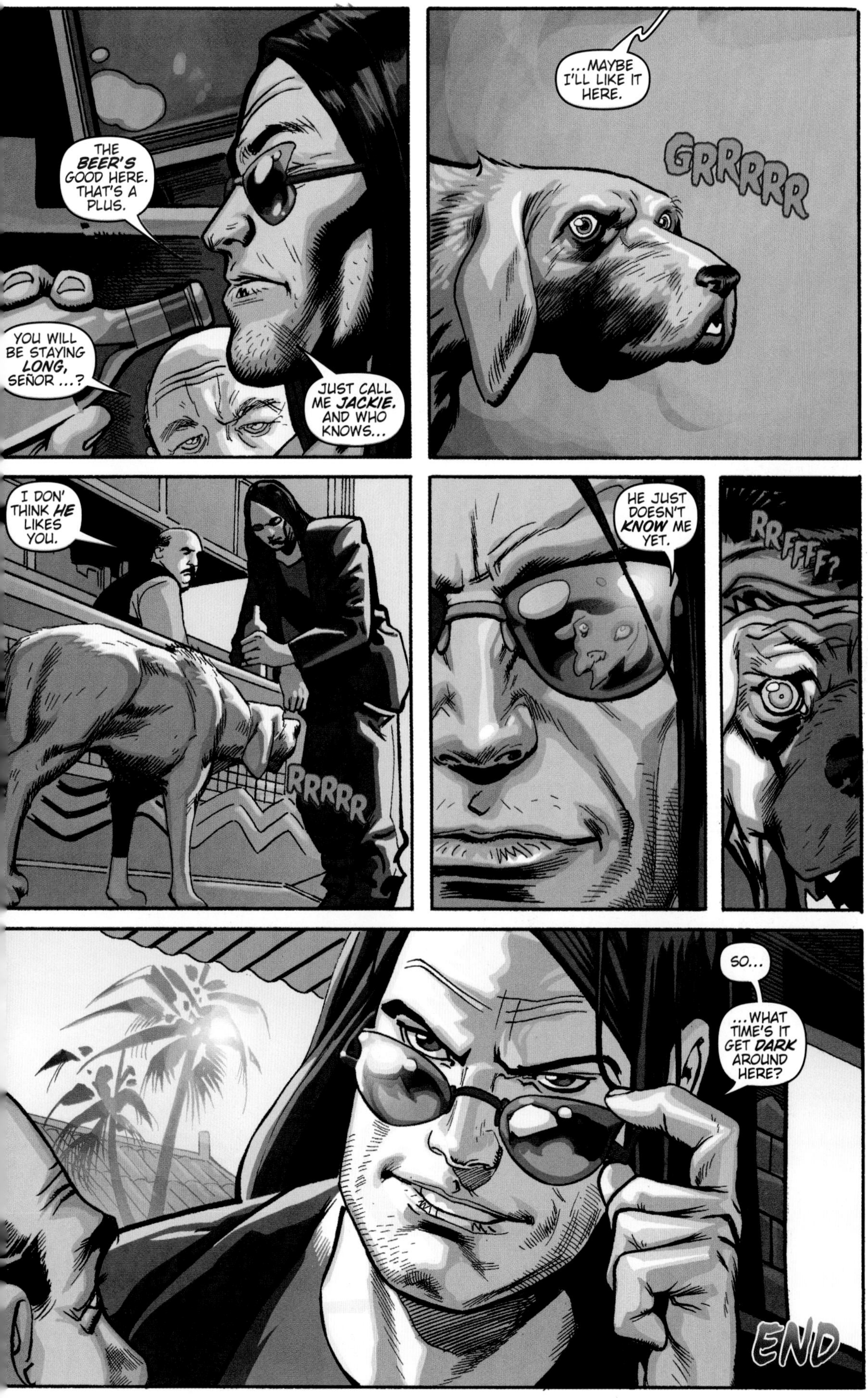
THE BEER'S GOOD HERE. THAT'S A PLUS.
YOU WILL BE STAYING LONG, SEÑOR ...?
JUST CALL ME JACKIE. AND WHO KNOWS...
...MAYBE I'LL LIKE IT HERE.
GRRRRR
I DON' THINK HE LIKES YOU.
RRRRR
HE JUST DOESN'T KNOW ME YET.
RRFFFF?
SO...
...WHAT TIME'S IT GET DARK AROUND HERE?
END

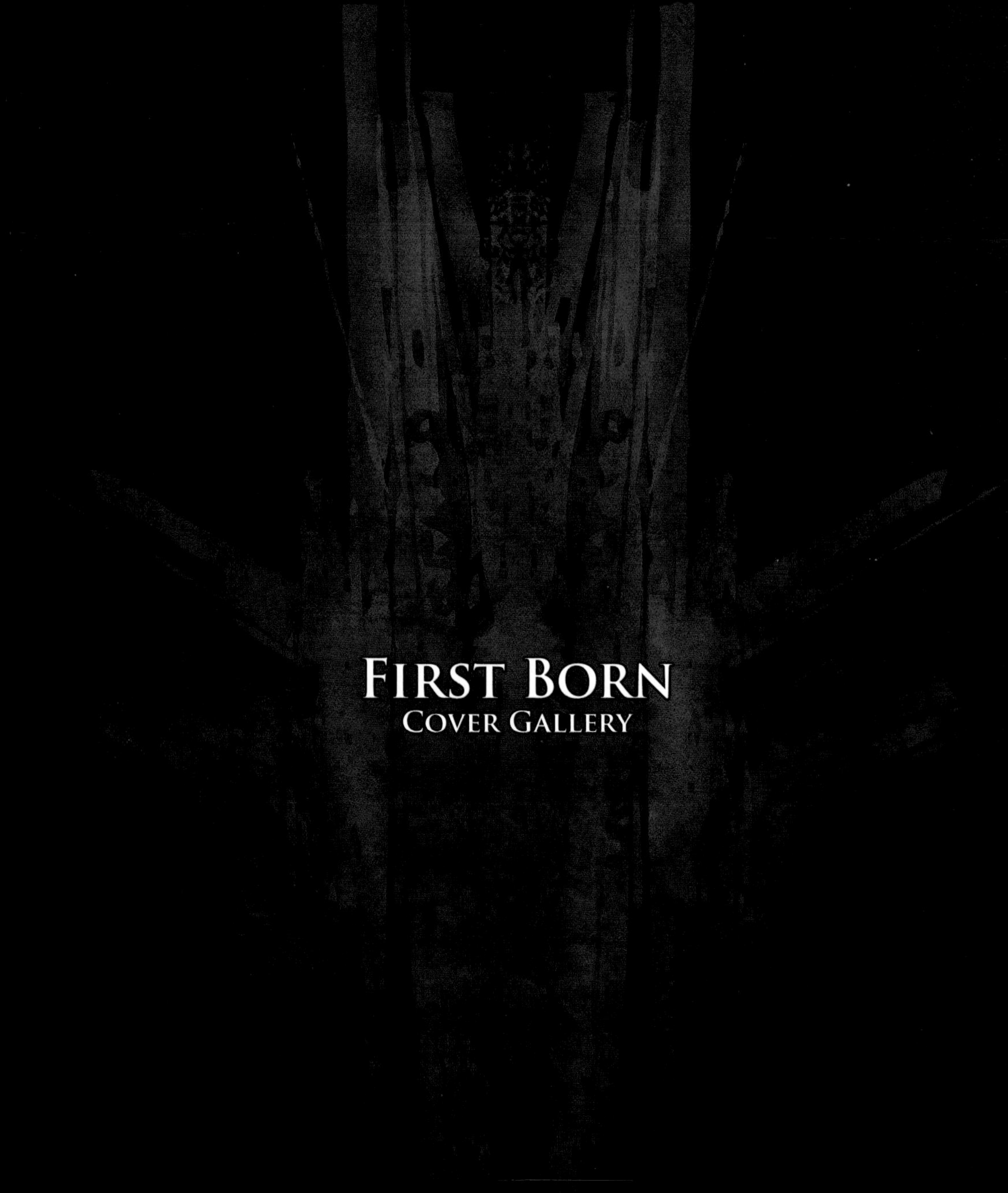

First Born
Cover Gallery

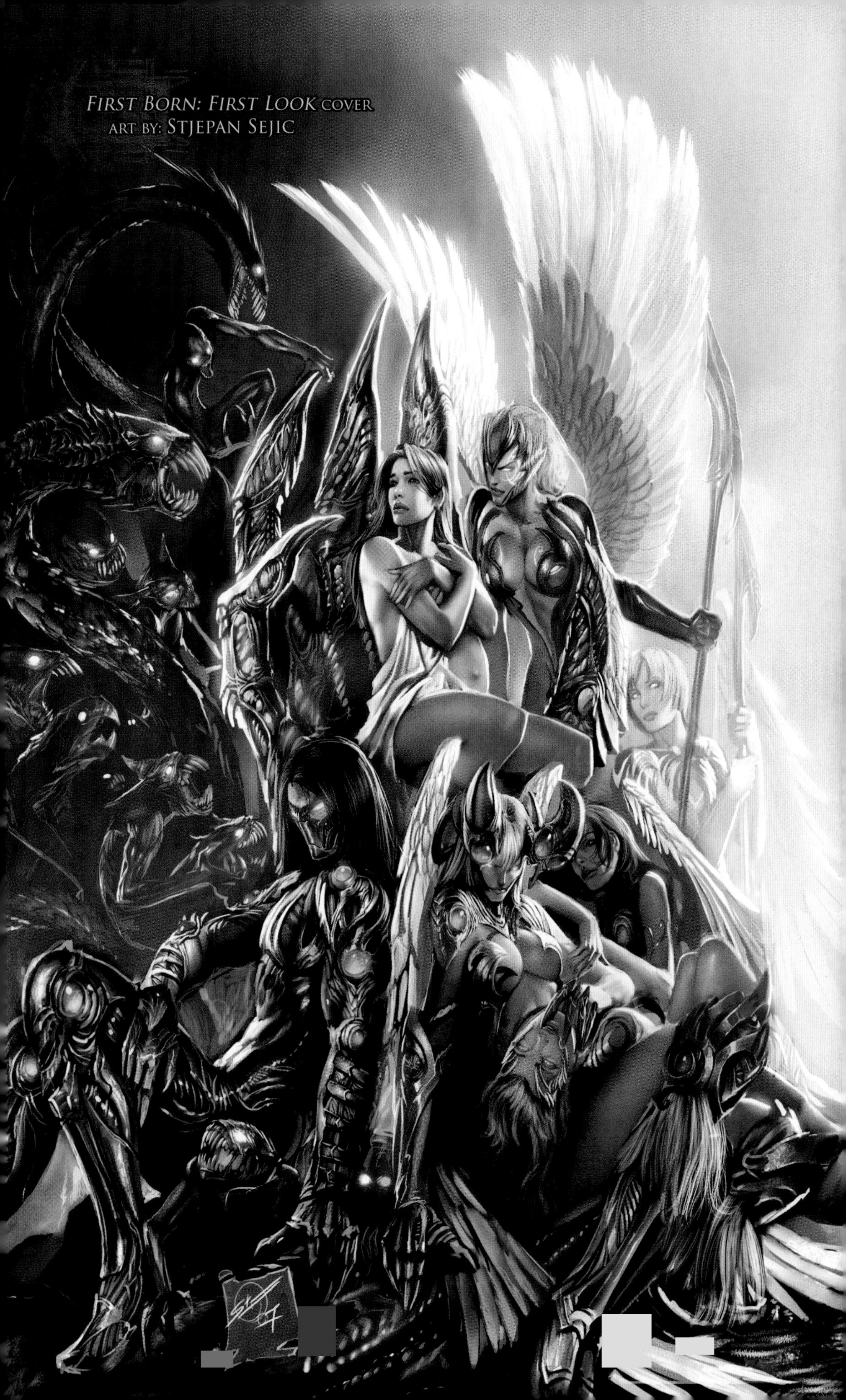

First Born: First Look cover
art by: Stjepan Sejic

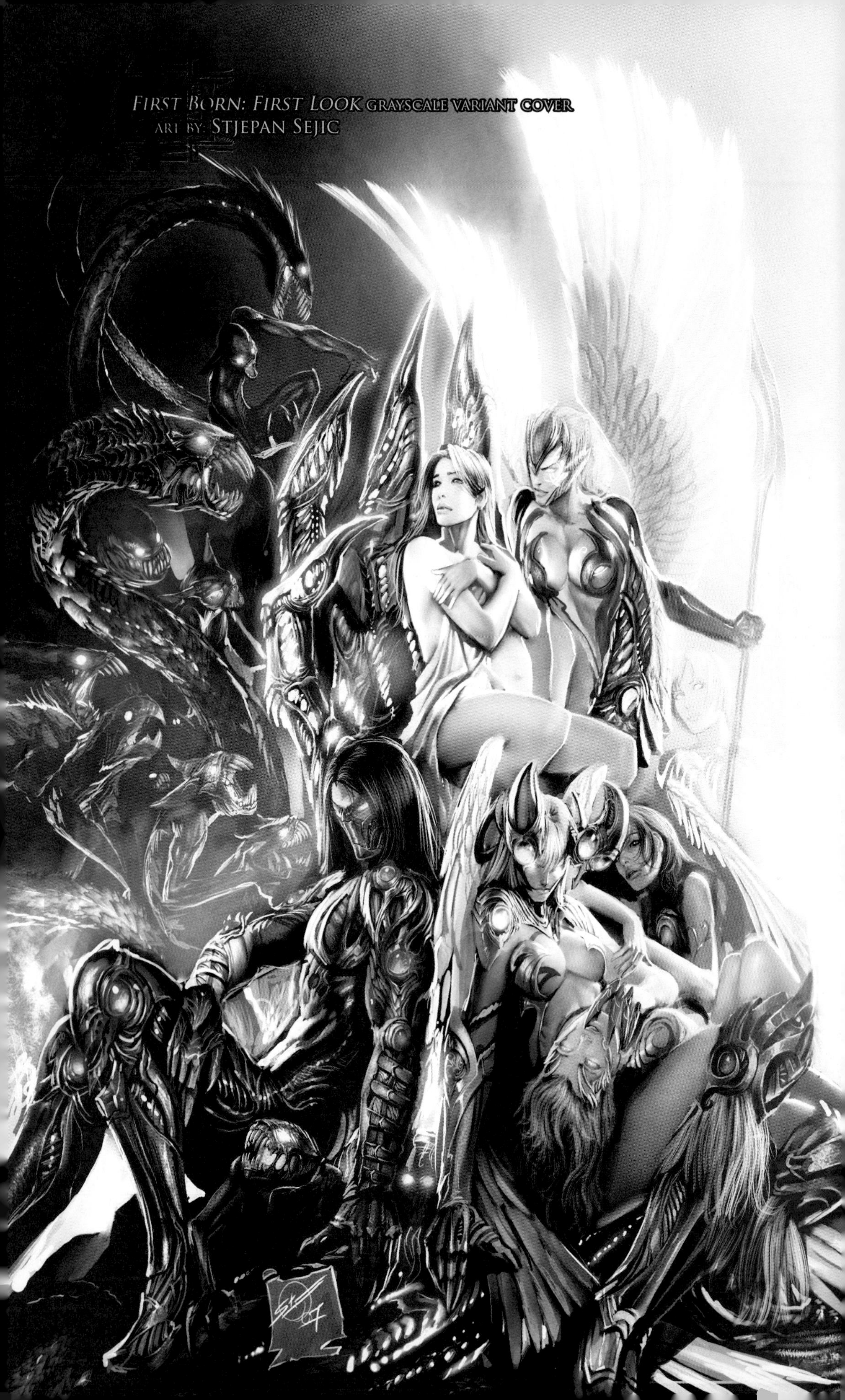

First Born: First Look grayscale variant cover
art by: Stjepan Sejic

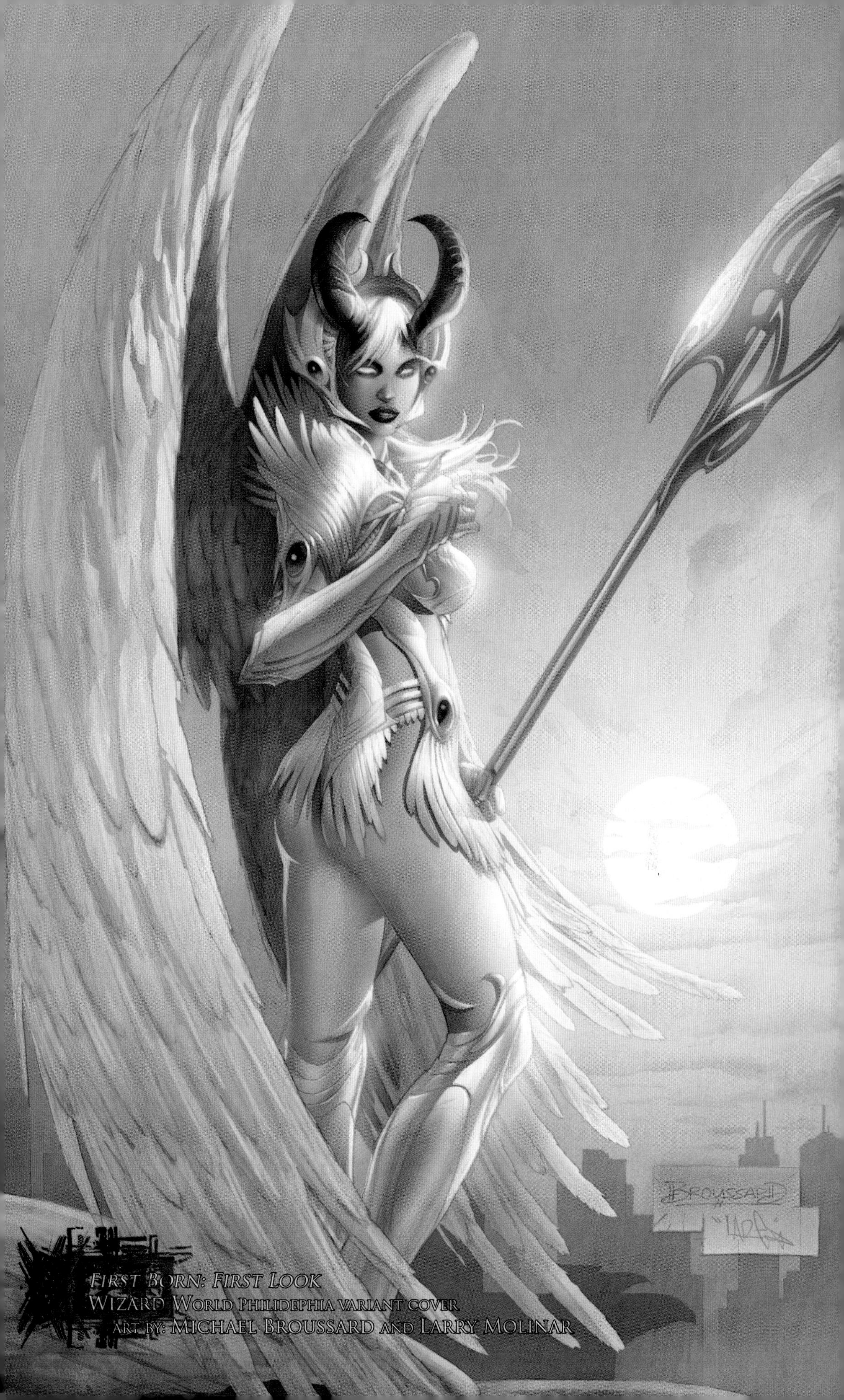
BROUSSARD

First Born: First Look
Wizard World Philidephia variant cover
Art by: Michael Broussard and Larry Molinar

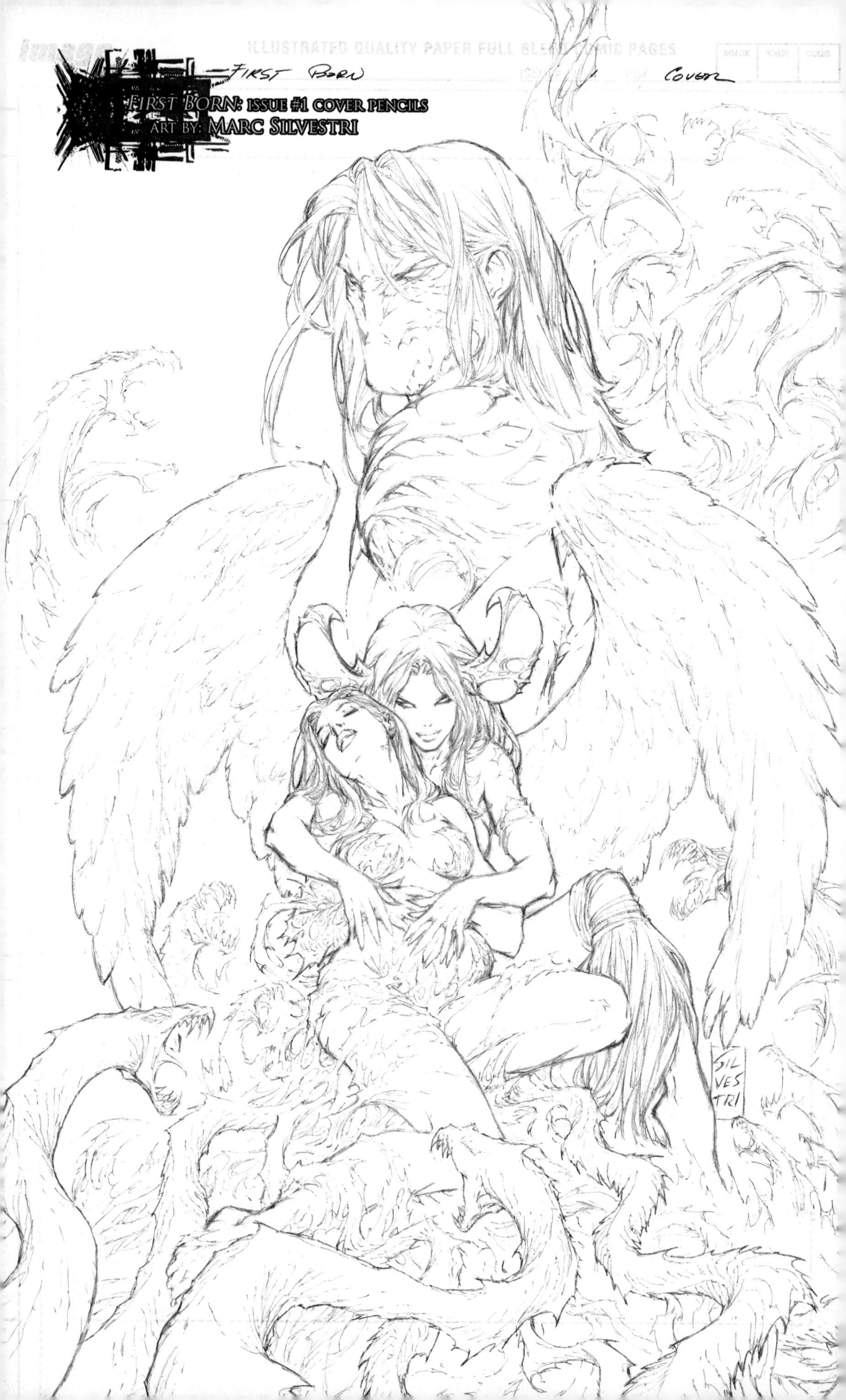
FIRST BORN
COVER
SIL VES TRI

FIRST BORN: issue #1 cover pencils
art by: Marc Silvestri

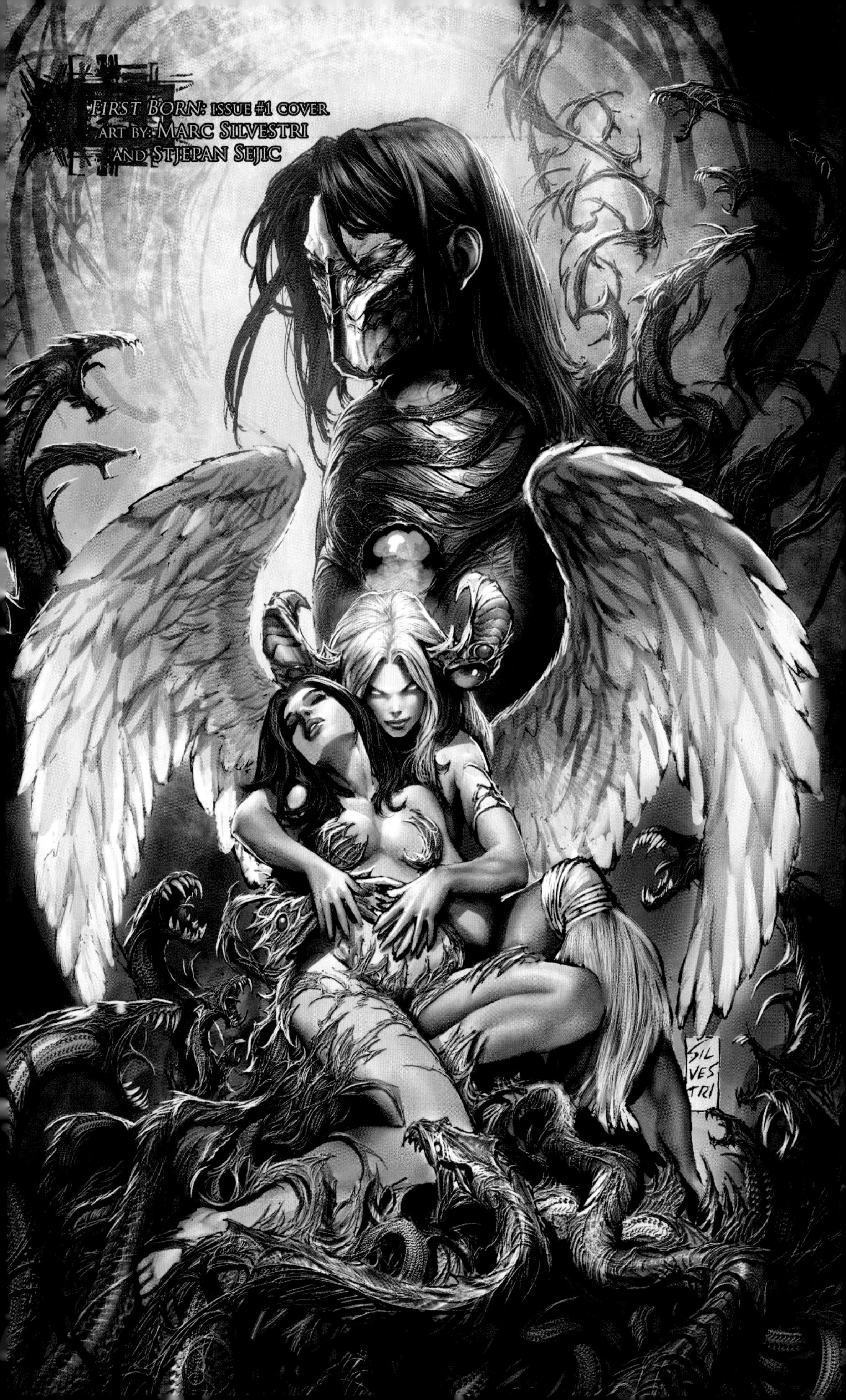
SIL
VES
TRI

FIRST BORN: issue #1 cover
art by: Marc Silvestri
and Stjepan Sejic

First Born: issue #1 Gatefold variant cover
art by: Stjepan Sejic

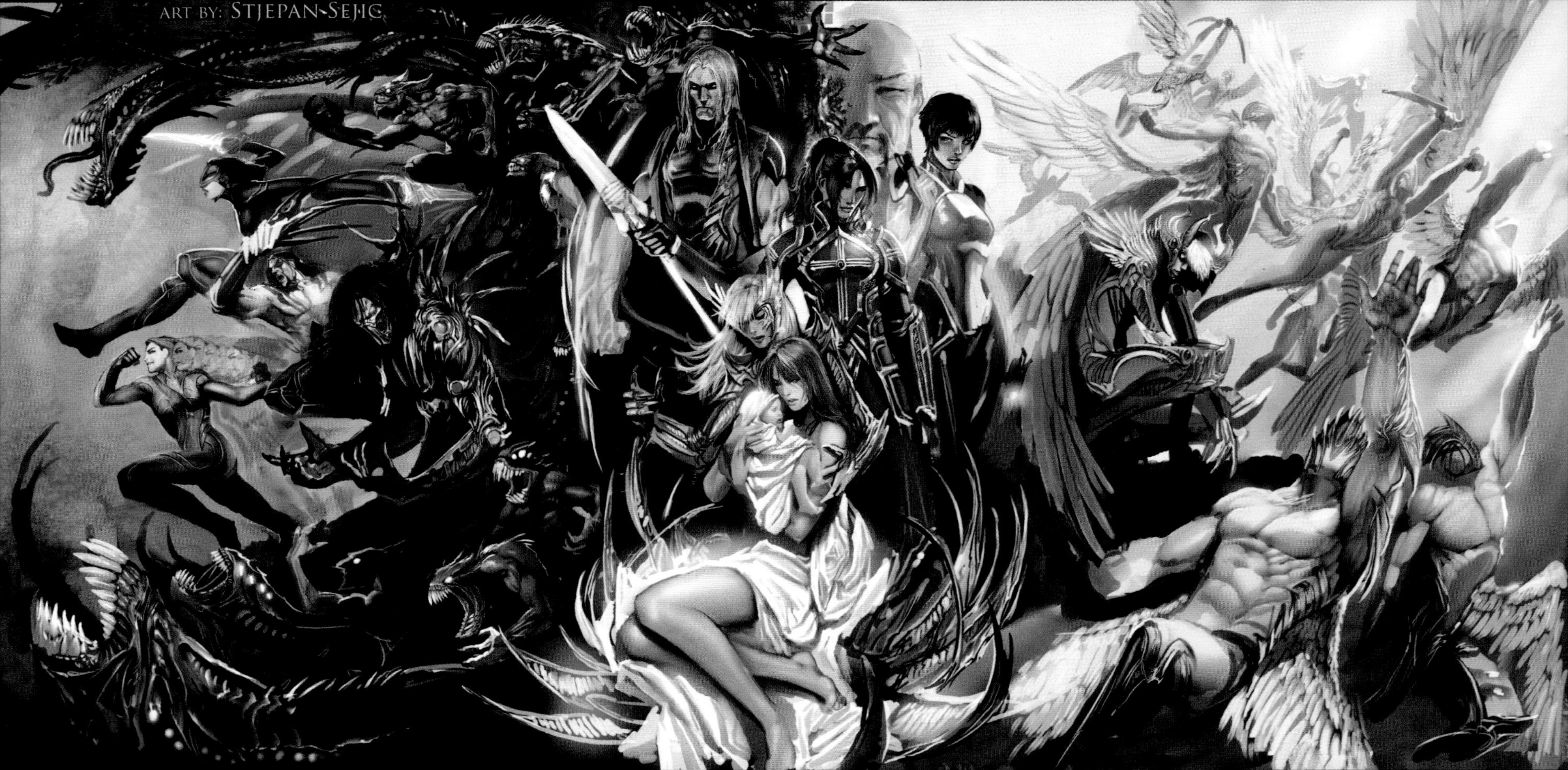

FIRST BORN: ISSUE #1
CONVENTION VARIANT COVER
ART BY: STJEPAN SEJIC

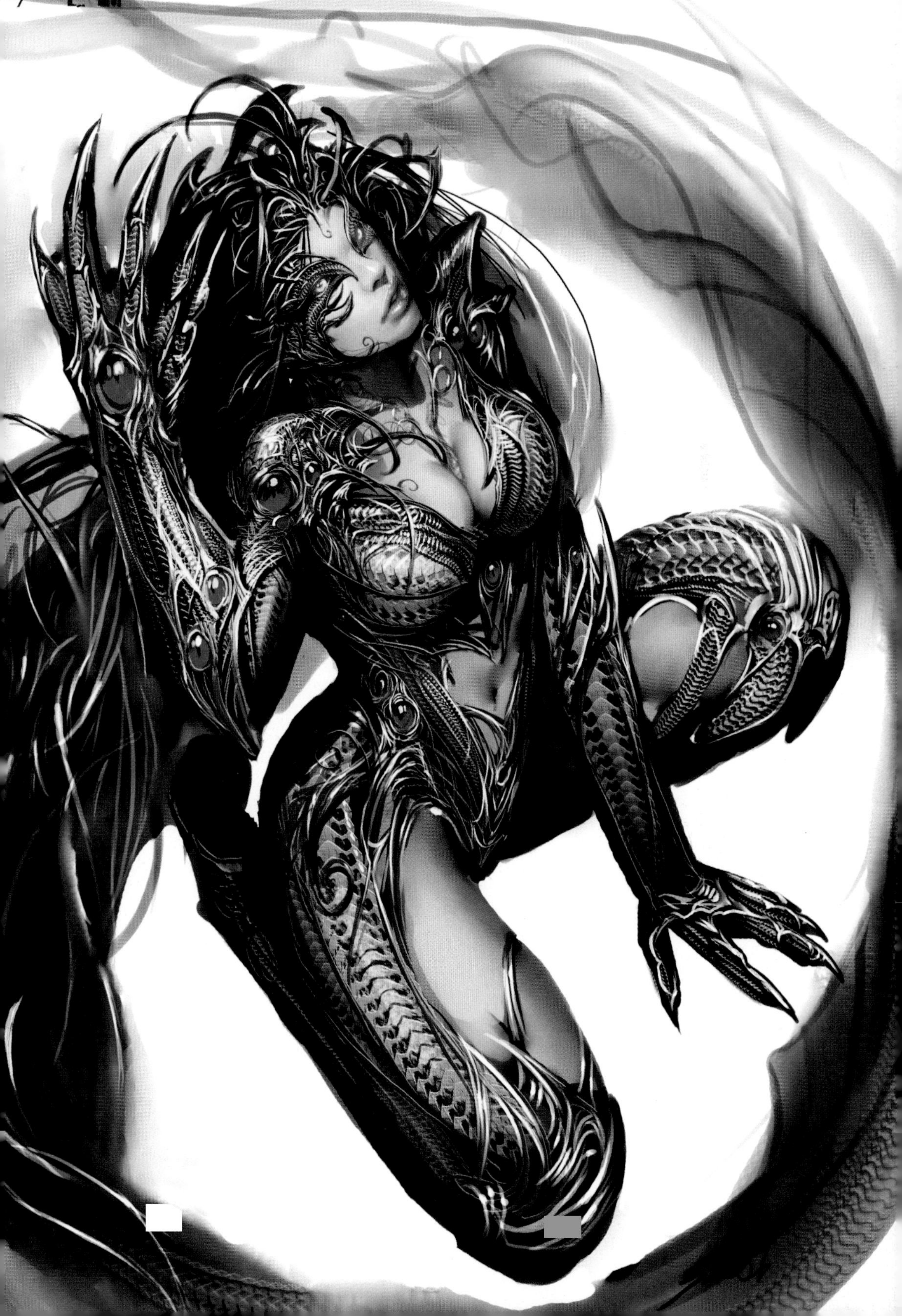

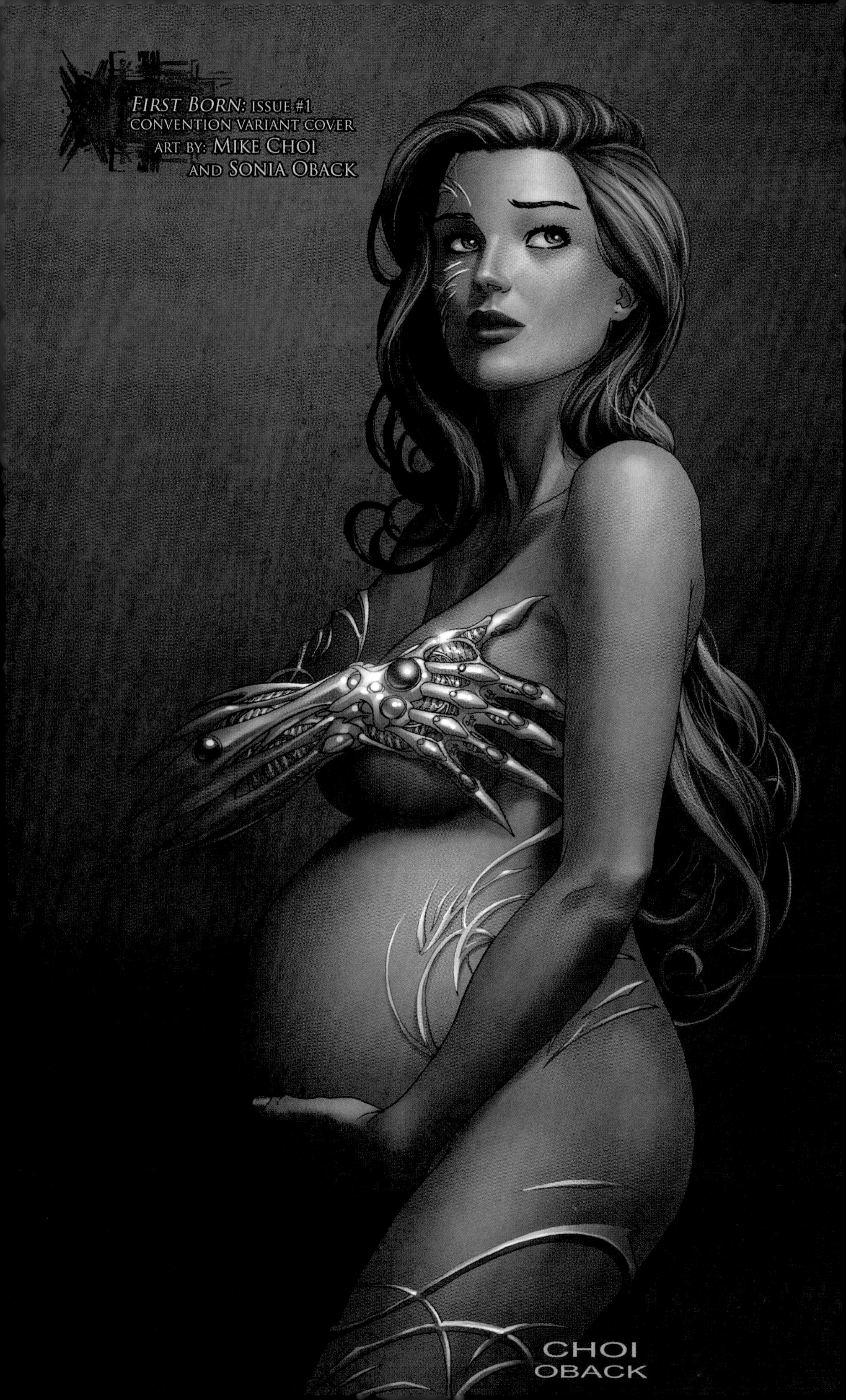
CHOI
OBACK

FIRST BORN: ISSUE #1
CONVENTION VARIANT COVER
ART BY: MIKE CHOI
AND SONIA OBACK

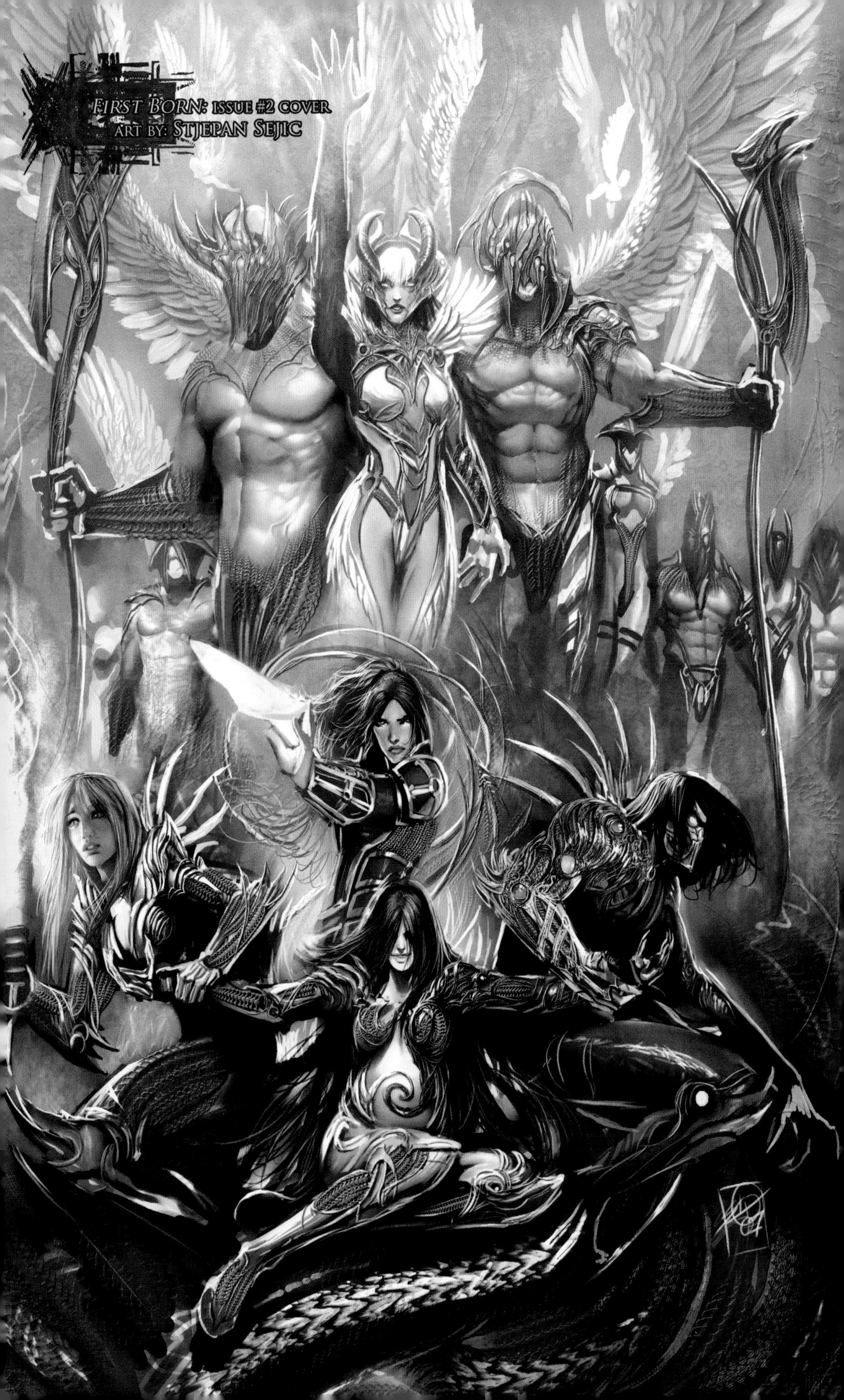

FIRST BORN: ISSUE #2 COVER
ART BY: STJEPAN SEJIC

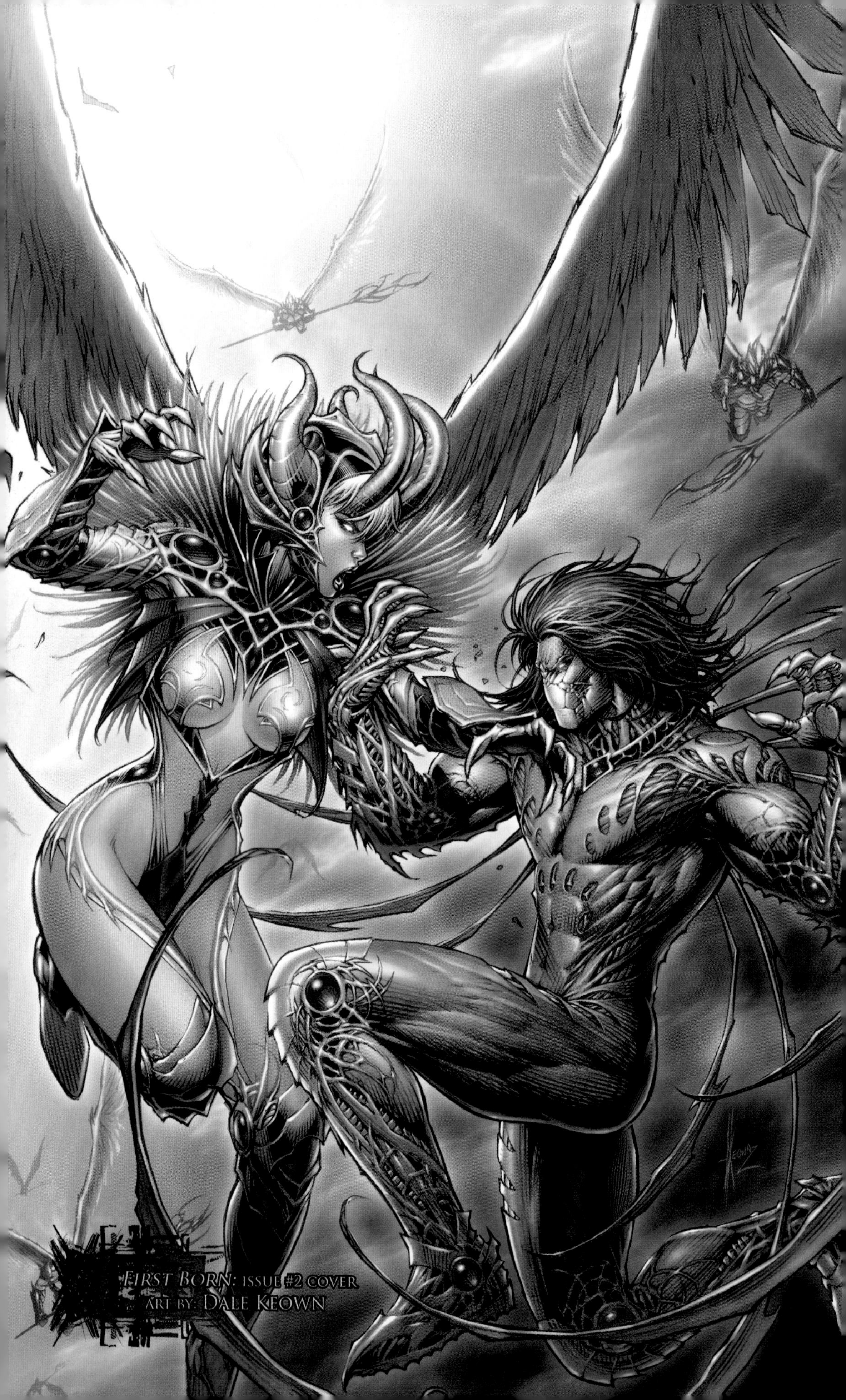

First Born: issue #2 cover
art by: Dale Keown

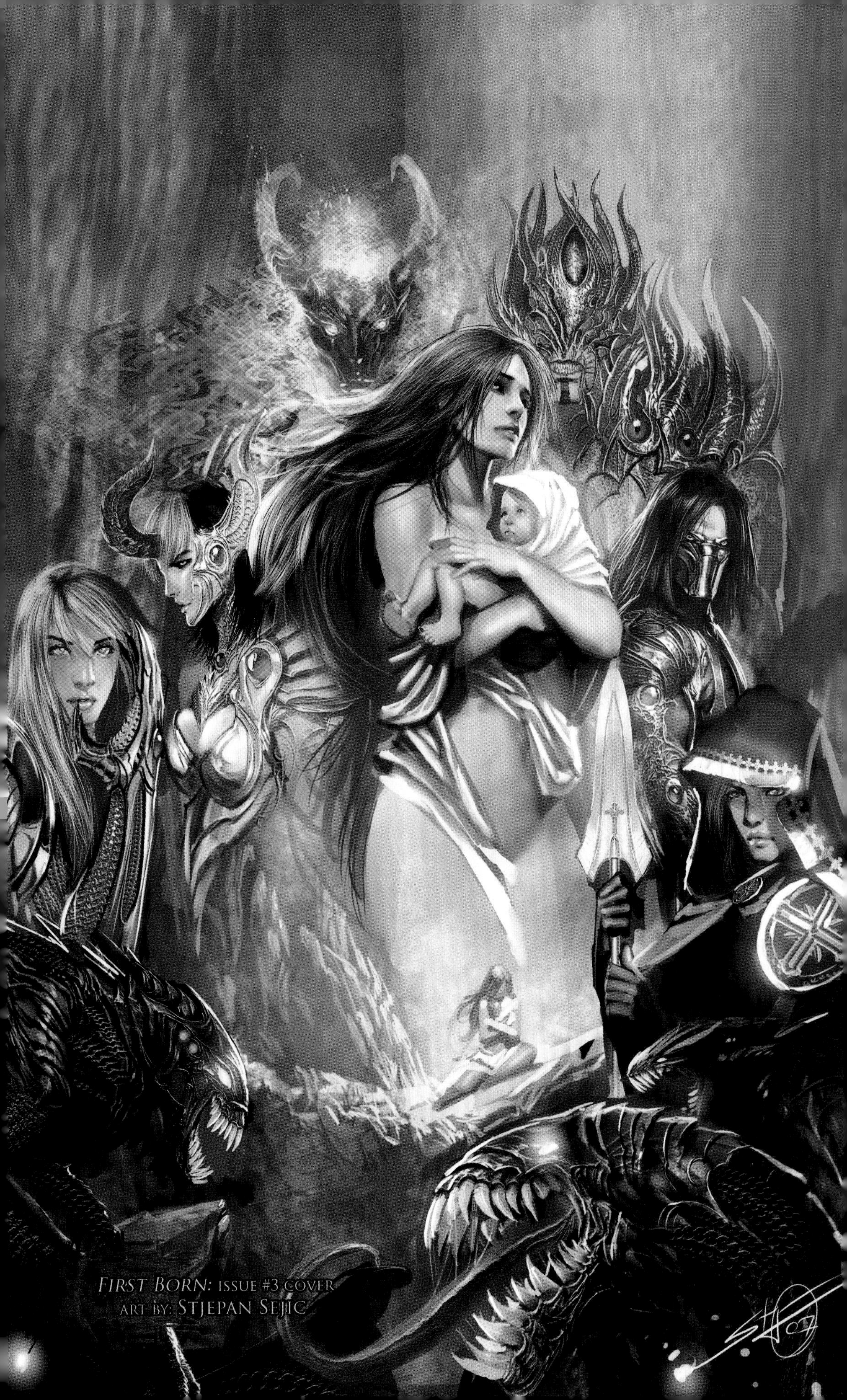

First Born: issue #3 cover
art by: Stjepan Sejic

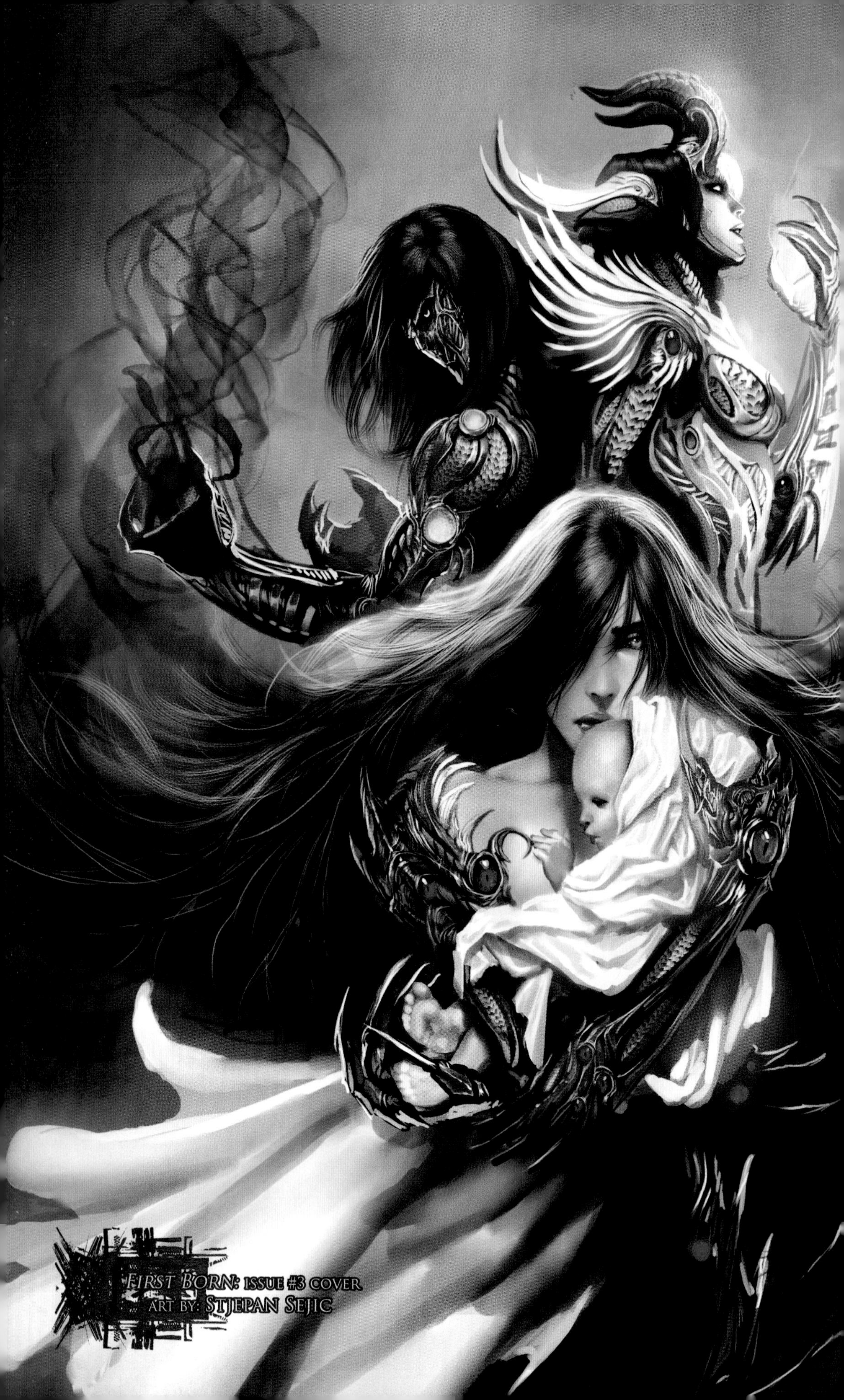

First Born: issue #3 cover
Art by: Stjepan Sejic

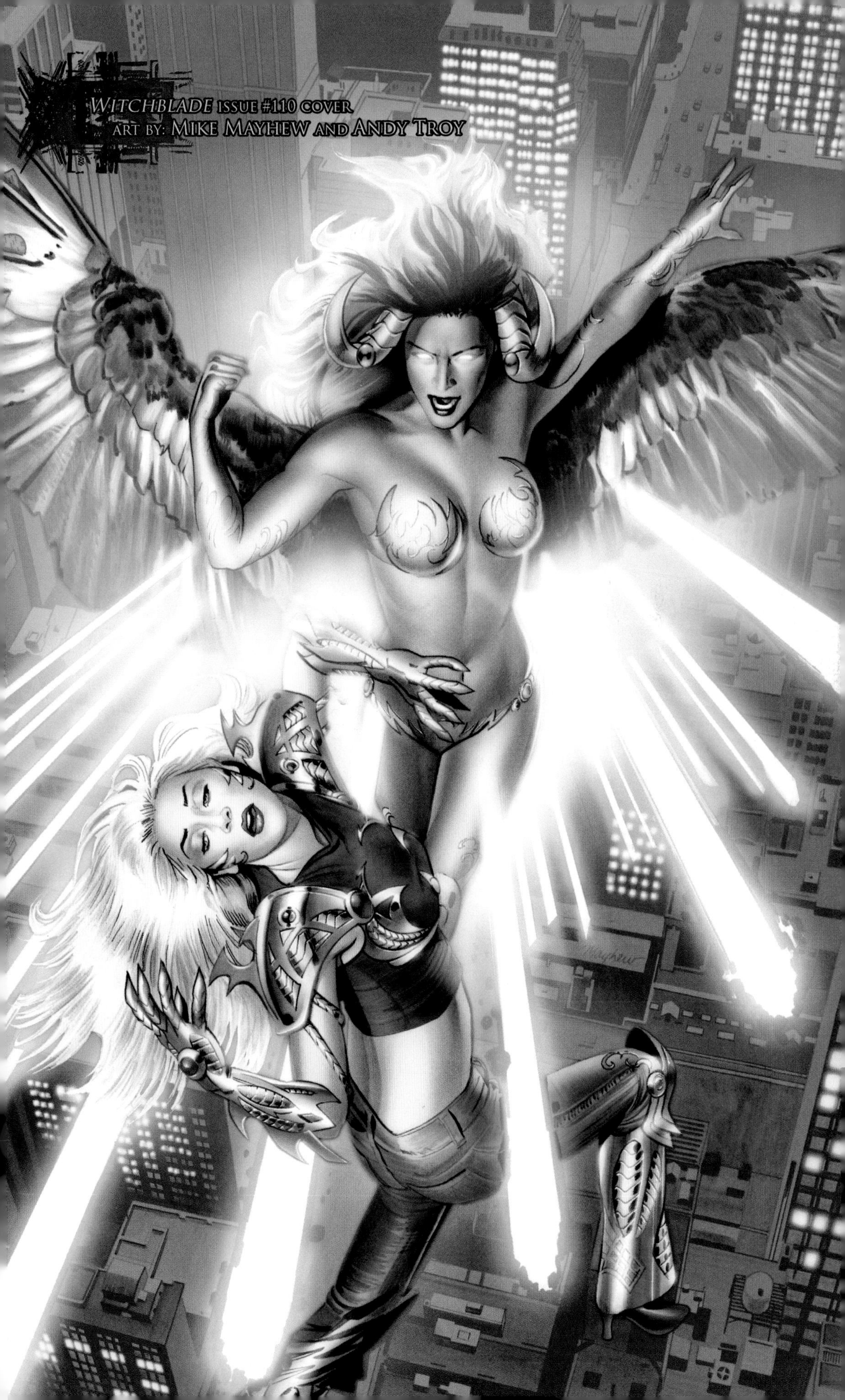

WITCHBLADE issue #110 cover
art by: Mike Mayhew and Andy Troy

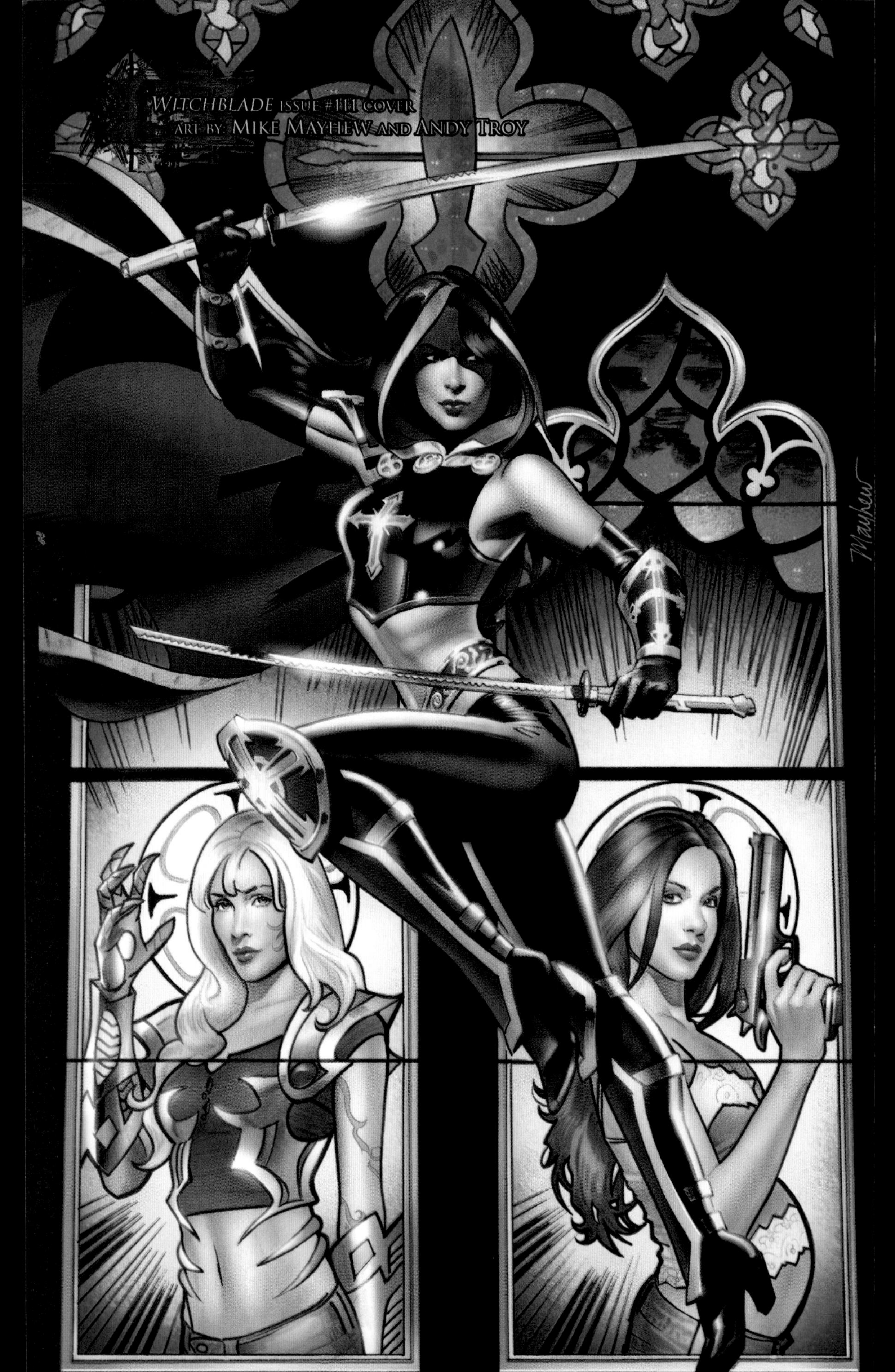
Mayhew

Witchblade issue #111 cover
art by: Mike Mayhew and Andy Troy

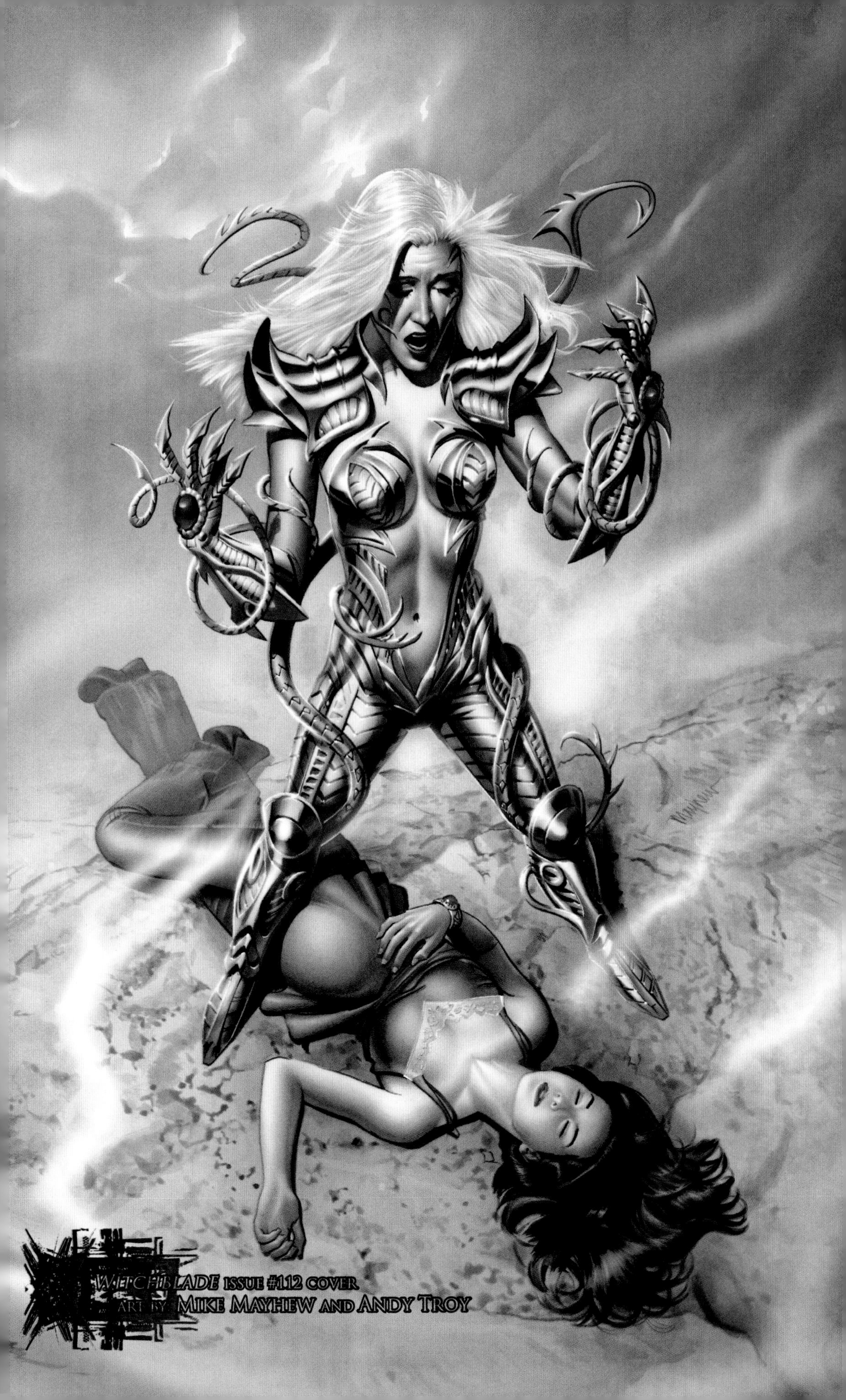

Witchblade issue #112 cover
Art by: Mike Mayhew and Andy Troy

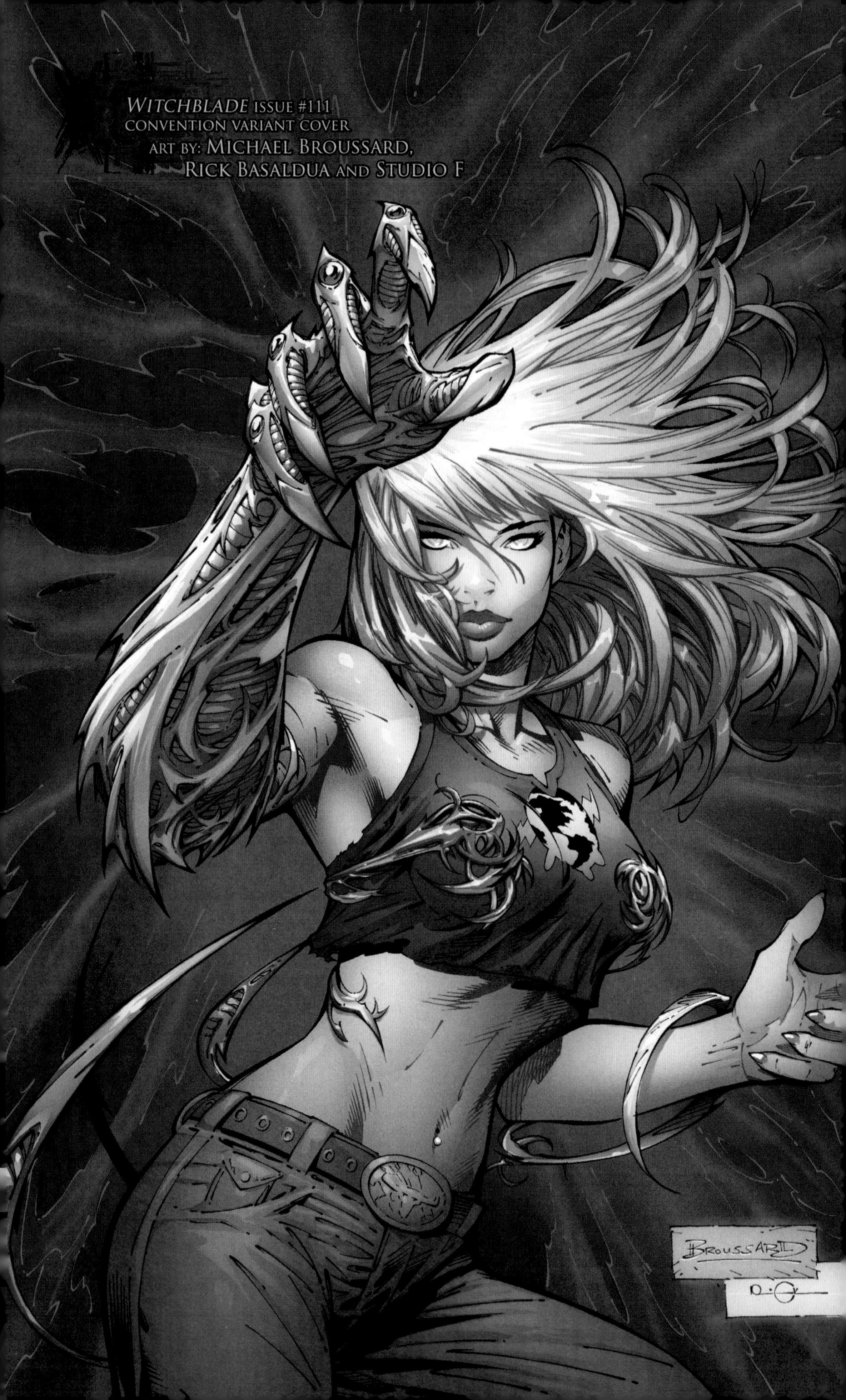
BROUSSARD

WITCHBLADE ISSUE #111
CONVENTION VARIANT COVER
ART BY: MICHAEL BROUSSARD,
RICK BASALDUA AND STUDIO F

STJEPAN SEJIC
SKETCHBOOK

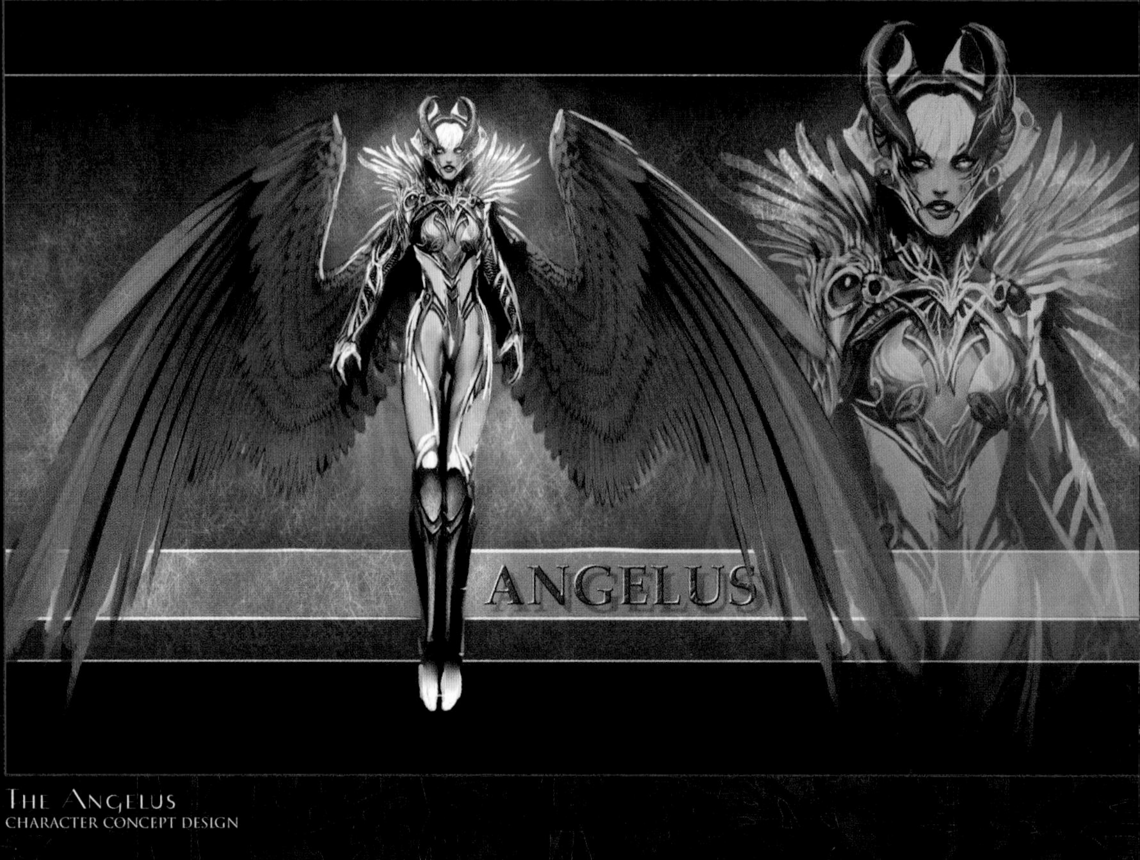
ANGELUS

The Angelus
CHARACTER CONCEPT DESIGN

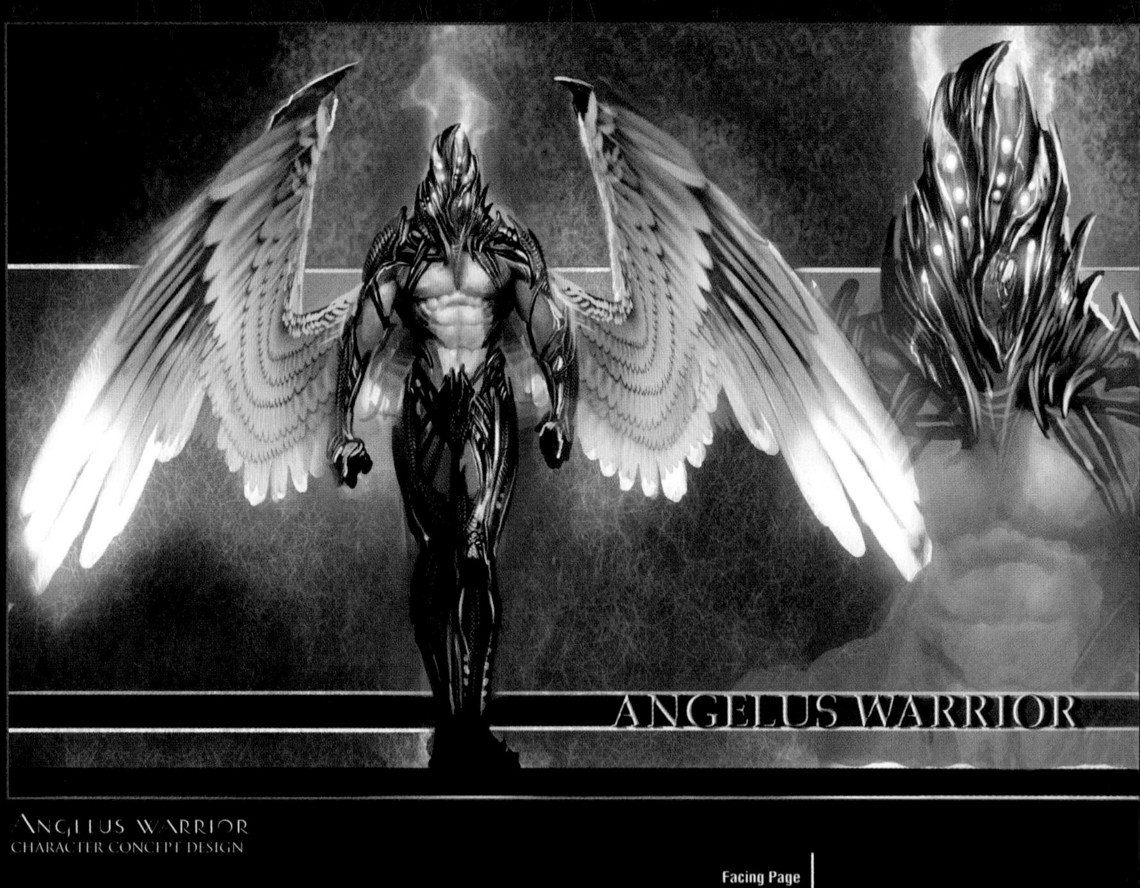
ANGELUS WARRIOR

Angelus Warrior
CHARACTER CONCEPT DESIGN

Facing Page

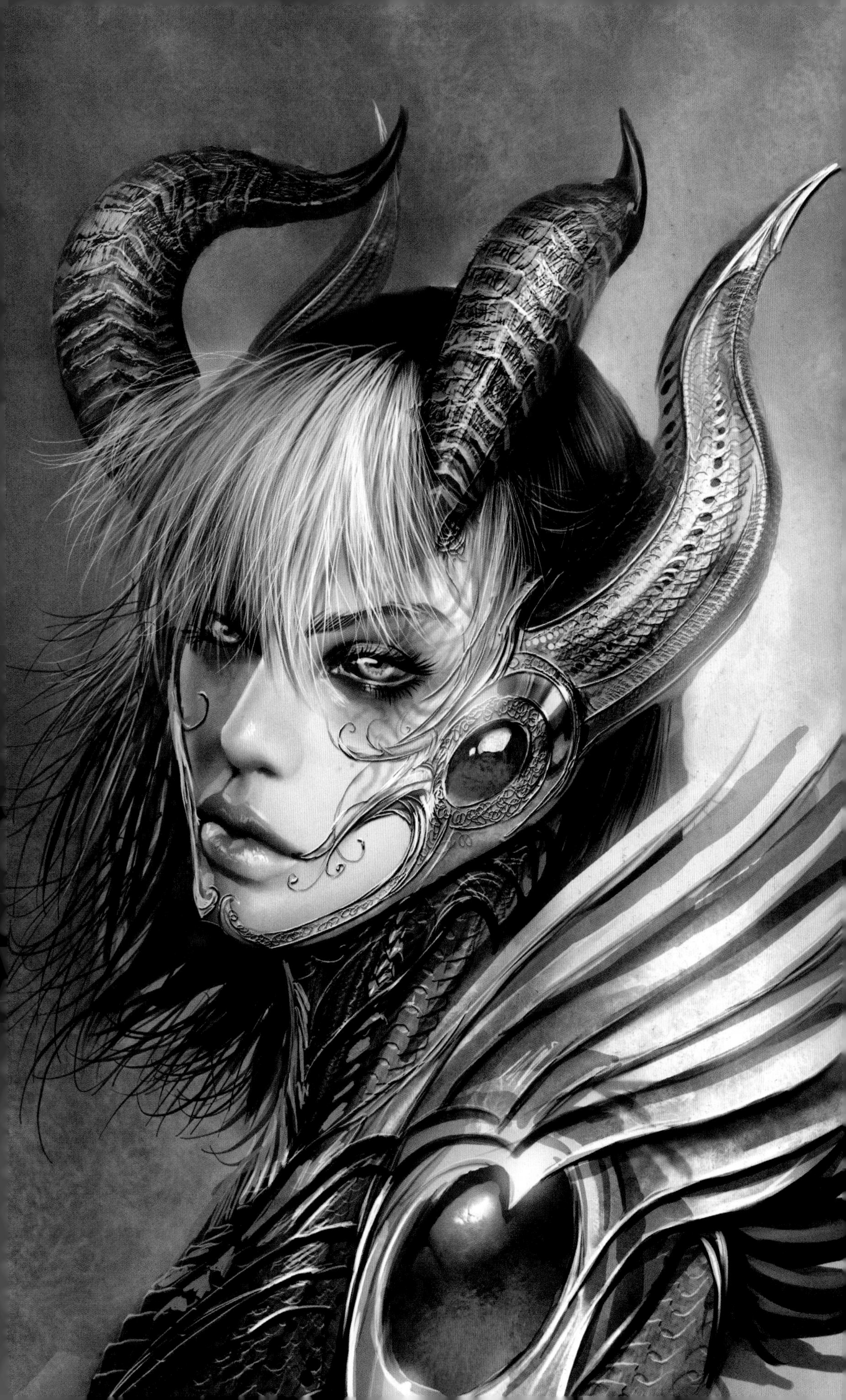

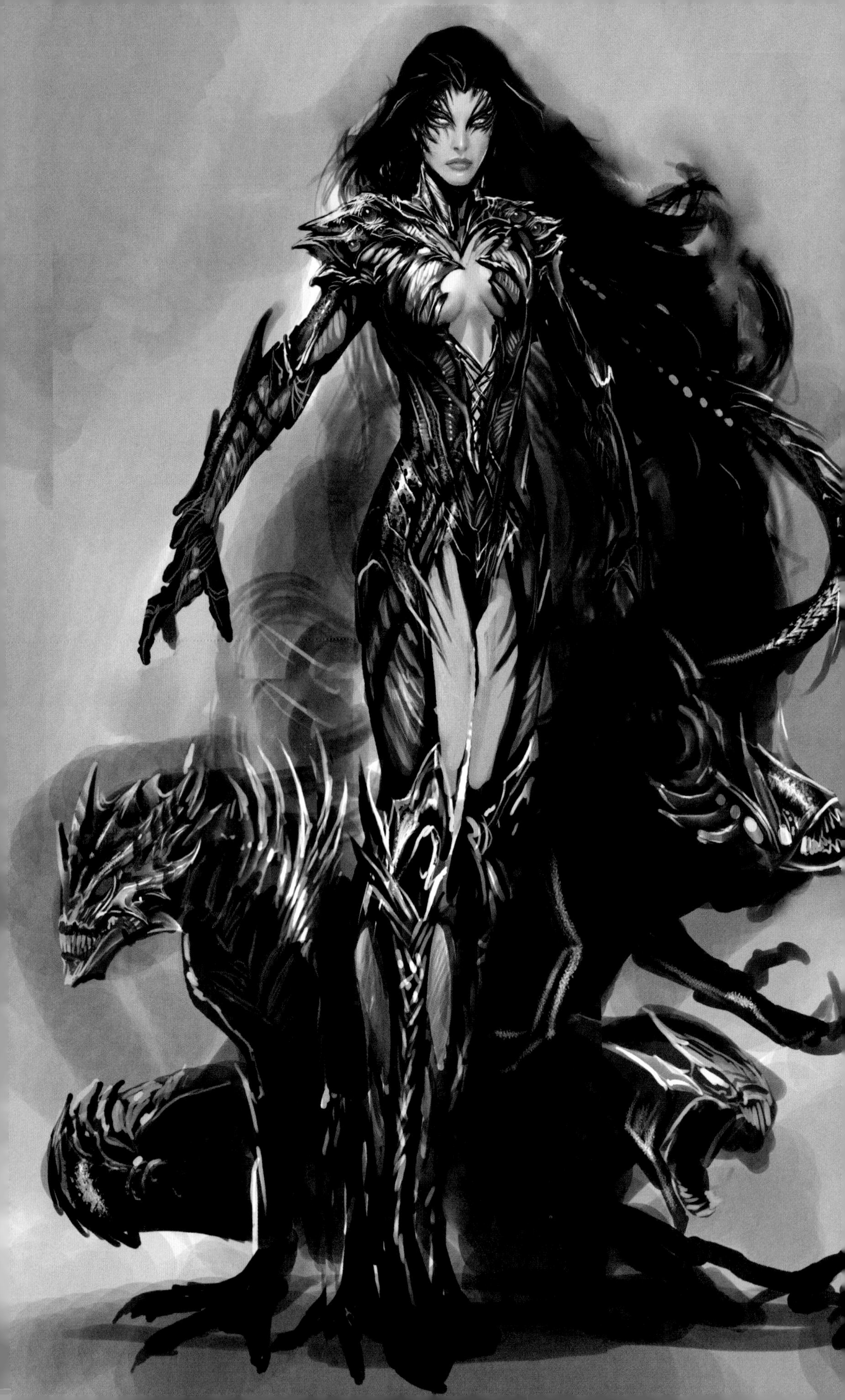

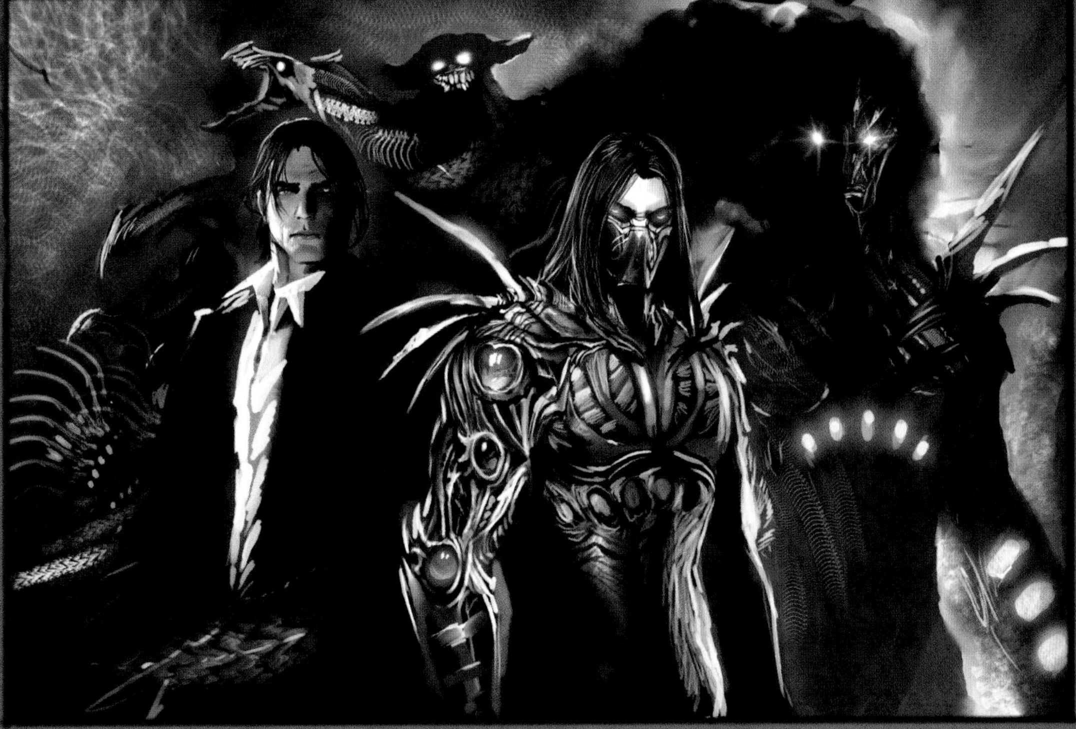

THE DARKNESS
CHARACTER CONCEPT DESIGN

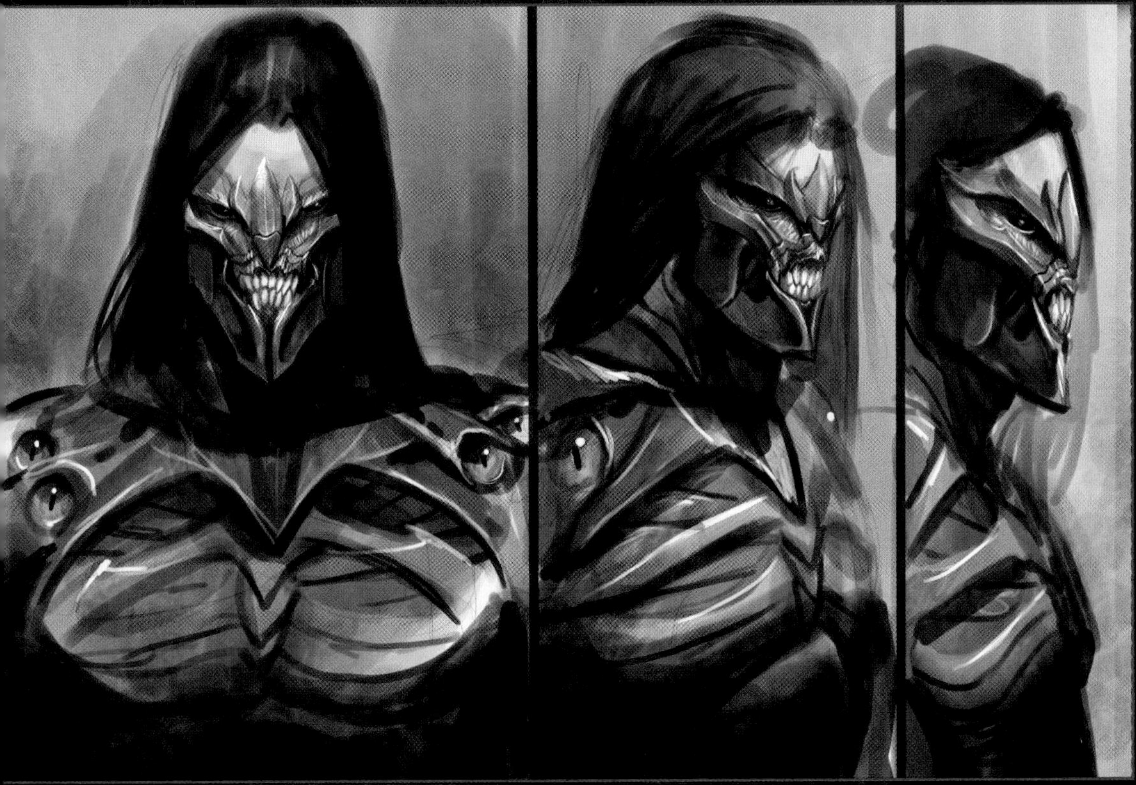

THE DARKNESS
CHARACTER CONCEPT TURNAROUNDS

Facing Page

"DARK WITCHBLADE"
CHARACTER CONCEPT DESIGN

FIRSTBORN
ENVIRONMENT DESIGN

CYBERFORCE
CHARACTER CONCEPT SKETCH

Facing Page

DANIELLE BAPTISTE

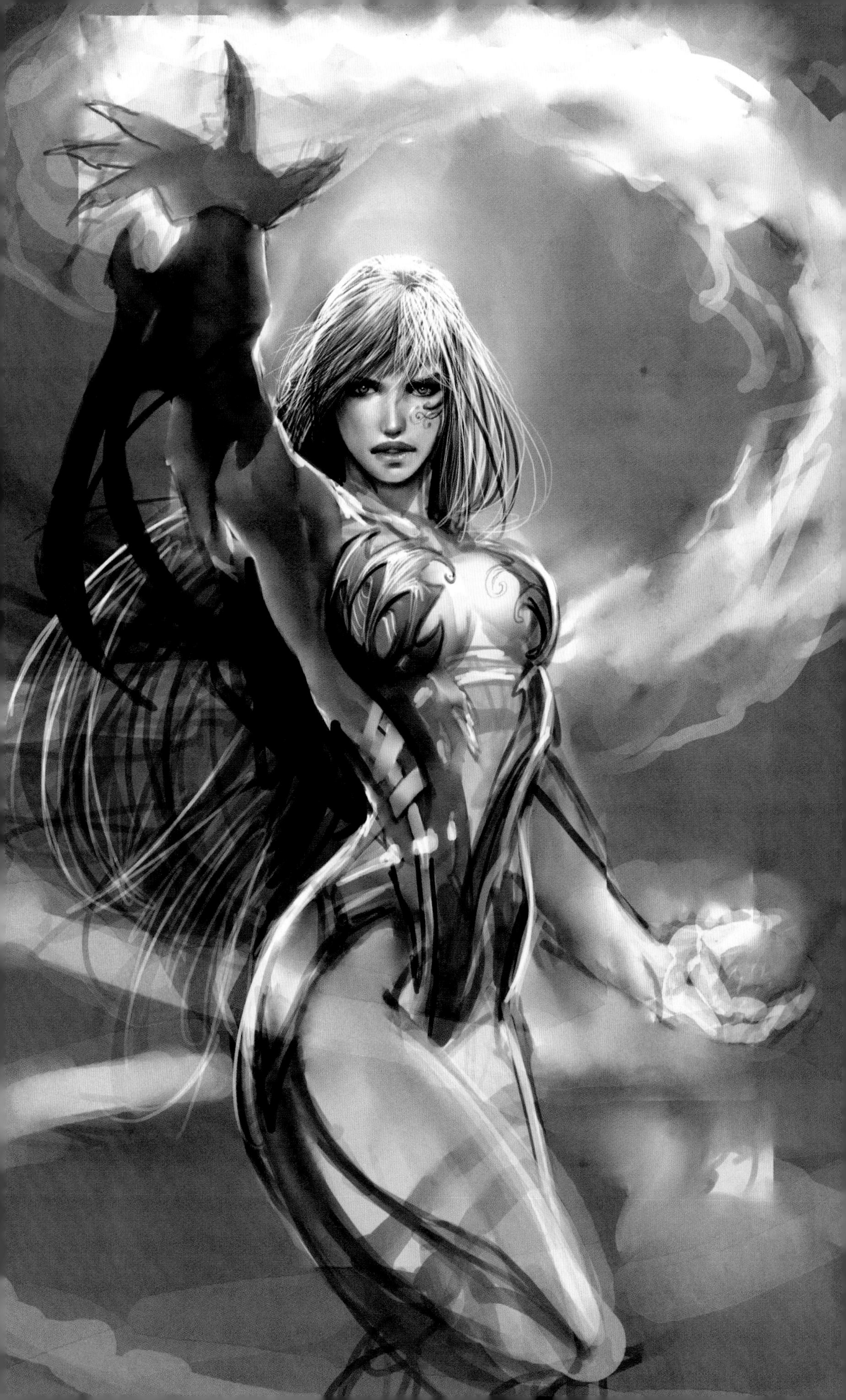

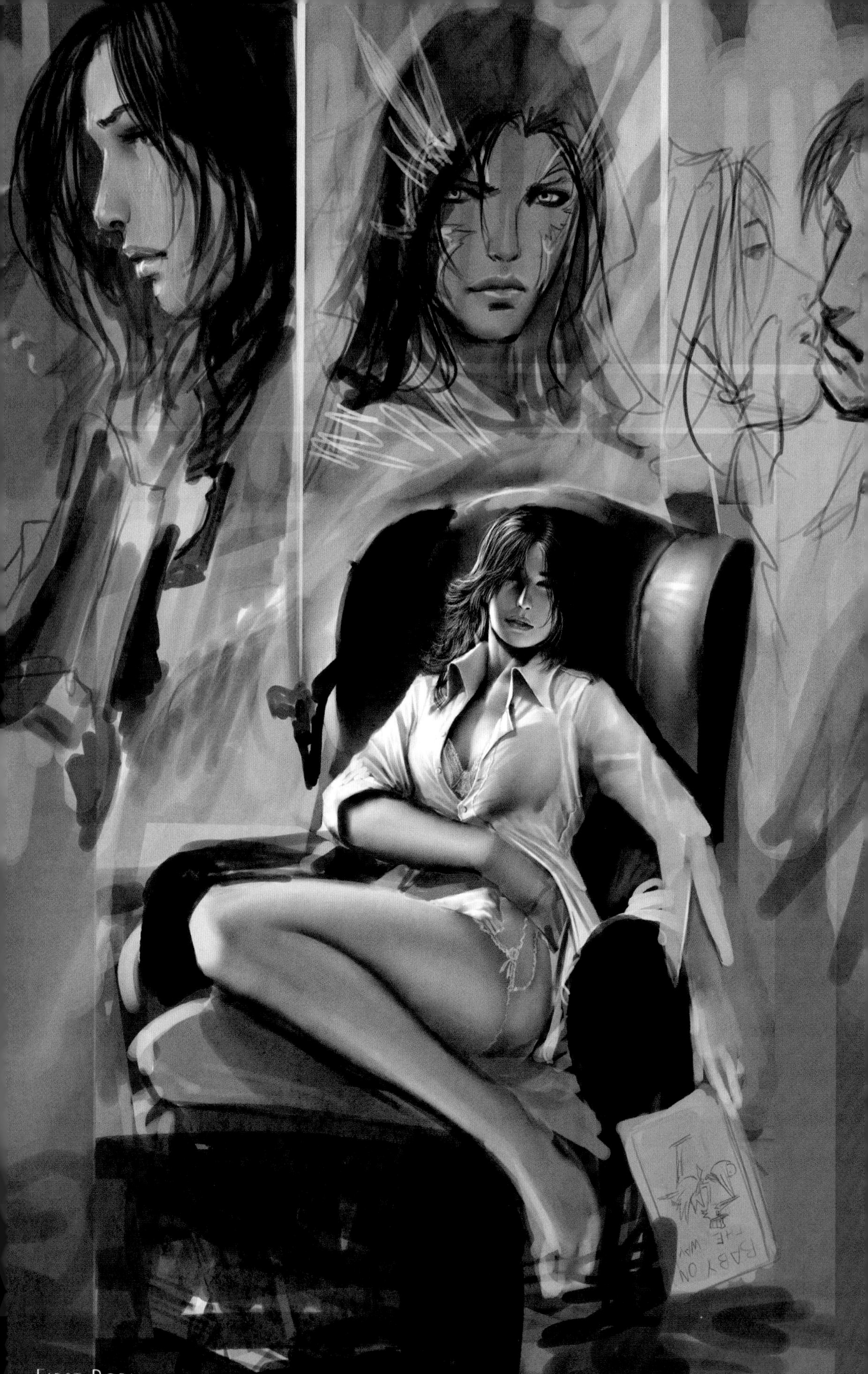
BABY ON THE WAY

First Born
character concept sketch, Sara and Gleason

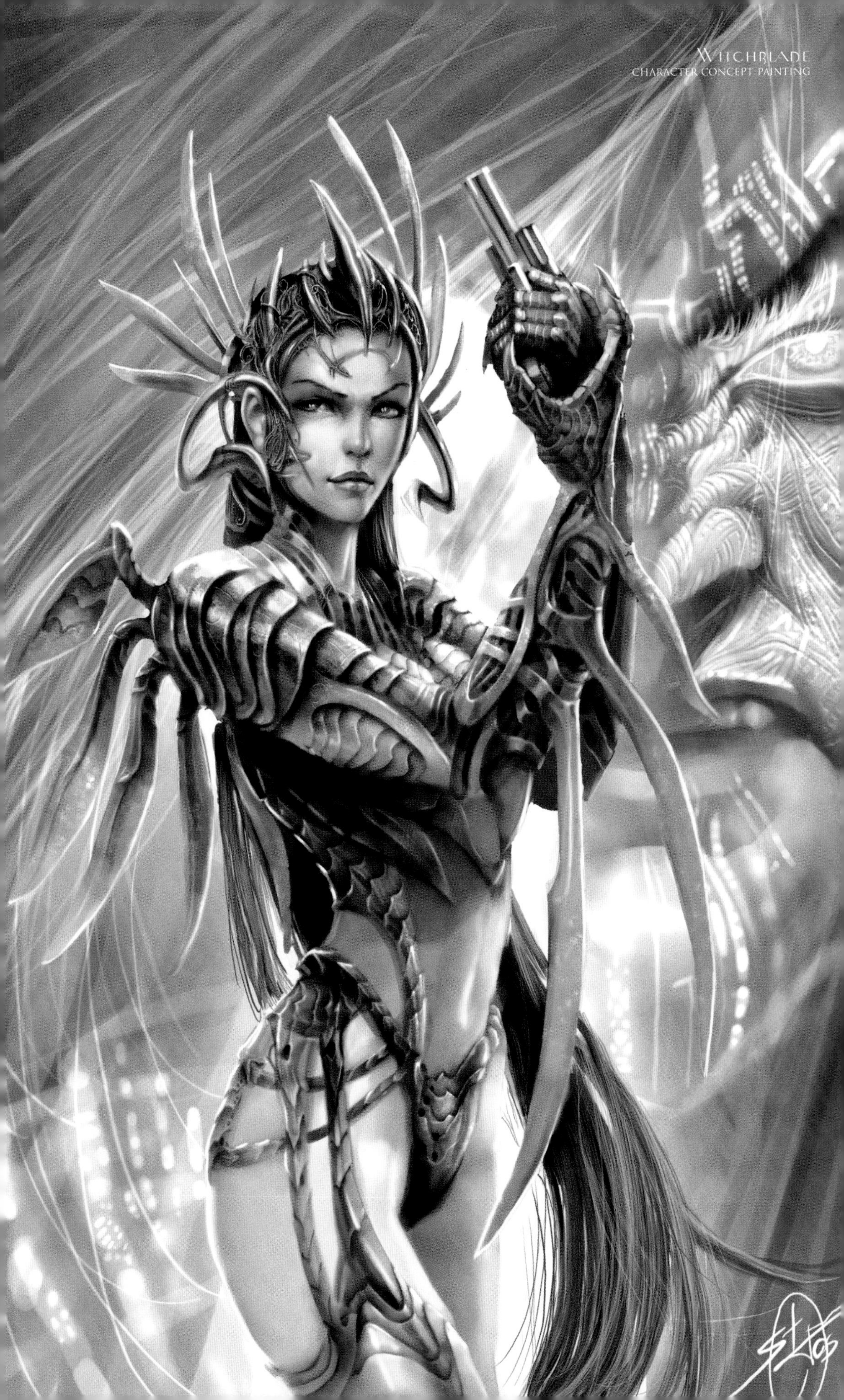
Witchblade
Character Concept Painting

First Born
First Look cover sketch and Final (inset)

Facing Page

First Born
Gatefold cover concept
and revised final sketch (inset)

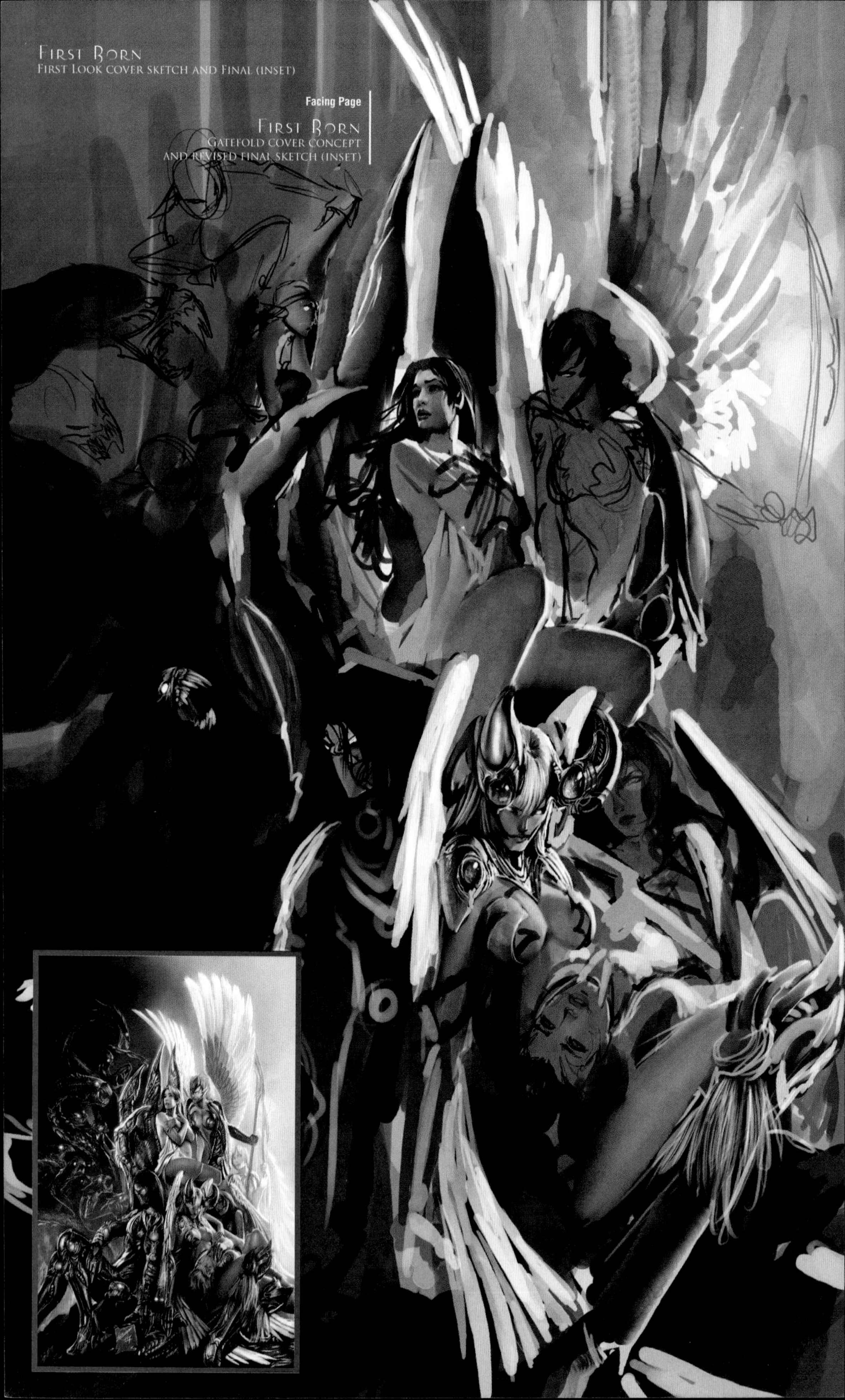

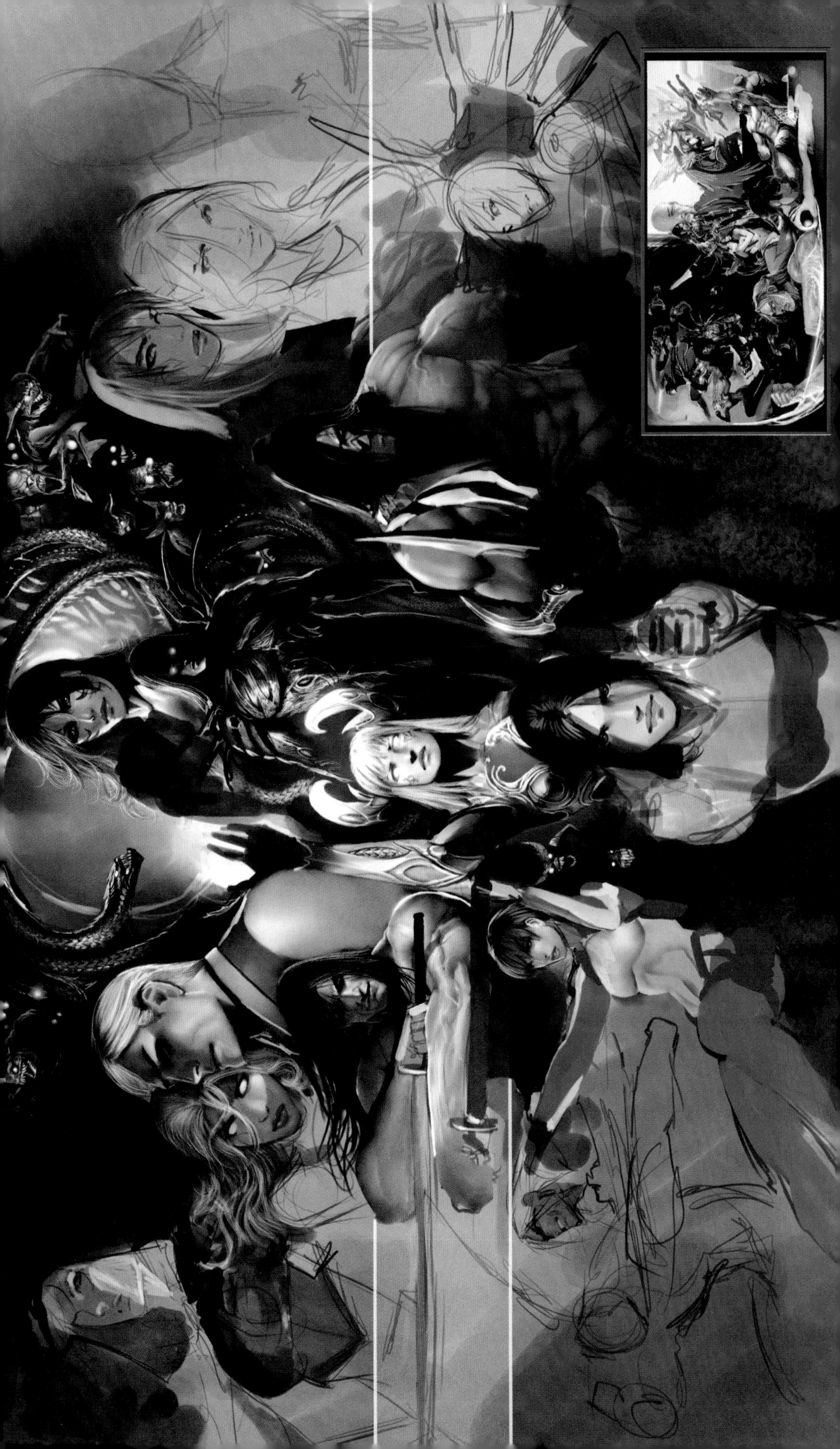

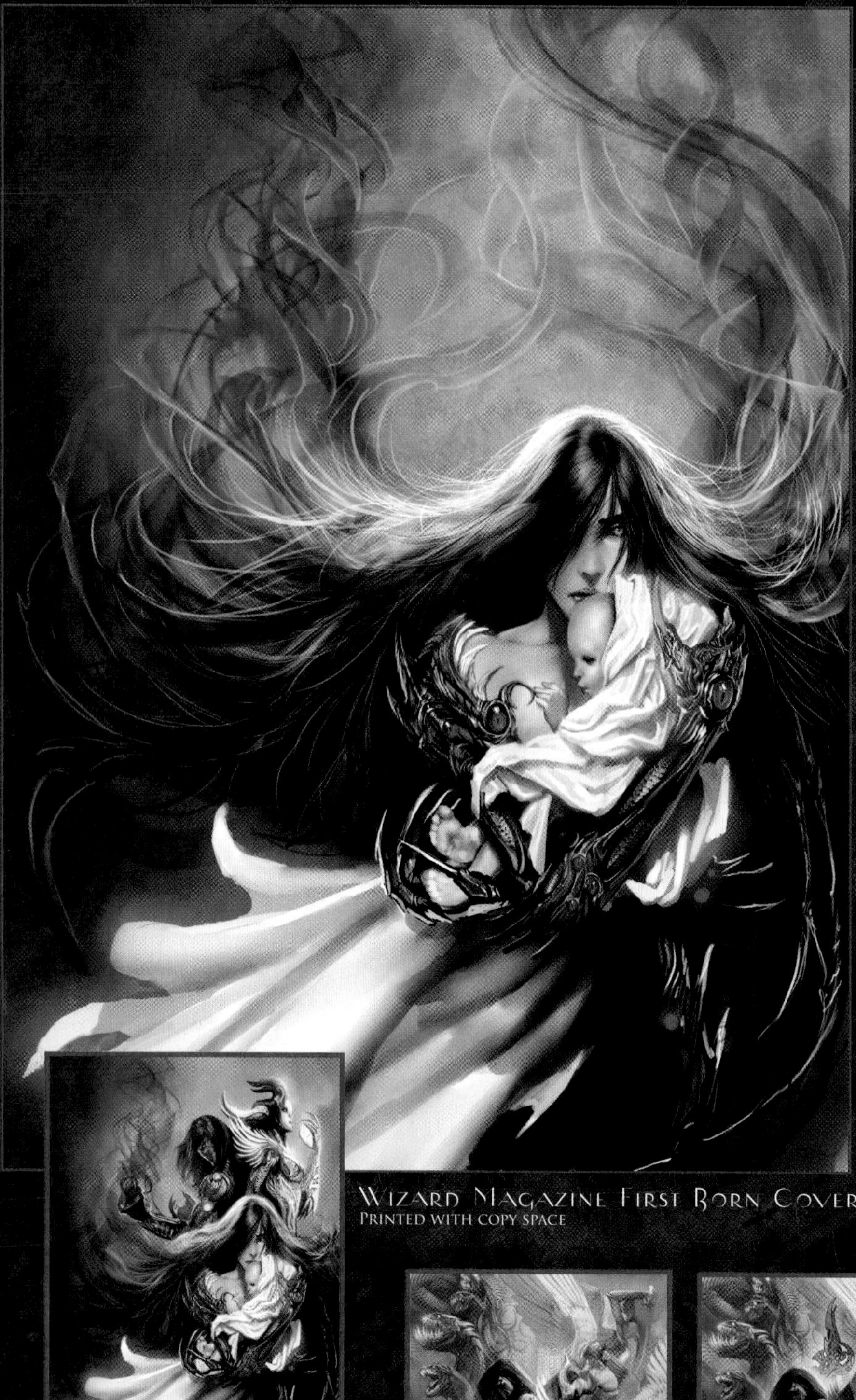

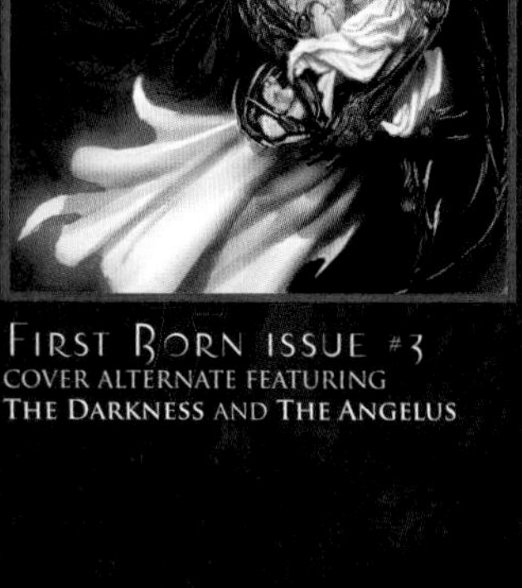

First Born issue #3
COVER ALTERNATE FEATURING
The Darkness and The Angelus

Wizard Magazine First Born Cover
PRINTED WITH COPY SPACE

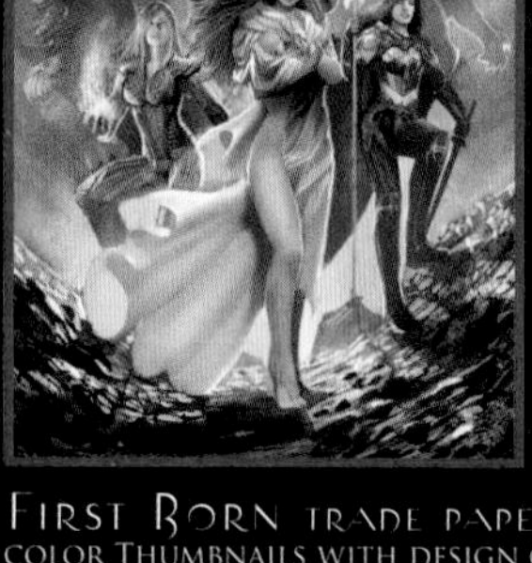

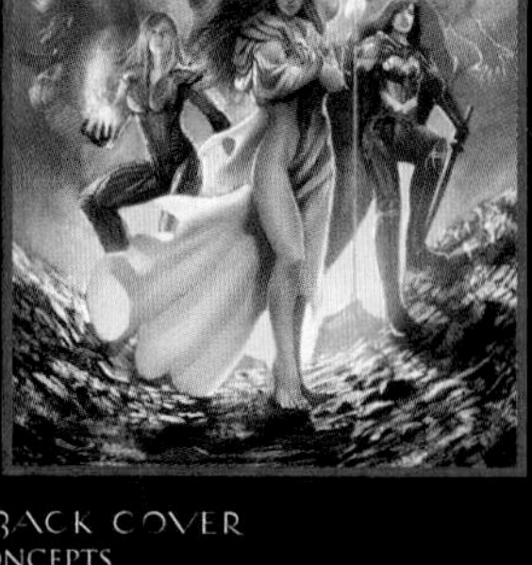

First Born trade paperback cover
COLOR THUMBNAILS WITH DESIGN CONCEPTS

Facing Page

First Born

trade paperback cover
Final

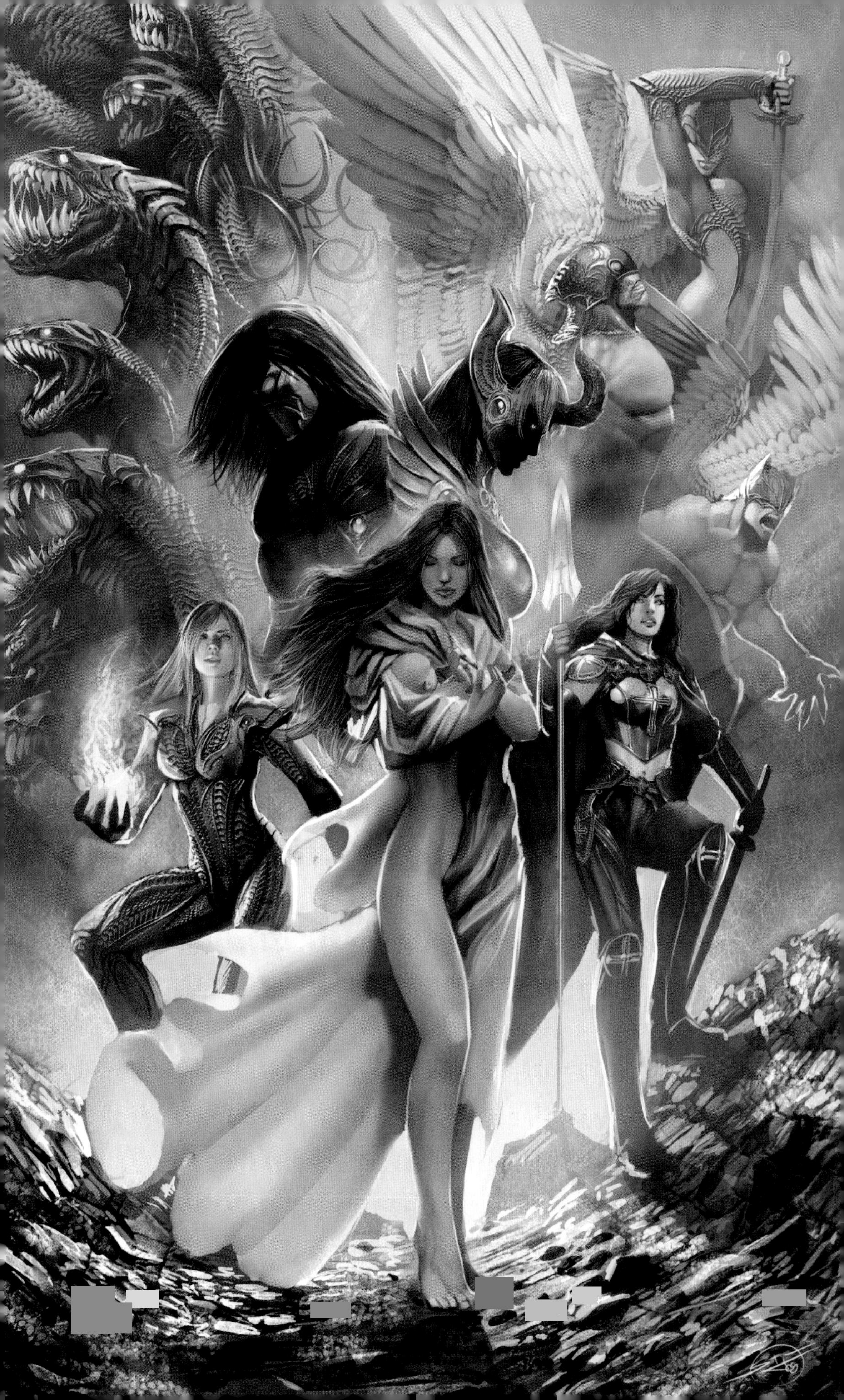

Take a look at our other trade paperbacks and special collections.

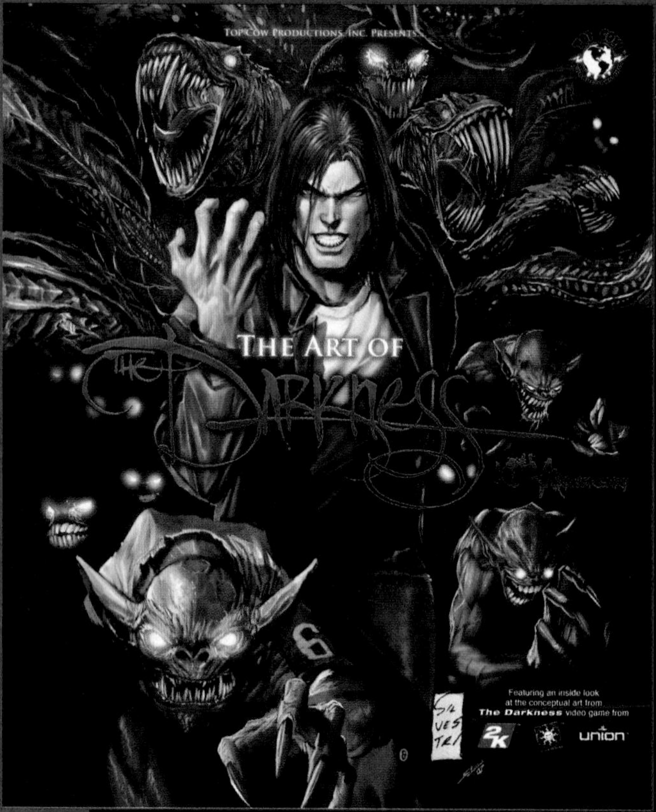

Top Cow Productions, Inc. Presents
The Art of
The Darkness
Featuring an inside look at the conceptual art from The Darkness video game from
2K
union

The Art of The Darkness

Celebrate the 10th Anniversary of The Darkness! Inspired by Art of books for video games and films, this oversized art book features glorious illustrations and commentary from the original creators, all contained in a glossy, thick-papered, beautifully designed book. Covers, splash pages, collectible cards, sketches--the best of the best *The Darkness* art! See it here in its unadulterated form. A decade of work to choose from, this is the definitive Art of book for *The Darkness*! Featuring art by the top names in comics including:

Marc Silvestri
Michael Turner
Dale Keown
Jae Lee
Stjepan Sejic
Dave Finch
Whilce Portacio
and many more!

(ISBN: 978-1-58240-649-7) $14.99

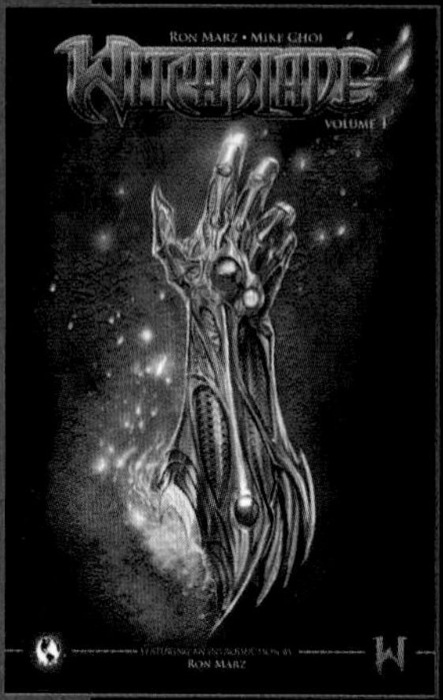

Ron Marz • Mike Choi
Witchblade
Volume 1

volume 1
collects issues #80-#85
(ISBN: 978-1-58240-906-1)
U.S.D. $9.99

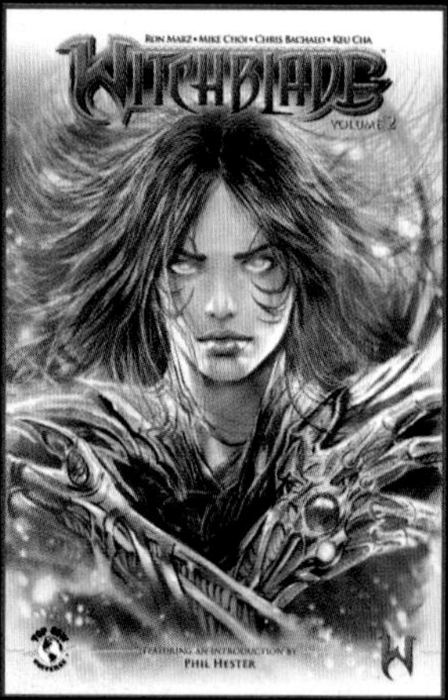

Witchblade
Volume 2

volume 2
collects issues #86-#92
(ISBN: 978-1-58240-886-6)
U.S.D. $14.99

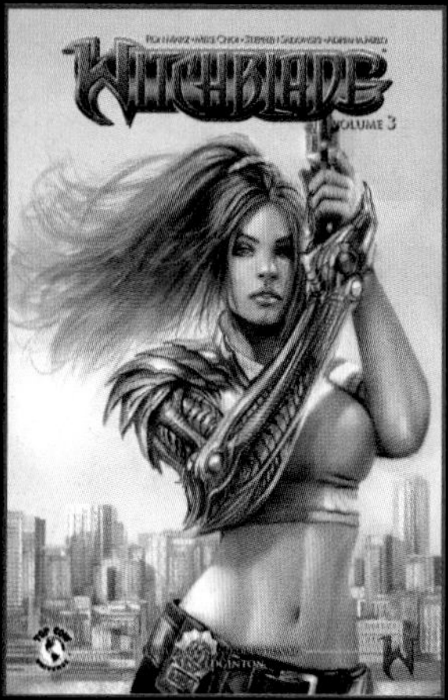

Witchblade
Volume 3

volume 3
collects issues #93-#100
(ISBN: 978-1-58240-887-3)
U.S.D. $14.99

Witchblade

volume 1 - volume 3

written by: Ron Marz
pencils by: Mike Choi, Stephen Sadowski, Keu Cha, Chris Bachalo and more!

Get in on the ground floor of Top Cow's flagship title with these affordable trade paperback collections from Ron Marz's series re-defining run on Witchblade! Each volume collects a key story arc in the continuing adventures of Sara Pezzini and the Witchblade.

Must have collected editions!

Hunter-Killer
vol.1

written by:
Mark Waid
pencils by:
**Marc Silvestri, Kenneth Rocafort,
and Eric Basaldua**

From the minds of visionary creators
Marc Silvestri (X-Men, The Darkness) and
Mark Waid (Kingdom Come, The Flash),
Hunter-Killer delivers high-octane action and
character-driven suspense in a world where
none of the standard rules of heroism apply.
This edition collects the complete Hunter-
Killer Season 1, the Hunter-Killer Dossier and
Hunter-Killer Script Book plus killer extras.
Also features art from Kenneth Rocafort
(Madame Mirage) and Eric Basaldua (The
Magdalena).

(ISBN: 978-1-58240-647-3) $24.99

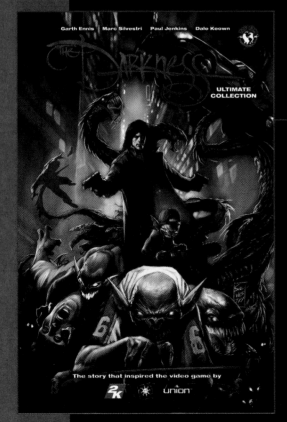

The Darkness
Ultimate Collection
written by:
Garth Ennis and **Paul Jenkins**
with art by:
Marc Silvestri and **Dale Keown**

The Darkness: Ultimate Collection trade paperback
spotlights the two storylines which inspired the hit video
game from 2K Games and made Jackie Estacado and the
Darkness an integral part of the Top Cow Universe.
Featuring the complete **Coming of Age** and
Resurrection storylines, this edition is a must-have for fans
of *The Darkness* and the video game.

(ISBN: 978-1-58240-780-7) $19.99

Ask your retailer for more information on the Top Cow trade paperback library.

DAVE FINCH DAVID WOHL
APHRODITE IX
TIME
•OUT OF•
MIND

Aphrodite IX

written by:
David Wohl
with art by:
Dave Finch

Collects *Aphrodite IX* vol. 1 issues #0 - #4 featuring the art of superstar **Dave Finch** (*Moon Knight, New Avengers*)!

Your name is Aphrodite IX. You've been programmed to kill then immediately erase all knowledge of your mission and former life, like someone hit a reset button on your mind. You are the perfect weapon—the perfect killing machine. You've toppled empires with a single shot. You just don't know it yet.

(ISBN: 978-1-58240-372-4) US $14.99

Joshua Ortega Francis Manapul
The Necromancer
BOOK I
Foreword by Mike Carey
Afterword by Matt Hawkins

The Necromancer

Book 1

written by:
Joshua Ortega
pencils by:
Francis Manapul

The Necromancer trade paperback, written by critically acclaimed novelist Joshua Ortega (*Frank Frazetta's Death Dealer*, *((Frequencies))*) and illustrated by fan-favorite penciler Francis Manapul (*Witchblade, Iron & the Maiden*), delivers a gothic supernatural adventure that is a must-have addition to any graphic novel collection.

(ISBN: 978-1-58240-648-0) $14.99

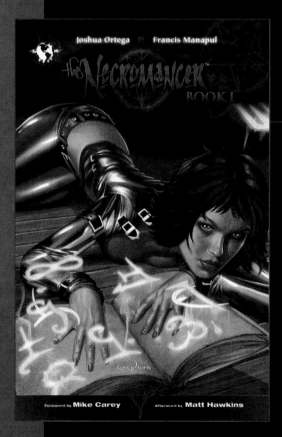